A Basic Course in Moroccan Arabic

Richard S. Harrell
with
Mohammed Abu-Talib and
William S. Carroll

Georgetown University Press
Washington, D.C.

Georgetown University Press, Washington, D.C.

Printed in the United States of America

10 9 8 7 6 5 4 3 2 1 2003

This book is printed on acid-free recycled paper meeting the requirements of the American National Standard for Permanence in Paper for Printed Library Materials.

The research reported herein was performed pursuant to a contract with the United States Office of Education, Department of Health, Education, and Welfare.

Library of Congress Cataloging-in-Publication Data

Harrell, Richard S. (Richard Slade), 1928–1964.
A basic course in Moroccan Arabic / Richard Harrell ; with Mohammed Abu-Talib, William S. Carroll.
p. cm. — (Georgetown classics in Arabic language and linguistics)
Originally published: Washington, D.C.: Georgetown University Press, 1965.
Includes bibliographical references (p.) and index.
ISBN 0-87840-387-6 (alk. paper)
1. Arabic language—Dialects—Morocco. I. Abu-Talib, Mohammed. II. Carroll, William S., 1935– III. Title. IV. Series.

PJ6770.23 .H37 2003
492.7′0964—dc21

2002033909

Georgetown Classics in Arabic Language and Linguistics
Karin C. Ryding and Margaret Nydell, series editors

For some time, Georgetown University Press has been interested in making available seminal publications in Arabic language and linguistics that have gone out of print. Some of the most meticulous and creative scholarship of the last century was devoted to the analysis of Arabic language, to producing detailed reference works and textbooks of the highest quality. Although some of the material is dated in terms of theoretical approaches, the content and methodology of the books considered for the reprint series is still valid and, in some cases, unsurpassed.

With global awareness now refocused on the Arab world, and with renewed interest in Arab culture, society, and political life, it is essential to provide easy access to classic reference materials such as dictionaries and reference grammars and language teaching materials. The key components of this series of classic reprints have been chosen for quality of research and scholarship, and have been updated with new bibliographies and introductions to provide readers with resources for further study. Where possible, the original authors have been involved in the reproduction and republication process.

Georgetown University Press hopes hereby to serve the growing national and international need for reference works on Arabic language and culture, as well as provide access to quality textbooks and audiovisual resources for teaching Arabic language in its written and spoken forms.

Contents

Arabic Research at Georgetown University

In the thirty-eight years since the original publication of *A Basic Course in Moroccan Arabic*, the world of research in Arabic theoretical linguistics has expanded, but the production of professional quality textbooks in colloquial Arabic has remained limited. Despite the passage of years, the Richard Slade Harrell Arabic Series has consistently been in demand from Georgetown University Press because of the quality of research that went into its composition, the solid theoretical foundations for its methodology, and the comprehensive coverage of regional Arabic speech communities.

The Arabic Department at Georgetown University (now Department of Arabic Language, Literature and Linguistics) recognizes the need to sustain the tradition of research and publication in Arabic dialects and has continued dialectology field research and textbook production, most notably with Margaret (Omar) Nydell's *Syrian Arabic Video Course*, a three-year research project funded by Center for the Advancement of Language Learning from 1991 to 1994. Currently, we are engaged in a four-year dialectology research project aimed at producing "conversion" courses to assist learners of Modern Standard Arabic in converting their knowledge and skills of written Arabic to proficiency in selected Arabic dialects. This project is part of a grant administered by the National Capital Language Resource Center under the directorship of Dr. James E. Alatis and Dr. Anna Chamot.

We pay tribute to the tradition initiated and led by Richard Harrell, the founder of this series, and of the original Arabic Research Program at Georgetown University. His scholarship and creative energy set a standard in the field and yielded an unprecedented and as yet unsurpassed series of, as he put it, "practical tools for the increasing number of Americans whose lives bring them into contact with the Arab world." We hope that this series of reprints, and our continuing efforts in applied Arabic dialectology research will yield a new crop of linguistic resources for Arabic language study.

For more information about the Department of Arabic Language, Literature and Linguistics at Georgetown University, its course offerings, its degree programs, and its research agenda, please consult our website at: www.georgetown.edu/departments/arabic.

Karin C. Ryding,
Sultan Qaboos bin Said Professor
of Arabic

The History of the Arabic Research Program School of Languages and Linguistics Georgetown University

The Arabic Research Program was established in June of 1960 as a contract between Georgetown University and the United States Office of Education under the provisions of the Language Development Program of the National Defense Education Act.

The first two years of the research program, 1960–62 (contract number SAE-8706), were devoted to the production of six books, a reference grammar, and a conversational English–Arabic dictionary in the cultivated spoken forms of Moroccan, Syrian, and Iraqi Arabic. The second two years of the research program, 1962–64 (contract number OE-2-14-029), have been devoted to the further production of Arabic–English dictionaries in each of the three varieties mentioned above, as well as comprehensive basic courses in the Moroccan and Iraqi varieties.

The eleven books of this series, of which the present volume is one, are designed to serve as practical tools for the increasing number of Americans whose lives bring them into contact with the Arab world. The dictionaries, the reference grammars, and the basic courses are oriented toward the educated American who is a layman in linguistic matters. Although it is hoped that the scientific linguist and the specialist in Arabic dialectology will find these books both of interest and of use, matters of purely scientific and theoretical importance have not been directly treated as such, and specialized scientific terminology has been avoided as much as possible.

As is usual, the authors or editors of the individual books bear final scholarly responsibility for the contents, but there has been a large amount of informal cooperation in our work. Criticism, consultation, and discussion have gone on constantly among the senior professional members of the staff. The contribution of more junior research assistants, both Arab and American, is also not to be underestimated. Their painstaking assembling and ordering of raw data, often in manners requiring considerable creative intelligence, has been the necessary prerequisite for further progress.

In most cases the books prepared by the Arabic Research Program are the first of their kind in English, and in some cases the first in any language. The preparation of them has been a rewarding experience. It is hoped that the public use of them will be equally so. The undersigned, on behalf of the entire staff, would like to ask the same indulgence of the reader as Samuel Johnson requested in his first English dictionary: To remember that although much has been left out, much has been included.

Richard S. Harrell
Professor of Linguistics
Georgetown University

Director,
Arabic Research Program

Before his death in late 1964, Dr. Harrell had done the major part of the work of general editor for the last five books of the Arabic Series, and to him is due the credit for all that may be found of value in that work. It remained for me only to make some minor editing decisions, and to see these books through the process of proofreading and printing; for any errors or inadequacies in the final editing, the responsibility is mine alone.

Wallace M. Erwin
Assistant Professor of
Linguistics and Arabic
Georgetown University

Contents of the CD Recordings

A set of eleven audio compact discs (CDs) accompany *A Basic Course in Moroccan Arabic*. They may be ordered from Georgetown University Press, ISBN 0-87840-388-4. These CDs were remastered from the original audiocassettes, and the sound quality reflects the early technology of the originals.

Disc	Track	Lesson	Time
1	1	Introduction	(1:44)
	2	Pronunciation Drill 1	(19:29)
	3	Drill 2	(9:26)
	4	Drill 3	(7:06)
	5	Drill 4	(9:33)
	6	Drill 5	(8:06)
	7	Drill 6	(8:03)
	8	Drill 7	(1:18)
	9	Drill 8	(3:54)
	10	Drill 9	(4:50)
	11	Drill 10	(1:52)
			Total: (75:35)
2	1	Drill 11	(7:50)
	2	Drill 12	(7:52)
	3	Drill 13	(7:22)
	4	Drill 14	(11:38)
	5	Drill 15	(7:31)
	6	Drill 16	(15:49)
	7	Drill 17	(9:42)
	8	Drill 18	(4:59)
	9	Drill 19	(5:39)
			Total: (78:22)

Disc	Track	Lesson	Time
3	1	Drill 20	(5:55)
	2	Drill 21	(7:22)
	3	Drill 22	(6:23)
	4	Drill 23	(4:28)
	5	Drill 24	(9:31)
	6	Drill 25	(7:10)
	7	Drill 26	(6:49)
	8	Drill 27	(9:40)
	9	Drill 28	(11:20)
	10	Drill 29	(8:09)
			Total: (76:47)
4	1	Drill 30	(6:40)
	2	Lesson 1	(3:53)
	3	Lesson 1-Exercise A	(1:49)
	4	Lesson 1-Exercise B	(1:17)
	5	Lesson 2	(5:32)
	6	Lesson 2-Exercise A	(2:27)
	7	Lesson 2-Exercise B	(1:25)
	8	Lesson 3	(8:25)
	9	Lesson 3-Exercises	(1:18)
	10	Lesson 4	(5:34)
	11	Lesson 4-Exercises	(6:12)
	12	Lesson 5	(5:23)
	13	Lesson 5-Exercises	(4:26)
	14	Lesson 6	(6:19)
	15	Lesson 7	(4:44)
	16	Lesson 7-Exercises	(5:01)
	17	Lesson 8	(3:53)
	18	Lesson 9	(3:52)
			Total: (88:10)

Disc	Track	Lesson	Time
5	1	Lesson 9-Exercises	(1:47)
	2	Lesson 10	(2:54)
	3	Lesson 10-Exercises	(2:44)
	4	Lesson 11	(3:02)
	5	Lesson 11-Exercise A	(8:05)
	6	Lesson 11-Exercise B	(2:13)
	7	Lesson 12	(4:38)
	8	Lesson 13	(4:04)
	9	Lesson 14	(3:11)
	10	Lesson 14-Exercises	(1:23)
	11	Lesson 15	(2:40)
	12	Lesson 15-Exercises	(7:35)
	13	Lesson 16	(4:23)
	14	Lesson 17	(2:25)
	15	Lesson 18	(5:49)
	16	Lesson 19	(6:24)
	17	Lesson 20	(8:35)
	18	Lesson 21	(2:43)
	19	Lesson 22	(3:53)
			Total: (78:28)
6	1	Lesson 23	(3:30)
	2	Lesson 24	(2:12)
	3	Lesson 25	(2:42)
	4	Lesson 26	(3:09)
	5	Lesson 27	(2:28)
	6	Lesson 28	(3:10)
	7	Lesson 29	(3:08)
	8	Lesson 30	(2:10)
	9	Lesson 31	(3:21)

Disc	Track	Lesson	Time
	10	Lesson 32	(3:03)
	11	Lesson 33	(1:59)
	12	Lesson 34	(2:16)
	13	Lesson 35	(3:37)
	14	Lesson 36	(4:34)
	15	Lesson 37	(4:36)
	16	Lesson 38	(6:31)
	17	Lesson 39	(2:45)
	18	Lesson 40	(5:31)
	19	Lesson 41	(4:25)
	20	Lesson 42	(4:41)
	21	Lesson 43	(6:20)
			Total: (76:08)
7	1	Lesson 44	(8:31)
	2	Lesson 45	(7:10)
	3	Lesson 46	(5:51)
	4	Lesson 47	(2:36)
	5	Lesson 47-Exercises	(5:11)
	6	Lesson 48	(4:55)
	7	Lesson 48-Exercises	(3:17)
	8	Lesson 49	(5:23)
	9	Lesson 49-Exercises	(2:09)
	10	Lesson 50	(3:07)
	11	Lesson 51	(5:00)
	12	Lesson 52	(5:51)
	13	Lesson 53	(4:34)
	14	Lesson 54	(3:58)
	15	Lesson 55	(4:03)
	16	Lesson 56	(5:46)
			Total: (77:26)

Disc	Track	Lesson	Time
8	1	Lesson 57	(6:41)
	2	Lesson 58	(4:01)
	3	Lesson 59	(6:24)
	4	Lesson 60	(8:49)
	5	Lesson 61	(4:47)
	6	Lesson 62	(4:30)
	7	Lesson 63	(6:05)
	8	Lesson 64	(2:52)
	9	Lesson 64-Exercises	(1:36)
	10	Lesson 65	(3:36)
	11	Lesson 66	(5:04)
	12	Lesson 67	(3:18)
	13	Lesson 68	(4:54)
	14	Lesson 69	(3:24)
	15	Lesson 70	(2:20)
	16	Lesson 71	(4:00)
	17	Lesson 72	(4:38)
			Total: (76:59)
9	1	Lesson 73	(3:56)
	2	Lesson 74	(3:02)
	3	Lesson 75	(3:05)
	4	Lesson 76	(3:58)
	5	Lesson 77	(3:12)
	6	Lesson 78	(3:25)
	7	Lesson 79	(2:25)
	8	Lesson 80	(2:50)
	9	Lesson 81	(3:14)
	10	Lesson 82	(3:34)

Disc	Track	Lesson	Time
	11	Lesson 83	(2:54)
	12	Lesson 84	(1:40)
	13	Lesson 85	(1:50)
	14	Lesson 86	(2:36)
	15	Lesson 87	(3:04)
	16	Lesson 88	(3:36)
	17	Lesson 89	(2:48)
	18	Lesson 90	(1:59)
	19	Lesson 91	(2:26)
	20	Lesson 92	(2:34)
	21	Lesson 93	(2:49)
	22	Lesson 94	(1:34)
	23	Lesson 95	(2:44)
	24	Lesson 96	(3:07)
	25	Lesson 97	(2:21)
	26	Lesson 98	(3:41)
	27	Lesson 99	(4:35)
			Total: (78:59)
10	1	Lesson 100	(4:05)
	2	Lesson 101	(5:49)
	3	Lesson 102	(5:01)
	4	Lesson 103	(4:58)
	5	Lesson 104	(3:41)
	6	Lesson 105	(2:57)
	7	Lesson 106	(3:47)
	8	Lesson 107	(3:54)
	9	Lesson 108	(3:32)
	10	Lesson 109	(4:32)
	11	Lesson 110	(4:42)

Disc	Track	Lesson	Time
	12	Lesson 111	(5:02)
	13	Lesson 112	(5:57)
	14	Lesson 113	(3:41)
	15	Lesson 114	(2:32)
	16	Lesson 115	(3:25)
	17	Lesson 116	(3:30)
	18	Lesson 117	(2:46)
	19	Lesson 118	(4:33)
			Total: (78:24)
11	1	Lesson 119	(3:48)
	2	Lesson 120	(4:00)
	3	Lesson 121	(8:20)
	4	Lesson 122	(3:56)
	5	Lesson 123	(3:59)
	6	Lesson 124	(3:04)
	7	Lesson 125	(4:08)
	8	Lesson 126	(4:20)
	9	Lesson 127	(4:48)
	10	Lesson 128	(3:13)
	11	Lesson 129	(5:23)
	12	Lesson 130	(3:17)
			Total: (52:16)

Foreword to the Georgetown Classics Edition

The Richard Harrell Arabic series was a ground-breaking project in the early 1960s because it was the first systematic study of several regional Arabic dialects: Moroccan, Egyptian, Syrian, and Iraqi. Dr. Richard Harrell, chair of Georgetown's Arabic department, and his assistants produced a series of grammars, dictionaries, and basic courses that set the standard. Since then, numerous scholars have supplemented the field of Arabic dialectology with their own research and publications, and most of them are designed with a strong influence from Harrell's original approach.

This book, one in the original Harrell series, is a text in spoken Moroccan Arabic written for beginners—those who do not know the Arabic language or alphabet. It is written in Latinate transcription for this reason.

This book is carefully designed to present vocabulary and grammatical points in a useful, cumulative order. After completion of the course, the user will have learned all of the essential information about the structure of Moroccan Arabic and will be prepared to continue through real-life practice. Vocabulary is presented in modules that describe common, everyday situations.

Richard Harrell died tragically in 1964 in Cairo while conducting research for an Egyptian reference grammar (which has not been written to this day). Some other parts of the original projected series of books are also missing: a Syrian–English dictionary, a basic course in Syrian, and an Egyptian–English dictionary (which was finally produced at the American University in Cairo in 1986). I have long thought that the assertion "Nobody is indispensable" was disproved in the case of Richard Harrell—he was truly indispensable and is still much missed after almost forty years.

Moroccan Arabic materials are essential tools for anyone studying or analyzing this dialect. Georgetown University Press is pleased to be reprinting this book, and other books in the Harrell series may follow, especially in light of recent increased demands for Arabic training.

MARGARET NYDELL

Preface

This book consists of two major parts, *Lessons* and *Dialogs*. Both the *Lessons* and the *Dialogs* are accompanied throughout with English translations. Preliminary material on pronunciation, with drills, precedes the *Lessons*. Appended to the *Lessons* are a glossary and an index of grammatical points covered.

Each lesson consists of four parts: **I. Text, II. Grammatical Notes, III. Exercises,** and **IV. Vocabulary.** Each text consists of a small number of phrases and sentences illustrating some grammatical point or points. The grammatical notes provide an explanation of the new grammatical material introduced in the text. The exercises are designed to drill the student on the new grammar and vocabulary of each lesson until they are fixed in his mind. The vocabulary lists the new words introduced in each lesson. The lessons are short, and each one should be mastered thoroughly before the next one is undertaken.

The *Lessons* are oriented entirely toward the point of teaching the basic structure of the language. In order not to distract the student from the primary task of learning the structure of Moroccan Arabic, considerations of cultural differences between the United States and Morocco have been avoided and the vocabulary has been restricted to fewer than 650 basic entries. The task of presenting the student a broader vocabulary and acquainting him with Moroccan culture are left to further works.

The second part of the book is a series of ninety-seven short dialogs. They are designed to provide conversational material for a variety of simple social situations. They have deliberately been made heavily repetitive. A minimal number of notes on grammatical and cultural points are attached to the dialogs.

The lessons and the dialogs are independent of one another. They can be combined in class in a variety of ways according to the judgment of the teacher. Whatever procedure is followed, the preliminary material on pronunciation, along with the drills, and at least the first twelve lessons should be worked through before the dialogs are undertaken. If the dialogs are undertaken prematurely, the common tendency of the beginner to focus on conversational content at the expense of a proper mastery of structure is likely to be reinforced.

The author wishes to make special acknowledgment of the roles of Mohammed Abu-Talib and William S. Carroll in the preparation of this *Basic Course in*

Moroccan Arabic. In the *Lessons*, Mr. Abu-Talib checked and verified the grammatical and idiomatic accuracy of the Arabic and in addition offered various constructive criticisms. Mr. Carroll relieved the author's work load by performing a variety of editorial functions. For example, one of the problems in the original manuscript was that a number of lessons were too long in terms of the type of pedagogical progression aimed at. One of Mr. Carroll's tasks was dividing some of these longer lessons in two and condensing others by deleting overly repetitious material.

The *Dialogs* are based on a collection of dialogs in Egyptian Arabic prepared by Dr. William Cowan at the Foreign Service Institute's Arabic School in Beirut, Lebanon. (These Egyptian Arabic dialogs exist in mimeographed form only and are not available to the public.) Mr. Abu-Talib took these dialogs and translated them into Moroccan Arabic, changing the scene from Egypt to Morocco and making various other cultural adjustments as necessary. The author edited and annotated the results of Mr. Abu-Talib's work, and Mr. Carroll subjected the dialogs to a final revision and condensation in view of the decision to include them in the book as an appendix to the preceding lessons. A final note of thanks is due to Mr. Ernest Ligon for reading the proofs.

RICHARD S. HARRELL
Washington, D.C.
August, 1964

PART ONE

THE LESSONS

PRONUNCIATION

1. Table of Sounds: Moroccan Arabic has thirty-one consonants and six vowels. The symbols for them are listed in the table below. Most of the consonants are classified according to the kinds of movements and positions of the lips, tongue, throat, and nasal passages which produce them.

CONSONANTS						
	Labial	**Dental**	**Palatal**	**Velar**	**Pharyngeal**	**Glottal**
Stops	*b ḅ*	*t ṭ d ḍ*		*k g q*		*ʔ*
Fricatives	*f*	*s ṣ z ẓ*	š ž	*x ġ*	ح ع	*h*
Nasals	*m ṃ*	*n*				
Resonants	*l ḷ r ṛ w y*					
VOWELS						
a ă e i o u						

Stops are those sounds which involve, momentarily, a complete blocking of the air stream in speech. For example, notice the complete closure of the lips in the pronunciation of the 'b' in English 'bed'. A fricative is a sound in which the air stream is partly blocked but not completely stopped, with a resulting noisy effect. For example, in the 'f' of English 'foot' note the way the air stream escapes through the partial closure of the lower lip against the upper front teeth. Nasals are sounds which involve a flow of air through the nasal passage, e.g. 'm', as in 'mad'.

The terms 'labial', 'dental', 'palatal', 'velar', 'pharyngeal', and 'glottal' refer, in going from front to back, to the parts of the mouth in which sounds are formed:

'Labial' refers to sounds which involve the lips.

'Dental' refers to sounds which involve the tip of the tongue in the area around the back of the upper front teeth.

'Palatal' refers to sounds formed with the upper surface of the tongue against the roof of the mouth.

'Velar' refers to sounds involving the rear part of the tongue against the rear portions of the roof of the mouth.

'Pharyngeal' refers to sounds formed in the area of the throat above the larynx ('Adam's apple').

'Glottal' refers to sounds formed in the larynx.

For practical teaching and learning purposes the sounds listed as 'resonants' are not usefully classifiable according to the system described above. The sound represented by letters with dots under them, e.g. *ṭ*, are referred to as 'emphatics'. They are discussed below.

There are six vowels, represented by the symbols *a, ă, e, i, o,* and *u*. Each one of these vowels has various pronunciations depending on the consonants they occur with. There is no single isolated pronunciation which can be learned for them. They are discussed individually in relation to the consonants in the following sections.

(Note: After reading sections 2 and 3 below, the student should proceed to Pronunciation Drill 1.)

2. Consonants Similar to English: Fifteen of the thirty-one Moroccan consonants are, for practical purposes, identical with consonants which occur in English. These are *b, f, m, t, d, s, z, n, š* (like the 'sh' in 'ship'), ž (like the 's' in 'pleasure'), *k, g, w, y,* and *h*.

For the student who wishes to be fully accurate, there is a small difference of detail to be noted between the Moroccan *t, d,* and *n* as opposed to the corresponding English sounds. In Moroccan these sounds are formed with the tip of the tongue against the back of the upper front teeth instead of against the gum ridge immediately above them. Note the tip of the tongue against the gum ridge above the teeth for English 't', 'd', and 'n', as in 'tea', 'day', 'no'.

A word about *w* and *y* is also necessary. The English speaker is familiar with them before vowels, as in words like 'well' and 'yes'. Moroccan *w* and *y* occur after vowels as well as before them. After vowels, the Moroccan *w* sounds to the English speaker somewhat like the vowel sound in 'who' and the *y* sounds somewhat like the vowel in '*he*'.

The occurrence of *h* in the middle and at the end of words may cause the student some difficulty. Practice is provided in Pronunciation Drill 10.

3. Vowel Sounds with Familiar Consonants: This section has to do with the pronunciation of some of the Moroccan vowels in combination with the consonants listed in **2** above. The descriptions below are accurate only for the vowels in combination with those Moroccan consonants which are similar to English. Elsewhere the vowels are pronounced differently.

(1) The *e:* Like the 'e' in English 'glasses', always very short.

(2) The *o:* Like the 'u' in English 'put', always very short.

(3) The *a:* Like the 'a' in English 'mad' except at the end of words. At the end of words, Moroccan *a* is pronounced about half-way between the 'a' of 'mad' and the 'a' of 'father".

(4) The *i:* Similar to the vowel of 'be' but without any gliding effect. By listening carefully the English speaker will note that from the beginning to the end of the vowel of 'be' there is a sort of gliding change in vowel quality. This gliding effect must be avoided in Moroccan. For the student who knows French, Italian, or Spanish, it may be helpful to point out that the 'i' in these languages is exactly equivalent to the Moroccan *i,* as in French *vite* 'quickly', Spanish *mi* 'my', or Italian *vino* 'wine'.

(5) The *u:* Similar to the vowel of 'do' but without any gliding effect. Compare the discussion of the *i* immediately above. The Moroccan *u* is like the French 'ou', as in *fou* 'insane', or Spanish and and Italian 'u', as in Spanish *luna* 'moon', Italian *luce* 'light'.

(NOTE: After reading sections **4**, **5**, and **6** below, the student should proceed to Pronunciation Drills **2** and **3**.)

4. The Emphatic Consonants: The easiest way for the English speaker to distinguish the emphatic consonants from the corresponding non-emphatic consonants is by the great difference in the sound of the vowels when they occur next to these consonants (see section **5. The Emphatic Vowels**). By paying careful attention to the vowel differences, which he hears relatively easily, the English speaker will arrive at an acceptable pronunciation of the difference between the plain and emphatic consonants, even if he feels that he can tell no difference between them.

The emphatic consonants are written with a subscript dot under the symbol for the corresponding plain consonants. There are eight emphatic consonants, *ḅ, ṃ, ṭ, ḍ, ṣ, ẓ, ḷ,* and *ṛ*. The first seven are discussed here, while the *ṛ* is considered in section **6** below. These sounds are lower in pitch than their non-emphatic counterparts. They are pronounced with greater muscular tension in the mouth and throat and with a raising of the back and root of the tongue toward the roof of the mouth. The English speaker can notice this contraction of the throat very easily by prolonging the 'l' in 'full', since this English 'l' is exactly like the Moroccan *ḷ* except that in the Moroccan sound the tip of the tongue is against the back of the upper front teeth instead of against the gum ridge above the teeth. After having acquired conscious control of the movement of the back and root of the tongue with *ḷ*, the English speaker can proceed to practice combining it with the other articulatory features of *ḅ, ṃ, ṭ, ḍ, ṣ, ẓ,* and *ṛ*. In addition to lower pitch and the contraction of the throat, *ṭ* differs from *t* by being released without any friction noise whereas the *t* usually has some, as in English.

The emphatics *ṭ, ḍ,* and *ṣ* are quite common, with or without other emphatic consonants in the words in which they occur. The *ṛ* also occurs widely in words without the presence of any other emphatic consonants, but it is limited to the neighborhood of the vowels *e* and *a* unless a *ṭ, ḍ,* or *ṣ* also occurs in the word. The occurrence of *ḅ, ṃ, ẓ,* or *ḷ* in words where no *ṭ, ḍ, ṣ,* or *ṛ* occurs is quite rare. Contrariwise, there is no occurrence of a plain *b* or *m* in a word in which one of the other emphatics occurs.

In order to avoid the repetition of subscript dots, the transcription employed here is to write *ḅ* and *ṃ* only if no other emphatic occurs in the word. Otherwise only *b* and *m* are written although they are to be interpreted as *ḅ* and *ṃ* if another emphatic consonant occurs in the word where they are found.

5. The Emphatic Vowels: The Moroccan vowels have special pronunciations in the neighborhood of the emphatic consonants. The emphatic pronunciations are:

(1) The *e:* Like the 'u' in English 'but', always very short.

(2) The *a:* Like the 'a' in English 'father.'

(3) The *i:* Similar to the vowel of 'they', but without any gliding effect. Cf. the comment on glides in section **3. Vowel Sounds with Familiar Consonants.** The Moroccan emphatic *i* is exactly like the French 'é' in *été* 'summer', the 'e' in Spanish *leche* 'milk', and the Italian 'e' in *le* 'the' (feminine plural).

(4) The *u:* Similar to the vowel of 'blow' but without any gliding effect. Cf. the comment on glides above. The Moroccan emphatic *u* is like the French 'ô' in *tôt* 'early', the Spanish 'o' in *tomo* 'I take', and the Italian 'o' in *come* 'how'.

(5) The *o:* Like the emphatic *u,* but always very short.

6. The Sounds *l, r,* and *ṛ*: A minor difference between English 'l' and Moroccan *l* is that, like the other Moroccan dentals, it is pronounced with the tip of the tongue against the upper front teeth instead of against the gum ridge above them. A more serious difference is that the usual American English 'l' is like the Moroccan emphatic *ḷ*. The Moroccan plain *l* is like the French, Spanish, and Italian 'l' in that it is pronounced with the tongue further forward in the mouth and without the back part of the tongue being raised toward the roof of the mouth.

The plain *r* is a flap of the tongue past the gum ridge above the upper front teeth, like the 'r' in Spanish *para* 'for' or the 't' in the usual American pronunciation of such words as 'water' and 'butter'. Emphatic ṛ bears exactly the same relation to plain *r* as the other emphatic consonants to the corresponding plain consonants, for which see section **4. The Emphatic Consonants.**

The vowels next to ṛ are pronounced the same as around the other emphatic consonants. Around plain *l* and *r* the vowels are pronounced the same as in the neighborhood of the various consonants which are similar to English, such as *f*, *š*, etc.

(NOTE: After reading section 7 below, the student should proceed to Pronunciation Drill 4.)

7. The Consonants q, x, and ġ. The *q* is similar to the *k* but is pronounced further back in the mouth. English 'k' ranges over a fairly wide area in the back of the mouth, and the English speaker must be careful to keep *k* more to the front part and *q* more to the back part of the rear of the mouth in order not to confuse them and pronounce *q* when he means *k* or vice versa.

The *x* and *ġ* are fricatives pronounced in approximately the same position as the *q*, with the rear of the tongue raised toward the roof of the mouth in the neighborhood of the uvula. The *ġ* is similar to the French 'r' and the *x* is the same sound as the 'ch' of German *Bach* or Scotch *loch*. If these sounds seem difficult to the English speaker he can approximate them by gargling gently. The *ġ* is similar to a light gargle accompanied by a musical buzz from the adam's apple ('voice' is the technical term for this musical buzz) whereas the *x* is the same sound without the musical buzz.

The vowels in the neighborhood of the consonants *q*, *x* and *ġ* are pronounced approximately the same as the vowels in the neighborhood of the emphatic consonants, see above, **5. The Emphatic Vowels.** This equivalence is only approximate, and the student's prime concern should be with exact imitation of the examples given in Pronunciation Drill 4.

(NOTE: After reading sections 8 and 9 below, the student should proceed to Pronunciation Drills 5, 6, 11, 12, and 13.)

8. The Consonants ح and ع. The ح and the ع are different from anything in English. Careful practice with a native speaker or with recordings is necessary for the English speaker to acquire a proper pronunciation of these consonants. These sounds are articulated by a simultaneous raising of the larynx and a movement of the root of the tongue toward the back wall of the thoat. The compression of the throat in this way gives rise to the particular sound quality of these two consonants.

The ح is somewhat similar to an English 'h' pronounced in a loud stage whisper, as opposed to Moroccan *h*, which is more like an English 'h' in ordinary conversation. The English speaker must exercise extreme care in learning to distinguish *h* and ح from each other, both in hearing and in pronunciation.

The ع is unlike any English sound, and a proper pronunciation of it can be acquired only by careful imitation. A useful articulatory description of the way to pronounce ع is difficult to give briefly and in simple terms. The student may approximate it by practicing the loud, prolonged stage whisper English 'h', as for ح. He should note the tension in his throat and the exact position of the adam's apple during the stage whisper 'h'. Then, with his adam's apple and throat in the exact position as for the stage whisper 'h', the student should try pronouncing the 'a' of 'father'. The result should be an acceptable approximation of ع. The student may contrast it with the normal pronunciation of the 'a' in 'father'.

9. The Vowels with ح and ع. In the neighborhood of ح and ع, the vowels *a, i, u,* and *o* are approximately the same as in the neighborhood of the emphatic consonants. The vowel *ă* is almost never found anywhere except next to ح or ع. It is pronounced about halfway between the 'a' of English 'mad' and the 'a' of English 'father', but always very short. It is especially important to note the shortness of *ă*. If it is lengthened, it will be confused with *a*. The only difference between *a* and *ă* is that *a* is held longer than *ă*. The vowel *e* next to ح and ع is similar to the 'e' in English 'set'.

10. The Glottal Stop. The glottal stop is represented by the symbol ˀ. This sound is as rare in Moroccan as it is in English. It is the break between vowels as heard in the exclamation 'uh oh'. The 'tt" in such a word as 'bottle' is also commonly pronounced as a glottal stop in some varieties of New York English ('Brooklynese') or Scotch English. Pronunciation Drill 7 provides illustrations. This sound offers no difficulties for the English speaker. The vowels around the glottal stop are pronounced the same as in the neighborhood of such plain consonants as *f, š, n* etc.

11. The Diphthongs *ăy* and *ăw*. These two diphthongs occur almost exclusively after ح or ع. The English speaker's principal difficulty in pronouncing them is to remember that they are always very short. Except for being pronounced much more quickly, the *ăy* is similar to the 'i' in English 'night' and the *ăw* is similar to the 'ou' in English 'about'. Pronunciation Drill 8 provides illustrations.

12. The Sequences *ay* and *aw*. The *a* in these sequences is pronounced as usual, i.e. similar to the 'a' of 'father' after the emphatics and the consonants *q, x, ġ,* ح, and ع, and similar to the 'a' of 'mad' after other consonants. In these sequences, the *y* is similar to the 'ee' of 'feed' and the *w* is similar to the 'oo' of 'food'. The sequences *aye* and *awe,* i.e. with an *e* after the *ay* and *aw,* are very common. The pronunciation of the *e* in these sequences is very fleeting, similar to the 'e' of 'towel' or the 'a' of 'trial'. An exception is that before ح or ع the *e* is fully pronounced. Pronunciation Drill 9 provides illustrations and practice for these sequences.

13. Double Consonants. Double consonants are an important feature of Moroccan pronunciation. In English the double writing of a consonant, as the 'dd' in 'middle', is simply a meaningless piece of spelling. In Moroccan, such a writing as *mm* as opposed to *m* or *dd* as opposed to *d* indicates an important difference in pronunciation. The writing of a consonant symbol twice indicates that the consonant is to be held twice as long as a single consonant. Genuine double consonants never occur in English in the middle of words, but they are very common from the end of one word to the beginning of another. Compare the difference between the single 'd' in 'lay down' and the double 'd+d' in 'laid down'. Many similar examples for other consonants can be found in English.

Medial double consonants are not particularly difficult for the English speaking student. More difficult is the occurrence of double consonants both at the beginning and the end of words. Careful attention and practice are necessary for the mastery of initial and final double consonants.

Pronunciation Drills **14** through **17** provide exercise material for the pronunciation of double consonants.

14. Sequences and Clusters. The preceding sections have discussed the various consonant and vowel sounds of Moroccan Arabic. Some of them are very similar to sounds which occur in English, others are quite different. Mastering the new sounds is only a first step for the student. There remains the task of learning to pronounce unfamiliar sequences. Sequences such as *bt-* at the beginning of a word or *-hd* at the end of a word strike the English speaking student as quite strange. Moroccan has a large number of such clusters, and the student must be prepared to deal with them, especially at the beginning and in the middle of words. Such sequences are actually not at all difficult, and they are easily mastered with attention and practice. As a matter of fact, similar clusters occur in rapid conversational English, for example the 'gb' in rapid pronunciations of 'good-bye'; the spelling 'g'bye' is sometimes used to represent this initial cluster in writing. A further example is the initial cluster 'tm' in casual pronunciations of 'tomorrow'. A close examination of spoken English at ordinary conversational speed reveals many such clusters. These can serve as a basis on which the student can build in mastering the pronunciation of seemingly unfamiliar Moroccan clusters.

The initial clusters are the greatest source of difficulty for the English speaking student. Once they are mastered the same clusters occurring medially are no problem. Pronunciation Drills **18** through **26** provide exercise material for various kinds of initial consonant clusters. There are relatively few different kinds of consonant clusters which occur at the end of words, but some of them are quite different from English. Pronunciation Drills **27**, **28**, and **29** provide exercise material for the most frequently encountered final consonant clusters.

15. Triple Consonants. Double consonants are held twice as long as single consonants. There are also cases of triple consonants, which are held even longer than double consonants. If the student has exercised the pronunciation of double consonants properly, learning to contrast them with triple consonants should not be difficult. Pronunciation Drill **30** provides exercise material for the pronunciation of triple consonants.

PRONUNCIATION DRILLS

Pronouncing and hearing sounds accurately is one of the most important factors in speaking and understanding a language. The ability to pronounce and hear the sounds of a new language is usually a skill which is acquired only with considerable practice. It is important for the student to devote his attention to pronouncing and hearing before beginning to learn vocabulary items and grammatical constructions. Once having reached the point of concentrating on meaning, the student is unlikely to concentrate sufficiently on an accurate pronunciation. Exercises on pronunciation must therefore precede the learning of vocabulary items and grammar.

In the drills below, the words used in illustrating pronunciation are numbered consecutively for reference purposes, but the meanings are not given. The student should not think of them as vocabulary items or even as words. He should focus his entire attention on them as sounds, to be listened to and to be imitated. By repeated practice in hearing and pronouncing sounds as sounds, the student will find he has made his later study of vocabulary and grammar much simpler. Once matters of pronunciation have been made automatic through practice, vocabulary and grammar are more easily learned since the student is able to devote his full conscious attention to them.

1. Consonants similar to English, with accompanying vowels. In connection with this pronunciation drill, the student should read section **2. Consonants Similar to English** and section **3. Vowel Sounds With Familiar Consonants** in the chapter on pronunciation.

b 1. *bab*
2. *biban*

f 3. *fas*
4. *kif-aš*
5. *šufu*
6. *šaf*

m 7. *men*
8. *mat*
9. *magana*
10. *huma*
11. *šafuhom*

t 12. *taman*
13. *matu*
14. *šefti*
15. *šeft*

d 16. *dwa*
17. *dak*
18. *hadi*
19. *wad*

s 20. *sinima*
21. *snin*
22. *kisan*
23. *kas*

z 24. *zaž*
25. *zit*
26. *wazen*
27. *daz*

n 28. *nas*
29. *snin*
30. *škun*

š 31. *šaf*
32. *šelya*
33. *maši*
34. *ma-šafu-š*

ž 35. *žib*
36. *ma-žabu-š*
37. *aži*
38. *zaž*

k 39. *kisan*
40. *kun*
41. *yakol*
42. *šeftek*

g 43. *gaz*
44. *gana*

w 45. *wad*
46. *wazen*
47. *ma-mšaw-š*
48. *nemšiw*

y 49. *yakol*
50. *mezyan*
51. *atay*

h 52. *hadi*
53. *huma*
54. *hiya*

a 55. *atay*
56. *maši*
57. *šelya*
58. *magana*
59. *sinima*

e 60. *šefti*
61. *šafet*
62. *zebna*
63. *wazen*

i 64. *sinima*
65. *zib*
66. *šefti*

o 67. *yakol*
68. *šefnahom*
69. *bihom*

2. The emphatic consonants and vowels. In connection with this and the following pronunciation drill, the student should read sections **4. The Emphatic Consonants, 5. The Emphatic Vowels,** and **6. The Sounds *l*, *r*, and *ṛ*** in the chapter on pronunciation.

ḅ 70. *ḅenk*
71. *ḅumbi*

ṭ 72. *ṭaksi*
73. *ṭebḷa*
74. *buṣṭa*
75. *šekḷaṭ*

ḍ 76. *ḍuṛuṣ*
77. *ḍṛeb*
78. *biḍa*
79. *naḍ*

ṣ 80. *ṣifeṭ*
81. *ṣabun*
82. *buṣṭa*
83. *ṛaṣ*

ẓ 84. *ẓeṛbiya*
85. *ẓaṛ*

ḷ 86. *ṭebḷa*
87. *buḷa*

ṛ 88. *ṛažel*
89. *muṛa*
90. *ṭiṛ*

e 91. *ṭeṛša*
92. *ṭebḷa*
93. *šeṛbu*
94. *ṣifeṭ*

a 95. *ṭaṛ*
96. *buḷa*
97. *ṛažel*
98. *ḍaṛ*

i 99. *ṣifeṭ*
100. *ṭiṛu*
101. *ḍaṛi*

u 102. *ṭubis*
103. *ḅumbi*
104. *buḷa*
105. *ṭaṛu*

o 106. *ṣoḷṭa*

3. Emphatic consonants and vowels compared with plain consonants and vowels.

b and *ḅ*
107. *bent* — *ḅenk*
108. *busa* — *ḅumbi*

t and *ṭ*
109. *taṛ* — *ṭaṛ*
110. *bat* — *baṭ*
111. *bitu* — *biṭan*

d and *ḍ*

112. *dar — ḍaṛ*
113. *derb — ḍeṛb*
114. *duza — ḍuṛa*

s and *ṣ*

115. *sif — ṣif*
116. *sum — ṣum*

z and *ẓ*

117. *zerba — ẓeṛbiya*

l and *ḷ*

118. *debla — ṭebḷa*
119. *fula — buḷa*

r and *ṛ*

120. *dar — ḍaṛ*
121. *rakeb — ṛazel*
122. *daru — ḍaṛu*

4. The consonants *q, x,* and *ġ*. Before proceeding with this pronunciation drill, the student should read section **7. The Consonants *q, x,* and *ġ*** in the chapter on pronunciation.

q

123. *qaḍi*
124. *qlam*
125. *qeṣmayn*
126. *qenṭṛa*
127. *qal*
128. *qṛa*
129. *qolt*
130. *qolti*
131. *iqul*
132. *iqama*
133. *weqt*
134. *fiqu*
135. *faq*
136. *fiq*
137. *ṣuq*

x

138. *xay*
139. *xawi*
140. *xud*
141. *xobz*
142. *xiba*
143. *xenša*
144. *xeržu*
145. *ixneq*
146. *menxaṛ*
147. *yaxod*
148. *ma-xda-š*
149. *xuxa*
150. *xux*
151. *šix*
152. *slex*

ġ

153. *ġali*
154. *ġiba*
155. *ġir*
156. *ġeslu*

157. *ġedda*
158. *ġul*
159. *ġonya*
160. *le-ġṭa*
161. *baġi*
162. *nebġi*
163. *ma-ġeslu-š*
164. *ka-iġenni*
165. *bleġ*
166. *baleġ*
167. *ẓaġ*
168. *iẓiġ*
169. *bluġ*

5. The consonant ح, with the various vowels. Before proceeding with this pronunciation drill, the student should read section **8. The Consonants ح and ع** and section **9. The Vowels with ح and ع** in the chapter on pronunciation.

170. *حanut*
171. *حal*
172. *حami*
173. *حaža*
174. *حit*
175. *حili*
176. *حimaya*
177. *حut*
178. *حumeq*
179. *حuf*
180. *حăbs*
181. *حălfa*
182. *حeft*
183. *حekma*
184. *ṛaحa*
185. *baحu*
186. *riحa*
187. *ṣiحa*
188. *iحiru*
189. *ibuحu*
190. *luحa*
191. *weحda*
192. *meحlul*
193. *meحtaṛem*
194. *ikoححu*
195. *rtaح*
196. *baح*
197. *luح*
198. *buح*
199. *tesriح*
200. *šiح*
201. *žnaweح*

6. The consonant ɛ, with the various vowels. Before proceeding with this pronunciation drill, the student should read section **8. The Consonants ḥ and ɛ** and section **9. The Vowels with ḥ and ɛ** in the chapter on pronunciation.

202. *ɛaš*
203. *ɛaqeb*
204. *ɛafya*
205. *ɛiš*
206. *ɛid*
207. *ɛisawa*
208. *ɛud*
209. *ɛumi*
210. *ɛăbdu*
211. *ɛăqli*
212. *ɛăsli*
213. *ɛămla*
214. *ɛers*
215. *ɛešrin*
216. *ɛonwan*
217. *ka-ibiɛu*
218. *biɛa*
219. *šiɛi*
220. *duɛa*
221. *meqluɛin*
222. *baɛu*
223. *saɛa*
224. *măɛmel*
225. *băɛdu*
226. *šăɛlu*
227. *šăɛṛa*
228. *moɛtabaṛ*
229. *inɛăs*
230. *baɛ*
231. *biɛ*
232. *žuɛ*
233. *meṣnuɛ*
234. *swayeɛ*
235. *ṛažeɛ*
236. *waseɛ*

7. The glottal stop. Section **10** of the chapter on pronunciation discusses the glottal stop.

237. *ma-ʔeddeb-š*
238. *fe-l-ʔislam*
239. *ka-iʔetteṛ*
240. *žaṛaʔid*

8. The diphthongs *ăy* and *ăw*. These diphthongs are discussed in section **11** of the chapter on pronunciation.

ăy	241.	*ɛăyn*	*ăw*	249.	*ɛăwd*
	242.	*ɛăyṭa*		250.	*ɛăwža*
	243.	*ɛăyyen*		251.	*ɛăwṛa*
	244.	*ɛăyyeṭ*		252.	*ɛăwwed*
	245.	*ɛăyyan*		253.	*ɛăwwež*
	246.	*ḥăyṭ*		254.	*ḥăwli*
	247.	*ḥăyyed*		255.	*ḥăwma*
	248.	*ḥăyyer*		256.	*ḥăwwel*
				257.	*ḥăwweṭ*

9. The sequences *ay* and *aw*. These sequences are discussed in section **12** of the chapter on pronunciation.

ay	258.	*fayn*		268.	*ṭayeš*
	259.	*qeṣmayn*		269.	*bayeɛ*
	260.	*yumayn*		270.	*ḍayeɛ*
	261.	*ɛamayn*	*aw*	271.	*ḥawlu*
	262.	*bayɛa*		272.	*ɛawnek*
	263.	*ḍayɛin*		273.	*ṣawbu*
	264.	*bayna*		274.	*ḍawyin*
	265.	*flayek*		275.	*srawel*
	266.	*kayen*		276.	*bṛaweṭ*
	267.	*mṛayeṛ*		277.	*žnaweḥ*

10. The consonant *h* in the middle and at the end of words. The student may experience some difficulty with a proper pronunciation of *h* in these positions. The illustrations below provide material for practice.

278.	*sahel*	282.	*šefnah*
279.	*ḍaheṛ*	283.	*beɛtih*
280.	*šahed*	284.	*šaryineh*
281.	*buhel*	285.	*žabuh*

11. The distinction between ḥ and *h*. Distinguishing ḥ and *h* from one another is one of the most difficult aspects of Moroccan pronunciation for speakers of English. The pairs below provide contrastive illustrations for practice.

286.	*ḥanut — hani*	297.	*kuḥel — šafuhom*
287.	*ḥalek — halek*	298.	*luḥa — qebluha*
288.	*ḥamel — hamel*	299.	*riḥa — šriha*
289.	*ḥaža — hažu*	300.	*meḥlul — mehluk*
290.	*ḥimaya — himan*	301.	*deḥša — dehša*
291.	*ḥin — hif*	302.	*žeḥdu — žehdu*
292.	*ḥuma — huma*	303.	*naḥ — šefnah*
293.	*ḥut — hul*	304.	*tesriḥ — tešrih*
294.	*ḥelfu — helku*	305.	*žnaweḥ — klaweh*
295.	*ḥetta — hetku*	306.	*buḥ — žabuh*
296.	*ṛaḥa — qṛaha*		

12. Exercise for the distinction between *h* and *x*. The following contrastive pairs illustrate the distinction.

307.	*xay — hayem*	316.	*ixneq — ihmez*
308.	*xadem — hadef*	317.	*ma-rxa-š — ma-darha-š*
309.	*xak — hak*	318.	*ma-xda-š — ma-hda-š*
310.	*xiba — hiba*	319.	*daxel — sahel*
311.	*xima — himan*	320.	*duxa — zaduha*
312.	*xenša — hemza*	321.	*dax — klah*
313.	*xumus — huma*	322.	*šix — nerših*
314.	*xud — hul*	323.	*slex — šaryineh*
315.	*xeržu — heṛbu*		

13. Exercise for the distinction between ح and *x*. The following contrastive pairs illustrate the distinction.

324. *حala — xala*
325. *حalek — xalek*
326. *حanut — xanu*
327. *حuti — xuti*
328. *حuf — xuf*
329. *حobb — xobz*
330. *حălfa — xălfa*
331. *حilat — xilan*
332. *حira — xira*
333. *riحa — šixa*
334. *luحa — duxa*
335. *laحu — daxu*
336. *baح — dax*
337. *šiح — slix*
338. *koحح — moxx*

14. Medial double consonants before a vowel, contrasted with single consonants.

339. *sebba — sba*
340. *deffa — dfa*
341. *semma — sma*
342. *ketbettu — ktebtu*
343. *beṭṭa — bṭa*
344. *xeddem — xdem*
345. *feḍḍa — fḍa*
346. *عăssel — عsel*
347. *qeṣṣeṛ — qṣeṛ*
348. *fezzeg — fzeg*
349. *qennet — qent*
350. *حeššem — حšem*
351. *عăžžel — عžel*
352. *sekket — sket*
353. *fegged — fged*
354. *beqqa — bqa*
355. *waxxa — daxu*
356. *šeġġal — šġal*
357. *ṣeححa — ṣحa*
358. *beععăd — băعd*
359. *zelleg — zleg*
360. *theḷḷa — ṭḷa*
361. *berred — bred*
362. *beṛṛa — bṛa*
363. *šuwwaš — šwaš*
364. *byeḍ — biyyeḍ*
365. *šehhed — šhed*

15. Medial double consonants before a consonant, contrasted with single consonants.

366. *šehhdu — šehdu*
367. *biyyḍu — biḍa*
368. *ṭuwwlu — ṭulu*
369. *berrdu — berdu*
370. *zellget — zelget*
371. *beɛɛdu — băɛdu*
372. *weqqfet — weqfet*
373. *sekktu — sektu*
374. *ɛeššmet — ɛešmet*
375. *qenntu — qentu*
376. *fezzgu — fezgu*
377. *feṣṣḷu — feṣḷu*
378. *xeddmet — xedmet*
379. *ṣemmṛu — ṣemṛu*
380. *ṣeffqu — ṣefqa*
381. *ṣebbṛu — ṣebṛu*

16. Initial double consonants, contrasted with initial single consonants.

382. *ḅḅaha — baṭ*
383. *b-bunya — bunya*
384. *f-fas — fas*
385. *f-fṛanṣa — fṛanṣa*
386. *mmellek — mellek*
387. *t-tilifun — tilifun*
388. *ṭ-ṭumubil — ṭumubil*
389. *ddar — dar*
390. *ḍḍaṛeb — ḍaṛeb*
391. *s-sira — sira*
392. *s-slam — slam*
393. *ṣ-ṣeɛɛa — ṣeɛɛa*
394. *ṣ-ṣṭeḷ — ṣṭeḷ*
395. *z-zit — zit*
396. *z-zbib — zbib*
397. *ẓ-ẓemmaṛa — ẓemmaṛa*
398. *ẓ-ẓṛaybi — ẓṛaybi*
399. *š-šekkaṛa — šekkaṛa*
400. *š-šhada — šhada*
401. *ž-žefna — žefna*
402. *ž-žben — žben*
403. *l-luz — luz*
404. *l-lsan — lsan*
405. *ḷḷah — ḷaṭif*
406. *r-rokba — rokba*
407. *r-ržel — ržel*
408. *ṛ-ṛažel — ṛažel*
409. *ṛ-ṛḍuma — ṛḍuma*

17. Final double consonants, contrasted with final single consonants.

410. *šabb — šab*
411. *leff — šaf*
412. *ka-išemm — žisem*
413. *u-bett — ketbet*

414. *skett — sket*
415. *qeṭṭ — saqeṭ*
416. *ka-iḥeṭṭ — šaḥeṭ*
417. *ka-imedd — žamed*
418. *ɛaḍḍ — faḍ*
419. *ka-imess — xames*
420. *feṣṣ — keṛfeṣ*
421. *dezz — xnez*
422. *ḍenn — qṭen*
423. *ṛešš — ṭṛeš*
424. *ḥažž — ɛwaž*
425. *fekk — skek*
426. *ṛeqq — bṛeq*
427. *moxx — fsex*
428. *ṣeḥḥ — nṣeḥ*
429. *qell — ɛqel*
430. *berr — kber*
431. *ḍeṛṛ — qḍeṛ*

18. Initial consonant clusters: Clusters of stop plus stop.

432. *bda*
433. *bqa*
434. *b-taman*
435. *dqiqa*
436. *kbir*
437. *kbeṛ*
438. *ktab*
439. *kteb*
440. *kteṛ*
441. *qbeḍ*
442. *qbel*
443. *qṭen*
444. *tkellem*
445. *tqaḍa*
446. *tqašeṛ*
447. *ṭbali*
448. *ṭbaṣel*
449. *ṭbib*

19. Initial consonant clusters: Clusters of stop plus fricative.

450. *bġa*
451. *bṣeḷ*
452. *bḥal*
453. *dheb*
454. *dxel*
455. *džuwwež*
456. *ḍheṛ*
457. *kfen*
458. *ksad*
459. *kḥăl*
460. *qṣem*
461. *qṣeṛ*
462. *tfahem*
463. *tfekk*
464. *tfeṛgăɛ*
465. *tfešš*

466. *theḷḷa*
467. *therres*
468. *tsenna*
469. *tsăɛṭaš*
470. *tṣaff*
471. *tṣaweṛ*
472. *txebba*
473. *tƈămmem*
474. *tɛăllem*
475. *tɛăṭṭeḷ*
476. *ṭfa*

20. Initial consonant clusters: Clusters of fricative plus stop.

477. *fḍuli*
478. *fqiha*
479. *ġda*
480. *ġṭa*
481. *hbel*
482. *hdiya*
483. *hḍeṛ*
484. *htemm*
485. *sbăɛṭaš*
486. *stilu*
487. *stexbeṛ*
488. *ṣbaƈ*
489. *ṣbiṭaṛ*
490. *škel*
491. *škun*
492. *xbaṛ*
493. *xda*
494. *xdem*
495. *xḍeṛ*
496. *xti*
497. *žbeṛ*
498. *ždid*
499. *ƈḍaš*
500. *ƈtaṛem*
501. *ɛṭa*

21. Initial consonant clusters: Clusters of fricative plus fricative.

502. *fsed*
503. *fṣeḷ*
504. *fšuš*
505. *fxeḍ*
506. *fƈula*
507. *fɛayel*
508. *ġfel*
509. *ġsil*
510. *ġsel*
511. *ġṣeb*
512. *ġšim*
513. *hšaš*
514. *hžuliya*
515. *sfina*

516. *shet*
517. *sxun*
518. *ṣfeṛ*
519. *ṣġiṛ*
520. *ṣġeṛ*
521. *šher*
522. *šحal*
523. *šحăl*
524. *šعăṛ*
525. *xfeq*
526. *xṣeṛ*
527. *xšin*
528. *حsab*
529. *حsen*
530. *حfaret*
531. *عfen*
532. *عsel*
533. *عṣiṛ*
534. *عšuṛ*
535. *عziz*

22. Initial consonant clusters: Clusters of stop plus nasal or resonant.

536. *blad*
537. *bṛawat*
538. *byeḍ*
539. *drari*
540. *dwa*
541. *dyal*
542. *ḍṛeb*
543. *ḍyeq*
544. *ḍyuṛ*
545. *gles*
546. *kla*
547. *knaneš*
548. *kriti*
549. *qlam*
550. *qleb*
551. *qnaṭeṛ*
552. *qṛa*
553. *tlata*
554. *tmenya*
555. *tnaber*
556. *tnayn*
557. *twessex*
558. *ṭḷeb*
559. *ṭnaš*
560. *ṭṛeš*
561. *ṭwil*
562. *ṭwel*

23. Initial consonant clusters: Clusters of nasal or resonant plus stop.

563. *lbes*
564. *mdabza*
565. *mkemmel*
566. *mkoħla*
567. *nqa*
568. *nqi*
569. *nta*
570. *ntaxeb*
571. *ntuma*
572. *ṛbaṭ*
573. *ṛbăɛṭaš*
574. *rkeb*
575. *rtaħ*
576. *wqef*
577. *wqid*

24. Initial consonant clusters: Clusters of fricative plus nasal or resonant.

578. *flayek*
579. *fnaṛ*
580. *ġleb*
581. *ġṛeq*
582. *hna*
583. *hlek*
584. *hṛeb*
585. *srawel*
586. *ṣḷaħ*
587. *smăɛ*
588. *ṣnăɛ*
589. *ṣyaḍa*
590. *š-men*
591. *šra*
592. *šṛeb*
593. *šṛib*
594. *šwiya*
595. *xlaq*
596. *xnaši*
597. *nxeq*
598. *xrež*
599. *xwatati*
600. *zlafa*
601. *znaqi*
602. *ẓṛabi*
603. *ẓṛeq*
604. *žnaweħ*
605. *žyub*
606. *ħla*
607. *ħlib*
608. *ħlu*
609. *ħmeṛ*
610. *ħna*
611. *ħrira*
612. *ħwanet*
613. *ɛla*
614. *ɛlaš*
615. *ɛmel*
616. *ɛwafi*

25. Initial consonant clusters: Clusters of nasal or resonant plus fricative.

617. *lfafa*
618. *lfuf*
619. *lġa*
620. *lhih*
621. *lsan*
622. *lṣeq*
623. *lzem*
624. *lžam*
625. *l-xir*
626. *lḥăm*
627. *lɛăb*
628. *mfafya*
629. *mġeṭṭi*
630. *mherres*
631. *msali*
632. *mṣaff*
633. *mṣaṛen*
634. *mša*
635. *mšaṭi*
636. *mwežžed*
637. *mxebbi*
638. *mžuwwež*
639. *mɛa*
640. *mɛăṭṭeḷ*
641. *nfăɛ*
642. *nhaṛ*
643. *nsa*
644. *nɛăs*
645. *rfed*
646. *ṛžăɛ*
647. *wsăɛ*
648. *wṣeḷ*
649. *wzen*

26. Initial consonant clusters: Clusters of nasals and resonants.

649. *l-mizan*
650. *l-mut*
651. *lmăɛ*
652. *lwaleb*
653. *lwan*
654. *lwaḥ*
655. *lyali*
656. *lyan*
657. *lyaqa*
658. *mlayen*
659. *mleḥ*
660. *mnin*
661. *mraya*
662. *mṛa*
663. *mṛiḍ*
664. *mwagen*
665. *mwessex*
666. *myatayn*
667. *nmel*
668. *nwa*

669. *nwayel*
670. *nyab*
671. *nyašen*
672. *ṛwayeḍ*
673. *ṛwiḍa*
674. *wlad*
675. *wṛaq*

27. Final consonant clusters ending in *t*. Clusters of this sort are very common, and the student should take care to learn them accurately. It is especially important for the student to avoid pronouncing them with an English accent by identifying them with similar sounding clusters in English.

676. *sebt*
677. *ḍṛebt*
678. *rfedt*
679. *žbedt*
680. *ʕăddedt*
681. *neḍt*
682. *qbeḍt*
683. *left*
684. *šeft*
685. *šerregt*
686. *ṣbeġt*
687. *šebbeht*
688. *teht*
689. *wežžeht*
690. *šebbekt*
691. *nzelt*
692. *tfahemt*
693. *fhemt*
694. *bent*
695. *kont*
696. *weqt*
697. *fiyyeqt*
698. *ġṛeqt*
699. *dert*
700. *žbeṛt*
701. *herrest*
702. *xelleṣt*
703. *ʕešt*
704. *ṣifeṭt*
705. *ġḷeṭt*
706. *twessext*
707. *slext*
708. *ddabezt*
709. *xrežt*
710. *džuwwežt*
711. *ṭeʕt*
712. *ṭiyyeʕt*
713. *beʕt*
714. *ṛžăʕt*

28. Final consonant clusters ending in *tš* preceded by another consonant. Clusters of this sort are very common. Since they are likely to cause the student some difficulty, they should be practiced very carefully.

715. *ma-ḍṛebt-š*
716. *ma-rfedt-š*
717. *ma-žbedt-š*
718. *ma-ḥăddedt-š*
719. *ma-neḍt-š*
720. *ma-qbeḍt-š*
721. *ma-šeft-š*
722. *ma-šerregt-š*
723. *ma-ṣbeġt-š*
724. *ma-šebbeht-š*
725. *ma-teht-š*
726. *ma-wežžeht-š*
727. *ma-šebbekt-š*
728. *ma-nzelt-š*
729. *ma-tfahemt-š*
730. *ma-fhemt-š*
731. *ma-kont-š*
732. *ma-fiyyeqt-š*
733. *ma-ġṛeqt-š*
734. *ma-dert-š*
735. *ma-žb^{e}ṛt-š*
736. *ma-herrest-š*
737. *ma-xeḷḷeṣt-š*
738. *ma-ɛešt-š*
739. *ma-ṣifeṭt-š*
740. *ma-ġḷeṭt-š*
741. *ma-twessext-š*
742. *ma-slext-š*
743. *ma-ddabezt-š*
744. *ma-xrežt-š*
745. *ma-džuwwežt-š*
746. *ma-ṭeḥt-š*
747. *ma-ṭiyyeḥt-š*
748. *ma-beɛt-š*
749. *ma-ṛžăɛt-š*
750. *ma-žeɛt-š*

29. Other final consonant clusters. Final consonant clusters ending in sounds other than *t* or *tš* are not frequent. However, some of them differ substantially from English, and practice is necessary for the student to achieve a proper pronunciation.

751. *kelb*
752. *denb*
753. *derb*
754. *berd*
755. *weld*
756. *ɛănd*
757. *ɛăbd*
758. *kebd*
759. *băɛd*
760. *derd*

761. *žehd*
762. *ḷeṛḍ*
763. *băɛḍ*
764. *ṣehḍ*
765. *wăɛḍ*
766. *ḍoɛf*
767. *welf*
768. *kăɛk*
769. *ḍăɛk*
770. *ḍoḷm*
771. *ṭoɛm*
772. *ṭeḷq*
773. *kebš*
774. *deɛš*
775. *wăɛš*
776. *keɛṭ*
777. *ḍebṭ*
778. *ḍeġṭ*
779. *šeṛṭ*
780. *beṣṭ*
781. *xobz*
782. *boṛž*
783. *šfenž*
784. *ṭeṛɛ*

30. Triple consonants, contrasted with double consonants.

785. *ɛăddu — ɛădddu*
786. *sebbu — sebbbu*
787. *feḍḍa — feḍḍḍu*
788. *žeffu — žefffu*
789. *ɛăžžet — fežžžet*
790. *fekku — fekkkom*
791. *dellu — delllu*
792. *ɛămmu — ɛămmmu*
793. *tmenna — mennna*
794. *ḍeṛṛu — ɛăṛṛṛu*
795. *messet — dessset*
796. *meṣṣu — qeṣṣṣu*
797. *betti — fetttu*
798. *xeṭṭu — xeṭṭṭu*
799. *feššet — fešššet*
800. *xezzi — xezzzet*

LESSON ONE

I. Text.

bab	door
l-bab	the door
magana	watch, clock
l-magana	the watch, the clock

xobz	bread
l-xobz	the bread
mdad	ink
le-mdad	the ink
ɛwayež	clothes
le-ɛwayež	the clothes
bit	room
l-bit	the room
konnaš	notebook
l-konnaš	the notebook
fe-l-konnaš	in the notebook
xenša	sack, bag
l-xenša	the sack, the bag
fe-l-xenša	in the bag
ktab	book
le-ktab	the book
f-le-ktab	in the book
ɛšiya	evening
le-ɛšiya	the evening
f-le-ɛšiya	in the evening

II. Grammatical Notes.

A. The form for 'the' is usually *l-*, as in *l-bab* 'the door'. The form is *le-* if the following word begins with two consonants, as in *le-ɛwayež* 'the clothes'.

B. The preposition usually translated as 'in' has the form *fe-* before two consonants, as in *fe-l-bit* 'in the room'; otherwise the form is *f-*, as in *f-le-ktab* 'in the book'.

III. Exercises.

A. Give the form for 'the' for each of the following words.

1. ——— *-bab.*
2. ——— *-bit.*
3. ——— *-ktab.*
4. ——— *-konnaš.*
5. ——— *-magana.*
6. ——— *-mdad.*
7. ——— *-xobz.*
8. ——— *-xenša.*
9. ——— *-ḥwayež.*
10. ——— *-ɛšiya.*

B. Give the form for 'in the' for each of the following words.

1. ——— *-bit.*
2. ——— *-ktab.*
3. ——— *-konnaš.*
4. ——— *-xenša.*
5. ——— *-ɛšiya.*

IV. Vocabulary.

bab	door
bit	room
f-, fe-	in
konnaš	notebook
ktab	book
l-, le-	the
magana	watch, clock
mdad	ink
xobz	bread
xenša	sack, bag
ḥwayež	clothes
ɛšiya	evening

The letters *e* and *o* are not taken into account when Moroccan words are alphabetized for vocabulary listings. Thus *xobz* 'bread' precedes *xenša* 'bag' in alphabetical listing.

LESSON TWO

I. Text.

ṛažel	man
ṛ-ṛažel	the man
šeṛžem	window
š-šeṛžem	the window
ṭebla	table
ṭ-ṭebla	the table
ḍaṛ	house
ḍ-ḍaṛ	the house
fe-ḍ-ḍaṛ	in the house
ṣif	summer
ṣ-ṣif	the summer
fe-ṣ-ṣif	in the summer
ṣbaḥ	morning
ṣ-ṣbaḥ	the morning
fe-ṣ-ṣbaḥ	in the morning
teṣwiṛa	picture
t-teṣwiṛa	the picture
fe-t-teṣwiṛa	in the picture
sefli	ground floor
s-sefli	the ground floor
fe-s-sefli	on the ground floor
ṛ-ṛažel fe-ḍ-ḍaṛ.	The man is in the house.
l-bit fe-ḍ-ḍaṛ.	The room is in the house.
l-bit fe-s-sefli.	The room is on the ground floor.
š-šeṛžem fe-l-bit.	The window is in the room.
ṭ-ṭebla fe-l-bit.	The table is in the room.
t-teṣwiṛa f-le-ktab.	The picture is in the book.
l-magana fe-l-xenša.	The clock is in the bag.
l-xobz fe-l-xenša.	The bread is in the bag.
l-xenša fe-ḍ-ḍaṛ.	The sack is in the house.
l-konnaš fe-l-bit.	The notebook is in the room.

II. Grammatical Notes.

A. When a word begins with a consonant made with the tip or front part of the tongue (the dentals and the palatals, plus *ḷ, r,* and *ṛ;* see the chapter on pronunciation), the form for 'the' is usually a repetition of the first consonant of the word it accompanies, as in *ḍ-ḍaṛ* 'the house'. There are fourteen such consonants. Seven of them are illustrated by the new words given in this lesson: *ḍ, ṛ, s, ṣ, š, t,* and *ṭ*. The remaining seven will be covered in the next lesson.

B. There is usually no Moroccan equivalent for English 'is', as exemplified by such sentences as *ṛ-ṛažel fe-ḍ-ḍaṛ* 'The man is in the house'.

C. The preposition *f-, fe-* is not always translated as 'in'. In many cases the proper translation is 'on', as in *fe-s-sefli* 'on the ground floor'. The student must be prepared to memorize such cases as they arise.

III. Exercises.

A. Supply the definite article for the following words:

1. ——— *-magana.*
2. ——— *-sefli.*
3. ——— *-ṭebla.*
4. ——— *-teṣwiṛa.*
5. ——— *-ṛažel.*
6. ——— *-ṣif.*
7. ——— *-bab.*
8. ——— *-mdad.*
9. ——— *-bit.*
10. ——— *-xenša.*
11. ——— *-konnaš.*
12. ——— *-ktab.*
13. ——— *-ḍaṛ.*
14. ——— *-ɛwayež.*
15. ——— *-šeṛžem.*
16. ——— *-xobz.*
17. ——— *-ɛšiya.*
18. ——— *-ṣbaɛ.*

B. Give the form for 'in the' for each of the following words.

1. ——— *-teṣwiṛa.*
2. ———*ɛšiya.*
3. ——— *-ktab.*
4. ——— *-ṣif.*
5. ——— *-ḍaṛ.*
6. ——— *-konnaš.*
7. ——— *-bit.*
8. ——— *-ṣbaɛ.*

C. Give the Moroccan equivalent for the English in parentheses and read the resulting sentence aloud.

1. *l-magana* (is in the) *bit.*
2. *l-bit* (is on the) *sefli.*
3. *le-mdad* (is in the) *xenša.*
4. *t-teṣwiṛa* (is in the) *konnaš.*
5. *š-šeṛžem* (is in the) *bit.*
6. *l-xobz* (is in the) *bit.*
7. *ṭ-ṭebla* (is in the) *ḍaṛ.*
8. *l-xenša* (is in the) *bit.*
9. *ṛ-ṛažel* (is in the) *ḍaṛ.*
10. (The room is) *fe-s-sefli.*
11. (The picture is) *fe-l-konnaš.*
12. (The table is) *fe-ḍ-ḍaṛ.*
13. (The man is) *fe-ḍ-ḍaṛ.*
14. (The bag is) *fe-ḍ-ḍaṛ.*
15. (The bread is) *fe-ḍ-ḍaṛ.*
16. (The ink is) *fe-ḍ-ḍaṛ.*
17. (The watch is) *fe-ḍ-ḍaṛ.*
18. (The window is) *fe-l-bit.*
19. *l-xenša fe-* (the room).
20. *ṛ-ṛažel fe-* (the house).
21. *l-xobz fe-* (the bag).
22. *ṭ-ṭebla fe-* (the room).
23. *le-mdad fe-* (the house).
24. *t-teṣwiṛa fe-* (the book).
25. *l-magana fe-* (the bag).
26. *l-bit fe-* (the ground floor).
27. *š-šeṛžem fe-* (the room).

IV. Vocabulary.

ḍaṛ	house
ṛažel	man
sefli	ground floor
ṣbaḥ	morning
ṣif	summer
šeṛžem	window
teṣwiṛa	picture
ṭebla	table

LESSON THREE

I. Text.

drari	children
d-drari	the children
nas	people
n-nas	the people

ržal	men
r-ržal	the men
šelya	chair
š-šelya	the chair
zit	oil
z-zit	the oil
ẓeṛbiya	rug, carpet
ẓ-ẓeṛbiya	the rug, the carpet
žib	pocket
ž-žib	the pocket
fayn	where
qeddam	in front of
ƈda	beside, next to
fayn le-ƈwayež?	Where are the clothes?
le-ƈwayež fe-l-xenša.	The clothes are in the bag.
fayn d-drari?	Where are the children?
d-drari fe-l-bit.	The children are in the room.
fayn r-ržal?	Where are the men?
r-ržal fe-ḍ-ḍaṛ.	The men are in the house.
fayn n-nas?	Where are the people?
n-nas fe-ḍ-ḍaṛ.	The people are in the house.
fayn t-teṣwiṛa?	Where is the picture?
t-teṣwiṛa fe-ž-žib.	The picture is in the pocket.
fayn l-xobz?	Where is the bread?
l-xobz fe-ž-žib.	The bread is in the pocket.
fayn le-mdad?	Where is the ink?
le-mdad fe-ž-žib.	The ink is in the pocket.
fayn ẓ-ẓeṛbiya?	Where is the rug?
ẓ-ẓeṛbiya fe-l-bit.	The rug is in the room.

fayn le-ktab?	Where is the book?
le-ktab ḥda l-konnaš.	The book is beside the notebook.
fayn ṭ-ṭebla?	Where is the table?
ṭ-ṭebla ḥda šeṛžem.	The table is next to the window.
fayn š-šelya?	Where is the chair?
š-šelya ḥda ṭ-ṭebla.	The chair is next to the table.
fayn ṛ-ṛažel?	Where is the man?
ṛ-ṛažel ḥda l-bab.	The man is next to the door.
fayn z-zit?	Where is the oil?
z-zit ḥda l-xobz.	The oil is next to the bread.
fayn d-drari?	Where are the children?
d-drari qeddam ḍ-ḍaṛ.	The children are in front of the house.
fayn ṛ-ṛažel?	Where is the man?
ṛ-ṛažel qeddam d-drari.	The man is in front of the children.
fayn n-nas?	Where are the people?
n-nas qeddam š-šeṛžem.	The people are in front of the window.

II. Grammatical Notes.

A. In Lesson 2 it was pointed out that the form for 'the' is usually a repetition of the first consonant of the word which follows if the word begins with *ḍ, ṛ, s, ṣ, š, t,* or *ṭ*. The same is true for words beginning with *d, n, r, z, ẓ,* and *ž*, as illustrated by the new words in this lesson. The same is also true for *ḷ*, but words beginning with *ḷ* are relatively rare. Illustrations will be given in subsequent lessons.

B. There is usually no Moroccan equivalent for English 'are', as exemplified by such sentences as *r-ržal fe-ḍ-ḍaṛ* 'The men are in the house'.

C. Note that the plural of *ṛažel* 'man' is *ržal* 'men'. In general, the plurals of Moroccan words are more different from the corresponding singulars than is the case in English. Moroccan plurals will be studied extensively in subsequent lessons.

III. Exercises.

A. Give the form for 'the' for each of the following words.

1. ——— *-šelya.*
2. ——— *-ṭebla.*
3. ——— *-teṣwiṛa.*
4. ——— *-ẓeṛbiya.*
5. ——— *-žib.*
6. ——— *-ṣif.*
7. ——— *-sefli.*
8. ——— *-drari.*
9. ——— *-ržal.*
10. ——— *-ṛažel.*
11. ——— *-šeṛžem.*
12. ——— *-ḍaṛ.*
13. ——— *-nas.*
14. ——— *-zit.*
15. ——— *-ṣbaᴤ.*

B. Give the Moroccan equivalent for the English in parentheses and read the resulting sentence aloud.

1. *fayn* (are the clothes)?
2. *fayn* (are the children)?
3. *fayn* (are the men)?
4. *fayn* (are the people)?
5. *fayn* (is the chair)?
6. *fayn* (is the pocket)?
7. *le-ᴤwayež* (are in the) *xenša.*
8. *d-drari* (are in the) *bit.*
9. *r-ržal* (are in the) *ḍaṛ.*
10. *n-nas* (are in the) *ḍaṛ.*
11. *t-teṣwiṛa* (is in the) *žib.*
12. *l-xobz* (is in the) *žib.*
13. *le-mdad* (is in the) *žib.*
14. *le-ktab* (is beside the) *konnaš.*
15. *ṭ-ṭebla* (is next to the) *šeṛžem.*
16. *š-šelya* (is next to the) *šeṛžem.*
17. *ṛ-ṛažel* (is next to the) *bab.*
18. *z-zit* (is next to the) *xobz.*
19. *d-drari* (are in front of the) *ḍaṛ.*
20. *ṛ-ṛažel* (is in front of the) *drari.*
21. *n-nas* (are in front of the) *šeṛžem*

IV. Vocabulary.

drari	children
fayn	where
nas	people
qeddam	in front of
ržal	men
šelya	chair
zit	oil
ẓeṛbiya	rug, carpet
žib	pocket
ᴤda	beside, next to

LESSON FOUR

I. Text.

mezyan	good
l-mezyan	the good one
xobz mezyan	good bread
l-xobz l-mezyan	the good bread
l-xobz mezyan.	The bread is good.
meɛlul	open
l-meɛlul	the open one
bit meɛlul	an open room
l-bit l-meɛlul	the open room
l-bit meɛlul.	The room is open.
mešdud	closed
l-mešdud	the closed one
šeṛžem mešdud	a closed window
š-šeṛžem l-mešdud	the closed window
š-šeṛžem mešdud.	The window is closed.
kbir	big
le-kbir	the big one
ṛažel kbir	a big man
ṛ-ṛažel le-kbir	the big man
ṛ-ṛažel kbir.	The man is big.
mwessex	dirty
le-mwessex	the dirty one
ktab mwessex	a dirty book
le-ktab le-mwessex	the dirty book
le-ktab mwessex.	The book is dirty.
ṣġiṛ	small, little
ṣ-ṣġiṛ	the little one
konnaš ṣġiṛ	a small notebook
l-konnaš ṣ-ṣġiṛ	the small notebook
l-konnaš ṣġiṛ.	The notebook is small.

nqi	clean
n-nqi	the clean one
šeṛžem nqi	a clean window
š-šeṛžem n-nqi	the clean window
š-šeṛžem nqi.	The window is clean.

II. Grammatical Notes.

A. The form for 'the' with adjectives is exactly the same as with nouns.

B. Adjectives come after the nouns they go with, just the opposite of English, as in *xobz mezyan* 'good bread'.

C. An adjective going directly with a noun must have the form for 'the' with it if the noun does. Notice such examples as *š-šeṛžem n-nqi* 'the clean window', where both *šeṛžem* 'window' and *nqi* 'clean' are accompanied by the form for 'the'.

D. Moroccan adjectives are commonly used as nouns, as in *le-kbir* 'the big one'. Note that there is no equivalent in Moroccan for 'one' in such uses.

III. Exercises.

A. Go through the pairs of nouns and adjectives below and combine them on the pattern of *ṛažel kbir* 'a big man'. Read the resulting phrase aloud for each pair.

B. Go through the pairs of nouns and adjectives below and combine them on the pattern of *ṛ-ṛažel kbir* 'The man is big'. Read the resulting sentence aloud for each pair.

1. *xobz* and *nqi.*
2. *bit* and *mešdud.*
3. *konnaš* and *meεlul.*
4. *ktab* and *kbir.*
5. *ṛažel* and *ṣġiṛ.*
6. *šeṛžem* and *mezyan.*
7. *žib* and *kbir.*
8. *xobz* and *mwessex.*
9. *ṛažel* and *mezyan.*
10. *ktab* and *mešdud.*
11. *šeṛžem* and *meεlul.*
12. *bit* and *mezyan.*
13. *žib* and *mwessex.*
14. *konnaš* and *mešdud.*

15. *ṛažel* and *nqi*.
16. *ktab* and *ṣġiṛ*.
17. *šeṛžem* and *mwessex*.
18. *bit* and *kbir*.
19. *žib* and *nqi*.
20. *konnaš* and *mezyan*.
21. *ṛažel* and *mwessex*.
22. *ktab* and *meƐlul*.
23. *bit* and *ṣġiṛ*.
24. *šeṛžem* and *nqi*.
25. *žib* and *ṣġiṛ*.
26. *konnaš* and *mwessex*.
27. *ktab* and *mezyan*.
28. *bit* and *nqi*.
29. *šeṛžem* and *kbir*.
30. *konnaš* and *nqi*.
31. *ktab* and *nqi*.
32. *bit* and *mwessex*.
33. *šeṛžem* and *ṣġiṛ*.
34. *konnaš* and *kbir*.

IV. Vocabulary.

kbir	big
mešdud	closed
mwessex	dirty
mezyan	good
meƐlul	open
nqi	clean
ṣġiṛ	small, little

LESSON FIVE

I. Text.

ḍyuṛ	houses
ḍ-ḍyuṛ	the houses
mwessxin	dirty (pl.)
le-mwessxin	the dirty ones
ḍyuṛ mwessxin	dirty houses
ḍ-ḍyuṛ le-mwessxin	the dirty houses
ḍ-ḍyuṛ mwessxin.	The houses are dirty.
biban	doors
l-biban	the doors
mešdudin	closed (pl.)

l-mešdudin	the closed ones
biban mešdudin	closed doors
l-biban l-mešdudin	the closed doors
l-biban mešdudin.	The doors are closed.
ktub	books
le-ktub	the books
mezyanin	good (pl.)
l-mezyanin	the good ones
ktub mezyanin	good books
le-ktub l-mezyanin	the good books
le-ktub mezyanin.	The books are good.
šṛažem	windows
š-šṛažem	the windows
meɛlulin	open (pl.)
l-meɛlulin	the open ones
šṛažem meɛlulin	open windows
š-šṛažem l-meɛlulin	the open windows
š-šṛažem meɛlulin.	The windows are open.
byut	rooms
le-byut	the rooms
nqiyin	clean (pl.)
n-nqiyin	the clean ones
byut nqiyin	clean rooms
le-byut n-nqiyin	the clean rooms
le-byut nqiyin.	The rooms are clean.

II. Grammatical Notes.

A. The plurals of Moroccan words are usually unpredictable and have to be memorized as individual vocabulary items, e.g., the plural of *ktab* 'book' is *ktub* 'books'.

B. Unlike English, Moroccan adjectives have separate plural forms. The plural of adjectives is also usually unpredictable, but a large number of adjectives which begin with *m-* form the plural by adding *-in,* as in *mezyan* 'good', plural *mezyanin.*

C. Adjectives which go with plural nouns must also be plural. Compare *ktab mezyan* 'a good book' and *ktub mezyanin* 'good books'.

III. Exercises.

A. Go through the pairs of nouns and adjectives below and combine them on the pattern of *ḍyuṛ mwessxin* 'dirty houses'. Read the resulting phrase aloud for each pair.

B. Go through the pairs of nouns and adjectives below and combine them on the pattern of *ḍ-ḍyuṛ le-mwessxin* 'the dirty houses'. Read the resulting phrase aloud for each pair.

C. Go through the pairs of nouns and adjectives below and combine them on the pattern of *ḍ-ḍyuṛ mwessxin* 'The houses are dirty'. Read the resulting sentence aloud for each pair.

1. *biban* and *mwessxin.*
2. *šṛažem* and *mešdudin.*
3. *ḍyuṛ* and *mezyanin.*
4. *byut* and *mwessxin.*
5. *ktub* and *meɛlulin.*
6. *byut* and *mešdudin.*
7. *ḍyuṛ* and *meɛlulin.*
8. *biban* and *mezyanin.*
9. *šṛažem* and *nqiyin.*
10. *ktub* and *mešdudin.*
11. *byut* and *meɛlulin.*
12. *ktub* and *mwessxin.*
13. *biban* and *nqiyin.*
14. *šṛažem* and *mezyanin.*
15. *ḍyuṛ* and *mešdudin.*
16. *ktub* and *nqiyin.*
17. *šṛažem* and *mwessxin.*
18. *biban* and *meɛlulin.*
19. *ḍyuṛ* and *nqiyin.*
20. *byut* and *mezyanin.*

IV. Vocabulary.

biban	doors
byut	rooms
ḍyuṛ	houses
ktub	books
mešdudin	closed (pl.)
mwessxin	dirty (pl.)
mezyanin	good (pl.)
meɛlulin	open (pl.)
nqiyin	clean (pl.)
šṛažem	windows

LESSON SIX

I. Text.

knaneš	notebooks
le-knaneš	the notebooks
kbaṛ	big (pl.)
le-kbaṛ	the big ones
knaneš kbaṛ	big notebooks
le-knaneš le-kbaṛ	the big notebooks
le-knaneš kbaṛ.	The notebooks are big.
šelyat	chairs
š-šelyat	the chairs
ṣġaṛ	small, little (pl.)
ṣ-ṣġaṛ	the small ones
šelyat ṣġaṛ	little chairs
š-šelyat ṣ-ṣġaṛ	the little chairs
š-šelyat ṣġaṛ.	The chairs are little.
mwagen	watches, clocks
le-mwagen	the watches, the clocks
mwagen kbaṛ	large clocks
le-mwagen le-kbaṛ	the large clocks
le-mwagen kbaṛ	The clocks are large.
xnaši	bags, sacks
le-xnaši	the bags, the sacks
xnaši ṣġaṛ	small bags
le-xnaši ṣ-ṣġaṛ	the small bags
le-xnaši ṣġaṛ.	The bags are small.
tṣaweṛ	pictures
t-tṣaweṛ	the pictures
tṣaweṛ kbaṛ	large pictures
t-tṣaweṛ le-kbaṛ	the large pictures
t-tṣaweṛ kbaṛ.	The pictures are large.
ṭbali	tables
ṭ-ṭbali	the tables

ṭbali ṣġaṛ	little tables
ṭ-ṭbali ṣ-ṣġaṛ	the little tables
ṭ-ṭbali ṣġaṛ.	The tables are little.
ẓṛabi	rugs
ẓ-ẓṛabi	the rugs
ẓṛabi kbaṛ	big rugs
ẓ-ẓṛabi le-kbaṛ	the big rugs
ẓ-ẓṛabi kbaṛ.	The rugs are big.
žyub	pockets
ž-žyub	the pockets
žyub ṣġaṛ	small pockets
ž-žyub ṣ-ṣġaṛ	the small pockets
ž-žyub ṣġaṛ.	The pockets are small.

II. Grammatical Notes.

Review the grammatical notes of Lesson 5.

III. Exercises.

Go through the exercises of Lesson 4 and, insofar as you have learned the proper forms, change all the singular forms to plurals. Read the resulting phrases and sentences out loud as you do them.

IV. Vocabulary.

kbaṛ	big, large (pl.)
knaneš	notebooks
mwagen	watches, clocks
ṣġaṛ	small, little (pl.)
šelyat	chairs
tṣaweṛ	pictures
ṭbali	tables
xnaši	bags, sacks
ẓṛabi	rugs, carpets
žyub	pockets

LESSON SEVEN

I. Text.

kbira	big, large (f.)
magana kbira	a big clock
l-magana le-kbira	the big clock
l-magana kbira.	The clock is big.
meɛlula	open (f.)
xenša meɛlula	an open bag
l-xenša l-meɛlula	the open bag
l-xenša meɛlula.	The bag is open.
nqiya	clean (f.)
ṭebḷa nqiya	a clean table
ṭ-ṭebḷa n-nqiya	the clean table
ṭ-ṭebḷa nqiya.	The table is clean.
mezyana	good (f.)
teṣwiṛa mezyana	a good picture
t-teṣwiṛa l-mezyana	the good picture
t-teṣwiṛa mezyana.	The picture is good.
ṣġiṛa	small, little (f.)
šelya ṣġiṛa	a little chair
š-šelya ṣ-ṣġiṛa	the little chair
š-šelya ṣġiṛa.	The chair is little.
mwessxa	dirty (f.)
ẓeṛbiya mwessxa	a dirty rug
ẓ-ẓeṛbiya le-mwessxa	the dirty rug
ẓ-ẓeṛbiya mwessxa.	The rug is dirty.
mešduda	closed (f.)
bab mešduda	a closed door
l-bab l-mešduda	the closed door
l-bab mešduda.	The door is closed.
ḍaṛ mezyana	a good house
ḍ-ḍaṛ l-mezyana	the good house
ḍ-ḍaṛ mezyana.	The house is good.

zit mwessxa	dirty oil
z-zit le-mwessxa	the dirty oil
z-zit mwessxa.	The oil is dirty.

II. Grammatical Notes.

A. All nouns in Moroccan fall into one of two classes, called 'masculine' (abbreviated 'm.') and 'feminine' (abbreviated 'f.'). This kind of difference is called 'gender'. Most nouns ending in *-a* are feminine, for example, *šelya* 'chair'. Most other nouns, not ending in *-a,* are masculine, for example *xobz* 'bread'. A few nouns not ending in *-a* are nonetheless feminine, for example *bab* 'door', *ḍaṛ* 'house', and *zit* 'oil'. The relatively few feminine nouns which do not end in *-a* must be learned as a matter of memory.

B. If a noun is feminine, the adjective going with it must also be feminine, for example *teṣwiṛa mezyana* 'a good picture'. This is true even if the feminine noun does not end in *-a,* for example *ḍaṛ mezyana* 'a good house'. Adjectives are regularly made feminine by adding *-a* to the masculine form, for example, masculine form *mezyan,* feminine form *mezyana* 'good'. Occasionally the masculine form is changed slightly when the feminine ending *-a* is added, as in masculine *mwessex* 'dirty', with feminine *mwessxa,* and masculine *nqi* 'clean', with feminine *nqiya.*

III. Exercises.

A. Give the appropriate Moroccan equivalent for the English in the parentheses. Read each resulting phrase aloud.

1. *ẓeṛbiya* (small).
2. *šelya* (dirty).
3. *ḍaṛ* (clean).
4. *teṣwiṛa* (big).
5. *ṭebla* (good).
6. *xenša* (closed).
7. *magana* (dirty).
8. *bab* (open).
9. *ṭebla* (big).
10. *teṣwiṛa* (dirty).
11. *xenša* (clean).
12. *ḍaṛ* (closed).
13. *magana* (good).
14. *šelya* (big).
15. *bab* (little).
16. *ẓeṛbiya* (clean).
17. *ẓeṛbiya* (good).
18. *šelya* (clean).
19. *ḍaṛ* (dirty).
20. *teṣwiṛa* (small).

21. *ṭebla* (dirty).
22. *xenša* (big).
23. *magana* (clean).
24. *bab* (good).
25. *ṭebla* (little).
26. *magana* (small).
27. *xenša* (dirty).
28. *teṣwiṛa* (clean).
29. *ẓeṛbiya* (big).
30. *šelya* (good).
31. *bab* (dirty).
32. *ḍaṛ* (open).
33. *xenša* (good).
34. *ḍaṛ* (little).
35. *bab* (big).
36. *zit* (good).

B. Go through the pairs of nouns and adjectives below and combine them on the pattern of *l-magana le-kbira* 'the big clock'. Read the resulting phrases aloud for each pair.

C. Go through the pairs of nouns and adjectives below and combine them on the pattern of *l-magana kbira* 'The clock is big'. Read the resulting sentence aloud for each pair.

1. *šelya* and *nqiya*.
2. *ẓeṛbiya* and *mezyana*.
3. *bab* and *kbira*.
4. *ẓeṛbiya* and *nqiya*.
5. *ḍaṛ* and *ṣġiṛa*.
6. *bab* and *ṣġiṛa*.
7. *xenša* and *mezyana*.
8. *šelya* and *kbira*.
9. *magana* and *mezyana*.
10. *ḍaṛ* and *meεlula*.
11. *bab* and *mwessxa*.
12. *ḍaṛ* and *mešduda*.
13. *šelya* and *mezyana*.
14. *xenša* and *nqiya*.
15. *ẓeṛbiya* and *kbira*.
16. *teṣwiṛa* and *mwessxa*.
17. *teṣwiṛa* and *nqiya*.
18. *ṭebla* and *kbira*.
19. *xenša* and *mwessxa*.
20. *bab* and *meεlula*.
21. *magana* and *ṣġiṛa*.
22. *magana* and *mwessxa*.
23. *ṭebla* and *ṣġiṛa*.
24. *xenša* and *mešduda*.
25. *bab* and *mezyana*.
26. *ṭebla* and *mezyana*.
27. *magana* and *nqiya*.
28. *teṣwiṛa* and *kbira*.
29. *xenša* and *kbira*.
30. *ḍaṛ* and *nqiya*.
31. *ṭebla* and *mwessxa*.
32. *šelya* and *mwessxa*.
33. *teṣwiṛa* and *ṣġiṛa*.
34. *ẓeṛbiya* and *ṣġiṛa*.
35. *ḍaṛ* and *mwessxa*.

IV. Vocabulary.

kbira	big, large (f.)
mešduda	closed (f.)
mwessxa	dirty (f.)
mezyana	good (f.)
meᶎlula	open (f.)
nqiya	clean (f.)
ṣġiṛa	small, little (f.)

LESSON EIGHT

I. Text.

fayn z-zit?	Where is the oil?
z-zit fe-l-bit.	The oil is in the room.
waš z-zit ᶓăl ṭ-ṭebla?	Is the oil on the table?
la, z-zit ᶎda š-šeṛžem.	No, the oil is beside the window.
le-ktab kbir.	The book is big.
waš le-knaneš kbaṛ?	Are the notebooks big?
iyeh, le-knaneš kbaṛ.	Yes, the notebooks are big.
waš š-šṛažem mwessxin?	Are the windows dirty?
la, š-šṛažem ma-ši mwessxin.	No, the windows aren't dirty.
waš l-magana teᶎt t-teṣwiṛa?	Is the watch under the picture?
iyeh, l-magana teᶎt t-teṣwiṛa.	Yes, the watch is under the picture.
d-drari ma-ši fe-l-bit.	The children aren't in the house.
fayn d-drari?	Where are the children?
d-drari muṛa ḍ-ḍaṛ.	The children are behind the house.
waš le-ᶎwayež fe-l-xenša?	Are the clothes in the bag?
la, le-ᶎwayež ma-ši fe-l-xenša.	No the clothes aren't in the bag.
le-ᶎwayež muṛa l-bab.	The clothes are behind the door.
waš le-mdad ᶓăl š-šelya?	Is the ink on the chair?
iyeh, le-mdad ᶓăl š-šelya.	Yes, the ink is on the chair.

II. Grammatical Notes.

A. Moroccan sentences which have no equivalent for English 'is' or 'are' (see Grammatical Note **B** of Lesson 2 and Grammatical Note **B** of Lesson 3) are called 'equational sentences', for example *ṛ-ṛažel fe-ḍ-ḍaṛ* 'The man is in the house'.

B. Equational sentences are made negative by inserting the word *ma-ši* 'not' at the point in the sentence where English 'is' or 'are' would come, for example, *ṛ-ṛažel ma-ši fe-ḍ-ḍaṛ* 'The man isn't in the house'.

C. Equational sentences can be turned into questions by prefixing the word *waš* to them, for example *waš ṛ-ṛažel fe-ḍ-ḍaṛ?* 'Is the man in the house?'.

III. Exercises.

A. Below is a list of equational sentences. Read each one out loud, then turn it into a question by prefixing *waš,* answer it affirmatively with a statement beginning with *iyeh,* and then answer it negatively with a statement beginning with *la.* Say each statement out loud.

Follow the sequence given in this example:

Equational sentence:	*ṛ-ṛažel fe-ḍ-ḍaṛ.*
Question:	*waš ṛ-ṛažel fe-ḍ-ḍaṛ?*
Affirmative answer:	*iyeh, ṛ-ṛažel fe-ḍ-ḍaṛ.*
Negative answer:	*la, ṛ-ṛažel ma-ši fe-ḍ-ḍaṛ.*

1. *l-bit fe-s-sefli.*
2. *š-šeṛžem fe-l-bit.*
3. *ṭ-ṭebla fe-l-bit.*
4. *t-teṣwiṛa fe-le-ktab.*
5. *l-xenša fe-ḍ-ḍar.*
6. *le-ktab ɛda l-konnaš.*
7. *l-xobz mezyan.*
8. *l-bit meɛlul.*
9. *ṛ-ṛažel kbir.*
10. *l-biban mešdudin.*
11. *ẓ-ẓṛabi kbaṛ.*
12. *l-magana kbira.*
13. *ḍ-ḍyuṛ mwessxin.*
14. *n-nas qeddam š-šeṛžem.*
15. *z-zit nqiya.*

B. Give the Moroccan equivalent for the English in the parentheses. Read the resulting sentences aloud.

1. *waš d-drari* (under the rug)?
2. (No, the children aren't) *teƐt ẓ-ẓeṛbiya.*
3. *waš d-drari* (on the rug)?
4. (Yes, the children are) *Ɛăl ẓ-ẓeṛbiya.*
5. *waš le-mdad* (behind the door)?
6. (No, the ink isn't) *muṛa l-bab.*
7. *waš le-mdad* (on the table)?
8. (Yes, the ink is) *Ɛăl ṭ-ṭebla.*
9. *waš ṛ-ṛažel* (behind the chair)?
10. (No, the man isn't) *muṛa š-šelya.*
11. *waš ṛ-ṛažel* (behind the house)?
12. (Yes, the man is) *muṛa ḍ-ḍaṛ.*
13. *waš t-teṣwiṛa* (under the notebook?)
14. (No, the picture isn't) *teƐt l-konnaš.*
15. *waš t-teṣwiṛa* (under the book?)
16. (Yes, the picture is) *teƐt le-ktab.*

IV. Vocabulary.

iyeh	yes
la	no
ma-ši	not
muṛa	behind
teƐt	under
waš	(see Grammatical Note C)
Ɛăl	on

The form *Ɛăl* occurs only before the various forms for 'the'. This word has another form when it occurs elsewhere. The other form will be given in a later lesson.

LESSON NINE

I. Text.

had ṛ-ṛažel	this man
had ḍ-ḍaṛ	this house
had š-šelyat	these chairs
had š-šṛažem	these windows

had le-mdad mezyan.	This ink is good.
had ẓ-ẓeṛbiya ṣġiṛa.	This rug is small.
had le-ɛwayež nqiyin.	These clothes are clean.
ktab u-konnaš	a book and a notebook
xobz u-zit	bread and oil
l-bab u-š-šeṛžem	The door and the window
ṭbali u-šelyat	tables and chairs
ṭ-ṭbali u-š-šelyat	the tables and chairs
z-zit u-l-xobz mezyanin.	The oil and the bread are good.
l-bab u-š-šeṛžem meɛlulin.	The door and the window are open.
had le-ktab u-had l-konnaš	this book and this notebook
had le-ktab u-had l-konnaš mwessxin.	This book and this notebook are dirty.
had le-ktab mwessex u-had l-konnaš mweṣsex.	This book is dirty and so is this notebook. (This book is dirty and this notebook is dirty.)
had š-šelyat u-had ṭ-ṭbali kbaṛ.	These chairs and these tables are big.
had š-šelyat kbaṛ u-had ṭ-ṭbali kbaṛ.	These chairs are big and so are these tables.

II. Grammatical Notes.

A. The equivalent for English 'this' and 'these' as in 'this book' and 'these clothes' is *had* placed before a word which already has the form for 'the', thus *le-ktab* 'the book', *had le-ktab* 'this book', *le-ɛwayež* 'the clothes', *had le-ɛwayež* 'these clothes'.

B. When two singular nouns or a singular noun and a plural noun are joined by *u* 'and', an adjective referring to both of them is plural, as in *l-xobz u-z-zit mezyanin* 'The bread and the oil are good' or *had ṭ-ṭebla u-had š-šelyat ṣġaṛ* 'This table and these chairs are little.'

C. When the form for 'the' is used with two nouns joined by *u* 'and', it must be repeated before each of them. In English it is possible to say either 'the bread and oil' or 'the bread and the oil', but Moroccan shows only the one pattern, as in *l-xobz u-z-zit.*

III. Exercises.

Given below are a number of triplets consisting of two nouns and an adjective. Form sentences out of them according to the pattern shown in the example.
Example:

Triplet:	*ktab, konnaš, kbaṛ*
Sentence:	*had le-ktab u-had l-konnaš kbaṛ.*

1. *bab, šeṛžem, meɛlulin.*
2. *bit, ẓeṛbiya, mwessħin.*
3. *teṣwiṛa, konnaš, nqiyin.*
4. *šelya, ṭebla, kbaṛ.*
5. *xobz, zit, mezyanin.*

IV. Vocabulary.

had	this, these (see Grammatical Note A)
u	and

LESSON TEN

I. Text.

l-weld	the boy
had l-weld	this boy
wlad	boys
l-ulad	the boys
had l-ulad	these boys
l-bent	the girl
had l-bent	this girl
le-bnat	the girls
had le-bnat	these girls
had le-bnat u-had l-ulad	these girls and boys (these girls and these boys)
weld mṛiḍ	a sick boy
l-weld le-mṛiḍ	the sick boy
bent mṛiḍa	a sick girl

had l-bent le-mṛiḍa	this sick girl
had le-bnat le-mṛaḍ	these sick girls
had l-ulad le-mṛaḍ	these sick boys
had l-ulad mṛaḍ.	These boys are sick.
had l-weld mṛiḍ u-had l-bent mṛiḍa.	This boy is sick and so is this girl.
had l-weld u-had l-bent mṛaḍ.	This boy and girl are sick.
had le-bnat u-had l-ulad mṛaḍ.	These girls and boys are sick.

II. Grammatical Notes.

A. In English one occurrence of 'this' or 'these' can refer to a number of following nouns, as in 'this boy and girl' or 'these boys and girls'. In Moroccan, *had* 'this, these' must be repeated before each noun it refers to, as in *had l-weld u-had l-bent* 'this boy and (this) girl' or *had l-ulad u-had le-bnat* 'these boys and (these) girls'.

B. Note that Moroccan adjectives in such expressions as *had l-bent le-mṛiḍa* 'this sick girl' have the form for 'the' when the noun they accompany has *had* 'this, these'.

C. If a word begins with *w* followed by a consonant, the *w* is changed to *u* after the word for 'the', e.g. *wlad* 'boys' and *l-ulad* 'the boys'.

III. Exercises.

A. Go through the following list of noun and adjective pairs and form phrases out of them on the pattern of *had l-weld le-mṛiḍ* 'this sick boy' and then change the phrase into the equational sentence *had l-weld mṛiḍ* 'this boy is sick'. Read each phrase and sentence aloud.

B. Go through the list of noun and adjective pairs again and form sentences on the pattern *had l-weld mṛiḍ* 'this boy is sick' and change them into negative sentences on the pattern *had l-weld ma-ši mṛiḍ* 'this boy is not sick'. Read each resulting sentence aloud.

1. *ṛažel, mṛiḍ.*
2. *weld, mṛiḍ.*
3. *weld, mezyan.*
4. *weld, mwessex.*
5. *bent, mwessxa.*
6. *bent, nqiya.*

7. *bent, kbira.*
8. *bent, mṛiḍa.*
9. *ṛžal, mṛaḍ.*
10. *drari, mṛaḍ.*
11. *nas, mṛaḍ.*
12. *wlad, mṛaḍ.*
13. *wlad, kbaṛ.*
14. *wlad, ṣġaṛ.*
15. *wlad, mezyanin.*
16. *bnat, mezyanin.*
17. *bnat, ṣġaṛ.*
18. *bnat, mwessxin.*
19. *bnat, nqiyen.*
20. *bnat, kbaṛ.*

C. Given below are a number of triplets consisting of two nouns and an adjective. Form sentences out of them according to the pattern shown in the example. Read each resulting sentence aloud.
Example:

Triplet: *weld, bent, mṛaḍ*
Sentence: *had l-weld u-had l-bent mṛaḍ.*

1. *ṛažel, weld, mṛaḍ.*
2. *ṛažel, bent, mṛaḍ.*
3. *ṛažel, bent, kbaṛ.*
4. *weld, bent, kbaṛ.*
5. *wlad, bnat, kbaṛ.*
6. *wlad, bnat, ṣġaṛ.*
7. *wlad, bnat, mṛaḍ.*
8. *ṛžal, bnat, mwessxin.*
9. *ṛžal, drari, mwessxin.*
10. *ṛžal, drari, nqiyin.*

IV. Vocabulary.

bent	girl
bnat	girls
mṛiḍ	sick
mṛiḍa (f.)	
mṛaḍ (pl.)	
weld	boy
wlad	boys

LESSON ELEVEN

I. Text.

l-weld l-feṛεan	the happy boy
had l-weld feṛεan.	This boy is happy.
l-bent l-feṛεana	the happy girl
had l-bent feṛεana.	This girl is happy.
had l-bent u-had l-weld feṛεanin.	This boy and this girl are happy.
ṛ-ṛažel l-keslan	the lazy man
ṛ-ṛažel keslan.	The man is lazy.
waš l-bent keslana?	Is the girl lazy?
iyeh, l-bent keslana.	Yes, the girl is lazy.
had ṛ-ṛažel u-had l-bent keslanin.	This man and this girl are lazy.
l-weld l-mešġul.	the busy boy
l-weld mešġul.	The boy is busy.
waš l-bent mešġula?	Is the girl busy?
iyeh, l-bent mešġula.	Yes, the girl is busy.
waš d-drari mešġulin?	Are the children busy?
iyeh, d-drari mešġulin.	Yes, the children are busy.

II. Grammatical Notes.

Reread the grammatical notes of Lessons 1 through 10.

III. Exercises.

A. Go through the following list of noun and adjective pairs and form questions on the pattern of *waš had l-weld mešġul?* 'Is this boy busy?' Then answer the question affirmatively on the pattern of *iyeh, had l-weld mešġul* 'Yes, this boy is busy'. Then answer the question negatively on the pattern of *la, had l-weld ma-ši mešġul* 'No, this boy isn't busy.' Read each resulting sentence aloud.

1. *ṛažel, mṛiḍ.*
2. *ṛažel, keslan.*
3. *weld, keslan.*
4. *weld, kbir.*
5. *weld, mwessex.*
6. *weld, ṣġiṛ.*
7. *bent, ṣġiṛa.*
8. *bent, feṛḥana.*
9. *bent, nqiya.*
10. *drari, nqiyin.*
11. *drari, mešġulin.*
12. *drari, mezyanin.*
13. *nas, mezyanin.*
14. *nas, mṛaḍ.*
15. *nas, keslanin.*
16. *nas, feṛḥanin.*
17. *wlad, feṛḥanin.*
18. *bnat, feṛḥanin.*
19. *bent, feṛḥana.*
20. *bent, mešġula.*

B. Given below are a number of triplets consisting of two nouns and an adjective. Form sentences out of them according to the pattern shown in the example. Read each resulting sentence aloud.

Example:

Triplet: *weld, bent, mṛaḍ*
Sentence: *had l-weld u-had l-bent mṛaḍ.*

1. *ṛažel, weld, mṛaḍ.*
2. *ṛažel, weld, feṛḥanin.*
3. *weld, bent, mešġulin.*
4. *weld, bent, keslanin.*
5. *bent, ṛažel, keslanin.*
6. *bent, ṛažel, kbaṛ.*
7. *ržal, drari, kbaṛ.*
8. *ržal, drari, feṛḥanin.*
9. *ržal, wlad, feṛḥanin.*
10. *ržal, wlad, kbaṛ.*

IV. Vocabulary.

feṛḥan	happy
feṛḥana (f.)	
feṛḥanin (pl.)	
keslan	lazy
keslana (f.)	
keslanin (pl.)	
mešġul	busy
mešġula (f.)	
mešġulin (pl.)	

LESSON TWELVE

I. Text.

mṛa feṛɛana	a happy woman
had le-mṛa feṛɛana.	This woman is happy.
ɛyalat mṛaḍ	sick women
had le-ɛyalat mṛaḍ.	These women are sick.
fqi mešġul	a busy schoolteacher (man)
had le-fqi mešġul.	This schoolteacher is busy.
fqiha mezyana	a good schoolteacher (woman)
had le-fqiha mezyana.	This schoolteacher is good.
mdad kɛăl	black ink
le-mdad kɛăl.	The ink is black.
ṭebla keɛla	a black table
ṭ-ṭebla keɛla.	The table is black.
biban kuɛăl	black doors
had l-biban kuɛăl.	These doors are black.
ktab ɛmeṛ	a red book
had le-ktab ɛmeṛ.	This book is red.
ẓeṛbiya ɛămṛa	a red rug.
had ẓ-ẓeṛbiya ɛămṛa.	This rug is red.
šelyat ɛumeṛ.	red chairs
had š-šelyat ɛumeṛ.	These chairs are red.
waš had le-fqi mešġul?	Is this schoolteacher busy?
la, le-fqi l-axoṛ mešġul.	No, the other schoolteacher is busy.
waš had le-mṛa mṛiḍa?	Is this woman sick?
la, le-mṛa le-x̂ṛa[1] mṛiḍa.	No, the other woman is.
waš had d-drari mwessxin?	Are these children dirty?
la, d-drari le-x̂ṛin mwessxin.	No, the other ones are.

II. Grammatical Notes.

Reread the Grammatical Notes of Lessons 1 through 10.

[1] The symbol ᵔ (or ˆ) over a consonant indicates labialization: the consonant is pronounced with rounded lips and followed by a slight *w*-sound.

III. Exercises.

There follows a list of noun and adjective pairs. Go through them successively according to the instructions below. In each case read the resulting phrase or sentence out loud.

A. Combine them on the pattern of *ktab kbir* 'a big book'.

B. Combine them on the pattern of *le-ktab le-kbir* 'the big book'.

C. Combine them on the pattern of *had le-ktab le-kbir* 'this big book'.

D. Combine them on the pattern of *had le-ktab kbir* 'This book is big'.

E. Combine them on the pattern of *waš had le-ktab kbir?* 'Is this book big?'

F. Combine them on the pattern of *la, had le-ktab ma-ši kbir* 'No, this book isn't big'.

1. *mṛa, xṛa.*
2. *mṛa, ṣġiṛa.*
3. *ɛyalat, keslanin.*
4. *ɛyalat, feṛḥanin.*
5. *ɛyalat, ṣġaṛ.*
6. *ɛyalat, xṛin.*
7. *fqi, axoṛ.*
8. *zit, keḥla.*
9. *magana, keḥla.*
10. *knaneš, xṛin.*
11. *fqi, mezyan.*
12. *fqiha, keslana.*
13. *konnaš, axoṛ.*
14. *mdad, ḥmeṛ.*
15. *zit, ḥămṛa.*
16. *ḥwayež, ḥumeṛ.*
17. *ktab, kḥăl.*
18. *ḍaṛ, xṛa.*
19. *ḥwayež, kuḥăl.*
20. *mwagen, kuḥăl.*

IV. Vocabulary.

axoṛ	other
xṛa (f.)	
xṛin (pl.)	
fqi (m.)	schoolteacher
fqiha (f.)	schoolteacher

kḥăl	black
keḥla (f.)	
kuḥăl (pl.)	
mṛa	woman
ẋṛa, ẋṛin	(see *axoṛ*)
ḥmeṛ	red
ḥămṛa (f.)	
ḥumeṛ (pl.)	
ɛyalat	women

LESSON THIRTEEN

I. Text.

ana	I
ana mešğul.	I'm busy.
ana fqi.	I'm a schoolteacher.
ana fe-l-bit.	I'm in the room.
ana muṛa ḍ-ḍaṛ.	I'm behind the house.
nta (m., sg.)	you
waš nta ṛažel?	Are you a man?
waš nta mṛiḍ?	Are you sick?
la, ana ma-ši mṛiḍ.	No, I'm not sick.
nti (f., sg.)	you
waš nti mṛa?	Are you a woman?
iyeh, ana mṛa.	Yes, I'm a woman.
waš nti feṛḥana?	Are you happy?
iyeh, ana feṛḥana.	Yes, I'm happy.
ḥna	we
ḥna kbaṛ.	We're big.
ḥna fe-ḍ-ḍaṛ.	We're in the house.
ḥna ḥda š-šeṛžem.	We're next to the window.
ntuma (pl.)	you
waš ntuma mwessxin?	Are you dirty?

la, ḥna ma-ši mwessxin, ḥna nqiyin.	No, we're not dirty, we're clean.
waš ntuma ɛyalat?	Are you women?
la, ḥna ṛžal.	No, we're men.

II. Grammatical Notes.

A. The pronoun *ana* 'I' takes a masculine or a feminine adjective depending on whether a man or a woman is speaking. A man says *ana mešġul* but a woman says *ana mešġula* for 'I'm busy'.

B. There are three Moroccan words corresponding to English 'you'. They are usually referred to as masculine, feminine, and plural. The masculine *nta* 'you' is used in speaking to a man or a boy, the feminine *nti* 'you' is used in speaking to a woman, and the plural *ntuma* 'you' is used in speaking to two or more people at once. For example:

To a man:	*waš nta feṛḥan?*
To a woman:	*waš nti feṛḥana?*
To two or more people:	*waš ntuma feṛḥanin?*

C. Plural forms are used with *ḥna* 'we' and *ntuma* 'you' as in *ḥna mešġulin* 'We're busy' and *ntuma mešġulin* 'You're busy'.

III. Exercises.

Listed below are a number of sentences. Change them according to the following instructions. With each change, read the resulting new sentence out loud.

A. Change each sentence into a question, changing each noun into *nta, nti,* or *ntuma,* whichever is appropriate.

B. To the questions formed in Exercise **A,** answer with *ana* or *ḥna,* whichever is appropriate. First answer affirmatively with *iyeh,* and then negatively with *la.*

1. *ṛ-ṛažel feṛḥan.*
2. *le-fqi mešġul.*
3. *l-weld mṛiḍ.*
4. *le-mṛa keslana.*
5. *le-fqiha mezyana.*
6. *l-bent ṣġiṛa.*
7. *r-ržal kbaṛ.*
8. *l-ulad mwessxin.*
9. *le-bnat feṛḥanin.*
10. *d-drari feṛḥanin.*
11. *n-nas mešġulin.*
12. *le-ɛyalat mṛaḍ.*

IV. Vocabulary.

ana	I
nta (m.)	you
nti (f.)	you
ntuma (pl.)	you
ḥna	we

LESSON FOURTEEN

I. Text.

huwa	he
fayn huwa?	Where is he?
fe-ḍ-ḍaṛ.	He's in the house.
waš huwa mešġul?	Is he busy?
iyeh, mešġul.	Yes, he is.
waš huwa fqi?	Is he a schoolteacher?
iyeh, huwa fqi.	Yes, he is.
la, huwa ma-ši fqi.	No, he isn't.
hiya	she
fayn hiya?	Where is she?
fe-l-bit.	She's in the room.
waš hiya mešġula?	Is she busy?
iyeh, mešġula.	Yes, she is.
waš hiya fqiha?	Is she a schoolteacher?
iyeh, hiya fqiha.	Yes, she is.
la, hiya ma-ši fqi.	No, she isn't.
huma	they
fayn huma?	Where are they?
fe-s-sefli.	They're on the ground floor.
waš huma mešġulin?	Are they busy?
iyeh, mešġulin.	Yes, they are.
waš huma ržal?	Are they men?
iyeh, huma ržal.	Yes, they are.
la, huma ma-ši ržal.	No, they aren't.

II. Grammatical Notes.

A. Just as with masculine and femine nouns (see the Grammatical Notes of Lesson 7), the masculine pronoun *huwa* 'he' takes masculine forms, for example *waš huwa kbir?* 'Is he big?', and the feminine pronoun *hiya* 'she' takes feminine forms, for example *waš hiya kbira?* 'Is she big?'.

B. The pronouns *huwa* 'he', *hiya* 'she', and *huma* 'they' are used in questions and in affirmative answers to these questions if the answer is an equational sentence containing a noun, for example *iyeh, huwa fqi.* 'Yes, he's a schoolteacher, versus *iyeh, mešġul* 'Yes, he's busy'. In the other instances cited, these pronouns are not used, contrary to the usual pattern in English.

III. Exercises.

A. Change the sentences below into questions and substitute *huwa* 'he', *hiya* 'she', or *huma* 'they', whichever is appropriate for the nouns. Then answer the questions affirmatively with *iyeh* and negatively with *la.*

1. *ṛ-ṛažel feṛɛan.*
2. *le-fqi mešġul.*
3. *l-weld mṛiḍ.*
4. *le-mṛa keslana.*
5. *le-fqiha mezyana.*
6. *l-bent ṣġiṛa.*
7. *r-ržal kbaṛ.*
8. *l-ulad mwessxin.*
9. *le-bnat feṛɛanin.*
10. *d-drari feṛɛanin.*
11. *n-nas mešġulin.*
12. *le-ɛyalat mṛaḍ.*

B. Form questions and answers from the following pairs of words on the pattern of the example.
Example:

Word pair:	*ṛažel, ḍaṛ*	
Question:	*fayn ṛ-ṛažel?*	Where is the man?
Answer:	*fe-ḍ-ḍaṛ.*	He's in the house.

1. *ɛwayež, xenša*
2. *bent, bit*
3. *konnaš, žib*
4. *weld, ḍaṛ.*
5. *byut, sefli*

IV. Vocabulary.

hiya	she
huma	they
huwa	he

LESSON FIFTEEN

I. Text.

le-ktab ždid.	The book is new.
le-ktab ž-ždid mezyan.	The new book is good.
had le-ktab ž-ždid ma-ši mezyan.	This new book isn't good.
l-meḍṛaṣa ždida.	The school is new.
had l-meḍṛaṣa ž-ždida ma-ši mezyana.	This new school isn't good.
le-mḍaṛeṣ ždidin.	The schools are new.
had le-mḍaṛeṣ ž-ždidin ma-ši kbaṛ.	These new schools aren't big.
l-kelb byeḍ.	The dog is white.
had l-kelb ma-ši byeḍ.	This dog isn't white.
š-šelya ma-ši biḍa.	The chair isn't white.
had š-šelya l-biḍa mwessxa.	This white chair is dirty.
le-klab ma-ši buyeḍ.	The dogs aren't white.

II. Grammatical Note.

Such English sequences as 'The book is new' and 'The new book is good' illustrate a pattern for building up increasingly larger and more complex sentences. Moroccan sentences can be built up in an exactly similar fashion, for example *le-ktab ždid* and *had le-ktab ž-ždid mezyan.*

III. Exercise.

Below are a number of triplets consisting of a noun and two adjectives, for example *ktab, ždid, kɛăl*. Make sentences from them on the pattern of *had le-ktab ž-ždid kɛăl* 'This new book is black'. Turn each resulting sentence into a question on the pattern of *waš had le-ktab ž-ždid kɛăl?* 'Is this new book black?', and answer each question on the pattern of *iyeh, kɛăl* 'Yes, it's black'. In each case, read the resulting sentence out loud.

1. *bit, kbir, mwessex.*
2. *konnaš, meɛlul, ṣġiṛ.*
3. *ktab, kɛăl, meɛlul.*
4. *mdad, ɛmeṛ, mezyan.*
5. *xobz, mwessex, kɛăl.*
6. *šeṛžem, kbir, mešdud.*
7. *žib, ṣġiṛ, mwessex.*
8. *kelb, kbir, mṛiḍ.*
9. *meḍṛaṣa, ždida, mezyana..*
10. *magana, ždida, mezyana.*
11. *bab, biḍa, meɛlula.*
12. *xenša, ɛămṛa kbira.*
13. *ḍaṛ, ždida, biḍa.*
14. *teṣwiṛa, sġiṛa, mezyana.*
15. *ṭebla, kbira, nqiya.*
16. *šelya, keɛla, ždida.*
17. *zit, ždida, mezyana.*
18. *ẓeṛbiya, kbira, mwessxa.*
19. *mḍaṛeṣ, sġaṛ, mešdudin.*
20. *klab, kbaṛ, mṛaḍ.*
21. *ɛwayež, nqiyin, ždad.*
22. *biban, ɛumeṛ, meɛlulin.*
23. *byut, ždad, mwessxin.*
24. *ḍyuṛ, buyeḍ, ždad.*
25. *ktub, kbaṛ, meɛlulin.*
26. *knaneš, ṣġaṛ, mešdudin.*
27. *knaneš, ṣġaṛ, mezyanin.*
28. *mwagen, ždad, mezyanin.*
29. *šelyat, ɛumeṛ, nqiyin.*
30. *ṭbali, kuɛăl, ždad.*

IV. Vocabulary.

byeḍ	white
biḍa (f.)	
buyeḍ (pl.)	
kelb	dog
klab (pl.)	
meḍṛaṣa	school
mḍaṛeṣ (pl.)	
ždid	new
ždida (f.)	
ždad (pl.)	

LESSON SIXTEEN

I. Text.

dak	that
dak le-ktab	that book
dak le-ktab le-kbir	that big book
dak le-ktab kbir.	That book is big.
dak le-ktab le-kbir ḥmeṛ.	That big book is red.
dak š-šelya	that chair
dak š-šelya l-biḍa	that white chair
dak š-šelya biḍa.	That chair is white.
dak š-šelya l-biḍa nqiya.	That white chair is clean.
duk n-nas	those people
duk n-nas l-mezyanin	those good people
duk n-nas mezyanin.	Those people are good
duk n-nas l-mezyanin feṛḥanin.	Those good people are happy.
žuž	two
žuž de-d-dari	two children
žuž de-d-drari feṛḥanin	two happy children
had ž-žuž de-d-drari	these two children
duk ž-žuž de-d-drari l-feṛḥanin	those two happy children
duk ž-žuž de-d-drari feṛḥanin.	Those two children are happy.
had ž-žuž d-le-byut n-nqiyin	these two clean rooms
duk ž-žuž d-le-byut n-nqiyin	those two clean rooms
had ž-ṣuž d-le-byut nqiyin.	These two rooms are clean.
duk ž-žuž d-le-byut nqiyin.	Those two rooms are clean.
had t-tlata de-š-šelyat kuḥăl.	These three chairs are black.
duk t-tlata de-š-šelyat kuḥăl.	Those three chairs are black.

II. Grammatical Notes.

A. The equivalent for English 'that' is *dak* placed before a word which already has the form for 'the', thus *le-ktab* 'the book', *dak le-ktab* 'that book', *š-šelya* 'the chair', *dak š-šelya* 'that chair'. The form for the plural is *duk* 'those', used in the same way, thus *le-mwagen* 'the clocks', *duk le-mwagen* 'those clocks'.

B. When used in counting with *žuž* 'two' and *tlata* 'three', nouns are plural and have the form for 'the' preceded by *d-* or *de-* (*d-* before a consonant plus a vowel, *de-* before two consonants). Thus *le-ktub* 'the books', *l-biban* 'the doors' and *žuž d-le-ktub* 'two books', *tlata d-le-ktub* 'three books', *žuž de-l-biban* 'two doors', *tlata de-l-biban* 'three doors'.

C. The forms for 'these' and 'those' are used with Moroccan numerals, just as in English, as in *had ž-žuž d-le-ktub* 'these two books', *duk t-tlata de-l-biban* 'those three doors'.

D. Unless the numeral itself is preceded by the form for 'the', 'these', or 'those', an adjective accompanying a counted noun does not take the form for 'the' even though the noun does, for example *kbaṛ* in *žuž de-r-ržal kbaṛ* 'two big men' and *had ž-žuž de-r-ržal le-kbaṛ* 'these two big men'.

III. Exercises.

A. Do the exercises of Lessons 10 and 11 substituting *dak* or *duk* for each occurrence of *had*.

B. From each of the noun-adjective pairs below form successively phrases and sentences on the pattern of the example. Read each resulting phrase and sentence out loud.

Example: *ktub, kbaṛ*
žuž d-le-ktub
žuž d-le-ktub kbaṛ
duk ž-žuž d-le-ktub le-kbaṛ
duk ž-žuž d-le-ktub kbaṛ.

1. *ḍyuṛ, mwessxin.*
2. *šṛažem, mešdudin.*
3. *knaneš, nqiyin.*
4. *mwagen, ždad.*
5. *šelyat, ḅuyeḍ.*
6. *tṣaweṛ, mezyanin.*
7. *ṭbali, ṣġaṛ.*
8. *ẓṛabi, ḥumeṛ.*
9. *žyub, kbaṛ*
10. *bnat, feṛḥanin.*
11. *wlad, keslanin.*
12. *ɛyalat, mešġulin.*
13. *klab, mṛaḍ.*
14. *mḍaṛeṣ, meḥlulin*

C. From each of the noun-adjective pairs below form successively phrases and sentences on the pattern of the example. Read each resulting phrase and sentence out loud.

Example: *šelyat, kuɛăl*

tlata de-š-šelyat

tlata de-š-šelyat kuɛăl

duk t-tlata de-š-šelyat l-kuɛăl

duk t-tlata de-š-šelyat kuɛăl.

1. *mḍaṛeṣ, mešdudin.*
2. *ḍyuṛ, meɛlulin.*
3. *klab, kbaṛ.*
4. *šṛažem, ṣġaṛ.*
5. *drari, mešġulin.*
6. *ṛžal, keslanin.*
7. *wlad, mṛaḍ.*
8. *biban, buyeḍ.*
9. *bnat, mezyanin.*
10. *byut, mwessxin.*
11. *tṣaweṛ, nqiyin.*
12. *žyub, ṣġaṛ.*
13. *xnaši, kuɛăl.*
14. *ktub, ždad.*

IV. Vocabulary.

d-, de-	(see Grammatical Note **B**)
dak	that (see Grammatical Notes **A** and **C**)
duk	those (see Grammatical Notes **A** and **C**)
tlata	three (see Grammatical Notes **B** and **D**)
žuž	two (see Grammatical Notes **B** and **D**)

LESSON SEVENTEEN

I. Text.

šuf had le-ktab!	Look at this book!
šuf dak le-ktab!	Look at that book!
hada ɛmeṛ be-l-ɛăqq hadak kɛăl.	This one is red but that one is black.

šuf had le-mdad!	Look at this ink!
šuf dak le-mdad!	Look at that ink!
hada mezyan be-l-ɛăqq hadak ma-ši mezyan.	This is good but that isn't.
šuf had š-šelya!	Look at this chair!
šuf dak š-šelya!	Look at that chair!
hadi nqiya be-l-ɛăqq hadik mwessxa.	This one's clean but that one's dirty.
šuf had r-ržal!	Look at these men!
šuf duk š-šṛažem!	Look at those windows!
hadu meɛlulin be-l-ɛăqq haduk mešdudin.	These are open but those are closed.

II. Grammatical Notes.

A. The text of this lesson illustrates the use of the pronouns ***hada*** (m.) 'this one', ***hadi*** (f.) 'this one', ***hadu*** 'these (ones)' and ***hadak*** (m.) 'that one', ***hadik*** (f.) 'that one', ***haduk*** 'those (ones)' as opposed to the adjectives ***had*** 'this, these' and ***dak*** 'that, those'. The forms ***had*** and ***dak*** are always directly connected with a following noun, adjective, or numeral (as in ***had le-ktab*** 'this book', ***dak ž-žuž*** 'those two', etc.), whereas the forms ***hada, hadi, hadu*** and ***hadak, hadik,*** and ***haduk*** are used independently like nouns. In traditional terms, the forms ***had*** and ***dak*** are demonstrative adjectives and the new forms learned in this lesson are demonstrative pronouns.

B. The form *šuf* 'See!', 'Look (at)!' is singular. It can be used only in speaking to one person, either male or female. The form appropriate for addressing two or more people at once will be learned in a later lesson.

III. Exercises.

A. Go through the texts of Lessons 10 and 11. Disregard the phrases, but in each sentence substitute ***hada*** (m.), ***hadi*** (f.), or ***hadu*** (pl.) for every noun and every case of ***had*** plus a noun. Read each resulting new sentence out loud.

B. Repeat Exercise **A** above but use ***hadak*** (m.), ***hadik*** (f.), and ***haduk*** (pl.) instead of ***hada, hadi,*** and ***hadu.***

IV. Vocabulary.

be-l-ɛăqq	but
hada (m.)	this, this one
hadi (f.)	
hadu (pl.)	
hadak (m.)	that, that one
hadik (f.)	
haduk (pl.)	
šuf!	See!, Look!, Look at!

LESSON EIGHTEEN

I. Text.

kas ɛameṛ	a full glass
l-kas l-ɛameṛ	the full glass
had l-kas l-ɛameṛ	this full glass
dak l-kas l-ɛameṛ	that full glass
had l-kas ɛameṛ.	This glass is full.
dak l-kas ɛameṛ.	That glass is full.
had l-kas ma-ši ɛameṛ.	This glass isn't full.
dak l-kas ma-ši ɛameṛ.	That glass isn't full.
hada ɛameṛ u-hadak ma-ši ɛameṛ.	This one's full and that one isn't (full).
kas xawi	an empty glass
l-kas l-xawi	the empty glass
had l-kas l-xawi	this empty glass
dak l-kas l-xawi	that empty glass
had l-kas xawi.	This glass is empty.
had l-kas ma-ši xawi.	This glass isn't empty.
dak l-kas xawi.	That glass is empty.
dak l-kas ma-ši xawi.	That glass isn't empty.
hada xawi u-hadak ma-ši xawi.	This one is empty and that one isn't (empty).

had ḍ-ḍaṛ ɛamṛa.	This house is full.
had ḍ-ḍaṛ ma-ši ɛamṛa.	This house isn't full.
dak ḍ-ḍaṛ ɛamṛa.	That house is full.
dak ḍ-ḍaṛ ma-ši ɛamṛa.	That house isn't full.
hadi ɛamṛa u-hadik ma-ši ɛamṛa.	This one is full and that one isn't (full).
had l-meḍṛaṣa xawya.	This school is empty.
had l-meḍṛaṣa ma-ši xawya.	This school isn't empty.
dak l-meḍṛaṣa xawya.	That school is empty.
dak l-meḍṛaṣa ma-ši xawya.	That school isn't empty.
hadi xawya u-hadik ma-ši xawya.	This one is empty and that one isn't (empty).
kisan	(drinking) glasses
l-kisan	the glasses
had l-kisan	these glasses
dak l-kisan	those glasses
had l-kisan ɛamṛin.	These glasses are full.
had l-kisan xawyin.	These glasses are empty.
duk l-kisan ɛamṛin.	Those glasses are full.
duk l-kisan xawyin.	Those glasses are empty.
hadu ɛamṛin u-haduk xawyin.	These are full and those are empty.

II. Grammatical Notes.

Review the grammatical notes of Lessons 16 and 17.

III. Exercises.

Combine the following noun-adjective pairs according to the pattern of the example. Read each resulting sentence out loud.
Example:

kas, ɛameṛ
had l-kas ɛameṛ.
dak l-kas ɛameṛ.
hada ɛameṛ u-hadak ɛameṛ.

1. *xenša, ɛamṛa.*
2. *xenša, xawya.*
3. *bit, ɛameṛ.*
4. *bit, xawi.*
5. *ḍaṛ, xawya.*
6. *meḍṛaṣa, ɛamṛa.*
7. *xnaši, ɛamṛin.*
8. *xnaši, xawyin.*
9. *byut, ɛamṛin.*
10. *byut, xawyin.*
11. *ḍyuṛ, xawyin.*
12. *mḍaṛes, ɛamṛin.*

IV. Vocabulary.

kas	(drinking) glass
kisan (pl.)	
xawi	empty
xawya (f.)	
xawyin (pl.)	
ɛameṛ	full
ɛamṛa (f.)	
ɛamṛin (pl.)	

LESSON NINETEEN

I. Text.

had le-ktab hada	this book here
had le-ktab le-kbir hada	this big book here
dak le-ktab hadak	that book there
dak le-ktab le-kbir hadak	that big book there
ɛṭini (sg., m, and f.)	Give me!
ɛṭini had le-ktab le-kbir hada, ma-ši dak le-ktab ṣ-ṣġiṛ hadak.	Give me this big book here, not that little book there.
ɛṭini dak le-ktab ṣ-ṣġiṛ hadak, ma-ši had le-ktab le-kbir hada.	Give me that little book there, not this big book here.
had š-šelya hadi	this chair here
had š-šelya l-ḥămṛa hadi	this red chair here

dak š-šelya hadik	that chair there
dak š-šelya l-ḥămṛa hadik	that red chair there
ɛṭini had š-šelya l-ḥămṛa hadi, ma-ši dak š-šelya l-biḍa hadik.	Give me this red chair here, not that white chair there.
ɛṭini dak š-šelya l-biḍa hadik, ma-ši had š-šelya l-ḥămṛa hadi.	Give me that white chair there, not this red chair here.
had le-ḥwayež hadu	these clothes here
had le-ḥwayež n-nqiyin hadu	these clean clothes here
duk le-ḥwayež haduk	those clothes there
duk le-ḥwayež n-nqiyin haduk	those clean clothes there
ɛṭini had le-ḥwayež n-nqiyin hadu, ma-ši duk le-ḥwayež le-mwessxin haduk.	Give me these clean clothes here, not those dirty clothes there.
ɛṭini duk le-ḥwayež le-mwess-xin haduk, ma-ši had le-ḥwayež n-nqiyin hadu.	Give me those dirty clothes there, not these clean clothes here.
ṛebɛa	four
had ṛ-ṛebɛa	these four
had ṛ-ṛebɛa hadu	these four here
duk ṛ-ṛebɛa	those four
duk ṛ-ṛebɛa haduk	those four there
ṛebɛa de-l-biban	four doors
ṛebɛa de-l-biban kbaṛ	four big doors
had ṛ-ṛebɛa de-l-biban le-kbaṛ	these four big doors
duk ṛ-ṛebɛa de-l-biban le-kbaṛ	those four big doors.
žuž ɛamṛin	two full ones
had ž-žuž l-ɛamṛin	these two full ones
had ž-žuž l-ɛamṛin hadu	these two full ones here
had ž-žuž l-xawyin hadu	these two empty ones here
duk ž-žuž l-xawyin haduk	those two empty ones there
ɛṭini had ž-žuž l-xawyin hadu.	Give me these two empty ones here.
ɛṭini duk ž-žuž l-xawyin haduk.	Give me those two empty ones there.

II. Grammatical Notes.

A. The demonstrative pronouns (see Grammatical Note **A** of Lesson 17) ***hada*** (m.), ***hadi*** (f.), ***hadu*** (pl.), and ***hadak*** (m.), ***hadik*** (f.), ***haduk*** (pl.) are used to reinforce expressions using ***had*** and ***dak,*** in exactly the same way as English 'here' and 'there' in such expressions as 'this book here' (Moroccan ***had le-ktab hada***) and 'that book there' (Moroccan ***dak le-ktab hadak***).

If the noun in the phrase is accompanied by an adjective, the demonstrative pronoun comes after the adjective, as in 'this big book here' (Moroccan ***had le-ktab le-kbir hada***) and 'that big book there' (Moroccan ***dak le-ktab le-kbir hadak***).

With the use of ***hada*** (m.), ***hadi*** (f.), ***hadu*** (pl.) and ***hadak*** (m.), ***hadik*** (f.), ***haduk*** (pl.) in this manner, the choice of the masculine, feminine or plural form depends on the noun involved, thus:

had le-ktab le-kbir hada
dak le-ktab le-kbir hadak

had š-šelya l-ɛămṛa hadi
dak š-šelya l-ɛămṛa hadik

had le-ɛwayež n-nqiyin hadu
duk le-ɛwayež n-nqiyin haduk

B. The form ***ɛṭini!*** 'Give me!' is singular. It can be used only in speaking to one person, either male or female. The form appropriate for addressing two or more people at once will be learned in a later lesson.

C. The numeral ***ṛebɛa*** is used exactly the same way as ***žuž*** and ***tlata.*** See Grammatical Notes **B, C,** and **D** of Lesson 16.

D. Adjectives going with numerals from 'two' on are always plural, for example ***žuž kbaṛ*** 'two big ones', ***ṛebɛa ṣġaṛ*** 'four little ones', etc.

III. Exercises.

A. Take the noun-adjective pairs of the exercises of Lesson 18 and combine them according to the pattern of the example below. In each case, read the resulting phrase or sentence out loud.

Example: ***ktab, kbir***
had le-ktab hada
had le-ktab le-kbir hada

dak le-ktab hadak
dak le-ktab le-kbir hadak
šuf had le-ktab hada!
ɛṭini had le-ktab hada!
šuf had le-ktab le-kbir hada!
ɛṭini had le-ktab le-kbir hada!
šuf dak le-ktab hadak!
ɛṭini dak le-ktab hadak!
šuf dak le-ktab le-kbir hadak!
ɛṭini dak le-ktab le-kbir hadak!

B. Go through the texts of Lessons 16, 17, and 18 and form new phrases and sentences by substituting *ṛebɛa* for every occurrence of *žuž* and *tlata*. Read the resulting new phrases and sentences out loud as each one is formed.

C. Go through the texts of Lesson 16, 17, and 18. For every occurrence of *žuž* or *tlata* with a noun plus an adjective, form a new phrase or sentence by omitting the noun. For example change *žuž de-r-ržal kbaṛ* 'two big men' into *žuž kbaṛ* 'two big ones'. In each case, read the resulting new phrases and sentences out loud as each one is formed.

IV. Vocabulary.

ṛebɛa	four (see Grammatical Note **C**)
ɛṭini!	Give me! (see Grammatical Note **B**)

LESSON TWENTY

I. Text.

had l-ġoṛṛaf xḍeṛ.	This pitcher is green.
dak l-ġoṛṛaf xḍeṛ.	That pitcher is green.
had l-ġoṛṛaf le-xḍeṛ ma-ši ɛameṛ.	This green pitcher isn't full.
dak l-ġoṛṛaf le-xḍeṛ ma-ši ɛameṛ.	That green pitcher isn't full.
had l-ġoṛṛaf le-xḍeṛ hada ma-ši ɛameṛ.	This green pitcher here isn't full.
dak l-ġoṛṛaf le-xḍeṛ hadak ma-ši ɛameṛ.	That green pitcher there isn't full.

ẓṛeq	blue
le-ẓṛeq	the blue (one)
had le-ẓṛeq	this blue (one)
dak le-ẓṛeq	that blue (one)
ġoṛṛaf ẓṛeq	a blue pitcher
l-ġoṛṛaf le-ẓṛeq	the blue pitcher
had l-ġoṛṛaf ẓṛeq.	This pitcher is blue.
dak l-ġoṛṛaf ẓṛeq.	That pitcher is blue.
had l-ġoṛṛaf hada ẓṛeq.	This pitcher here is blue.
dak l-ġoṛṛaf hadak ẓṛeq.	That pitcher there is blue.
had l-ġoṛṛaf le-ẓṛeq ma-ši ždid.	This blue pitcher isn't new.
dak l-ġoṛṛaf le-ẓṛeq ma-ši ždid.	That blue pitcher isn't new.
had l-ġoṛṛaf le-ẓṛeq hada ma-ši ždid.	This blue pitcher here isn't new.
dak l-ġoṛṛaf le-ẓṛeq hadak ma-ši ždid.	That blue pitcher there isn't new.
buḷa xeḍṛa	a green light-bulb
had l-buḷa xeḍṛa.	This light-bulb is green.
dak l-buḷa xeḍṛa.	That light-bulb is green.
had l-buḷa hadi xeḍṛa.	This light-bulb here is green.
dak l-buḷa hadik xeḍṛa.	That light-bulb there is green.
had l-buḷa l-xeḍṛa ma-ši mezyana.	This green light-bulb isn't good.
dak l-buḷa l-xeḍṛa ma-ši mezyana.	That green light-bulb isn't good.
had l-buḷa l-xeḍṛa hadi ma-ši mezyana.	This green light-bulb here isn't good.
dak l-buḷa l-xeḍṛa hadik ma-ši mezyana.	That green light-bulb there isn't good.
ẓeṛqa (f.)	blue
ẓ-ẓeṛqa	the blue (one)
buḷa ẓeṛqa	a blue light-bulb
l-buḷa ẓ-ẓeṛqa	the blue light-bulb
had l-buḷa ẓeṛqa.	This light-bulb is blue.
dak l-buḷa ẓeṛqa.	That light-bulb is blue.

had l-buḷa ẓ-ẓerqa ṣġiṛa.	This blue light-bulb is little.
dak l-buḷa ẓ-ẓerqa ṣġiṛa.	That blue light-bulb is little.
had l-buḷa ẓ-ẓerqa hadi ṣġiṛa.	This blue light-bulb here is little.
dak l-buḷa ẓ-ẓerqa hadik ṣġiṛa	That blue light-bulb there is little.
ġraṛef xuḍeṛ	green pitchers
had le-ġraṛef xuḍer.	These pitchers are green.
duk le-ġraṛef xuḍer.	Those pitchers are green.
had le-ġraṛef hadu xuḍer.	These pitchers here are green.
duk le-ġraṛef haduk xuḍer.	Those pitchers there are green.
had le-ġraṛef l-xuḍer xawyin.	These green pitchers are empty.
duk le-ġraṛef l-xuḍer xawyin.	Those green pitchers are empty.
had le-ġraṛef l-xuḍer hadu xawyin.	These green pitchers here are empty.
duk le-ġraṛef l-xuḍer haduk xawyin.	Those green pitchers there are empty.
buḷat ẓuṛeq	blue light-bulbs
l-buḷat ẓ-ẓuṛeq	the blue light-bulbs
had l-buḷat ẓuṛeq.	These light-bulbs are blue.
duk l-buḷat ẓuṛeq.	Those light-bulbs are blue.
had l-buḷat hadu ẓureq.	These light-bulbs here are blue.
duk l-buḷat haduk ẓuṛeq.	Those light-bulbs there are blue.
had l-buḷat ẓ-ẓuṛeq ždad.	These blue light-bulbs are new.
duk l-buḷat ẓ-ẓuṛeq ždad.	Those blue light-bulbs are new.
had l-buḷat ẓ-ẓuṛeq hadu ždad.	These blue light-bulbs here are new.
duk l-buḷat ẓ-ẓuṛeq hadu ždad.	Those blue light-bulbs there are new.

II. Grammatical Notes.

In the Grammatical Notes of Lessons 2 and 3 a special form of the Moroccan equivalent for 'the' was discussed. This involved a repetition of the first consonant of the following word for a certain list of consonants, for example *šeržem* 'window' and *š-šeržem* 'the window'. One of the consonants so listed is *ẓ*, but there are a few words which are exceptions to the general rule. One exception is *ẓreq* 'blue' and *le-ẓreq* 'the blue (one)'. These exceptions have to be memorized one by one as they appear. Note that the feminine and plural forms are regular for this particular exception, thus *ẓerqa* (f.) 'blue', *ẓ-ẓerqa* (f.) 'the blue (one)', and *ẓuṛeq* (pl.) 'blue (ones)', *ẓ-ẓuṛeq* (pl.) 'the blue (ones)'.

III. Exercise.

Combine each of the listed noun-adjective pairs into sentences on the pattern of the example given below. Read each resulting sentence out loud.

Example: *ġoṛṛaf, xḍeṛ*
had l-ġoṛṛaf hada xḍeṛ.
dak l-ġoṛṛaf hadak xḍeṛ.

1. *bab, xḍer.*
2. *ġoṛṛaf, mwessex.*
3. *bab, ẓṛeq.*
4. *ġoṛṛaf, mezyan.*
5. *bit, xḍeṛ.*
6. *ġoṛṛaf, nqi.*
7. *bit, ẓṛeq.*
8. *ġoṛṛaf, ṣġiṛ*
9. *konnaš, xḍeṛ.*
10. *ġoṛṛaf, kbir.*
11. *magana, xeḍṛa.*
12. *buḷa, kbira.*
13. *magana, ẓeṛqa.*
14. *buḷa, mwessxa.*
15. *xenša, xeḍṛa.*
16. *buḷa, mezyana.*
17. *xenša, ẓeṛqa.*
18. *buḷa, nqiya.*
19. *ḍaṛ, xeḍṛa.*
20. *buḷa, ṣġiṛa.*
21. *buḷat, kbaṛ.*
22. *εwayež, ẓuṛeq.*
23. *ġṛaṛef, ždad.*
24. *ktub, ẓuṛeq.*
25. *ġṛaṛef, xawyin.*
26. *šṛažem, xuḍeṛ.*
27. *ġṛaṛef, εamṛin.*
28. *šṛažem, ẓuṛeq.*
29. *knaneš, xuḍeṛ.*
30. *knaneš, ẓuṛeq.*

IV. Vocabulary.

buḷa	electric light-bulb
buḷat (pl.)	
ġoṛṛaf	pitcher
ġṛaṛef (pl.)	
xḍeṛ	green
xeḍṛa (f.)	
xuḍeṛ (pl.)	
ẓṛeq	blue
ẓeṛqa (f.)	
ẓuṛeq (pl.)	

LESSON TWENTY-ONE

I. Text.

l-konnaš dyali	my notebook
ḍ-ḍaṛ dyali	my house
l-magana dyali	my watch
le-ɛwayež dyali	my clothes
l-xobz dyali.	The bread is mine.
l-xobz dyali mezyan.	My bread is good.
ḍ-ḍaṛ dyali.	The house is mine.
ḍ-ḍaṛ dyali biḍa.	My house is white.
le-ɛwayež dyali.	The clothes are mine.
le-ɛwayež dyali nqiyin.	My clothes are clean.
le-mdad dyalek	your ink
š-šelya dyalek	your chair
t-tṣaweṛ dyalek	your pictures
waš le-mdad dyalek?	Is the ink yours?
waš le-mdad dyalek zṛeq?	Is your ink blue?
waš š-šelya dyalek?	Is the chair yours?
waš š-šelya dyalek ždida?	Is your chair new?
waš t-tṣaweṛ dyalek?	Are the pictures yours?
waš t-tṣaweṛ dyalek mezyanin?	Are your pictures good?

II. Grammatical Notes.

A. The Moroccan equivalent of English 'my' is *dyali.* It is placed after a noun which has the word for 'the', thus *le-ktab* 'the book' and *le-ktab dyali* 'my book'. The Moroccan equivalent for 'your' (singular) is *dyalek,* used in the same way as *dyali;* thus *le-mdad* 'the ink' and *le-mdad dyalek* 'your ink'.

B. In case a noun is accompanied by an adjective, the forms *dyali* and *dyalek* go after the adjective; thus *l-magana ž-ždida* 'the new watch', *l-magana ž-ždida dyali* 'my new watch', and *l-magana ž-ždida dyalek* 'your new watch'.

C. The forms *dyali* and *dyalek* also mean 'mine' and 'yours', for example *had le-ɛwayež dyali* 'these clothes are mine' and *dak ẓ-ẓeṛbiya dyalek* 'That rug is yours'. Note that an utterance consisting of a noun with 'the' followed by *dyali* or *dyalek* can have two meanings. Thus *le-gṛaṛef dyali* can be translated either as 'my pitchers' or 'The pitchers are mine'. Similarly *le-klab dyalek* can be translated either as 'your dogs' or 'The dogs are yours'. Which sense is intended in a given situation must be deduced from context.

D. When *dyali* or *dyalek* is used with a noun which has *had* or *dak,* the most accurate English translations are 'of mine' or 'of yours', for example *dak l-weld dyalek* 'that boy of yours', *duk š-šelyat dyalek* 'those chairs of yours', *had l-ulad dyali* 'these boys of mine', *duk le-ktub ž-ždad dyali* 'those new books of mine'. Note the same possibility of double translation as mentioned in Grammatical Note C above, for example *duk š-šelyat dyalek* is translatable as 'Those chairs are yours' in addition to the translation 'those chairs of yours', etc.

E. The form *dyalek* 'you, yours' can be used in speaking only to one person (either male or female); that is, it is singular in meaning. Note that the forms *dyali* and *dyalek* can be used with either singular or plural nouns (*ṭ-ṭebḷa dyali, ṭ-ṭebḷa dyalek, ṭ-ṭbali dyali, ṭ-ṭbali dyalek*). The form *dyalek* is singular only in the sense that it refers to one but not two or more persons.

III. Exercise.

Take the list of noun-adjective pairs in the exercise of Lesson 20 and combine them on the pattern of the example below. Read each resulting phrase or sentence out loud as it is formed.

Example: *ktab, kbir*
le-ktab dyali
le-ktab dyalek
le-ktab le-kbir dyali
le-ktab le-kbir dyalek
had le-ktab dyali
had le-ktab dyalek
had le-ktab le-kbir dyali
had le-ktab le-kbir dyalek

IV. Vocabulary.

dyali	my, mine (see the Grammatical Notes)
dyalek	your, yours (see the Grammatical Notes)

LESSON TWENTY-TWO

I. Text.

ṣ-ṣenḍuq dyalu	his box
le-ṣfeṛ dyalu	his yellow one
ṣ-ṣenḍuq le-ṣfeṛ	the yellow box
had ṣ-ṣenḍuq le-ṣfeṛ dyalu.	this yellow box of his
dak ṣ-ṣenḍuq le-ṣfeṛ dyalu.	that yellow box of his
ṣ-ṣenḍuq dyalu.	The box is his.
had ṣ-ṣenḍuq dyalu.	This box is his.
dak ṣ-ṣenḍuq dyalu.	That box is his.
l-kuṛa dyalha	her ball
l-kuṛa ṣ-ṣefṛa	the yellow ball
l-kuṛa dyalha.	The ball is hers.
had l-kuṛa dyalha.	This ball is hers.
dak l-kuṛa dyalha.	That ball is hers.
l-kuṛat dyalu.	The balls are his.
ṣ-ṣnaḍeq dyalha.	The boxes are hers.
had l-kuṛat dyalu.	These balls are his.
had ṣ-ṣnaḍeq dyalha.	These boxes are hers.
ṣ-ṣnaḍeq ṣ-ṣufeṛ dyalha.	The yellow boxes are hers.
had l-kuṛat ṣ-ṣufeṛ dyalu.	These yellow balls are his.
duk l-kuṛat ṣ-ṣufeṛ dyalha.	Those yellow balls are hers.
le-ktab l-bali dyalu	his worn book
le-ktab l-bali dyalha	her worn book
ẓ-zeṛbiya l-balya dyalu mwessxa.	His worn-out rug is dirty.
dak ẓ-zeṛbiya l-balya dyalha mwessxa.	That worn-out rug of hers is dirty.
le-ɛwayež l-balyin dyalha ma-ši nqiyin.	Her old clothes aren't clean.
duk le-ɛwayež l-balyin dyalu ma-ši nqiyin.	Those old clothes of his aren't clean.

II. Grammatical Notes.

A. The forms *dyalu* 'his' and *dyalha* 'her, hers' are used in exactly the same way as the forms *dyali* and *dyalek*. See the Grammatical Notes of Lesson 21.

B. Note that the form for 'the' before *ṣfeṛ* (m.) 'yellow' is *le-*. Compare the Grammatical Notes of Lesson 20.

III. Exercise.

A. Go through the following list of noun-adjective pairs and form phrases and sentences on the pattern of the example. Read each phrase and sentence out loud.

Example: *magana, ždida*
l-magana dyalu
l-magana dyalha
l-magana dyalu ždida.
l-magana dyalha ždida.

1. *ṣenḍuq, byeḍ.*
2. *kuṛa, biḍa.*
3. *goṛṛaf, ṣfeṛ.*
4. *konnaš, bali.*
5. *ṣenḍuq, kbir.*
6. *kuṛa, ždida.*
7. *bit, ṣfeṛ.*
8. *ktab, bali.*
9. *ṣnaḍeq, xawyin.*
10. *kuṛat, kbaṛ.*
11. *ḍaṛ, ṣefṛa.*
12. *ẓeṛbiya, balya.*
13. *knaneš, ṣufeṛ.*
14. *ɛwayež, balyin.*

B. Go through the list of noun-adjective pairs in the exercise of Lesson 20 and combine them according to the pattern prescribed for Exercise **A** above.

IV. Vocabulary.

bali	old, used, worn, worn-out
balya (f.)	
balyin (pl.)	
dyalha	her, hers

dyalu	his
kuṛa	ball
kuṛat (pl.)	
ṣfeṛ	yellow
ṣefṛa (f.)	
ṣufeṛ (pl.)	
ṣenḍuq	box
ṣnaḍeq (pl.)	

LESSON TWENTY-THREE

I. Text.

had l-bakit dyalna.	This package is ours.
l-bakit dyalna ṣġiṛ.	Our package is small.
l-bakit le-kbir dyalna fe-ḍ-ḍaṛ.	Our large package is in the house.
waš had le-fluka dyalkom?	Is this boat yours?
waš le-fluka dyalkom ح̣ămṛa?	Is your boat red?
waš le-fluka ṣ-ṣġiṛa dyalkom ح̣ămṛa?	Is your little boat red?
had ṭ-ṭumubil dyalhom.	This car is theirs.
ṭ-ṭumubil dyalhom ždida.	Their car is new.
ṭ-ṭumubil ž-ždida dyalhom ṣġiṛa.	Their new car is small.
dak ṭ-ṭumubil ž-ždida dyalhom ma-ši kbira.	That new car of theirs isn't big.
waš l-bakitat dyalkom fe-ḍ-ḍaṛ?	Are your packages in the house?
la, l-bakitat dyalna ma-ši fe-ḍ-ḍaṛ.	No, our packages aren't in the house.
l-bakitat dyalhom fe-ḍ-ḍaṛ.	Their packages are in the house.
šuf ṭumubil ž-ždida dyalna!	Look at our new car!
ṭ-ṭumubil ž-ždida dyalkom kbira.	Your new car is big.
waš ṭ-ṭumubil dyalhom kbira?	Is their car big?

waš le-flayek dyalna ɛamṛin?	Are our boats full?
iyeh, le-flayek dyalna ɛamṛin.	Yes, our boats are full.
waš had ž-žuž de-ṭ-ṭumubilat xawyin?	Are these two cars empty?
la, had ž-žuž de-ṭ-ṭumubilat ma-ši xawyin.	No, these two cars aren't empty.

II. Grammatical Notes.

A. The forms *dyalna, dyalkom,* and *dyalhom* are used in exactly the same way as the forms *dyali, dyalek, dyalu,* and *dyalha.* Compare the Grammatical Notes of Lesson Nineteen.

B. The form *dyalkom* 'your, yours' is plural and is used only in speaking to two or more people at once. Contrast it with the singular *dyalek* 'your, yours', which is used only in speaking to one person.

III. Exercises.

Repeat the exercises of Lessons 21 and 22 but using *dyalna, dyalkom,* and *dyalhom* instead of *dyali, dyalek, dyalu,* and *dyalha.*

IV. Vocabulary.

bakit	package
bakitat (pl.)	
dyalhom	their, theirs
dyalkom	your, yours (pl.)
dyalna	our, ours
fluka	boat
flayek (pl.)	
ṭumubil (f.)	car, automobile
ṭumubilat (pl.)	

LESSON TWENTY-FOUR

I. Text.

dak ẓ-ẓeṛbiya l-keƐla balya šwiya.	That black rug is sort of worn.
waš nta mṛid šwiya?	Are you a little bit sick?
iyeh, ana mṛid šwiya.	Yes, I'm sort of sick.
le-fluka dyalna nqiya bezzaf.	Our boat is real clean.
waš l-bakit dyalkom kbir bezzaf?	Is your package very big?
la, l-bakit dyalna ma-ši kbir bezzaf.	No, our package isn't very big.
Ɛăndek bezzaf de-z-zit?	Do you have a lot of oil?
la, Ɛăndi ġir ši-šwiya de-z-zit.	No, I've only got a little bit of oil.
šuf, Ɛăndi ši-ẓṛabi.	Look, I've got some rugs.
Ɛṭini ši-ẓṛabi ždad.	Give me some new rugs.
Ɛăndek bezzaf de-t-tṣaweṛ?	Do you have a lot of pictures?
iyeh, Ɛăndi bezzaf de-t-tṣaweṛ mezyanin.	Yes, I have a lot of good pictures.

II. Grammatical Notes.

A. Both *šwiya* 'a little, somewhat, sort of' and *bezzaf* 'very, real' come immediately after adjectives. The function of *šwiya* is to diminish the meaning of the adjective, e.g. *mṛiḍ* 'sick' and *mṛiḍ šwiya* 'a little sick, sort of sick'. The function of *bezzaf* is to intensify the meaning of the adjective, e.g. *kbir* 'big' and *kbir bezzaf* 'very big, real big'.

B. In Grammatical Note **B** of Lesson 16, the student was introduced to the form *d-, de-* going before a noun with the word for 'the', as in *žuž de-ṭ-ṭumubilat* 'two cars'. This same form plus 'the' is used before nouns with *ši-šwiya* 'a little, a little bit' and *bezzaf* 'a lot, many' preceding, as in *ši-šwiya de-z-zit* 'a little (bit of) oil' and *bezzaf de-l-bakitat* 'a lot of packages'.

C. Although nouns after *ši-šwiya* and *bezzaf* invariably have 'the', adjectives accompanying these nouns occur regularly without 'the', for example *ši-šwiya d-le-mdad Ɛmeṛ* 'a little (bit of) red ink', *bezzaf de-ṣ-ṣnaḍeq xawyin* 'a lot of empty boxes'.

D. Note that *bezzaf* is used with both singular and plural nouns, e.g. *bezzaf de-z-zit* 'a lot of oil', *bezzaf d-le-flayek* 'a lot of boats'. This use of *bezzaf* is similar to English 'a lot of'. On the other hand, *ši-šwiya* is used only with singular nouns, e.g. *ši-šwiya de-l-xobz* 'a little bread'. In this lesson, *ši* 'some, a few' has been given as occurring only with plural nouns. Its use with singular nouns will be explained later.

E. It is not always necessary to have *waš* at the beginning of a sentence to indicate a question. Often only a rising tone of voice is used, without *waš*. Thus both *waš ɛăndek le-ktab dyali?* and *ɛăndek le-ktab dyali?* mean 'Do *you have my book?*'. If said with a falling tone of voice, *ɛăndek le-ketab dyali* is simply a statement meaning 'You have my book'.

F. The form *ɛăndek* 'you have, you've got' is singular and is used only in speaking to one person at a time.

III. Exercises.

Go through the noun-adjective pairs below and combine them on the patterns of the example. Do the same with the list of noun-adjective pairs in the exercises of Lesson 20. Read each resulting sentence out loud as it is formed.

Example: *ktub, kbaṛ*
ɛăndi bezzaf d-le-ktub kbaṛ.
ɛăndi ġir ši-šwiya de-le-ktub kbaṛ.
ɛăndek ši-ktub kbaṛ?
ɛăndek bezzaf d-le-ktub kbaṛ?

1. *bakitat, mwessxin.*
2. *flayek, ṣġaṛ.*
3. *ṭumubilat, ždad.*
4. *ṣnaḍeq, xawyin.*
5. *kuṛat, kbaṛ.*
6. *knaneš, ṣufeṛ.*
7. *ɛwayež, balyin.*
8. *bakitat, xawyin.*
9. *flayek, kuɛăl.*
10. *ṭumubilat, ṣġaṛ.*

IV. Vocabulary.

bezzaf	very, "real"; much, many, a lot
ġir	only, just
ši	some, a few

ši-šwiya	a little, a little bit
šwiya	a little (bit), somewhat, sort of
ɛăndi	I have, I've got
ɛăndek	you (sg.) have, you've got

LESSON TWENTY-FIVE

I. Text.

šṛeb le-ɛlib.	He drank the milk.
ṛ-ṛažel šṛeb le-ɛlib.	The man drank the milk.
šeṛbet l-qehwa.	She drank the coffee.
le-mṛa šeṛbet l-qehwa.	The woman drank the coffee.
ḍṛeb l-kelb.	He hit the dog.
le-fqi ḍṛeb l-kelb.	The teacher hit the dog.
ḍeṛbet l-kuṛa.	She hit the ball.
l-bent ḍeṛbet l-kuṛa.	The girl hit the ball.
gles ɛăl š-šelya dyali.	He sat down in my chair.
l-weld gles ɛăl š-šelya dyali.	The boy sat down in my chair.
lbes had le-ɛwayež ž-ždad.	He wore these new clothes.
ṛ-ṛažel lbes had le-ɛwayež ždad.	The man wore these new clothes.
rfed l-bakitat dyalna.	He carried our packages.
le-fqi rfed l-bakitat dyalna.	The teacher carried our packages.
žbeṛ le-ktub dyalek fe-ṣ-ṣenḍuq.	He found your books in the box.
l-weld žbeṛ le-ktub dyalek fe-ṣ-ṣenḍuq.	The boy found your books in the box.

II. Grammatical Notes.

A. The usual way of citing Moroccan verbs is in the he-form of the perfect tense, e.g. *šṛeb* 'he drank', *ḍṛeb* 'he hit', *gles* 'he sat, he sat down', *lbes* 'he put on, he wore', *rfed* 'he carried', and *žbeṛ* 'he found'. This form is taken as the basic form of the verb, and other forms are treated as being derived from it.

The he-form of the perfect is also the one which is used for dictionary listings. For dictionary purposes, *šṛeb* is listed as 'to drink', and vice versa.

This procedure is simply a short-hand device whereby the base form of the English verb and the base form of the Moroccan verb are identified for citation purposes. The actual translation meaning of *šṛeb* is, of course, 'he drank'. There is no direct translation meaning for 'to drink', since the Moroccan verb has no infinitive form.

B. It is not necessary to use the pronouns *huwa* 'he' or *hiya* 'she' with verb forms like *šṛeb* and *šeṛbet,* since the meanings 'he' and 'she' are included in the verb forms.

C. A large number of Moroccan verbs have the pattern shown in *šṛeb* 'he drank' and *ḍṛeb* 'he hit'; that is, two consonants, followed by the vowel *e,* followed by another consonant. Using the capital letter *C* to stand for 'consonant', this pattern can be indicated by the formula *CCeC.* Verbs of this sort may be referred to as 'sound verbs'.

D. The ending for 'she' is *-et.* This ending is attached to the end of the he-form. As this ending is added, the pattern of the he-form is changed to *CeCC-,* e.g. *ḍṛeb* 'he hit' and *ḍeṛbet* 'she hit'. This change of position of the *e* is called 'inversion'.

III. Exercises.

Go through the text of this lesson and change each he-form encountered to the corresponding she-form, e.g. change *šṛeb* 'he drank' to *šeṛbet* 'she drank'. In the sentences with nouns as the subject, substitute *le-mṛa* 'the woman' for *ṛ-ṛažel* 'the man', *l-bent* 'the girl' for *l-weld* 'the boy', and *le-fqiha* 'the (woman) teacher' for *le-fqi* 'the (man) teacher', to correspond to each verb change of a he-form to a she-form.

IV. Vocabulary.

ḍṛeb	to hit ('he hit')
gles	to sit, to sit down ('he sat, he sat down')
lbes	to put on, to wear ('he put on, he wore')
qehwa	coffee
rfed	to carry ('he carried')
šṛeb	to drink ('he drank')
žbeṛ	to find ('he found')
ɛlib	milk

LESSON TWENTY-SIX

I. Text.

kteb l-ɛonwan fe-l-konnaš dyali.	He wrote the address in my notebook.
le-fqi kteb l-ɛonwan fe-l-konnaš dyali.	The teacher wrote the address in my notebook.
ketbu le-ɛanawin fe-l-konnaš.	They wrote the addresses in the notebook.
l-feqya ketbu l-ɛanawin fe-l-konnaš.	The teachers wrote the addresses in the notebook.
ġsel le-mraya.	He washed the mirror.
le-fqi ġsel le-mraya.	The teacher washed the mirror.
ġeslu le-mraya.	They washed the mirror.
l-feqya ġeslu le-mraya.	The teachers washed the mirror.
le-fqihat ketbu.	The teachers (f.) wrote.
le-fqihat ġeslu le-ɛwayež.	The teachers washed the clothes.
hḍeṛ bezzaf l-bareɛ.	He talked a lot yesterday.
ṛ-ṛažel hḍeṛ bezzaf l-bareɛ.	The man talked a lot yesterday.
hedṛu bezzaf l-bareɛ.	They talked a lot yesterday.
r-ržal hedṛu bezzaf l-bareɛ.	The men talked a lot yesterday.
xdem bezzaf l-bareɛ.	He worked a lot yesterday.
l-weld xdem bezzaf l-bareɛ.	The boy worked a lot yesterday.
xedmu bezzaf l-bareɛ.	They worked a lot yesterday.
r-ržal xedmu bezzaf l-bareɛ.	The men worked a lot yesterday.

II. Grammatical Notes.

A. The they-form of the perfect tense is formed by adding *-u* to the *he*-form, e.g. *kteb* 'he wrote' and *ketbu* 'they wrote'. The same inversion of the he-form from *CCeC* to *CeCC-* occurs with the addition of *-u* 'they' as with the addition of *-et* 'she'. Compare Grammatical Note **D** of Lesson 25.

B. Note that the use of the pronoun *huma* 'they' is not necessary with such forms as *ketbu* 'they write'. Compare Grammatical Note **B** of Lesson 25.

III. Exercises.

A. Go through the text of Lesson 25 and form new phrases and sentences by changing every occurrence of a he-form or a she-form to a they-form. In those cases where the sentences have singular nouns as subjects, change the nouns to the corresponding plural form. For example, *ṛ-ṛažel šṛeb le-ɛlib* 'The man drank the milk' should be changed to read *r-ržal šeṛbu le-ɛlib* 'The men drank the milk'. In every case, read the resulting new sentences out loud.

B. Go through the text of this lesson and change every occurrence of a he-form or a they-form into a she-form. As the situation requires, substitute feminine nouns for masculine nouns (e.g. occurrences of *ṛ-ṛažel* 'the man' should be replaced by *le-mṛa* 'the woman') and substitute singular nouns for plural nouns (e.g. *fqiha* for *fqihat* and *le-mṛa* for *r-ržal*. Read each resulting new sentence out loud.

IV. Vocabulary.

fqihat	(women) teachers (pl. of *fqiha*)
feqya	(men) teachers (pl. of *fqi*)
ġsel	to wash ('he washed')
hḍeṛ	to talk ('he talked')
kteb	to write ('he wrote')
l-bareɛ	yesterday
mraya	mirror
xdem	to work ('he worked')
ɛonwan	address
ɛanawin (pl.)	

LESSON TWENTY-SEVEN

I. Text.

waš ḍṛebti l-kelb?	Did you (sg.) hit the dog?
iyeh, ḍṛebt l-kelb.	Yes, I hit the dog.
waš glesti ɛăl ṣ-ṣenḍuq?	Did you sit down on the box?
la, glest ɛăl š-šelya.	No, I sat on the chair.

waš lbesti le-ɛwayež ž-ždad dyalek l-bareɛ?	Did you wear your new clothes yesterday?
iyeh, lbest l-ɛwayež ž-ždad dyali l-bareɛ.	Yes, I wore my new clothes yesterday.
waš rfedti l-bakatit dyalhom?	Did you carry their packages?
la, rfedt le-ktub dyalha.	No, I carried her books.
waš šṛebti ši-šwiya de-l-qehwa?	Did you drink a little coffee?
la, šṛebt ši-šwiya d-leɛlib.	No, I drank a little milk.
ɛăndu bezzaf d-le-ɛlib.	He has a lot of milk.
ɛăndha bezzaf de-l-qehwa.	She has a lot of coffee.
ɛăndu l-mešṭa ž-ždida dyali.	He has my new comb.
ɛăndha le-mšaṭi dyalna.	She has our combs.

II. Grammatical Note.

The equivalent for 'I' in the perfect tense is *-t* added directly to the he-form, e.g. ***kteb*** 'he wrote' and ***ktebt*** 'I wrote'. The equivalent for 'you' (sg., m. and f.) in the perfect tense is ***-ti*** added to the he-form, e.g. ***kteb*** 'he wrote' and ***ktebti*** 'you (sg., m. and f.) wrote'. As with the forms for 'he', 'she', and 'they' it is not necessary to use the pronouns *ana* 'I', ***nta*** (m. sg.) 'you', and ***nti*** (f. sg.) 'you' with these verb forms.

III. Exercises.

A. Go through the following set of pairs and form them into sentences on the pattern of *ḍṛebt l-kuṛa* 'I hit the ball' and *waš ḍṛebti l-kuṛa?* 'Did you (sg., m. and f.) hit the ball?' Read each sentence out loud.

1. *žbeṛ — l-mešṭa dyali*
2. *ġsel — le-ɛwayež dyalhom*
3. *hḍeṛ — bezzaf l-bareɛ*
4. *kteb — le-ɛanawin fe-l-konnaš*
5. *xdem — ġir ši-šwiya l-bareɛ*

B. Go through the texts of Lessons 25 and 26 and substitute the forms for 'I' and 'you' (sg., m. and f.) for every verb form encountered. In those cases where sentences have noun subjects, the noun subjects should be dropped. Read each new sentence out loud.

C. Go through the text and exercises of Lesson 24. For every occurrence of *ɛăndi* 'I have' or *ɛăndek* 'you (sg., m. and f.) have' form a new sentence by using *ɛăndu* 'he has' instead. Repeat the process with *ɛăndha* 'she has'. Read each new sentence formed out loud.

IV. Vocabulary.

mešṭa	comb
mšaṭi (pl.)	
ɛăndha	she has
ɛăndu	he has

LESSON TWENTY-EIGHT

I. Text.

ḍṛebtiw ṣ-ṣeṛṛaq?	Did you (pl.) hit the thief?
iyeh, ḍṛebna ṣ-ṣeṛṛaq.	Yes, we hit the thief.
glestiw ɛăl n-namusiya?	Did you sit down on the bed?
la, glesna ɛăl ḷ-ḷeṛḍ.	No, we sat down on the ground.
ġseltiw s-serwal?	Did you wash the (pair of) trousers?
la, ġselna ẓ-ẓṛabi.	No, we washed the rugs.
lbesna le-kbabeṭ dyalna.	We put on our coats.
lbesna t-tqašeṛ ž-ždad dyalna.	We wore our new socks.
lbestiw t-tqašeṛ ž-ždad dyalkom?	Did you wear your new socks?
hḍeṛtiw bezzaf l-bareɛ?	Did you talk a lot yesterday?
la, hḍeṛna ġir ši-šwiya had ṣ-ṣbaɛ.	No, we only talked a little this morning.
ktebtiw dak le-bṛa l-bareɛ?	Did you write that letter yesterday?
iyeh, ktebna dak le-bṛa l-bareɛ.	Yes, we wrote that letter yesterday.
ktebtiw ž-žwab had ṣ-sbaɛ?	Did you write the answer this morning?
la, ktebna ž-žwab l-bareɛ.	No. we wrote the answer yesterday.
šṛebtiw bezzaf de-l-qehwa?	Did you drink a lot of coffee?
la, šṛebna ġir ši-šwiya d-atay.	No, we just drank a little tea.

II. Grammatical Notes.

A. The equivalent for 'we' in the perfect tense is *-na* added directly to the he-form, e.g. *xdem* 'he worked' and *xdemna* 'we worked'. The equivalent for 'you' (pl.) in the perfect tense is *-tiw* added to the he-form, e.g. *xdem* 'he worked' and *xdemtiw* 'you (pl.) worked'. As with the others, it is not necessary to use the pronouns *ح na* 'we' and *ntuma* 'you' (pl.) with these verb forms.

B. The word *atay* 'tea' has the peculiarity that the word for 'the' is never used with it. Context determines whether a given occurrence of *atay* is to be translated into English as 'tea' or 'the tea'. The word is used exactly as other nouns except for this peculiarity, e.g. *had atay* 'this tea', *atay dyalu* 'his tea', etc.

C. The word *lẹṛḍ* 'ground' is another example of a feminine word not ending in *-a*. (See Grammatical Note **A** of Lesson 7).

D. Note that the word *serwal* '(pair of) trousers' is singular, e.g. *had s-serwal ṣġiṛ* 'These trousers are ('this pair of trousers is') small'.

III. Exercises.

A. Go through Exercise **A** of Lesson 27 using the forms for 'we' and 'you' (pl.) instead of the forms for 'I' and 'you' (sg., m. and f.).

B. Go through the texts of Lessons 25, 26, and 27, and substitute the forms for 'we' and 'you' (pl.) for every verb form encountered. In those cases where sentences have noun subjects, the noun subjects should be dropped. Read each new sentence out loud.

C. Go through the text of this lesson and substitute successively the forms 'I', 'you' (sg., m, and f.), 'he', 'she', and 'they' for the we-forms and the plural you-forms encountered. Wherever necessary to make sense change *dyalna* 'our' to *dyali* 'my', etc.

IV. Vocabulary.

atay	tea
bṛa	letter
kbabeṭ	coats

leṛḍ	ground
namusiya	bed
serwal (sg.)	(pair of) trousers
ṣeṛṛaq	thief
tqašeṛ	socks
žwab	answer

LESSON TWENTY-NINE

I. Text.

šaf duk n-nas l-bareč.	He saw those people yesterday.
šafet l-mešṭa dyali.	She saw my comb.
šaf l-qaḍi l-bareč f-le-čšiya.	He saw the judge yesterday evening.
šafet l-qaḍi l-bareč f-le-čšiya.	She saw the judge yesterday evening.
l-weld šaf n-nežžar.	The boy saw the carpenter.
bač ṭ-ṭumubil dyalu.	He sold his car.
bačet bezzaf d-atay.	She sold a lot of tea.
l-qaḍi bač ḍ-ḍaṛ dyalu.	The judge sold his house.
dar l-kebbuṭ fe-ṭ-ṭumubil.	He put the coat in the car.
daret l-kebbuṭ čăl n-namusiya.	She put the coat on the bed.
naḍ men š-šelya.	He got up out of the chair.
naḍ men ṭ-ṭebla.	He got up from the table.
naḍet men l-leṛḍ.	She got up from the ground.
naḍet men n-namusiya.	She got up out of bed.
žab le-bṛa men ḍ-ḍaṛ.	He brought the letter from the house.
žabet atay l-bareč f-le-čšiya.	She brought (some) tea yesterday evening.

II. Grammatical Notes.

Another very common verb pattern in Moroccan is for the he-form in the perfect tense to consist of the vowel *a* between two consonants, e.g. *šaf* 'he saw'. Such verbs are commonly referred to as 'hollow verbs'. The she-form is arrived at by adding *-et* directly to the he-form, e.g. *žab* 'he brought' and *žabet* 'she brought'. Unlike sound verbs (cf. the Grammatical Notes of Lesson 25), there is no change such as inversion involved in the he-form when the ending *-et* 'she' is added.

III. Exercises.

A. Go through the sentences in the text of this lesson. Change every he-form encountered into a she-form. In those cases where the verbs have noun subjects, substitute an appropriate feminine noun such as *bent, mṛa,* or *fqiha* for the masculine nouns such as *ṛažel,* etc. Read the new sentences formed out loud.

B. Reverse Exercise A above by substituting he-forms for she-forms and replacing feminine nouns with masculine nouns.

IV. Vocabulary.

baɛ	to sell ('he sold')
dar	to put ('he put')
kebbuṭ	coat
l-bareḥ f-le-ɛšiya	yesterday evening
men	from
naḍ	to get up ('he got up')
nežžaṛ	carpenter
qaḍi	judge
šaf	to see ('he saw')
žab	to bring ('he brought')

LESSON THIRTY

I. Text.

ṭaḥ men š-šelya.	He fell out of the chair.
ṭaḥu men n-namusiya.	They fell out of the bed.
ẓaṛ l-medṛaṣa l-bareḥ fe-ṣ-ṣbaḥ.	He visited the school yesterday morning.
ẓaṛu l-qaḍi had ṣ-ṣbaḥ.	They visited the judge this morning.
ɛaš fe-ḍ-ḍaṛ l-biḍa.	He lived in Casablanca.

n-nežžaṛ ع*aš f-had ḍ-ḍaṛ.*	The carpenter lived in this house.
ع*ašu fe-l-meġṛib.*	They lived in Morocco.
*had le-*ع*yalat* ع*ašu fe-l-meġṛib.*	These women lived in Morocco.
*kan fe-ḍ-ḍaṛ l-bare*ح *fe-ṣ-ṣba*ح.	He was at home yesterday morning.
*l-qaḍi kan fe-ḍ-ḍaṛ l-biḍa l-bare*ح.	The judge was in Casablanca yesterday.
*kanu fe-ḍ-ḍaṛ had ṣ-ṣba*ح.	They were at home this morning.
*n-nežžaṛa kanu fe-l-medṛaṣa l-bare*ح.	The carpenters were at the school yesterday.

II. Grammatical Notes.

A. The they-form of hollow verbs is arrived at by adding *-u* to the he-form, e.g., *kan* 'he was' and *kanu* 'they were'.

B. The preposition *f-, fe-* is often translated as 'at', especially with reference to places and in idioms. Two examples given in this lesson are *fe-l-medṛaṣa* 'at the school' and *fe-ḍ-ḍaṛ* 'at home'.

III. Exercises.

A. Go through the text of Lesson 29 and change every verb encountered into a they-form. In those cases where the verbs have nouns as subjects, use the corresponding plural noun along with the change of a he-form or a she-form to a they-form.

B. Go through the text of this lesson and change each he-form and they-form into a she-form. In those cases where the verbs have noun subjects, substitute an appropriate feminine singular noun to correspond to the she-form verb.

IV. Vocabulary.

ḍ-ḍaṛ l-biḍa	Casablanca
fe-ḍ-ḍaṛ	at home ('in the house')
fe-l-medṛaṣa	at the school
kan	to be ('he was')

l-bareḥ fe-ṣ-ṣbaḥ	yesterday morning
l-meġṛib	Morocco
nežžaṛa	carpenters
ṭaḥ	to fall ('he fell')
ẓaṛ	to visit ('he visited')
ɛaš	to live ('he lived')

LESSON THIRTY-ONE

I. Text.

beɛt ḍ-ḍaṛ dyali wel-l-bareḥ.	I sold my house day before yesterday.
beɛt ṭ-ṭumubil dyali.	I sold my car.
beɛti l-kebbuṭ?	Did you sell the coat?
dert s-serwal fe-ṣ-ṣenḍuq.	I put the trousers in the box.
derti le-mdad ɛăl ṭ-ṭebḷa?	Did you put the ink on the table?
neḍt bekri l-bareḥ.	I got up early yesterday.
neḍt deġya had ṣ-ṣbaḥ.	I got up quickly this morning.
neḍti bekri?	Did you get up early?
neḍti deġya?	Did you get up quickly?
šeft l-qaḍi fe-ḍ-ḍaṛ l-biḍa.	I saw the judge in Casablanca.
šefti ṣ-ṣeṛṛaq?	Did you see the thief?
žebt le-mkoḥla le-ḍ-ḍaṛ.	I brought the rifle home.
žebti had le-mkoḥla men l-meġṛib?	Did you bring this rifle from Morocco?
ṭeḥt men l-biškliṭa.	I fell off the bicycle.
ṭeḥti men ṭ-ṭumubil?	Did you fall out of the car?
ẓeṛt ṣ-ṣbiṭaṛ wel-l-bareḥ.	I visited the hospital day before yesterday.
ẓeṛt ḍ-ḍaṛ l-biḍa l-bareḥ.	I visited Casablanca yesterday.
ẓeṛti ṣ-ṣbiṭaṛ?	Did you visit the hospital?
kont fe-l-meġṛib ɛam luwwel.	I was in Morocco last year.
kont fe-ṛ-ṛbaṭ l-bareḥ.	I was in Rabat yesterday.
konti fe-l-meġṛib ɛam luwwel?	Were you in Morocco last year?
konti fe-ṛ-ṛbaṭ wel-l-bareḥ?	Were you in Rabat day before yesterday?

II. Grammatical Notes.

The endings for 'I' and 'you' (sg., m. and f.) for hollow verbs are the same as for sound verbs, namely *-t* 'I' and *-ti* 'you' (sg., m. and f.). As these endings are added, the medial *a* of the he-form is changed to *e*, e.g., *šaf* 'he saw', *šeft* 'I saw', and *šefti* 'you' (sg., m. and f.) saw'. A rare exception is *kan* 'he was', in which the *a* is changed to *o*, thus *kont* 'I was' and *konti* 'you (sg., m. and f.) were'.

III. Exercises.

Go through the texts of Lessons 29 and 30 and change every verb form encountered first to an I-form and then to a you-form (sg., m. and f.). In the case of verbs with noun subjects, the nouns should be dropped. If cases arise where the substitution of an I-form or a you-form would not make sense contextually, the sentence may be omitted or the student may make appropriate changes in the sentence. Read each new sentence out loud.

IV. Vocabulary.

bekri	early
biškliṭa	bicycle
deǧya	quick(ly), in a hurry
le-ḍ-ḍaṛ	(to) home, to the house
mkoḥla	rifle
ṛ-ṛbaṭ	Rabat
ṣbiṭaṛ	hospital
wel-l-bareḥ	day before yesterday
ʕam luwwel	last year

LESSON THIRTY-TWO

I. Text.

beʕna le-mkoḥla l-bareḥ.	We sold the rifle yesterday.
beʕtiw l-biškliṭa?	Did you sell the bicycle?
derna s-sarut ʕăl ṭ-ṭebla.	We put the key on the table.
dertiw le-ḥwayež fe-l-xenša?	Did you put the clothes in the bag?
neḍna men ṭ-ṭebla.	We got up from the table.
neḍtiw bekri had ṣ-ṣbaḥ?	Did you get up early this morning?

šeftiw ṛ-ṛbaṭ εam luwwel?	Did you see Rabat last year?
žebna s-swaret men l-εanut.	We brought the keys from the shop.
žebtiw had l-makla men ṛ-ṛbaṭ?	Did you bring this food from Rabat?
konna f-fas εam luwwel.	We were in Fez last year.
kontiw f-fas εam luwwel?	Were you in Fez last year?
ṭeεna men l-biškliṭat dyalna.	We fell off our bicycles.
ṭeεtiw men š-šelyat dyalkom?	Did you fall off your chairs?
ẓeṛna d-drari fe-ṣ-ṣbiṭaṛ.	We visited the children in the hospital.
ẓeṛtiw n-nežžaṛ fe-l-εanut dyalu?	Did you visit the carpenter in his shop?
εešna εamayn f-fas.	We lived in Fez for two years.
εešna telt snin fe-l-meġṛib.	We lived in Morocco for three years.
εeštiw fe-ṛ-ṛbaṭ?	Did you live in Rabat?

II. Grammatical Notes.

A. The endings for 'we' and 'you' (pl.) are the same for hollow verbs as for sound verbs, namely *-na* 'we' and *-tiw* 'you' (pl.). As these endings are added, the medial *a* of the he-form is changed to *e*, e.g. *εaš* 'he lived', *εešna* 'we lived', and *εeštiw* 'you (pl.) lived'. The verb *kan* 'to be' is an exception. The *a* of the he-form is changed to *o*, thus *kan* 'he was', *konna* 'we were', and *kontiw* 'you (pl.) were'.

B. Note that expressions of time in Moroccan often occupy a different place in the sentence from what is usual in English, e.g. *εešna εamayn f-fas* 'We lived in Fez for two years.'

III. Exercises.

A. Go through the texts of Lessons 29, 30, and 31 and change every verb form encountered into a we-form first and then into a you-form (pl.). In the case of sentences with noun subjects, the nouns are to be dropped. In the cases where the use of a we-form for a you-form (pl.) would not be in harmony with the rest of the sentence, the student should make whatever changes are necessary to make a reasonable sentence. Read each new sentence out loud.

B. Go through the text of this lesson and substitute I-forms, you-forms (sg.), and they-forms for the we-forms and the plural you-forms encountered.

IV. Vocabulary.

biškliṭat	bicycles
fas	Fez
makla	food
sarut	key
swaret (pl.)	
telt snin	three years, for three years
ḥanut (f.)	shop, store
ɛamayn	two years

LESSON THIRTY-THREE

I. Text.

ža bekri.	He came early.
l-qaḍi ža.	The judge came.
le-fqiha žat.	The teacher came.
žat l-bareḥ fe-ṣ-ṣbaḥ.	She came yesterday morning.
n-nežžaṛa žaw l-bareḥ.	The carpenters came yesterday.
žaw fe-ṣ-ṣbaḥ.	They came in the morning.
šra žuž de-l-buḷat.	He bought two light bulbs.
šrat bezzaf d-atay.	She bought a lot of tea.
šraw ši-biškliṭat.	They bought some bicycles.
l-weld xella l-bab meḥlula.	The boy left the door open.
l-bent xellat atay fe-l-ḥanut.	The girl left the tea at the shop.
d-drari xellaw le-kbabeṭ dyalhom ɛăl ḷ-leṛḍ.	The children left their coats on the ground.

II. Grammatical Notes.

A large number of Moroccan verbs end in *-a* in the he-form of the perfect tense, e.g. *šra* 'he bought'. For such verbs the she-form is made by adding *-t*, e.g. *šrat* 'she bought', and the they-form is made by adding *-w*, e.g. *šraw* 'they bought'.

III. Exercises.

Go through the sentences of this lesson and:

1. Change every she-form and they-form to a he-form.
2. Change every he-form and they-form to a she-form.
3. Change every he-form and she-form to a they form.

In following the above instructions, make appropriate substitutions among masculine, feminine, and plural nouns to correspond to the verb changes. Each new sentence formed by these changes should be read out loud.

IV. Vocabulary.

šra	to buy ('he bought')
xella	to leave ('he left')
ža	to come ('he came')

LESSON THIRTY-FOUR

I. Text.

ɛṭa le-ktab le-ṛ-ṛažel.	He gave the man the book.
n-nežžaṛ ɛṭa ṣ-ṣenḍuq l-l-bent.	The carpenter gave the box to the girl.
ɛṭat le-bṛa l-l-qaḍi.	She gave the judge the letter.
l-bent ɛṭat s-sarut le-n-nežžaṛ.	The girl gave the key to the carpenter.
ɛṭaw l-makla l-le-mṛa.	They gave the woman the food.
werra le-mkoḥla l-l-qaḍi.	He showed the rifle to the judge.
werrat le-ḥwayež l-l-bent.	She showed the clothes to the girl.
werraw l-ḥanut le-ṛ-ṛažel.	They showed the shop to the man.
ža bekri l-l-meḍṛaṣa	He came to school early.
le-fqiha žat l-l-meġṛib ɛam luwwel.	The teacher came to Morocco last year.
n-nas žaw l-l-meḍṛaṣa l-bareḥ.	The people came to the school yesterday.

II. Grammatical Notes.

The Moroccan equivalent for 'to' is *le-* if the following form begins with two consonants and the first of the two consonants is other than *l* itself, e.g. *ṛ-ṛažel* 'the man' and *le-ṛ-ṛažel* 'to the man'. Otherwise the form is *l-*, e.g. *l-l-bent* 'to the girl', *l-le-fqi* 'to the teacher'.

III. Exercises.

Go through the sentences of this lesson and:

1. Change every she-form and they-form to a he-form.

2. Change every he-form and they-form to a she-form.

3. Change every he-form and she-form to a they-form.

In following the above instructions, make appropriate substitutions among masculine, feminine, and plural nouns to correspond to the verb changes. Each new sentence formed by these changes should be read out loud.

IV. Vocabulary.

l-, le	to
werra	to show ('he showed')
ɛṭa	to give ('he gave')

LESSON THIRTY-FIVE

I. Text.

ɛṭit le-mkaḥel l-l-quḍat.	I gave the rifles to the judges.
ɛṭiti s-swaret l-l-quḍat?	Did you give the keys to the judges?
ɛṭina le-flus l-l-xeddam.	We gave the money to the worker.
ɛṭitiw le-flus le-ṣ-ṣeṛṛaq?	Did you give the thief the money?
šrit had s-sella l-bareḥ.	I bought this basket yesterday.
fayn šriti had l-žarida?	Where did you buy this newspaper?

šrina had s-sella fe-l-meġrib.	We bought this basket in Morocco.
fayn šritiw had le-mkaḥel?	Where did you buy these rifles?
žit l-bareḥ fe-ž-žuž.	I came yesterday at two o'clock.
žiti fe-ṭ-ṭumubil dyalek?	Did you come in your car?
žina wel-l-bareḥ fe-t-tlata.	We came day before yesterday at three o'clock.
žitiw bekri l-l-meḍṛaṣa?	Did you come to school early?
werrit l-žarida l-l-xeddama.	I showed the newspaper to the workers.
werriti s-sella l-le-bnat?	Did you show the basket to the girls?
werrina s-sellat le-n-nas.	We showed the people the baskets.
werritiw l-žarida l-l-qaḍi?	Did you show the judge the newspaper?
xellit l-werqa ḥăl ṭ-ṭebla.	I left the ticket on the table.
xelliti l-werqa fe-ḍ-ḍaṛ?	Did you leave the ticket at home?
xellina l-makla fe-s-sella.	We left the food in the basket.
fayn xellitiw l-werqa?	Where did you leave the ticket?

II. Grammatical Notes.

A. The endings *-t* 'I', *-na* 'we', *-ti* 'you' (sg., m. and f.), and *-tiw* 'you' (pl.) remain constant. But for verbs with he-forms ending in *a,* this final *a* is changed to *i* before these endings. Note the examples below:

šra to buy ('he bought')		*werra* to show ('he showed')	
šrit	I bought	*werrit*	I showed
šrina	we bought	*werrina*	we showed
šriti	you (sg.) bought	*werriti*	you (sg.) showed
šritiw	you (pl.) bought	*werritiw*	you (pl.) showed

B. Note that the word *flus* 'money' is plural, although singular in meaning. Compare such English words as 'scissors' and '(eye)glasses'.

III. Exercises.

A. Go through the sentences of the text of Lessons 33 and 34 and successively substitute the forms for 'I', 'you' (both sg. and pl.), and 'we' for the verb forms encountered. Make whatever further changes in the sentences, if any, that are necessary to have them make good sense.

B. Reverse the procedures of Exercise **A** above by substituting he-forms, she-forms, and they-forms for the verbs in the sentences of the text of this lesson.

IV. Vocabulary.

flus (pl.)	money
fe-t-tlata	at three o'clock
fe-ž-žuž	at two o'clock
mkaɛel	rifles
quḍat	judges
sella	basket
sellat (pl.)	
weṛqa	ticket
xeddam	worker
xeddama (pl.)	
žarida	newspaper

LESSON THIRTY-SIX

I. Text.

šedd le-ɛwanet fe-ž-žuž.	He closed the shops at two o'clock.
le-fqi šedd l-meḍṛaṣa fe-t-tlata.	The teacher closed the school at three o'clock.
šeddet l-bab fe-ṛ-ṛebɛa.	She closed the door at four o'clock.
l-metɛăllma šeddet ḍ-ḍaṛ.	The maid closed the house.
šeddu ḍ-ḍaṛ fe-l-xemsa.	They closed the housε at five o'clock.
n-nežžaṛa šeddu l-ɛanut f-le-ɛšiya.	The carpenters closed the shop in the evening.
kebb l-ma men l-ġoṛṛaf.	He poured the water out of the pitcher.

l-xeddam kebb atay men l-kisan.	The worker poured the tea out of the glasses.
kebbet l-ma fe-l-qeṛƹa.	She poured the water into the bottle.
l-bent kebbet ši-šwiya de-l-qehwa men l-qeṛƹa.	The girl poured a little coffee out of the bottle.
kebbu le-ḥlib fe-l-kisan.	They poured the milk into the glasses.
le-fqihat kebbu l-ma fe-l-kisan.	The teachers poured the water into the glasses.
ḥăll le-qṛaƹi.	He opened the bottles.
l-qaḍi ḥăll l-bakit.	The judge opened the package.
ḥăllet ḍ-ḍaṛ.	She opened the house.
xti ḥăllet ṣ-ṣnadeq.	My sister opened the boxes.
ḥăllu ṣ-ṣbiṭaṛ ž-ždid l-bareḥ.	They opened the new hospital yesterday.
n-nežžaṛa ḥăllu l-ḥanut fe-l-xemsa.	The carpenters opened the shop at five o'clock.
medd l-qeṛƹa l-l-weld.	He handed the bottle to the boy.
ṭ-ṭebbax medd l-makla l-l-xeddam.	The cook handed the food to the worker.
meddet l-žarida l-l-xeddam.	She handed the newspaper to the worker.
l-metƹăllma meddet l-weṛqa l-l-qaḍi.	The maid handed the ticket to the judge.
d-drari meddu l-xobz l-l-xeddama.	The children handed the bread to the workers.
le-bnat meddu le-knaneš dyalhom le-xti.	The girls handed their notebooks to my sister.

II. Grammatical Notes.

The endings *-et* 'she' and *-u* 'they' are added without change to he-forms which end in two identical consonants, e.g. ***kebb*** 'he poured', ***kebbet*** 'she poured', and ***kebbu*** 'they poured'.

III. Exercises.

Go through the sentences of this lesson and:

1. Change every she-form and they-form to a he-form.
2. Change every he-form and they-form to a she-form.
3. Change every he-form and she-form to a they-form.

In following the above instructions, make appropriate substitutions among masculine, feminine, and plural nouns to correspond to the verb changes. Each new sentence formed by these changes should be read out loud.

IV. Vocabulary.

fe-l-xemsa	at five o'clock
fe-ṛ-ṛebƐa	at four o'clock
kebb	to pour ('he poured')
ma	water
medd	to hand ('he handed')
metƐăllma	maid
qeṛƐa	bottle
qṛaƐi (pl.)	
šedd	to close ('he closed')
ṭebbax	cook
xemsa	five
xti	my sister
Ɛăll	to open ('he opened')
Ɛwanet	shops, stores

LESSON THIRTY-SEVEN

I. Text.

kebbit le-Ɛrira fe-z-zlafa.	I poured the soup into the bowl.
kebbiti l-ma fe-z-zlafa?	Did you pour the water into the bowl?
kebbina d-dwa fe-l-kas.	We poured the medicine into the glass.
kebbitiw l-qehwa fe-l-kisan?	Did you pour the coffee into the glasses?
meddit d-dwa le-ṭ-ṭbib.	I handed the medicine to the doctor.
medditi l-weṛqa l-l-metƐăllma?	Did you hand the ticket to the maid?

meddina le-mkaɛel l-l-xeddama.	We handed the rifles to the workers.
medditiw z-zlafa le-ṭ-ṭebbax?	Did you hand the bowl to the cook?
šeddit ḍ-ḍaṛ fe-s-setta.	I closed the house at six o'clock.
šedditi š-šeṛžem?	Did you close the window?
šeddina le-ɛwanet fe-s-setta.	We closed the shops at six o'clock.
šedditiw le-ktub dyalkom?	Did you close your books?
ɛăllit setta d-le-brawat.	I opened six letters.
ɛălliti d-dwa?	Did you open the medicine?
ɛăllina xemsa d-le-bṛawat.	We opened five letters.
ɛăllitiw duk s-setta d-le-bṛawat dyali?	Did you open those six letters of mine?
ṭ-ṭbib leff d-dwa.	The doctor wrapped up the medicine.
l-gezzar leff l-makla.	The butcher wrapped up the food.
l-metɛăllma leffet l-lɛăm.	The maid wrapped up the meat.
xti leffet setta d-le-ktub.	My sister wrapped up six books.
l-gezzara leffu l-lɛăm.	The butchers wrapped up the meat.
xwatati leffu bezzaf de-l-bakitat.	My sisters wrapped up a lot of packages.
leffit ṣ-ṣiniya.	I wrapped up the tray.
leffiti d-dwa?	Did you wrap up the medicine?
leffina bezzaf de-ṣ-ṣwani.	We wrapped up a lot of trays.
leffitiw duk l-xemsa de-ṣ-ṣwani dyali?	Did you wrap up those five trays of mine?

II. Grammatical Notes.

A. The endings *-t* 'I', *-ti* 'you' (sg.), *-na* 'we', and *-tiw* 'you' (pl.) remain constant. With he-forms ending in two identical consonants, an *i* is added to the he-forms before the endings. Note the examples below:

kebb to pour ('he poured')	*ɛăll* to open ('he opened')
kebbit I poured	*ɛăllit* I opened
kebbina we poured	*ɛăllina* we opened
kebbiti you (sg.) poured	*ɛălliti* you (sg.) opened
kebbitiw you (pl.) poured	*ɛăllitiw* you (pl.) opened

B. Note that the word *dwa* 'medicine' is masculine despite its *a* ending. As a consequence it takes masculine adjectives, etc., e.g. *dwa mezyan* 'good medicine'.

III. Exercises.

A. Go through the sentences of the text of Lesson 36 and successively substitute the forms for 'I', 'you' (both sg. and pl.), and 'we' for the verb forms encountered. Make whatever further changes in the sentences, if any, that are necessary to have them make good sense.

B. Reverse the procedure of Exercise **A** by substituting he-forms, she-forms, and they-forms for the verbs in the sentences of the text of this lesson.

IV. Vocabulary.

bṛawat	letters
dwa (m.)	medicine
fe-s-setta	at six o'clock
gezzar	butcher
gezzara (pl.)	
leff	to wrap up ('he wrapped up')
lẓăm	meat
setta	six
ṣiniya	tray
ṣwani (pl.)	
ṭbib	doctor
xwatati	my sisters
zlafa	bowl
ẓrira	soup

LESSON THIRTY-EIGHT

I. Text.

ṛežžăɛ ṣ-ṣwani le-xwatati.	He brought the trays back to my sisters.
ṭ-ṭebbax ṛežžăɛ l-makla le-ḍ-ḍaṛ.	The cook took the food back to the house.
ṣ-ṣeṛṛaq ṛežžăɛ le-flus.	The thief returned the money.
ṛežžɛet le-ɛrira le-ṭ-ṭebbax.	She sent the soup back to the cook.
xti ṛežžɛet l-lɛăm l-l-gezzar	My sister sent the meat back to the butcher.
l-metɛăllma ṛežžɛet d-dwa le-ṭ-ṭbib.	The maid took the medicine back to the doctor.
ṛežžɛu le-bṛawat.	They sent the letters back.
l-gezzara ṛežžɛu l-lɛăm.	The butchers sent the meat back.
l-xeddama ṛežžɛu ṭ-ṭumubil l-bareɛ fe-s-setta.	The workers brought the car back yesterday at six o'clock.
siyyeb z-zlayef l-balyin.	He threw the old bowls away.
l-gezzar siyyeb l-lɛăm l-l-kelb.	The butcher threw the meat to the dog.
siyybet le-bṛawat dyalu.	She threw away his letters.
l-metɛăllma siyybet le-ɛwayež fe-ṣ-ṣenduq.	The maid threw the clothes into the box.
siyybu l-žarida dyali.	They threw my newspaper away.
l-metɛăllmat siyybu s-sellat dyalhom ɛăl ḷ-ḷeṛd.	The maids threw their baskets on the ground.
ṣifeṭ ṭ-ṭbib le-ḍ-ḍaṛ l-biḍa.	He sent the doctor to Casablanca.
ṣifṭet s-sokkaṛ le-ṭ-ṭebbax.	She sent the sugar to the cook.
xti ṣifṭet setta de-z-zlayef ždad l-l-metɛăllma.	My sister sent six new bowls to the maid.
ṣifṭu l-uṛaq le-ṛ-ṛbaṭ.	They sent the tickets to Rabat.
l-metɛăllmat ṣifṭu le-flus dyalhom le-ḍ-ḍaṛ.	The maids sent their money home.

ɛawen l-metɛăllmat fe-l-xedma dyalhom.	He helped the maids in their work.
xay ɛawen l-quḍat fe-l-xedma dyalhom.	My brother helped the judges in their work.
ɛawnet xak fe-l-xedma dyalu.	She helped your brother in his work.
had l-bent ɛawnet xay bezzaf.	This girl helped my brother a lot.
ɛawnu xwatatek bezzaf.	They helped your sisters a lot.
xwatati ɛawnu ṭ-ṭobba fe-ṣ-ṣbiṭaṛ.	My sisters helped the doctors at the hospital.
ɛaqeb ṣeṛṛaqa.	He punished the thieves.
l-qaḍi ɛaqeb duk ž-žuž de-ṣ-ṣeṛṛaqa.	The judge punished those two thieves.
ɛaqbet l-metɛăllma.	She punished the maid.
le-fqiha ɛaqbet xwatati.	The teacher punished my sisters.
ɛaqbu ṣ-ṣeṛṛaqa.	They punished the thieves.
l-feqya ɛaqbu d-drari.	The teachers punished the children.

II. Grammatical Notes.

Other than verbs on the pattern of *CCeC* (see the Grammatical Notes of Lessons 25 and 26), verbs which end in *-eC* or *-ăC* lose the vowel before their final consonant when the endings *-et* 'she' and *-u* 'they' are added, for example *ṣifeṭ* 'he sent', *ṣifṭet* 'she sent', and *ṣifṭu* 'they sent', or *ṛežžăɛ* 'he gave back', *ṛežžɛet* 'she gave back', and *ṛežžɛu* 'they gave back'.

III. Exercises.

Go through the sentences of this lesson and:

1. Change every she-form and they-form to a he-form.
2. Change every he-form and they-form to a she-form.
3. Change every he-form and she-form to a they-form.

In following the above instructions make appropriate substitutions among masculine, feminine, and plural nouns to correspond to the verb changes. Each new sentence formed by these changes should be read out loud.

IV. Vocabulary.

metɛăllmat	maids
ṛeẓẓăɛ	to return (send back, take back, bring back, give back)
siyyeb	to throw, to throw away
sokkaṛ	sugar
ṣifeṭ	to send
ṣeṛṛaqa	thieves
ṭobba	doctors
ṭebbaxa	cooks
wṛaq (*l-uṛaq*)	tickets (the tickets)
xak	your (sg., m. and f.) brother
xay	my brother
xedma	work
xwatatek	your (sg., m. and f.) sisters
zlayef	bowls
ɛaqeb	to punish
ɛawen	to help

LESSON THIRTY-NINE

I. Text.

teṛžemt le-bṛawat men n-negliza.	I translated the letters from English.
teṛžemti l-žarida?	Did you translate the newspaper?
teṛžemna le-bṛa dyalha le-n-negliza.	We translated her letter into English.
teṛžemtiw ž-žwab l-l-ɛăṛbiya?	Did you translate the answer into Arabic?
ɛămmeṛt z-zlayef b-le-ḥrira.	I filled the bowls with soup.
ɛămmeṛt l-ġoṛṛaf be-l-ma.	I filled the pitcher with water.
ɛămmeṛti l-kisan?	Did you fill the glasses?
ɛămmeṛna z-zlafa be-z-zit.	We filled the bowl with oil.
ɛămmeṛtiw le-xnaši?	Did you fill the bags?

weqqeft ṭ-ṭumubil fe-ẓ-ẓenqa.	I stopped the car in the street.
weqqeft le-mkoƐla fe-l-qent.	I stood the rifle in the corner.
weqqefti l-qeṛƐa?	Did you stand the bottle up?
weqqefna le-mraya fe-l-qent.	We stood the mirror up in the corner.
weqqeftiw ṭ-ṭumubil Ɛda l-bab?	Did you stop the car next to the door?

II. Grammatical Notes.

A. The endings *-t* 'I', *-ti* 'you (sg., m. and f.), *-na* 'we', and *-tiw* 'you' (pl.) are added directly to the he-form of verbs ending in *-eC* and *-ăC*. There is no modification of the he-form upon the addition of the endings, e.g.: *teṛžem* 'he translated', *teṛžemt* 'I translated', etc.

B. The preposition *b-, be-* has the form *be-* before a following cluster of consonants (*be-l-ma* 'with water') and *b-* before a consonant plus vowel (*b-le-Ɛlib 'with milk'*). The usual meaning of this preposition is 'with', e.g. *Ɛămmeṛ z-zlafa b-le-Ɛrira* 'He filled the bowl with soup'. Note that this preposition is equal to English 'with' only in the sense of referring to an instrument, a tool, or something else by means of which something is done (*b-le-Ɛrira* 'with soup', i.e. using the soup for a purpose). The Moroccan equivalent for 'with' in the sense of accompaniment or association (e.g. 'I saw the boy with the girl.') will be learned in a later lesson.

C. The names of languages in Moroccan are always accompanied by the word for 'the', e.g. *n-negliza* 'English', *l-Ɛăṛbiya* 'Arabic'. Note that with the names of languages, 'into' is translated as *l-*, e.g. *le-n-negliza, l-l-Ɛăṛbiya.*

III. Exercises.

A. Go through the sentences of the text of Lesson 38 and successively substitute the forms 'I', 'you' (both sg. and pl.), and 'we' for the he-forms, she-forms, and they-forms encountered there. Noun subjects of the sentences should be dropped and any other changes made which are necessary to good sense. Each new sentence formed by these substitutions should be read out loud.

B. Go through the sentences of this lesson and successively substitute he-forms, she-forms, and they-forms for the verbs encountered. Appropriate masculine, feminine, and plural nouns should be added as the subjects of the verbs as the changes of form are made.

IV. Vocabulary.

b-, be-	(see Grammatical Note **B**)
(n-)negliza	(the) English (language)
qent	corner
teṛžem	to translate
weqqef	to stop, to stand, to stand up
ẓenqa	street
ɛămmeṛ	to fill
(l-)ɛăṛbiya	(the) Arabic (language)

LESSON FORTY

I. Text.

had l-kebbuṭ meṣnuɛ men ṣ-ṣuf.	This coat is made out of wool.
had s-serwal meṣnuɛ men le-qṭen.	This pair of trousers is made out of cotton.
had l-xenša meṣnuɛa men ṣ-ṣuf.	This bag is made out of wool.
had ẓ-ẓeṛbiya meṣnuɛa men le-qṭen.	This rug is made out of cotton.
had t-tqašeṛ meṣnuɛin men ṣ-ṣuf.	These socks are made out of wool.
had le-ḥwayež meṣnuɛin men le-qṭen.	These clothes are made out of cotton.
ɛămmeṛ l-qeṛɛa b-le-mdad.	He filled the bottle with ink.
šrina le-ḥlib u-l-lḥăm had ṣ-ṣbaḥ.	We bought some milk and meat this morning.
daru s-sokkaṛ fe-l-kisan.	They put sugar in the glasses.
kebbina l-ma ɛăl ẓ-ẓeṛbiya.	We poured water on the rug.
šritiw le-ḥrira?	Did you (pl.) buy soup?
žebṛet z-zit fe-l-qeṛɛa.	She found some oil in the bottle.
ṣifeṭti l-qehwa l-xay?	Did you (sg.) send some coffee to my brother?

aš, š-, še-	what (see Grammatical Note **B**)
ʕăndna	we have
ʕăndkom	you (pl.) have
ʕăndhom	they have
š-šritiw men dak l-ʕanut?	What did you (pl.) buy in that shop?
šrina d-dwa.	We bought some medicine.
š-ʕăndkom f-had l-bakit?	What do you have in this package?
ʕăndna l-makla f-had l-bakit.	We have food in this package.
š-ʕăndhom f-had l-xenša?	What've they got in this bag?
ʕăndhom l-lʕăm f-had l-xenša.	They've got meat in this bag.
ʕăndkom le-flus?	Do you (pl.) have any money?
iyeh, ʕăndna le-flus.	Yes, we have some money.
ṭ-ṭbib žab d-dwa le-ṣ-ṣbiṭaṛ.	The doctor brought some medicine to the hospital.
š-ʕăndhom f-had ṣ-ṣenduq?	What've they got in this box?
ʕăndhom le-ktub u-le-knaneš u-t-tṣaweṛ f-had ṣ-ṣenduq.	They've got books, notebooks, and pictures in this box.
š-ʕăndkom fe-l-ʕanut dyalkom?	What do you (pl.) have in your shop?
ʕăndna ṣ-ṣnadeq u-š-šelyat u-ṭ-ṭbali.	We have boxes, chairs, and tables.
glesna ʕăl š-šelyat, ma-ši ʕăl l-leṛḍ.	We sat on chairs, not on the ground.

II. Grammatical Notes.

A. The English word 'the' and its Moroccan equivalent are usually referred to as 'the definite article'. The use and meaning of the Moroccan definite article differ in many ways from the English definite article.

To understand the difference in use between the English and the Moroccan definite articles, a distinction must be made between 'count nouns' and 'mass nouns'. Count nouns are nouns which usually refer to individual objects which have plurals and which can be counted, e.g. ***ktab*** 'book', ***ktub*** 'books', and ***ṛebʕa d-le-ktub*** 'four books'. Mass nouns are nouns which typically refer to continuous substances which have no plurals and which cannot be counted, e.g. ***zit*** 'oil.'

In Moroccan, mass nouns almost always take the definite article. Thus *le-ɛlib,* depending on context, is variously translated into English as 'milk', 'some milk', or 'the milk'. Moroccan mass nouns occur without the definite article only in a very limited number of special circumstances. These special circumstances will be discussed in detail in later lessons. Note in passing that there are a small number of nouns which never take the definite article under any circumstances. These nouns, which constitute exceptions to the general rule, must be memorized one by one. The only noun of this type given so far is *atay* 'tea'. Note also that the names of languages are classifiable as mass nouns and therefore take the definite article regularly, e.g. *n-negliza* 'English' and *l-ɛăṛbiya* 'Arabic'.

B. The three forms *aš, š-,* and *še-* all mean 'what?'. The form *aš* is generally usable, and *š-* and *še-* are abbreviations of it. The form *š-* is used before a consonant plus a vowel or before the consonant *š* itself, e.g. *š-ɛăndkom fe-ṣ-ṣenduq?* 'What've you (pl.) got in the box?', or *š-šriti?* 'What did you (sg.) buy?' The form *še-* is generally used if the following word begins with two or more consonants, e.g. *še-kteb?* 'What did he write?' The full form *aš* is used without reference to how the following word begins.

III. Exercises.

Change the following sentences into questions by deleting the underlined form and prefixing a form of *aš* 'what' to the verb. Read the resulting new sentence out loud. For example, *lbes le-ɛwayež ž-ždad dyalu* 'He wore his new clothes' should be changed to *še-lbes?* 'What did he wear?'

1. *ɛṭa le-ktab le-ṛ-ṛažel.*
2. *ɛṭal-biškliṭa l-l-bent.*
3. *ɛṭat le-bṛa l-l-qaḍi.*
4. *ɛṭat n-namusiya le-n-nežžaṛ.*
5. *ɛṭaw l-makla l-le-mṛa.*
6. *ɛṭaw le-knaneš l-le-fqi.*
7. *šra žuž de-l-buḷat.*
8. *šrat bezzaf d-atay.*
9. *šraw ši-biškliṭat.*
10. *xella ṣ-ṣenduq meɛlul.*
11. *xellat s-swaret fe-ḍ-ḍaṛ.*
12. *xellaw le-kbabeṭ dyalhom ɛăl ḷ-ḷeṛḍ.*
13. *werra le-bṛa l-le-mṛa.*
14. *werra le-mkoɛla l-l-qaḍi.*
15. *werrat le-ɛwayež l-l-bent.*
16. *werra l-ɛanut le-ṛ-ṛažel.*
17. *werraw ṭ-ṭebla le-n-nežžaṛ*
18. *ɛṭiti s-swaret l-l-quḍat?*
19. *ɛṭiti le-ɛwayež le-ṣ-ṣeṛṛaq?*
20. *ɛṭina le-flus l-l-xeddam.*
21. *ɛṭitiw le-flus le-ṣ-ṣeṛṛaq?*
22. *šriti s-sella men dak l-ɛanut?*
23. *šriti l-žarida men had l-weld?*
24. *šrina had s-sella fe-l-meġṛib.*
25. *šrina l-žarida had ṣ-ṣbaɛ.*

IV. Vocabulary.

aš, š-, še-	what (see Grammatical Note C)
meṣnuع	made, manufactured
meṣnuعa (f.)	
meṣnuعin (pl.)	
qṭen	cotton
ṣuf	wool
عăndhom	they have
عăndkom	you (pl.) have
عăndna	we have

LESSON FORTY-ONE

I. Text.

ka-iṛežžăع	he returns (sends back, gives back, takes back, brings back)
dima ka-iṛežžăع d-drari dyalu l-l-meġṛib fe-ṣ-ṣif.	He always sends his children back to Morocco in the summer.
dima ka-iṛežžăع le-ktub l-l-mektaba fe-l-weqt.	He always returns books to the library on time.
ka-iṣifeṭ	he sends
dima ka-iṣifeṭ d-drari dyalu l-l-medṛaṣa fe-l-weqt.	He always sends his children to school on time.
dima ka-iṣifeṭ le-bṛawat le-xti fe-ṣ-ṣif.	He always sends my sister letters in the summer.
dima ka-iعămmeṛ z-zlafa dyalu b-le-حrira.	He always fills his bowl with soup.
dima ka-iعămmeṛ ž-žib dyalu be-š-šekḷaṭ.	He always fills his pocket with chocolate.
dima ka-tsiyyeb le-حwayež dyalha عăl ḷ-leṛḍ.	She always throws her clothes on the floor.
dima ka-tsiyyeb le-bṛawat dyalha.	She always throws her letters away.

ka-tƐawen xay fe-l-mektaba.	She helps my brother at the library.
ka-tƐawen l-feqya fe-l-medṛaṣa.	She helps the teachers at school.
Ɛlaš ka-tsiyyeb le-bṛawat dyalek?	Why do you throw away your letters?
waš dima ka-tsiyyeb d-dwa dyalek?	Do you always throw away your medicine?
ka-tƐawen xak fe-l-medṛaṣa?	Do you help your brother at school?
waš ka-tƐawen l-xeddama fe-l-mektaba?	Do you help the workers at the library?
ka-nteṛžem ž-žwabat fe-l-mektaba.	I translate answers at the library.
dima ka-nteṛžem ž-žwabat dyalu l-l-Ɛăṛbiya.	I always translate his answers into Arabic.
dima ka-nweqqef ṭ-ṭumubil qeddam ḍ-ḍaṛ.	I always stop the car in front of the house.
ka-nweqqef l-biškliṭa dyali muṛa ḍ-ḍaṛ.	I park my bicycle behind the house.

II. Grammatical Notes.

A. Lessons 25 through 39 were primarily concerned with the forms of the perfect tense. Five basic kinds of verbs were studied:

1. Those on the pattern *CCeC* (e.g. *kteb* 'to write'), which show inversion when a vowel ending is added. (Lessons 25-28).
2. Those on the pattern of *CaC* (e.g. *šaf* 'to see'), which show a change of the medial *a* to *e* in some forms. (Lessons 29-32).
3. Those ending in *-a* (e.g. *šra* 'to buy'), which change the final *a* to *i* in some forms. (Lessons 33-35).
4. Those ending in two identical consonants (e.g. *kebb* 'to pour'), which show the addition of *i* before certain endings. (Lessons 36-37).
5. Those ending in *-eC* or *-ăC* other than the pattern *CCeC* (e.g. *Ɛămmeṛ* 'to fill') which lose the *e* or *ă* before their final consonant when a vowel ending is added. (Lessons 38-39).

This lesson and those immediately following concern themselves with the forms of the durative tense. The simplest form of the durative tense is found with the kind of verbs listed as number 5 above, those ending in *-eC* or *-ăC*. The he-form of the perfect is prefixed with *n-* for 'I', *t-* for 'you' (sg.), *i-* for 'he' and *t-* for 'she', and these prefixes are always preceded by *ka-*. The forms presented in this lesson are summarized below:

ka-nteṛžem	(from *teṛžem*)	I translate
ka-nweqqef	(from *weqqef*)	I stop, I park
ka-tsiyyeb	(from *siyyeb*)	you (sg.) throw, you throw away
ka-tɛawen	(from *ɛawen*)	you (sg.) help
ka-iṛežžăɛ	(from *ṛežžăɛ*)	he sends back, he returns
ka-iṣifeṭ	(from *ṣifeṭ*)	he sends
ka-iɛămmeṛ	(from *ɛămmeṛ*)	he fills
ka-tsiyyeb	(from *siyyeb*)	she throws, she throws away
ka-tɛawen	(from *ɛawen*)	she helps

Note that the forms for 'you' (sg.) and 'she' are identical; both have the form *t-*, as in *ka-tsiyyeb* and *ka-tɛawen*. Only context or the actual use of the pronouns *nta* 'you' (m.sg.), *nti* 'you' (f.sg.), or *hiya* 'she' can distinguish whether 'you' (sg.) or 'she' is the intended subject of such a verb form.

B. Lesson 40 pointed out some differences between the use of the Moroccan definite article and the English definite article. An important difference that applies to both mass nouns and count nouns is that the Moroccan definite article is almost always used (rare exceptions will be noted later) in exactly those cases where English calls for a simple noun with no definite article or such modifiers as a possessive pronoun or demonstrative such as 'this', 'these', etc. A number of examples are given in this lesson. They are listed below:

fe-l-weqt	on time
dima ka-iṛežžăɛ le-ktub l-l-mektaba fe-l-weqt.	He always sends books back to the library on time.
fe-l-meḍṛaṣa	at school
l-l-meḍṛaṣa	to school
dima ka-iṣifeṭ le-bṛawat le-xti fe-ṣ-ṣif.	He always sends letters to my sister in the summer.
ka-nteṛžem le-bṛawat fe-l-mektaba.	I translate letters at the library.

Note how accurately this general rule holds for mass nouns:

Ɛămmeṛ ž-žib dyalu be-š-šekḷaṭ.	He filled his pocket with chocolate.
be-l-Ɛăṛbiya	in Arabic
be-n-negliza	in English
meṣnuƐ men ṣ-ṣuf	made out of wool
meṣnuƐ men le-qṭen	made out of cotton

This is perhaps the single most important rule for the use of the Moroccan definite article, that it is required in exactly those cases where English excludes the definite article. Note that Moroccan equivalents for possession ('my', 'his', etc.) and demonstratives ('this', 'that', 'those') have already been given. This rule must be taken as applying only to English nouns in those circumstances where they stand without the definite article, without a possessive, and without a demonstrative, as in the examples given above.

III. Exercises.

A. Go through the sentences of this lesson and change all 'he', 'she', and 'you' forms to 'I' forms. Make any other changes necessary in the sentences, e.g. *d-drari dyalu* 'his children' should be changed to *d-drari dyali* 'my children' as a 'he' form is changed to an 'I' form.

B. Repeat **A.**, changing all 'I', 'you', and 'she' forms to 'he' forms.

C. Repeat **A.**, changing all 'I', 'he', and 'she' forms into 'you' forms.

D. Go through the sentences of this lesson and insert appropriate nouns as subjects for the he-forms and the she-forms.

Each new sentence formed in following the directions above should be read out loud as it is formed.

IV. Vocabulary.

dima	always
fe-l-weqt	on time
ḷeṛḍ	floor
mektaba	library
šekḷaṭ	chocolate
žwabat	answers
Ɛlaš	why

LESSON FORTY-TWO

I. Text.

ka-iṛežžăʕ d-drari fe-l-weqt.	He sends the children back on time.
ka-iṛežžʕu d-drari l-l-meḍṛaṣa băʕd le-ġda.	They send the children back to school after dinner.
ka-iṛežžʕu r-ržal l-l-xedma băʕd le-ġda.	They send the men back to work after dinner.
ka-iʕămmeṛ l-berrad.	He fills the teapot.
d-drari dima ka-iʕămmṛu ž-žyub dyalhom be-š-šeklaṭ.	The children always fill their pockets with chocolate.
dima ka-iʕămmṛu l-berrad be-n-neʕnaʕ.	They always fill the teapot with mint.
ka-iweqqef ṭ-ṭumubil muṛa ḍ-ḍaṛ.	He parks the car behind the house.
ka-iweqqfu ṭ-ṭumubil dyalhom qeddam ḍ-ḍaṛ.	They park their car in front of the house.
ka-iweqqfu l-biškliṭat dyalhom muṛa l-meḍṛaṣa.	They park their bicycles behind the school.
dima ka-nsiyyeb le-ʕwayež l-balyin.	I always throw old clothes away.
dima ka-nsiyybu le-bṛawat dyalhom.	We always throw their letters away.
dima ka-nsiyybu le-ʕwayež l-balyin.	We always throw old clothes away.
ka-nṣifeṭ d-drari l-l-meḍṛaṣa.	I send the childen to school.
ka-nṣifṭu d-drari l-l-meḍṛaṣa fe-t-tesʕud.	We send the children to school at nine o'clock.
ka-nṣifṭu l-žarida le-ḍ-ḍaṛ koll nhaṛ.	We send the newspaper to the house every day.
waš ka-tteṛžem ž-žwabat dyalhom?	Do you translate their answers?
waš ka-tteṛžmu ž-žwabat dyalhom l-l-ʕăṛbiya?	Do you translate their answers into Arabic?

ɛlaš dima ka-tteṛžmu ž-žwabat dyalkom?	Why do you always translate your answers?
waš ka-tɛawen d-drari?	Do you help the children?
waš ka-tɛawnu d-drari fe-l-xedma dyalhom?	Do you help the children in their work?
ɛlaš ka-tɛawnu l-metɛăllma fe-l-xedma dyalha?	Why do you help the maid in her work?

II. Grammatical Notes.

A. In the durative tense, the forms for 'we', 'you' (pl.), and 'they' are derived by adding *-u* to the forms for 'I', 'you' (sg.), and 'he' respectively, e.g.:

ka-nṣifeṭ	I send
ka-nṣifṭu	we send
ka-tṣifeṭ	you(sg.) send
ka-tṣifṭu	you (pl.) send
ka-iṣifeṭ	he sends
ka-iṣifṭu	they send

B. The verb forms for 'I', 'you (sg.), 'he' and 'she' are collectively referred to as 'singular forms'. The verb forms for 'we' 'you' (pl.), and 'they' are collectively referred to as 'plural forms'. A summary of the pattern given in **A** above is that the plural forms are arrived at by adding *-u* to the corresponding singular forms. Note that there is no specific plural form corresponding to the singular 'she'.

C. As the plural ending *-u* is added to the verbs given in this lesson, the *ă* or *e* preceding the final consonant of the singular form is dropped, e.g. *ka-iɛawen* 'he helps' and *ka-iɛawnu* 'they help'. The technical name for this dropping out of a vowel is 'elision'.

Both elision and inversion (for 'inversion' cf. Grammatical Note **D**, Lesson 25) are processes which occur throughout the language and are not limited to verbs. The prevailing pattern is that when a vowel ending is added to a word ending in *-eC* or *-ăC,* either elision or inversion occurs. Usually, inversion occurs only with quite short words, e.g. the verb forms *kteb* 'he write' and *ketbet* 'she wrote', or the adjective forms *ṣfeṛ* (m.) and *ṣefṛa* (f.) 'yellow'. Elision occurs with longer words, as in the verbs studied in this lesson or as in such adjective forms as *mwessex* (m.) and *mwessxin* (pl.) 'dirty'.

D. Note further examples in this lesson of Moroccan nouns taking the definite article where the patterns of English call for the noun by itself:

băɛd le-ġda	after dinner
l-l-meḍṛaṣa	to school
l-l-xedma	to work
be-š-šekḷaṭ	with chocolate
be-n-neɛnaɛ	with mint
le-ḥwayež l-balyin	old clothes

Additional English phrases with the definite article, and consequently with a different meaning, are possible in each case, e.g. 'after dinner' and 'after the dinner' are both good English and mean different things in different contexts. Moroccan makes no such distinction and translates both 'after dinner' and 'after the dinner' as *băɛd le-ġda,* etc.

III. Exercises.

A. Go through the text of Lesson 41 and form new sentences by substituting plural forms for singular forms. Make any further changes in the sentences that are logically necessary to accompany the change of a singular verb form to a plural verb form. Read each new sentence out loud as it is formed.

B. Go through the text of this lesson and successively:

1. Change all 'we' and 'you' (pl.) forms to 'they' forms.
2. Change all 'we' and 'they' forms to 'you' (pl.) forms.
3. Change all 'you' (pl.) and 'they' forms to 'we' forms.
4. In 1, 2, and 3 above make any other changes in the sentences that are logically necessary to accompany the verb form changes.
5. Read each new sentence formed out loud.

C. Take the 'they' forms of this lesson and instead of 'they' use an appropriate plural noun as subject, e.g. from *ka-iteṛžmu* 'they translate' form *r-ržal ka-iteṛžmu* 'the men translate'.

D. Go through the texts of Lessons 41 and 42, changing every statement into a question and every question into a statement.

IV. Vocabulary.

berrad	teapot
băƐd	after
fe-t-tesƐud	at nine o'clock
ġda	dinner, mid-day meal
koll nhaṛ	every day
neƐnaƐ	mint
tesƐud	nine

Note: In Morocco, the midday meal (*le-ġda*) is the main meal of the day; thus 'dinner' is a more appropriate translation than 'lunch'.

Note: Moroccans drink great quantities of tea. A customary part of tea-making is usually to stuff the pot completely full of mint.

LESSON FORTY-THREE

I. Text.

ka-imedd l-konnaš dyalu l-le-fqi koll ṣbaḥ.	He hands his notebook to the teacher every morning.
ka-imedd l-makla l-l-xeddama f-le-ġda.	He hands the food to the workers at dinner.
ka-išedd l-bab koll nhaṛ fe-s-sebƐa.	He closes the door every day at seven o'clock.
ka-išedd l-ḥanut fe-t-tmenya.	He closes the shop at eight o'clock.
ka-ileff l-bakitat fe-l-ḥanut dyali.	He wraps packages in my shop.
ka-ileff le-ḥwayež n-nqiyin koll ṣbaḥ.	He wraps up the clean clothes every morning.
koll ṣbaḥ ka-iḥoll l-bab fe-t-tmenya.	Every morning he opens the door at eight o'clock.
dima ka-iḥoll š-šṛažem fe-s-sebƐa.	He always opens the windows at seven o'clock.
ka-nmedd	I hand

dima ka-nmedd ṭ-ṭbaṣel l-oṃṃi[1] *băεd le-ġda.*	I always hand my mother the dishes after dinner.
ka-nmedd l-makla l-l-xeddama koll ṣbaε.	I hand the food to the workers every morning.
dima ka-nšedd š-šṛažem f-le-εšiya.	I always close the windows in the evening.
ka-nšedd ḍ-ḍaṛ fe-t-tmenya.	I close the house at eight o'clock.
ka-nleff le-ktub fe-l-εanut dyalu.	I wrap books in his shop.
ka-nleff le-εwayež fe-ṣ-ṣbiṭaṛ.	I wrap clothes at the hospital.
dima ka-nkobb atay fe-s-sebεa.	I always pour tea at seven o'clock.
dima ka-nkobb bezzaf de-s-sokkaṛ f-atay dyali.	I always pour a lot of sugar in my tea.
ka-nεoll l-bakitat fe-l-buṣṭa.	I open packages at the post office.
ka-nεoll l-medṛaṣa fe-s-sebεa.	I open the school at seven o'clock.
ka-tmedd t-tṣaweṛ le-d-drari meṛṛa fe-l-ˀusbuε.	She hands pictures to the children once a week.
ṃṃi ka-tmedd ṭ-ṭbaṣel le-mwessxin l-l-metεăllma.	My mother hands the dirty dishes to the maid.
ka-tšedd had l-bit băεd le-ġda.	She closes this room after dinner.
ka-tšedd l-mektaba fe-t-tesεud.	She closes the library at nine o'clock.
ka-tleff t-tṣaweṛ f-dak l-εanut.	She wraps pictures in that shop.
ka-tleff l-bakitat fe-l-buṣṭa.	She wraps packages at the post office.
ka-tkobb bezzaf d-le-εlib fe-l-qehwa dyalha.	She pours a lot of milk into her coffee.
ka-tkobb ġir ši-šwiya de-atay fe-l-kas.	She only pours a little bit of tea in the glass.
ka-tεoll le-qṛaεi fe-ṣ-ṣbiṭaṛ.	She opens bottles at the hospital.
dima ka-tεoll le-bṛawat dyalha băεd le-ġda.	She always opens her letters after dinner.

II. Grammatical Notes.

A. The durative tense prefixes *n-* 'I', *t-* 'you' (sg.), *i-* 'he', and *t-* 'she' learned in Lessons 41 and 42 remain the same for verbs ending in two identical consonants (verbs of this sort were first discussed in Lessons 36-37).

[1] See footnote p. 55.

Usually these are added directly to the he-form of the perfect tense without change of any kind, e.g.:

šedd to close
ka-nšedd I close
ka-tšedd you (sg.) close
ka-išedd he closes
ka-tšedd she closes

Note once again that the forms for 'she' and 'you' (sg.) are identical in the durative tense.

B. In a few cases the vowel of the perfect tense he-form changes in the durative tense. Such cases must be individually memorized. Two examples are *kebb and* ح*ăll,* both of which have the vowel *o* in the present tense:

ka-nkobb I pour
ka-tkobb you (sg.) pour
ka-ikobb he pours
ka-tkobb she pours

*ka-n*ح*oll* I open
*ka-t*ح*oll* you (sg.) open
*ka-i*ح*oll* he opens
*ka-t*ح*oll* she opens

C. Plural forms are arrived at by adding *-u* to the singular, as explained in 42. The singular forms of this class of verbs undergo no changes as the plural *-u* is added. An illustration:

ka-nkobb I pour
ka-tkobb you (sg.) pour
ka-ikobb he pours
ka-tkobb she pours

ka-nkobbu we pour
ka-tkobbu you (pl.) pour
ka-ikobbu they pour

III. Exercises

Go through the sentences of the text of this lesson and:

1. Change every verb form encountered to a 'you (sg.) form. Turn the new sentences resulting into questions.
2. Change every 'I' and 'he' form into a 'she' form.
3. Change every 'I' and 'she' form into a 'he' form.
4. Change every 'he' form and 'she' form into an 'I' form.
5. Change every verb form encountered into a 'they' form.
6. Change every verb form encountered into a 'we' form.

7. Change every verb form encountered into a 'you' (pl.) form.
8. Supply an appropriate masculine noun as subject for each 'he' form encountered.
9. Supply an appropriate feminine noun as subject for each 'she' form encountered.
10. Repeat number 5 above using appropriate plural nouns as subjects of the verb forms.

In making the verb changes directed above, any further modifications necessary to make good sense should be made in the sentences. Each new sentence formed should be read out loud.

IV. Vocabulary.

buṣṭa	post office
fe-s-sebƐa	at seven o'clock
fe-t-tmenya	at eight o'clock
koll ṣbaƐ	every morning
l-om̃m̃i	to my mother
m̃m̃i	my mother
meṛṛa	one time, once
sebƐa	seven
tmenya	eight
ṭbaṣel	dishes
ˀusbuƐ	week

LESSON FORTY-FOUR

I. Text.

baƐ	to sell
ka-ibiƐ ṭ-ṭumubilat.	He sells cars.
ka-ibiƐ bezzaf de-š-šekḷaṭ.	He sells a lot of chocolate.
dar	to put
ka-idir bezzaf de-s-sokkaṛ f-atay dyalu.	He puts a lot of sugar in his tea.

ka-idir bezzaf de-l-mleɛ f-le-ɛrira dyalu.	He puts a lot of salt in his soup.
žab	to bring
ka-ižib le-flus l-om̃m̃u koll ʔusbuɛ.	He brings money to his mother every week.
ka-ižib d-drari dyalu l-ḍaṛna meṛṛa fe-l-ʔusbuɛ.	He brings his children to our house once a week.
naḍ	to get up.
dima ka-inuḍ bekri fe-ṣ-ṣbaɛ.	He always gets up early in the morning.
ka-inuḍ fe-t-tesɛud nhaṛ s-sebt.	He gets up at nine o'clock on Saturdays.
ẓaṛ	to visit
ka-iẓur xtu meṛṛa fe-š-šheṛ.	He visits his sister once a month.
ka-iẓuṛ m̃m̃u koll ʔusbuɛ.	He visits his mother every week.
šaf	to see
ka-išuf xah koll nhaṛ.	He sees his brother every day.
ka-išuf ḅḅah koll ṣbaɛ.	He sees his father every morning.
ka-nbiɛ le-qṭen u-ṣ-ṣuf f-had l-ɛanut.	I sell cotton and wool in this shop.
dima ka-nbiɛ l-uṛaq dyali.	I always sell my tickets.
dima ka-ndir le-flus dyali fe-l-benk.	I always put my money in the bank.
dima ka-ndir ṭ-ṭbaṣel fe-l-keššina băɛd le-ġda.	I always put the dishes in the kitchen after dinner.
ka-nžib le-ktub dyali le-ḍ-ḍaṛ koll nhaṛ.	I bring my books home every day.
ka-nžib d-drari le-ḍ-ḍaṛ l-biḍa meṛṛa fe-š-šheṛ.	I bring the children to Casablanca once a month.
ka-nnuḍ bekri nhaṛ s-sebt.	I get up early on Saturdays.
ka-nnuḍ fe-s-setta koll nhaṛ.	I get up at six o'clock every day.
ka-nẓuṛ xtu koll nhaṛ.	I visit his sister every day.
ka-nẓuṛ ḅḅah f-fas meṛṛa fe-š-šher.	I visit his father in Fez once a month.
ka-nšuf ṭ-ṭbib meṛṛtayn fe-š-šheṛ.	I see the doctor twice a month.

ka-nšuf d-drari meṛṛtayn fe-n-nhaṛ.	I see the children twice a day.
ka-tbiɛ l-uṛaq meṛṛa fe-l-ˀusbuɛ.	She sells tickets once a week.
ka-tbiɛ le-ḥrira l-l-xeddama.	She sells soup to the workers.
dima ka-ddir ši-swiya de-š-šekḷaṭ fe-ž-žib dyalha fe-ṣ-ṣbaḥ.	She always puts a little chocolate in her pocket in the morning.
ka-ddir ši-flus fe-l-ḅenk meṛṛa fe-š-šheṛ.	She puts some money in the bank once a month.
ka-džib d-drari l-ḍaṛna koll nhaṛ.	She brings the children to our house every day.
ka-džib bezzaf d-le-ktub men l-mektaba nhaṛ s-sebt.	She brings a lot of books from the library on Saturdays.
ka-tnuḍ fe-t-tmenya nhaṛ s-sebt.	She gets up at eight o'clock on Saturdays.
dima ka-tnuḍ bekri.	She always gets up early.
ka-dẓuṛ xtu meṛṛa fe-l-ˀusbuɛ.	She visits his sister once a week.
ka-dẓuṛ ṃṃi fe-ṛ-ṛbaṭ meṛṛa fe-š-šheṛ.	She visits my mother in Rabat once a month.
ka-tšuf xah meṛṛa fe-l-ˀusbuɛ.	She sees his brother once a week.
ka-tšuf d-drari bezzaf.	She sees the children a lot.

II. Grammatical Notes.

A. Before *d, ž,* or *ẓ,* the prefix for 'she' and 'you' is *d-,* not *t.* Thus: ***ka-ddir*** 'she puts', or 'you (sg.) put', ***ka-džib*** 'she brings', or 'you (sg.) bring', ***ka-dẓuṛ*** 'she visits' or 'you (sg.) visit'.

B. Except for the change noted above, the prefixes for 'I', 'you' (sg.), 'he', and 'she' are the same for verbs of the pattern *CaC* (verbs of this sort were first discussed in Lessons 29-32) as for the verbs discussed in Lessons 41-43. Note once again that the forms for 'she' and 'you' (sg.) are identical in the durative tense.

C. Some verbs on the pattern of *CaC* change the medial *a* of the perfect to *u* in the durative, e.g. *šaf* 'to see', ***ka-nšuf*** 'I see', ***ka-tšuf*** 'you see (sg.)', etc. Others change the medial *a* to *i,* e.g. ***žab*** 'to bring', ***ka-nžib*** 'I bring', ***ka-ižib***

'he brings' etc. From the perfect tense form with *a,* there is no way of predicting whether the vowel of the durative tense will be *u* or *i.* Whether the durative tense vowel is *u* or *i* must be memorized as a vocabulary item for each individual verb of this sort encountered.

D. Plural forms are arrived at by adding *-u* to the singular, as explained in Lesson 42. The singular forms of this class of verbs undergo no change as the plural *-u* is added. Illustrations:

šaf	to see		
ka-nšuf	I see	*ka-nšufu*	we see
ka-tšuf	you (sg.) see	*ka-tšufu*	you (pl.) see
ka-išuf	he sees	*ka-išufu*	they see
ka-tšuf	she sees		
žab	to bring		
ka-nžib	I bring	*ka-nžibu*	we bring
ka-džib	you (sg.) bring	*ka-džibu*	you (pl.) bring
ka-ižib	he brings	*ka-ižibu*	they bring
ka-džib	she brings		

III. Exercises.

Take the instructions given for the exercises in Lesson 43 and apply them to this lesson.

IV. Vocabulary.

ḅḅah	his father
ḅenk	bank
ḍaṛna	our house
fe-n-nhaṛ	in the day, per day, a day
koll ʔusbuع	every week
keššina	kitchen
l-oṃ̂ṃ̂u	to his mother
mleح	salt
ṃ̂ṃ̂u	his mother

meṛṛa fe-š-šheṛ	once a month
meṛṛtayn	two times, twice
nhaṛ s-sebt	on Saturday(s)
šheṛ	month
xah	his brother
xtu	his sister

LESSON FORTY-FIVE

I. Text.

šra	to buy
ka-išri bezzaf d-le-qṭen fe-ṣ-ṣif.	He buys a lot of cotton in the summer.
ka-išri l-qehwa dyalu f-had l-ʕanut.	He buys his coffe in this shop.
werra	to show
dima ka-iwerri t-tṣaweṛ dyalu le-d-drari.	He always shows his pictures to the children.
dima ka-iwerri l-xedma dyalu le-ḅḅah.	He always shows his work to his father.
xella	to leave
ka-ixelli d-drari f-ḍaṛna nhaṛ s-sebt.	He leaves the children at our house on Saturdays.
dima ka-ixelli le-ʕwayež dyalu ʕăl l-ḷeṛḍ.	He always leaves his clothes on the floor.
ža	to come
dima ka-iži l-l-medṛaṣa bekri.	He always comes to school early.
ka-iži l-fas meṛṛtayn fe-š-šheṛ.	He comes to Fez twice a month.
ʕṭa	to give
ka-yeʕṭi bezzaf d-le-flus le-ṃṃu.	He gives a lot of money to his mother.
ka-yeʕṭi bezzaf de-l-xedma l-xah.	He gives his brother a lot of work.
ka-nešri l-žarida koll nhaṛ.	I buy the newspaper every day.
ka-nešri žuž de-l-uṛaq fe-š-šheṛ.	I buy two tickets a month.
dima ka-nwerri l-xedma le-ḅḅa.	I always show the work to my father.

dima ka-nwerri t-tṣawer ž-ždad dyali le-xtu.	I always show my new pictures to his sister.
ka-nxelli l-bišklịta dyali f-ḍaṛhom nhaṛ s-sebt.	I leave my bicycle at their house on Saturdays.
dima ka-nxelli le-ktub dyali fe-l-medṛaṣa.	I always leave my books at school.
ka-nži f-le-ɛḍaš nhaṛ le-xmis.	I come at eleven o'clock on Thursdays.
dima ka-nži bekri nhaṛ le-xmis.	I always come early on Thursdays.
ka-neɛṭi le-flus le-ḅḅa koll šheṛ.	I give my father money every month.
ka-neɛṭi ši-šwiya de-š-šekḷaṭ le-d-drari koll nhaṛ.	I give the children a little bit of chocolate every day.
ka-tešri atay nhaṛ le-xmis.	She buys tea on Thursday.
ka-tešri le-ɛwayež dyalha f-had l-ɛanut le-kbira.	She buys her clothes in this big store.
dima ka-twerri le-ɛwayež ž-ždad dyalha l-xetha.	She always shows her new clothes to her sister.
ka-twerri le-ktub le-n-nas fe-l-mektaba.	She shows books to people at the library.
ka-txelḷi d-drari f-ḍaṛhom nhaṛ le-xmis.	She leaves the children at their house on Thursdays.
dima ka-txelli ṭ-ṭbaṣel mwessxin.	She always leaves the dishes dirty.
ka-dži bekri nhaṛ s-sebt.	She comes early on Saturdays.
ka-dži l-had l-medṛaṣa meṛṛtayn fe-š-šheṛ.	She comes to this school twice a month.
ka-teɛṭi bezzaf d-le-ɛwayež l-xetha.	She gives her sister a lot of clothes.
dima ka-teɛṭi atay l-l-xeddama.	She always gives tea to the workers.

II. Grammatical Notes.

A. Before two consonants, the prefix for 'I' is usually *ne-* instead of *n-*, e.g. *ka-nešri* 'I buy', *ka-neɛṭi* 'I give'. Similarly the prefix for 'she' and 'you' (sg.) is usually *te-* and not *t-*, e.g. *ka-tešri* 'she buys' or 'you (sg.) buy', *ka-teɛṭi* 'she gives' or 'you (sg.) give'. Observe again that the forms for 'she' and 'you' (sg.) are identical.

B. Before ɛ plus another consonant, the prefix for 'he' is *ye-* instead of *i-*, e.g. *ka-yeɛti* 'he gives'.

C. Some verbs which end in *-a* in the 'he' form of the perfect tense (verbs of this sort were first discussed in Lessons 33-35) change this *-a* to *-i* in the durative tense, e.g. *šra* 'to buy', *ka-išri* 'he buys'. All the verbs used in this lesson show the change of final perfect *-a* to *-i* in the present. Some verbs retain the *-a* without change in the durative and examples of them will be given in later lessons.

D. Plural forms for verbs of this sort are formed by adding *-w* to the singular. An illustration:

ža	to come		
ka-nži	I come	*ka-nžiw*	we come
ka-dži	you (sg.) come	*ka-džiw*	you (pl.) come
ka-iži	he comes	*ka-ižiw*	they come
ka-dži	she comes		

III. Exercises.

Take the instructions given for the exercises in Lesson 43 and apply them to this lesson.

IV. Vocabulary.

ḅḅa	my father
ḍaṛhom	their house
f-le-ɛḍaš	at eleven o'clock
koll šheṛ	every month
nhaṛ le-xmis	on Thursdays
xetha	her sister

LESSON FORTY-SIX

I. Text.

xdem	to work
ka-ixedmu	they work
ḅḅa ka-ixdem fe-l-mektaba.	My father works in the library.
had n-nas ka-ixedmu fe-l-meḍṛaṣa.	These people work at the school.
šṛeb	to drink
ka-išeṛbu	they drink
ka-išṛeb عăšṛa de-l-kisan d-atay fe-n-nhaṛ.	He drinks ten glasses of tea a day.
ka-išeṛbu atay fe-l-عăšṛa.	They drink tea at ten o'clock.
kteb	to write
ḅḅa ka-ikteb le-xti koll nhaṛ.	My father writes to my sister every day.
dima ka-iketbu b-le-mdad.	They always write with ink.
ġsel	to wash
ka-iġsel ṭ-ṭumubil dyalu meṛṛa fe-l-ʔusbuع.	He washes his car once a week.
ka-iġeslu le-حwayež dyalhom meṛṛtayn fe-l-ʔusbuع.	They wash their clothes twice a week.
ka-nxedmu	we work
ka-nexdem f-ṭanža.	I work in Tangier.
ka-nxedmu f-had l-حanut le-kbira.	We work in this big store.
ka-nšeṛbu	we drink
dima ka-nešṛeb le-حlib f-le-ġda.	I always drink milk at dinner.
ka-nšeṛbu ġir ši-šwiya de-l-qehwa f-ḍaṛna.	We only drink a little coffee at our house.
ka-nekteb le-ḅḅa koll nhaṛ.	I write to my father every day.
ka-nketbu le-ḅḅana koll nhaṛ.	We write to our father every day.
ka-neġsel l-berrad meṛṛtayn fe-n-nhaṛ.	I wash the teapot twice a day.

ka-nġeslu le-ḥwayež dyalna nhaṛ le-xmis.	We wash our clothes on Thursdays.
ka-nġeslu ṭ-ṭbaṣel meṛṛa fe-n-nhaṛ.	We wash the dishes once a day.
ka-texdem	you (sg.) work
ka-txedmu	you (pl.) work
ka-texdem fe-l-meḍṛaṣa?	Do you work at the school?
ka-texdem f-ṭanža?	Do you work in Tangier?
ka-txedmu bezzaf?	Do you work a lot?
ka-txedmu nhaṛ le-xmis?	Do you work on Thursdays?
ka-tešṛeb	you (sg.) drink
ka-tšeṛbu	you (pl.) drink
ka-tešṛeb le-ḥlib?	Do you drink milk?
ka-tešṛeb bezzaf d-atay f-ḍaṛkom?	Do you drink a lot of tea at your house?
waš ka-tšeṛbu atay f-le-ġda?	Do you drink tea at dinner?
waš ka-tekteb bezzaf d-le-bṛawat?	Do you write a lot of letters?
waš ka-tketbu bezzaf le-ḅḅakom?	Do you write your father a lot?
ka-teġsel ṭ-ṭbaṣel tlata de-l-meṛṛat fe-n-nhaṛ.	She washes dishes three times a day.
ka-teġsel ṣ-ṣwani meṛṛa fe-š-šheṛ	She washes the trays once a month.

II. Grammatical Notes.

A. As was mentioned in Lesson 45, the prefix for 'I' is usually *ne-* instead of *n-* before two consonants, e.g. *ka-nekteb* 'I write', etc. Similarly, the prefix for 'she' and 'you' (sg.) is usually *te-* and not *t-* before two consonants, e.g. *ka-tekteb* 'she writes' or 'you write'.

B. Verbs on the pattern of *CCeC* (verbs of this sort were first discussed in Lessons 25-28) form their plurals by adding *-u* to the corresponding singular forms. With the addition of plural *-u,* inversion (for inversion, cf. Grammatical Note **D** of Lesson 35 and Grammatical Note **C** of Lesson 42) takes place, e.g. *ka-ikteb* 'he writes' and *ka-iketbu* 'they write'.

With inversion, the prefixes *ne-* for 'I' and *te-* for 'she' and 'you' (sg.) required before two consonants become *n-* for 'we' and *t-* for 'you' (pl.) since they no longer stand before two consonants, e.g. ***ka-nekteb*** 'I write', ***ka-nketbu*** 'we write', or ***ka-tekteb*** 'she writes', 'you (sg.) write' and ***ka-tketbu*** 'you (pl.) write'.

III. Exercises.

Go through the text of this lesson and:

1. Change all 'you' (sg.), 'he' and 'she' forms to 'I' forms.
2. Change all 'he', 'she', and 'I' forms to 'you' (sg.) forms.
3. Change all 'I', 'you' (sg.), and 'he' forms to 'she' forms.
4. Change all 'I', 'you' (sg.), and 'she' forms to 'he' forms.
5. Change every singular form encountered to a 'we' form.
6. Change every singular form encountered to a 'you' (pl.) form.
7. Change every singular form encountered to a 'they' form.
8. Change every plural form encountered to an 'I' form.
9. Change every plural form encountered to a 'you' (sg.) form.
10. Change every plural form encountered to a 'he' form.
11. Change every plural form encountered to a 'she' form.

As these directions are followed, each new sentence formed should be read out loud. With the changes in the verb forms, make any other changes necessary in the sentences to make good sense.

IV. Vocabulary.

ḅḅakom	your (pl.) father
ḅḅana	our father
ḍaṛkom	your (pl.) house
fe-l-ɛăšṛa	at ten o'clock
tlata de-l-meṛṛat	three times
ṭanža	Tangier
ɛăšṛa	ten

LESSON FORTY-SEVEN

I. Text.

qṛa	to read, to study
ka-iqṛa l-žarida de-ḅḅa.	He's reading my father's newspaper.
dda	to take
dak l-weld dda l-kuṛa dyal xti.	That boy took my sister's ball.
f-had s-saɛa ka-iddi xtu l-l-meḍṛaṣa	At this time, he takes his sister to school.
dima ka-iddi ṭ-ṭumubil de-ḅḅah nhaṛ s-sebt.	He always takes his father's car on Saturdays.
f-had s-saɛa ka-neqṛa le-bṛa dyal ṁṁi.	I'm reading my mother's letter right now.
ka-neqṛa l-konnaš dyali koll nhaṛ.	I study my notebook every day.
ṣ-ṣeṛṛaq dda l-weṛqa de-l-weld.	The thief took the boy's ticket.
ṣ-ṣeṛṛaqa ddaw le-flus dyal le-mṛa.	The thieves took the woman's money.
nsa	to forget
l-metɛăllma nsat l-ɛonwan de-ṭ-ṭbib.	The maid forgot the doctor's address.
had l-weld dima ka-insa d-dwa dyal xtu.	This boy always forgets his sister's medicine.

II. Grammatical Notes.

A. A common way of indicating possession between two nouns is by joining them with *d-, de-,* or *dyal,* as in *l-weṛqa de-l-weld* or *l-weṛqa dyal l-weld* 'the boy's ticket'. Note that this is another important use for *d-, de-,* and *dyal.* Previous lessons have shown *dyal* only with endings, e.g. *dyali* 'my, mine' (cf. Lessons 21-23). Likewise, *d-, de-,* has been used up to now only with numerals (cf. Lesson 16).

The forms *d-, de-,* and *dyal* are interchangeable with no difference in meaning. In slower, more deliberate speech there is a tendency for *dyal* to occur more often than *d-, de-,* and in more rapid speech *d-, de-* predominate over *dyal.*

The possessed term is always placed first. The list below summarizes the examples given in the text of this lesson.

l-žarida de-ḅḅa	my father's newspaper
l-kuṛa dyal xti	my sister's ball
ṭ-ṭumubil de-ḅḅah	his father's car
le-bṛa dyal ṃṃi	my mother's letter
l-weṛqa de-l-weld	the boy's ticket
le-flus dyal le-mṛa	the woman's money
l-Ɛonwan de-ṭ-ṭbib	the doctor's address
d-dwa dyal xtu	his sister's medicine

B. Since the final vowel of the durative tense for verbs which end in *-a* in the perfect tense is not predictable (cf. Lesson 45, Grammatical Note C), it will be given as a part of the vocabulary in future lessons e.g. *nsa* (*ka-nsa*) 'to forget', *dda* (*ka-iddi*) 'to take'.

C. Moroccan makes no such distinctions as English 'he works' and 'he is working'; both are rendered by the durative tense, e.g. *ka-ixdem* 'he works, he is working,' or *ka-ikteb* 'he writes, he is writing'. Only context and the general situation show which translation is appropriate in a given case.

III. Exercises.

A. Combine the following word pairs on the pattern of *l-weṛqa de-l-weld* and *l-weṛqa dyal l-weld* 'the boy's ticket'. Read the resulting phrases out loud.

1. *xedma, bent*
2. *tṣaweṛ, fqi.*
3. *šelya, fqiha.*
4. *kbabeṭ, ržal.*
5. *Ɛanut, nežžaṛ.*
6. *Ɛwayež, nas.*
7. *atay, mṛa.*
8. *flus, xay.*
9. *biškliṭa, xak.*
10. *knaneš, qaḍi.*
11. *magana, xeddam.*
12. *mraya, metƐăllma.*
13. *bit, ṭebbax.*
14. *bṛawat, ẋtu.*
15. *ġda, xeddama.*
16. *ẓeṛbiya, ṃṃu.*
17. *mkoƐla, ṣeṛṛaq.*
18. *makla, bnat.*
19. *flayek, ḅḅana.*
20. *knaneš, wlad.*
21. *lƐăm, gezzar.*
22. *bakit, ṃṃi.*
23. *serwal, xah.*
24. *berrad, xti.*
25. *Ɛwayež, drari.*

B. Go through the texts of Lessons 41 through 46. For every sentence in which *dima* 'always' is used with a durative tense, substitute *f-had s-saεa* 'right now, at this moment', and re-interpret the English meaning accordingly. For example, the sentence *dima ka-ikobb ši-šwiya d-le-ḥlib fe-l-qehwa dyalu* is translated 'He always pours a little milk in his coffee.' It should be changed to *f-had s-saεa ka-ikobb ši-šwiya d-le-ḥlib fe-l-qehwa dyalu* and re-translated as 'Right now he's pouring a little milk into his coffee. In those cases where a simple substitution of *f-had s-saεa* for *dima* would result in absurdity, further changes should be made. For example, in such a sentence as *dima ka-iḥoll š-šṛažem fe-s-sebεa,* the phrase *fe-s-sebεa* should be deleted along with the substitution of *f-had s-saεa* for *dima.*

IV. Vocabulary.

dda	to take
f-had s-saεa	right now, at this moment
nsa (*ka-insa*)	to forget
qṛa (*ka-iqṛa*)	to read, to study

LESSON FORTY-EIGHT

I. Text.

f-had s-saεa ka-iġsel š-šṛažem de-l-medṛaṣa.	Right now, he's washing the windows of the school.
ka-irfed waḥed l-xenša de-ṣ-ṣuf le-ḍ-ḍaṛ.	He's carrying a bag of wool to the house.
dar l-xenša de-ṣ-ṣuf εăl ḷ-ḷeṛḍ.	He put the bag of wool on the floor.
ka-ižib waḥed l-berrad d-atay.	He's bringing a pot of tea.
ka-ikobb l-berrad d-atay fe-l-kisan.	He's pouring the pot of tea into the glasses.
l-lun de-l-kuṛa ḥmeṛ.	The color of the ball is red.
l-lun d-le-mdad kḥăl.	The color of the ink is black.
l-lun de-šεăṛha ma-ši kḥăl.	The color of her hair isn't black.
bġa waḥed t-teṣwiṛa de-l-ḅenk.	He wants a picture of the bank.
bġa had t-teṣwiṛa de-l-ḅenk.	He wants this picture of the bank.
bġa waḥed z-zlafa d-le-ḥrira.	He wants a bowl of soup.

bġa z-zlafa d-le-ɛrira dyali.	He wants my bowl of soup.
bġat waɛed l-qeṛɛa de-z-zit.	She wants a bottle of oil.
bġat dak l-qeṛɛa de-z-zit hadik.	She wants that bottle of oil there.
bġat waɛed l-kas de-l-ma.	She wants a glass of water.
bġat had l-kas de-l-ma.	She wants this glass of water.
bġat ši-kisan de-l-ma.	She wants some glasses of water.
bġat had l-kisan de-l-ma.	She wants these glasses of water.
bġit waɛed ṣ-ṣenḍuq de-š-šekḷaṭ.	I want a box of chocolate.
bġit ṣ-ṣenḍuq de-š-šekḷaṭ dyalek.	I want your box of chocolate.
bġina waɛed s-sella d-le-qṭen.	We want a basket of cotton.
bġina had s-sella d-le-qṭen.	We want this basket of cotton.
bġina ši-sellat d-le-qṭen.	We want some baskets of cotton.
bġina had s-sellat d-le-qṭen.	We want these bags of cotton.

II. Grammatical Notes.

A. The particle *d-, de-* (interchangeable with *dyal;* see Grammatical Note A, Lesson 47) is also used to translate English 'of' in the broadest range of meanings and contexts. An example such as *š-šṛažem de-l-meḍṛaṣa* 'the windows of the school' is typical. In some cases there is ambiguity, e.g. *l-xenša de-ṣ-ṣuf* 'the bag of wool' can mean either a bag which has wool in it or one which is made out of wool. Context is the only clue to which meaning is intended.

The list below summarizes the examples which occur in this lesson:

š-šṛažem de-l-meḍṛaṣa	the windows of the school
l-xenša de-ṣ-ṣuf	the bag of wool
l-berrad d-atay	the pot of tea
l-lun de-l-kuṛa	the color of the ball
l-lun de-le-mdad	the color of the ink
l-lun de-šɛăṛha	the color of her hair
t-teṣwiṛa de-l-ḅenk	the picture of the bank
z-zlafa d-le-ɛrira	the bowl of soup
l-qeṛɛa de-z-zit	the bottle of oil
l-kas de-l-ma	the glass of water
l-kisan de-l-ma	the glasses of water

ši-kisan de-l-ma	some glasses of water
ṣ-ṣenduq de-š-šeklat	the box of chocolates
s-sella d-le-qṭen	the basket of cotton
s-sellat d-le-qṭen	the baskets of cotton
ši-sellat d-le-qṭen	some baskets of cotton

B. The Moroccan indefinite article equivalent to English 'a' or 'an' is formed by placing *waƐed* before the definite article, e.g *l-kas de-l-ma* 'the glass of water', *waƐed l-kas de-l-ma* 'a glass of water', etc.

C. The verb *bġa* 'to want' is regular in form, but the perfect tense is translated by the English present tense, e.g. *bġit* 'I want', *bġaw* 'they want', *bġiti* 'you (sg.) want', etc.

III. Exercises.

Go through the following list of pairs and combine them on the pattern of *l-qeṛƐa de-z-zit* 'the bottle of oil'. Repeat the process using *dyal* instead of *d-, de-*.

1. *bab, busṭa.*
2. *lun, ṭbaṣel.*
3. *ṣenduq, sokkaṛ.*
4. *Ɛonwan, bṛa.*
5. *tṣaweṛ, ḍaṛ.*
6. *ṣiniya, makla.*
7. *kas, dwa.*
8. *bakit, Ɛwayež.*
9. *byut, meḍṛaṣa.*
10. *xenša, xobz.*
11. *ḷeṛḍ, Ɛanut.*
12. *ḅenk, ṛ-ṛbaṭ.*
13. *swaret, ḍaṛ.*
14. *sella, Ɛwayež.*
15. xnaši, *ṣuf.*

IV. Vocabulary.

bġa	to want (see Grammatical Note C)
lun	color
šƐăṛha	her hair
waƐed	a, an, (see Grammatical Note B)

LESSON FORTY-NINE

I. Text.

ḅḅa šra waḥed le-mkoḥla de-ṣ-ṣyaḍa.	My father bought a hunting rifle.
weqqeft le-mkoḥla de-ṣ-ṣyaḍa dyal ḅḅa fe-l-qent.	I stood my father's hunting rifle in the corner.
ɛăndi waḥed le-ktab d-le-ḥsab ždid.	I have a new arithmetic book.
bġit waḥed le-ktab d-le-ḥsab ždid.	I want a new arithmetic book.
fayn le-ktab d-le-ḥsab?	Where is the arithmetic book?
ṃṃi šrat waḥed le-ktab de-l-ɛăṛbiya l-yum.	My mother bought an Arabic book today.
ddit le-ktab de-l-ɛăṛbiya l-l-medṛaṣa l-yum.	I took the Arabic book to school today.
ɛăndna waḥed le-fqi de-le-ḥsab ždid fe-l-medṛaṣa dyalna.	We have a new arithmetic teacher in our school.
le-fqi d-le-ḥsab ž-ždid ža men ḍ-ḍaṛ l-biḍa.	The new arithmetic teacher came from Casablanca.
bġit ši-kisan d-atay ždad.	I want some new tea glasses.
xaha šra waḥed s-serwal d-le-qṭen.	Her brother bought a pair of cotton trousers.
šriti l-magana de-d-dheb f-had l-ḥanut?	Did you buy the gold watch in this shop?
žbeṛt waḥed l-žarida fṛanṣiya fe-ḍ-ḍaṛ l-biḍa.	I found a French newspaper in Casablanca.
žebti waḥed l-žarida mġeṛbiya mɛak?	Did you bring a Moroccan newspaper with you?
daret waḥed l-ġoṛṛaf de-l-feḍḍa ɛăl ṭ-ṭebla.	She put a silver pitcher on the table.
daret l-ma fe-l-ġoṛṛaf de-l-feḍḍa.	She put water in the silver pitcher.
žabet waḥed l-ġoṛṛaf de-z-zaž men l-keššina.	She brought a glass pitcher from the kitchen.
ɛṭat l-ġoṛṛaf de-z-zaž l-l-bent ṣ-ṣġiṛa.	She gave the glass pitcher to the little girl.

ka-ixdem f-waɛed l-măɛmel de-l-biškliṭat.	He works in a bicycle factory.
ka-ixdem f-had l-măɛmel de-l-biškliṭat.	He works in this bicycle factory.

II. Grammatical Notes.

A. Review the comments on *d-, de-* and *dyal* in the Grammatical Notes of Lessons 47 and 48.

B. The construction with *d-, de-,* and *dyal* is also widely used to translate those cases in English where one noun is used adjectivally to modify another, as in a hunting rifle', 'an arithmetic book', etc. A number of examples are given in the text of this lesson. They are summarized below:

le-mkoɛla de-ṣ-ṣyaḍa	the hunting rifle
le-ktab d-le-ɛsab	the arithmetic book
le-ktab de-l-ɛăṛbiya	the Arabic book
le-fqi d-le-ɛsab	the arithmetic teacher
l-kisan d-atay	the tea glasses
s-serwal d-le-qṭen	the cotton trousers
l-magana de-d-dheb	the gold watch
l-ġoṛṛaf de-z-zaž	the glass pitcher
l-ġoṛṛaf de-l-feḍḍa	the silver pitcher
l-măɛmel de-l-biškliṭat	the bicycle factory

Note the ambiguity of such expressions as *l-kisan d-atay,* which can mean either 'the tea glasses' or 'the glasses of tea'.

C. When a noun has the indefinite article, an adjective accompanying it does not take the definite article, e.g. *waɛed l-magana ždida* 'a new watch', *waɛed s-serwal d-le-qṭen ždid* 'a new pair of cotton trousers', etc. Unlike the definite article, adjectives never have the indefinite article prefixed to them.

III. Exercises.

Combine the following noun pairs on the pattern of *l-măƐmel de-l-biškliṭat* 'the bicycle factory'.

1. *kebbuṭ, ṣuf.*
2. *fqi, negliza.*
3. *ṣenduq, dheb.*
4. *ṣiniya, feḍḍa.*
5. *ṣenduq, Ɛwayež.*
6. *măƐmel, ṭumubilat.*
7. *kbabeṭ, qṭen.*
8. *kisan, feḍḍa.*
9. *zlafa, Ɛrira.*
10. *tqašeṛ, ṣuf.*
11. *qeṛƐa, zit.*
12. *bab, keššina.*
13. *žarida, fas.*
14. *ṣenduq, bṛawat.*
15. *ṣbiṭaṛ, drari.*

IV. Vocabulary.

dheb	gold
feḍḍa	silver
fṛanṣi, (m.)	French
fṛanṣiya (f.)	
fṛanṣiyin (pl.)	
l-yum	today
mġeṛbi (m.)	Moroccan
mġeṛbiya (f.)	
mġeṛbiyin (pl.)	
mƐak	with you
măƐmel	factory
ṣyaḍa	hunting
xaha	her brother
zaž	glass (the material)
Ɛsab	arithmetic

LESSON FIFTY

I. Text.

ma-ḍṛeb-š l-kelb.	He didn't hit the dog.
l-weld ma-ḍṛeb-š l-kelb.	The boy didn't hit the dog.
ma-gelset-š Ɛăl š-šelya dyali.	She didn't sit down in my chair.
r-ržal ma-lebsu-š le-kbabeṭ dyalhom.	The men didn't put on their coats.
ma-rfedt-š le-ktub dyalu l-l-meḍṛaṣa.	I didn't carry his books to school.
ma-šṛebna-š bezzaf de-l-qehwa.	We didn't drink very much coffee.
ma-žbeṛti-š xak fe-ḍ-ḍaṛ?	Didn't you find your brother at home?
ma-ġseltiw-š ṭ-ṭbaṣel?	Didn't you wash the dishes?
ṣ-ṣeṛṛaq ma-hḍeṛ-š.	The thief didn't talk.
ṃṃi ma-ketbet-š fe-l-konnaš dyali.	My mother didn't write in my notebook.
le-bnat ma-ketbu-š le-ḅḅahom.	The girls didn't write to their father.
ma-ktebt-š le-xwatati.	I didn't write to my sisters.
ma-ktebna-š l-xana l-yum.	We didn't write to our brother today.
Ɛlaš ma-ktebti-š le-ḅḅak?	Why didn't you write to your father?
ma-ktebtiw-š l-Ɛanawin f-had l-konnaš?	Didn't you write the addresses in this notebook?

II. Grammatical Notes.

A. Negation of verb forms is usually expressed by placing *ma-* before the verb and *-š* after it, e.g. *šṛebna* 'we drank',*ma-šṛebna-š* 'we didn't drink', etc.

B. Note that in English, 'not very much' is usually used in negative expressions instead of 'a lot of', e.g. 'We drank a lot of coffee' and 'We didn't drink very much coffee'. The word *bezzaf* is used in both cases in Moroccan, e.g. *šṛebna bezzaf de-l-qehwa* and *ma-šṛebna-š bezzaf de-l-qehwa.*

C. In English it is possible to say either 'The girls didn't write to their father' or 'The girls didn't write their father'. In Moroccan the equivalent for 'to' must always be included, thus, *le-bnat ma-ketbu-š le-ḅḅahom.*

III. Exercises.

Go through the texts of Lessons 25-28 and make every verb form negative, e.g. change *xdem* 'he worked' to *ma-xdem-š* 'he didn't work'. Read each form and sentence out loud as the changes are made.

IV. Vocabulary.

ḅḅahom	their father
ḅḅak	your (sg.) father
xana	our brother

LESSON FIFTY-ONE

I. Text.

ma-xdem-š bezzaf l-yum.	He didn't work very much today.
ḅḅa ma-xdem-š l-yum.	My father didn't work today.
ma-baɛet-š l-bišklița l-xana.	She didn't sell the bicycle to our brother.
le-mṛa ma-baɛet-š ḍaṛha.	The woman didn't sell her house.
ma-daru-š d-dheb fe-ṣ-ṣenḍuq.	They didn't put the gold in the box.
le-ɛyalat ma-daru-š l-makla ɛăl ṭ-ṭebla.	The women didn't put the food on the table.
ma-neḍt-š fe-l-weqt.	I didn't get up on time.
ma-neḍt-š fe-t-tmenya l-yum.	I didn't get up at eight o'clock today.
ma-šefna-š ḍaṛu l-yum.	We didn't see his house today.
ma-šefna-š ḍaṛek l-bareḥ.	We didn't see your house yesterday.
ɛlaš ma-žebti-š le-ktub le-ḅḅaha?	Why didn't you bring her father the books?
ma-žebti-š le-flus le-ḅḅaha?	Didn't you bring her father the money?
ma-kontiw-š fe-ḍ-ḍaṛ?	Weren't you at home?
ɛlaš ma-kontiw-š fe-l-medṛaṣa l-bareḥ?	Why weren't you at school yesterday?

ma-ẓaṛ-š ḍaṛi.	He didn't visit my house.
ɛlaš xakom ma-ẓaṛ-š ḍaṛi l-bareɛ?	Why didn't your brother visit my house yesterday?
waš ma-ɛašu-š xwatatek telt snin f-fas?	Didn't your sisters live in Fez for three years?
waš ma-ɛašu-š xwatatek fe-ṛ-ṛbaṭ?	Didn't your sisters live in Rabat?
ma-šrit-š ṭ-ṭumubil.	I didn't buy the car.
ma-šrit-š ḍaṛhom.	I didn't buy their house.
ma-werrina-š le-ktab l-xakom.	We didn't show the book to your brother.
ma-werrina-š t-tṣawer le-xwatatek.	We didn't show the pictures to your sisters.
ma-xelliti-š le-flus le-xwatatu?	Didn't you leave the money for his sisters?
ɛlaš ma-xelliti-š ṭ-ṭumubil l-xak?	Why didn't you leave the car for your brother?
ma-žitiw-š fe-l-weqt?	Didn't you come on time?
ɛlaš ma-žitiw-š bekri?	Why didn't you come early?

II. Grammatical Notes.

A. Note that the preposition *l-, le-,* which is usually translated as 'to' can also be equivalent to English 'for' in some contexts, e.g. *ɛlaš ma-xelliti-š ṭ-ṭumubil l-xak?* 'Why didn't you leave the car for your brother?'

B. Note the word order in *waš ma-ɛašu-š xwatatek telt snin f-fas?* 'Didn't your sisters live in Fez for three years?'

C. For such sentences as *ma-žebti-š le-flus le-ḅḅaha?* 'Didn't you bring her father the money?', see Grammatical Note **C,** Lesson 50.

III. Exercises.

Go through the texts of Lessons 29-32 and make every verb form negative. Read each form and sentence out loud as the changes are made.

IV. Vocabulary.

ḅḅaha	her father
ḍaṛha	her house
ḍaṛi	my house
ḍaṛek	your (sg.) house
ḍaṛu	his house
xakom	your (pl.) brother
xwatatu	his sisters

LESSON FIFTY-TWO

I. Text.

baqi ma-ɛṭa l-konnaš l-le-fqi.	He still hasn't given the notebook to the teacher.
l-weld ma-ɛṭa-š le-flus le-ḅḅah.	The boy hasn't given the money to his father.
xtek ma-kebbet-š atay.	Your sister hasn't poured the tea.
xtek baqi ma-kebbet atay.	Your sister still hasn't poured the tea.
ma-šeddu-š l-biban.	They haven't closed the doors.
l-gezzara baqi ma-šeddu le-ḥwanet dyalhom.	The butchers still haven't closed their shops.
ma-ḥăllit-š ṣ-ṣenḍuq.	I haven't opened the box.
baqi ma-ḥăllit l-bakit.	I still haven't opened the package.
ma-siyyebna-š ṭ-ṭbaṣel.	We haven't thrown the dishes away.
baqi ma-siyyebna duk le-ḥwayež l-balyin.	We still haven't thrown those old clothes away.
ma-ṣifeṭti-š le-flus l-om̃m̃ek?	Haven't you sent your mother the money?
baqi ma-ṣifeṭti l-bakit?	Haven't you sent the package yet?
ɛlaš ma-teṛžemtiw-š had le-bṛawat?	Why haven't you translated these letters?
baqi ma-teṛžemtiw le-ktab dyalu?	Haven't you translated his book yet?

ma-weqqef-š l-biškliṭa dyalu qeddam ḍ-ḍaṛ.	He didn't park his bicycle in front of the house.
waš ṭ-ṭbib baqi ma-weqqef ṭ-ṭumubil dyalu?	Hasn't the doctor parked his car yet?
waš ṃ̃ṃ̃ek ma-Ɛămmṛet-š l-berrad?	Hasn't your mother filled the teapot?
waš ṃ̃ṃ̃ek baqi ma-Ɛămmṛet l-berrad?	Hasn't your mother filled the teapot yet?
ma-ddaw-š le-bṛawat l-l-buṣṭa.	They haven't taken the letters to the post office.
xwatatha baqi ma-ddaw le-ktub dyalhom le-ḍ-ḍar.	Her sisters still haven't taken their books home.
ma-nsit-š dak n-nhaṛ.	I haven't forgotten that day.
baqi ma-nsit l-Ɛonwan dyalha.	I still haven't forgotten her address.
ma-nsina-š ṃ̃ṃ̃na.	We haven't forgotten our mother.
baqi ma-nsina ž-žwab dyal ṃ̃ṃ̃na.	We still haven't forgotten our mother's answer.
ma-qṛiti-š l-žarida?	Haven't you read the newspaper?
baqi ma-qṛiti ž-žwab dyalu?	Haven't you read his answer yet?

II. Grammatical Notes.

A. Moroccan makes no such distinctions as English 'I worked' versus 'I have worked', 'I went' versus 'I have gone', etc. The Moroccan perfect tense renders both of these English forms. Thus *žit* can be translated as either 'I came' or 'I have come', depending on the context.

B. In English two such sentences as 'I still haven't sent the package' and 'I haven't sent the package yet' are equivalent in meaning. However, in many types of questions, only 'yet' occurs, e.g. 'Haven't you sent the package yet?' In Moroccan the one word *baqi* covers the range of both 'still' and 'yet'.

C. The final *-š* of negation is dropped if *baqi* is used, e.g. *ma-ža-š* 'he didn't (hasn't) come', but *baqi ma-ža* 'he still hasn't come'.

III. Exercises.

A. Go through the texts of Lessons 33-40 and make every verb form negative. Read each form and sentence out loud as the changes are made.

B. Go through the texts of Lessons 25-32 and, insofar as makes good sense, re-interpret the past tense verb forms as meaning, 'I have done', etc. instead of 'I did', etc.

C. Go through the texts of Lessons 50 and 51 and, insofar as makes good sense, insert *baqi* into the sentences, drop the final *-š* from negative verb forms, and re-interpret the meanings accordingly.

IV. Vocabulary.

baqi	still, yet
ṃṃek	your (sg.) mother
ṃṃna	our mother
xtek	your (sg.) sister
xwatatha	her sisters

LESSON FIFTY-THREE

I. Text.

ḍṛebni	he hit me
ṣ-ṣeṛṛaq ḍṛebni.	The thief hit me.
mƐaha	with her
žbeṛni	he found me
ḅḅa žbeṛni mƐaha.	My father found me with her.
mƐahom	with them
šafni	he saw me
xaha šafni mƐahom.	Her brother saw me with them.
ẓaṛni	he visited me
ḅḅak ẓaṛni fe-ṣ-ṣbitaṛ.	Your father visited me in the hospital.
xellani	he left me
xay xellani fe-ḍ-ḍaṛ.	My brother left me at home.

ḍeṛbetni	she hit me
xtek ḍeṛbetni.	Your sister hit me.
mɛah	with him
žebṛetni	she found me
ṃ̂ṃ̂i žebṛetni mɛah.	My mother found me with him.
(s-)sinima	(the) movies, (the) theater
šafetni	she saw me
šafetni fe-s-sinima.	She saw me at the movies.
ẓaṛetni fe-l-meḍṛaṣa.	She visited me at school.
mṛati xellatni fe-l-ɛanut.	My wife left me at the store.
ṣ-ṣeṛṛaqa ḍeṛbuni	The thieves hit me.
xwatatek žebṛuni fe-s-sinima.	Your sisters found me at the movies.
n-nas šafuni mɛah.	The people saw me with him.
d-drari ẓaṛuni fe-ṣ-ṣbiṭaṛ.	The children visited me in the hospital.
xellawni fe-s-sinima fe-t-tmenya.	They left me at the movies at eight o'clock.
ḍṛebtina	you (sg.) hit us
ɛlaš ḍṛebtina?	Why did you hit us?
žbeṛtina fe-ḍ-ḍar.	You found us at home.
waš šeftina mɛaha?	Did you see us with her?
ẓeṛtina meṛṛtayn l-yum.	You've visited us twice today.
ɛlaš xellitina mɛah?	Why did you leave us with him?

II. Grammatical Notes.

A. The Moroccan equivalent for 'me' with verb forms is *-ni* added as an ending, e.g. *šaf* 'he saw' and *šafni* 'he saw me'. The ending for 'us' is *-na,* e.g. *šefti* 'you (sg.) saw', and *šeftina* 'you (sg.) saw us'.

B. The endings *-ni* 'me' and *-na* 'us' are integral parts of the verb forms. The negation of such forms is regular, with *ma-* preceding the entire form and *-š* following it, e.g. *ṣifeṭni* 'he sent me' and *ma-ṣifeṭni-š* 'he didn't send me'.

III. Exercises.

Go through the text of this lesson and

1. Change all occurrences of *-ni* 'me' to *-na* 'us'.
2. Change all occurrences of *-na* 'us' to *-ni* 'me'.
3. Change all singular 'you' forms to plural 'you' forms.
4. Make every verb form negative.

IV. Vocabulary.

mɛah	with him
mɛaha	with her
mɛahom	with them
sinima	movies, theater

LESSON FIFTY-FOUR

I. Text.

le-fqi ɛaqeb l-weld.	The teacher punished the boy.
le-fqi ɛaqbu.	The teacher punished him.
ḅḅaha ɛawen xay.	Her father helped my brother.
ḅḅaha ɛawnu.	Her father helped him.
xak weqqef l-weld.	Your brother stopped the boy.
xak weqqfu.	Your brother stopped him.
ṛ-ṛažel rfed l-weld le-ḍ-ḍaṛ.	The man carried the boy to the house.
ṛ-ṛažel refdu le-ḍ-ḍaṛ.	The man carried him to the house.
l-weld žbeṛ ḅḅah fe-s-sinima.	The boy found his father at the movies.
l-weld žebṛu fe-s-sinima.	The boy found him at the movies.
ḅḅa ḍṛeb ṣ-ṣeṛṛaq.	My father hit the thief.
ḅḅa ḍeṛbu.	My father hit him.

xahom šaf ṭ-ṭbib l-bareḥ.	Their brother saw the doctor yesterday.
xahom šafu l-bareḥ.	Their brother saw him yesterday.
ṭ-ṭbib žab xahom le-ḍ-ḍaṛ	The doctor brought their brother home.
ṭ-ṭbib žabu le-ḍ-ḍaṛ.	The doctor brought him home.
ddit xay mɛaya.	I took my brother with me.
dditu mɛaya.	I took him with me.
nsit le-fqi dyalna.	I've forgotten our teacher.
nsitu.	I've forgotten him.
ɛawent l-weld f-le-ḥsab.	I helped the boy in arithmetic.
ɛawentu f-le-ḥsab.	I helped him in arithmetic.
ġsel	he washed
ġeslu	he washed it
ma-ġeslu-š	he didn't wash it
ẓaṛ	he visited
ẓaṛu	he visited him
ma-ẓaṛu-š	he didn't visit him

II. Grammatical Notes.

A. The ending for 'him' or 'it' is *-u* after verb forms ending in consonants, e.g. *šaf* 'he saw' and *šafu* 'he saw him'.

B. Inversion and elision (cf. Lessons 25 and 42) occur regularly with the ending *-u* 'him', e.g. *rfed* 'he carried' and *refdu* 'he carried it', *ṣifeṭ* 'he sent' and *ṣifṭu* 'he sent him'.

C. Negation is regular, e.g. *nsitu* 'I forgot him' and *ma-nsitu-š* 'I didn't forget him'.

D. The ending *-u* 'him' is the same in form as the ending *-u* 'they' in the formation of the perfect tense (cf. Lesson 26) and the plural forms in the durative tense. Consequently some individual forms out of context are ambiguous, e.g. *šafu* means either 'he saw him' or 'they saw', *ɛawnu* means either 'he helped him' or 'they helped', etc.

III. Exercises.

A. Make all verb forms in the text of this lesson negative.

B. Insofar as makes good sense

1. Change all the 'him' endings in the text of this lesson to 'me' endings.
2. Change all the 'him' endings in the text of this lesson to 'us' endings.

IV. Vocabulary.

mƐaya	with me
xahom	their brother

LESSON FIFTY-FIVE

I. Text.

l-feqya Ɛawnu xay f-le-ḥsab.	The teachers helped my brother in arithmetic.
l-feqya Ɛawnuh f-le-ḥsab.	The teachers helped him in arithmetic.
weqqefna ṣ-ṣaṛeq fe-ẓ-ẓenqa.	We stopped the thief in the street.
weqqefnah fe-ẓ-ẓenqa.	We stopped him in the street.
waš šeftih mƐana?	Did you see him with us?
xay dda l-weld mƐah.	My brother took the boy with him.
xay ddah mƐah.	My brother took him with him.
xti ṣifṭet weldha l-l-ḥanut.	My sister sent her son to the store.
xti ṣefṭettu l-l-ḥanut.	My sister sent him to the store.
benti šafet weldha l-yum.	My daughter saw her son today.
benti šafettu l-yum	My daughter saw him today.
l-bent žebṛet ḅḅaha mƐana.	The girl found her father with us.
l-bent žebṛettu mƐana.	The girl found him with us.
xwatatu xellaweh fe-ḍ-ḍaṛ.	His sisters left him at home.

ddaw weldhom mƐahom le-s-sinima.	They took their son with them to the movies.
ddaweh mƐahom le-s-sinima.	They took him with them to the movies.
šeftiw weldhom mƐahom?	Did you see their son with them?
šeftiweh mƐahom?	Did you see him with them?
nsitiw le-fqi dyalkom?	Did you forget your teacher?
nsitiweh?	Did you forget him?

II. Grammatical Notes.

A. After vowels, the ending for 'him' is *-h, e.g. šefna* 'we saw', *šefnah* 'we saw him'.

B. After a final *w,* the ending for 'him' is *-eh,* e.g. *ddaw* 'they took' and *ddaweh* 'they took him', *šeftiw* 'you (pl.) saw' and *šeftiweh 'you* (pl.) saw him', etc.

C. The ending *-et* 'she' in the past tense becomes *-ett* before *-u* 'him', e.g. *šafet* 'she saw' and *šafettu* 'she saw him'.

D. Negation is regular, e.g. *šefnah* 'we saw him' and *ma-šefnah-š* 'we didn't see him'.

III. Exercises.

A. Make all the verb forms in the text of this lesson negative.

B. Go through the text of Lesson 53 and change all the 'me' and 'us' endings to 'him' endings.

C. Go through the text of this lesson and, insofar as makes good sense, change all the 'him' endings to 'me' and 'us' endings.

IV. Vocabulary.

benti	My daughter
mƐana	with us
weldi	my boy, my son

LESSON FIFTY-SIX

I. Text.

nsit bentek.	I forgot your daughter.
nsitha.	I forgot her.
dditi bentu mƐak le-s-sinima?	Did you take his daughter to the movies with you?
dditiha mƐak le-s-sinima?	Did you take her to the movies with you?
waš Ɛawen bentek fe-l-xedma dyalha?	Did he help your daughter in her work?
waš Ɛawenha fe-l-xedma dyalha?	Did he help her in her work?
le-fqiha Ɛaqbet bentha.	The teacher punished her daughter.
le-fqiha Ɛaqbetha.	The teacher punished her.
ṣifeṭna bentna le-ḍ-ḍaṛ fe-t-tesƐud.	We sent our daughter home at nine o'clock.
ṣifeṭnaha le-ḍ-ḍaṛ fe-t-tesƐud.	We sent her home at nine o'clock.
xellitiw d-drari fe-s-sinima?	Did you leave the children at the movies?
xellitiwhom fe-s-sinima?	Did you leave them at the movies?
ẓeṛt duk n-nas f-fas l-bareƐ	I visited those people in Fez yesterday.
ẓeṛthom f-fas l-bareƐ.	I visited them in Fez yesterday.
lbest le-Ɛwayež ž-ždad dyali l-yum.	I wore my new clothes today.
lbesthom l-yum.	I wore them today.
beƐti duk ž-žuž de-ṭ-ṭumubilat dyalek?	Did you sell those two cars of yours?
beƐtihom?	Did you sell them?
waš daret ṭ-ṭbaṣel Ɛăl ṭ-ṭebla?	Has she put the dishes on the table?
waš darethom Ɛăl ṭ-ṭebla?	Has she put them on the table?

waš žab weldek le-ktub dyali men l-medṛaṣa?	Did your son bring my books from school?
waš žabhom weldek men l-medṛaṣa?	Did your son bring them from school?
šeft l-măɛmel ž-ždid l-yum.	I saw the new factory today.
šeftu l-yum.	I saw it today.
dditi l-kebbuṭ dyalek mɛak?	Did you take your coat with you?
dditih mɛak?	Did you take it with you?
nsaw s-sarut dyalhom fe-ḍ-ḍaṛ.	They forgot their key at home.
nsaweh fe-ḍ-ḍaṛ.	They forgot it at home.
qṛit dak l-žarida l-bareɛ fe-ṣ-ṣbaɛ.	I read that newspaper yesterday morning.
qṛitha l-bareɛ fe-ṣ-ṣbaɛ.	I read it yesterday morning.

II. Grammatical Notes.

A. The equivalent for English 'her' as an object of a verb is the ending *-ha, e.g. šeft* 'I saw' and *šeftha* 'I saw her'. The equivalent for 'them' is *-hom,* e.g. *žab* 'he brought, and *žabhom* 'he brought them'.

B. There is no specific Moroccan equivalent for 'it' as the object of verbs. Depending on whether a masculine or a feminine object is referred to, the form for 'him' or 'her' is used. Thus, referring to *bṛa,* which is feminine, 'I read it' is *qṛitha.*

III. Exercises.

A. Go through the exercise of Lesson 40. Delete the underlined portions of the sentences and add the ending for 'him', 'her' or 'them' to the verb, depending on whether the deleted noun is masculine, feminine or plural. For example, *werraw t-ṭebla le-n-nežžaṛ* should be changed to read *werrawha le-n-nežžar*. As each change is made, read the resulting new sentence out loud.

B. Go through the text of this lesson and

1. Change all statements to questions.
2. Change all questions to statements.
3. Make all verb forms negative.

IV. Vocabulary.

bentha	her daughter
bentek	your (sg.) daughter
bentna	our daughter
bentu	his daughter
weldek	your (sg.) son

LESSON FIFTY-SEVEN

I. Text.

waš ddak ḅḅak le-s-sinima mʕah?	Did your father take you to the movies with him?
waš ddak xak le-ḍ-ḍaṛ l-biḍa?	Did your brother take you to Casablanca?
waš ʕawnuk xutek fe-l-xedma dyalek?	Did your brothers help you in your work?
ṣifeṭnak l-l-medṛaṣa mʕa xutek u-xwatatek.	We sent you to school with your brothers and sisters.
ʕlaš xellak ṭ-ṭbib mʕa xutek?	Why did the doctor leave you with your brothers?
ẓeṛtek meṛṛtayn l-bareḥ.	I visited you twice yesterday.
waš ẓaṛettek le-fqiha dyalek?	Did your teacher visit you?
waš ẓaṛettek xtek l-yum?	Did your sister visit you today?
waš šafettek ṃṃek?	Did your mother see you?
waš šafettek xtek?	Did your sister see you?
ma-žbeṛtek-š fe-l-ḥanut had ṣ-ṣbaḥ.	I didn't find you at the shop this morning.
ʕlaš ḍeṛbek l-weld?	Why did the boy hit you?
waš ḍeṛbek ṣ-ṣeṛraq?	Did the thief hit you?
waš ddakom ḅḅakom l-l-meġrib mʕah?	Did your father take you to Morocco with him?
ma-ṣifeṭkom-š mʕa ṃṃkom?	Didn't he send you with your mother?

šeftkom fe-ṛ-ṛbaṭ.	I saw you in Rabat.
ma-šeftkom-š fe-l-meḍṛaṣa l-yum.	I didn't see you at school today.
ka-iddini mʕah koll nhaṛ.	He takes me with him every day.
ma-ka-iddini-š l-l-meḍṛaṣa nhaṛ le-xmis.	He doesn't take me to school on Thursdays.
waš ka-iddik l-l-xedma fe-ṣ-ṣbaʕ?	Does he take you to work in the morning(s)?
ʕlaš ma-ka-iddik-š l-l-meḍṛaṣa fe-ṭ-ṭumubil?	Why doesn't he take you to school in the car?
f-had s-saʕa ka-nʕawenha fe-l-xedma dyalha.	Right now I'm helping her with her work.
f-had s-saʕa ma-ka-nʕawenha-š.	I'm not helping her right now.
ma-ka-nʕawenha-š nhaṛ s-sebt.	I don't help her on Saturdays.
waš dima ka-txelliweh mʕa xah?	Do you always leave him with his brother?
ʕlaš ma-ka-txelliweh-š mʕa xtu nhaṛ le-xmis?	Why don't you leave him with his sister on Thursdays?
ka-nẓuṛuha meṛṛtayn fe-š-šheṛ.	We visit her twice a month.
waš ka-iẓuṛukom bezzaf?	Do they visit you a lot?
ka-nšufuhom bezzaf fe-ṣ-ṣif.	We see them a lot in the summer.
waš ka-iʕawnek le-fqi bezzaf?	Does the teacher help you a lot?

II. Grammatical Notes.

A. The ending for 'you' (sg.) is *-k* after vowels and *-ek* after consonants, e.g. *ṣifeṭna* 'we sent' and *ṣifeṭnak* 'we sent you' (sg.), *ẓeṛt* 'I visited' and *ẓeṛtek* 'I visited you (sg.).

B. The ending for 'you' (pl.) is *-kom,* e.g. *šeft* 'I saw' and *šeftkom* 'I saw you'.

C. With the addition of *-ek* 'you' (sg.), inversion and elision occur regularly, e.g., *ḍreb* 'he hit' and *ḍeṛbek* 'he hit you (sg.)' show inversion, while *ka-iʕawen* 'he helps' and *ka-iʕawnek* 'he helps you' show elision.

D. An exception to the pattern of elision is that the ending *-et* 'she' in the past tense changes to *-ett* before *-ek* 'you (sg.)', e.g. *šafet* 'she saw' and *šafettek* 'she saw you (sg.)'.

E. Until this lesson, the endings for 'me', 'you', 'him', etc. have been shown only with verb forms in the perfect tense. Exactly the same forms are added to the durative tense, e.g. *ka-nƐawen* 'I am helping' and *ka-nƐawenha* 'I am helping her.'

F. Negation is completely regular in durative tense forms as well as in perfect tense forms, e.g. *ka-iddini* 'he takes me' and *ma-ka-iddini-š* 'he doesn't take me.'

III. Exercises.

A. Go through the text of this lesson and

1. Turn all statements into questions.
2. Turn all questions into statements.
3. Make all positive forms negative.

B. Go through the texts of Lessons 53-54 and, insofar as makes good sense, change the endings on the verbs from 'me', 'us', and 'him' to the ending for 'you' (sg.).

C. Go through the texts of Lessons 55-56 and, insofar as makes good sense, change the endings on the verbs from 'him', 'her', and 'them' to the endings for 'you' (pl.).

D. Go through the texts of Lessons 53-57 and change every perfect tense verb form to the corresponding durative tense verb form. Make whatever other changes are necessary to achieve good sense in the sentences as the tense of the verb forms is changed.

E. Repeat Exercise **D** above and in the process make every positive verb form negative and every negative verb form positive. As these changes are made, make any other changes necessary to achieve good sense in the individual sentences.

IV. Vocabulary.

ṃṃkom	your (pl.) mother
mƐa	with
xutek	your (sg.) brothers

NOTE: The preposition *mƐa* 'with' is used only to denote accompaniment, never instrument. Compare the comments on the preposition *b-, be-* in Grammatical Note **B** of Lesson 39.

LESSON FIFTY-EIGHT

I. Text.

xedmu bin l-qenṭṛa u-l-medṛaṣa.	They worked between the bridge and the school.
z-zlafa ṭaƐet binu u-binha.	The bowl fell between him and her.
xdemna bin ṭ-ṭebla u-š-šeṛžem.	We worked between the table and the window.
siyyeb l-kuṛa binek u-bini.	He threw the ball between you and me.
l-kuṛa ṭaƐet binathom.	The ball fell between them.
dak l-weld bƐal ḅḅah.	That boy is like his father.
hiya bƐal xti.	She is like my sister.
dak l-bent lebset bƐalek u-bƐal xtek.	That girl dressed like you and your sister.
xdem bƐal ḅḅah.	He worked like his father.
ma-kont-š bƐalu.	I was not like him.
d-drari xedmu bƐalhom bƐal r-ržal u-le-Ɛyalat.	The children worked like the men and women.
ḍ-ḍaṛ kbira bƐalha bƐal l-medṛaṣa.	The house is as big as the school.
Ɛežbetni dak ẓ-ẓeṛbiya l-Ɛămṛa.	I liked that red rug. (That red rug pleased me.)
Ɛežbethom ḍ-ḍaṛ l-biḍa bezzaf.	They liked Casablanca a lot.
t-tṣaweṛ ma-Ɛežbuh-š.	He didn't like the photographs.
waš Ɛežbek l-lun de-z-zlafa?	Did you like the color of the bowl?

II. Grammatical Notes.

A. The details of endings such as those shown in *bini u-binek* 'between me and you' and *bƐalu* 'like him' are discussed in a later lesson.

B. When used with two objects, both *bin* 'between' and *bƐal* 'like, as' are repeated before each object unless both objects are nouns, e.g. *bini u-binek* 'between me and you', *bini u-bin xay* 'between me and my brother', *bƐal xtek u-bƐalek* 'like your sister and you'. However, when two nouns follow *bin,* the structure is similar to English, e.g. *bin ṭ-ṭebla u-š-šeṛžem* 'between the table and the window'. The form *binat* is used, instead of *bin,* before a plural ending, e.g. *binathom* 'between them'.

C. In comparisons, a second *bƐal* is often inserted with a pronoun ending agreeing with the subject, e.g. *d-drari mešġulin bƐalhom bƐal r-ržal* 'The children are as busy as the men', *l-bent xedmet bƐalha bƐal le-mṛa* 'The girl worked like (as much as) the woman'.

D. To say 'I liked that book' in Moroccan, one says 'That book pleased me'. In other words, the thing that a person likes is the subject of the verb and the person who likes it is the object of the verb, e.g. *l-magana Ɛežbetni* 'I liked the watch', *š-šelya Ɛežbethom* 'They liked the chair'.

IV. Vocabulary.

bin, binat	between
ḅḅah	his father
bƐal	like, as, as . . . as
qenṭṛa	bridge
xtek	your (sg.) sister

LESSON FIFTY-NINE

I. Text.

ma-tegles-š Ɛăl š-šelya dyali.	Don't sit in my chair.
gles Ɛda š-šeṛžem.	Sit next to the window.
ma-teġsel-š ṭ-ṭumubil ġedda.	Don't wash the car tomorrow.
ġsel ḷ-ḷeṛḍ l-yum.	Wash the floor today.

ma-tekteb-š fe-l-konnaš dyali.	Don't write in my notebook.
kteb waƐed le-bṛa le-ḅḅak.	Write your father a letter.
ma-trefdu-š l-bakitat dyalkom fe-ḍ-ḍaṛ.	Don't carry your packages into the house.
refdu had ṣ-ṣnaḍeq l-l-buṣṭa ġedda.	Carry these boxes to the post office tomorrow.
ma-tbiƐ-š ḍ-ḍaṛ dyalek!	Don't sell your house!
biƐ ṭ-ṭumubil dyalek b-taman mezyan.	Sell your car for a good price.
ma-ddiru-š le-ktub dyalkom Ɛla had ṭ-ṭebla.	Don't put your books on this table.
diru le-Ɛwayež dyalkom f-had l-bit.	Put your clothes in this room.
ma-tkun-š keslan.	Don't be lazy.
kun ražel.	Be a man.
ma-tešri-š ṭumubil balya.	Don't buy an old car.
šri l-lƐăm u-z-zit.	Buy some meat and oil.
ma-džiw-š l-l-meḍṛaṣa nhaṛ le-xmis.	Don't come to school Thursday.
ažiw ġedda fe-t-tmenya.	Come at eight o'clock tomorrow.
ažiw băƐd ġedda fe-l-Ɛăšṛa.	Come day after tomorrow at ten o'clock.
ma-teƐṭi-š le-flus l-had ṛ-ṛažel.	Don't give this man the money.
Ɛṭi l-žarida le-ḅḅak.	Give the newspaper to your father.
ma-teqṛa-š l-žarida daba.	Don't read the newspaper now.
qṛa had le-bṛa.	Read this letter.
ma-tkobb-š l-ma Ɛla had ẓ-ẓeṛbiya.	Don't pour water on this rug.
kobb atay f-had l-kisan.	Pour the tea into these glasses.
ma-tšedd-š l-bab qbel l-xemsa.	Don't close the door before five o'clock.
šedd š-šeṛžem daba.	Close the window now.

ma-tleff-š had le-ɛwayež.	Don't wrap up these clothes.
leff had l-bakit.	Wrap up this package.
ma-tsiyyeb-š dak l-weṛqa.	Don't throw that ticket away.
siyyeb le-ɛwayež l-balyin dyalek.	Throw your old clothes away.
ma-tweqqfu-š l-biškliṭat dyalkom qeddam ḍ-ḍar.	Don't park your bicycles in front of the house.
weqqfu ṭ-ṭumubilat dyalkom hna.	Park your cars here.

II. Grammatical Notes.

A. The negative imperative is formed by taking the durative tense forms for 'you', dropping the *ka-* and using the regular negative form *ma-* plus *-š* e.g. *ka-tegles* 'you (sg.) sit' and *ma-tegles-š* 'don't sit', or *ka-ddiru* 'you (pl.) put' and *ma-ddiru-š* 'don't put'.

B. The positive imperative is arrived at by dropping both the *ka-* and the *t-* (*te-, d-* as the case may be, cf. Grammatical Note A of Lesson 44 and Grammatical Note A of Lesson 45) from the sg. and pl. 'you' forms of the durative tense, as in sg. *ka-tekteb* 'you write' with imperative *kteb,* and pl. *ka-tketbu* 'you write' with imperative *ketbu.*

Quite often the imperative is identical in form with the 'he' form and the 'they' form of the perfect tense, e.g. *xdem* means both 'he worked' and 'work!' and *xedmu* means both 'they worked' and 'work!' This similarity of form does not hold true for verbs which show changes of the basic verb stem in the durative, e.g. *šra* 'he bought', durative tense *ka-tešri,* imperative *šri.*

C. The imperative of *ža* 'to come' is irregular. The singular imperative is *aži* and the plural imperative is *ažiw.* The imperative of *mša* 'to go' is irregular and will be given in a later lesson.

D. The form *ɛla* instead of *ɛăl* is used unless the definite article follows, e.g. *ɛla had š-šelya* 'on this chair' as opposed to *ɛăl š-šelya* 'on the chair'.

III. Exercises.

A. Go through the text of this lesson and change all singular imperative forms to the plural.

B. Go through the text of this lesson and, insofar as makes sense, successively add the endings for 'him' (it), 'her' (it), and 'them' to the imperative forms.

C. Go through the texts of Lessons 41-44 and give the imperative form—singular, plural, positive, and negative—for every verb encountered.

D. Apply the instructions of Exercise **B** to the results of Exercise **C.**

IV. Vocabulary.

b-taman mezyan	at a good price, for a good price
băƐd ġedda	day after tomorrow
ġedda	tomorrow
hna	here
qbel	before
taman	price
Ɛla	on (see Grammatical Note **D**)

LESSON SIXTY

I. Text.

ġad-iṣifeṭ	he will send, he's going to send
ġad-iṣifeṭ-li	he's going to send (to) me
ġad-iṣifeṭha-li.	He's going to send it (f.) to me.
ġad-iṣifeṭ-li t-teṣwiṛa băƐd ġedda.	He's going to send me the picture day after tomorrow.
ġedda fe-ṣ-ṣbaƐ	tomorrow morning
ġad-nekteb	I'll write, I'm going to write
ġad-nekteb-lu	I'll write (to) him
ġad-nketbu	I'll write it (m.)
ġad-nketbu-lu	I'll write it to him
ġad-nekteb ž-žwab le-ḅḅak ġedda fe-ṣ-ṣbaƐ.	I'll write the answer to your father tomorrow morning.
ġad-nketbu l-xak l-yum.	I'll write it to your brother today.
ġad-nekteb-lu ž-žwab daba.	I'll write the answer to him now.
ġad-nketbu-lu ġedda fe-ṣ-ṣbaƐ.	I'll write it to him tomorrow morning.

žib-li	bring (sg.) (to) me
žibu	bring it (m.)
žibu-li	bring it to me
žib-li dak le-ktab.	Bring me that book.
žibu-li qbel t-tesɛud.	Bring it to me before nine o'clock.
ġad-nteṛžem	I'll translate
ġad-nteṛžem-lek	I'll translate for you (sg.)
ġad-nteṛžemhom	I'll translate them
ġad-nteṛžemhom-lek	I'll translate them for you
ġad-nteṛžem-lek duk le-bṛawat ġedda fe-ṣ-ṣbaɛ.	I'll translate those letters for you tomorrow morning.
ġad-nteṛžemhom-lek qbel s-setta.	I'll translate them for you before six o'clock.
meddit l-uṛaq le-d-drari.	I handed the tickets to the children.
meddit-lhom l-uṛaq nhaṛ s-sebt.	I handed them the tickets on Saturday.
medditthom-lhom l-bareɛ.	I handed them to them yesterday.
meddu l-uṛaq l-dak l-bent.	Hand the tickets to that girl.
medduhom l-dak l-bent.	Hand them to that girl.
meddu-lha l-uṛaq.	Hand her the tickets.
medduhom-lha daba.	Hand them to her now.
ḅḅa u-m̩m̩i ġad-išriw-li had l-kebbuṭ.	My father and mother are going to buy me this coat.
ḅḅa u-m̩m̩i ġad-išriweh-li.	My father and mother are going to buy it for me.
žabu-li s-sarut l-bareɛ fe-ṣ-ṣbaɛ.	They brought me the key yesterday morning.
ɛad žabuh-li.	They just now brought it to me.
ġad-nqeddem mṛatek le-ḅḅa ġedda.	I'll introduce your wife to my father tomorrow.
ġad-nqeddemha le-ḅḅa băɛd le-ġda.	I'll introduce her to my father after dinner.
ġad-nqeddemha-lu l-yum.	I'll introduce her to him today.

ɛlaš ma-qeddemti-lna-š duk n-nas?	Why didn't you introduce those people to us?
ɛlaš ma-qeddemtihom-lna-š?	Why didn't you introduce them to us?
ġad-ixelli-lkom duk le-ktub ɛăl ṭ-ṭebla.	He's going to leave those books on the table for you.
ġad-ixellihom-lkom ɛăl ṭ-ṭebla.	He's going to leave them on the table for you.
siyyeb l-kuṛa le-d-drari.	Throw the ball to the children.
siyyebha le-d-drari.	Throw it to the children.
siyyeb-lhom l-kuṛa.	Throw them the ball.
siyyebha-lhom!	Throw it to them!
ɛṭani le-flus l-bareḥ.	He gave me the money yesterday.
ɛṭahom-li l-bareḥ.	He gave it to me yesterday.*
ɛṭitha l-ɛonwan dyal xti.	I gave her my sister's address.
ɛṭitu-lha.	I gave it to her.
waš ɛṭawek t-tṣaweṛ?	Did they give you the pictures?
waš ɛṭawhom-lek?	Did they give them to you?
werrini l-xedma dyalek.	Show me your work.
werriha-li.	Show it to me.
ma-ġad-nwerriweh-š le-ḥwayež ž-ždad dyalna.	We're not going to show him our new clothes.
ma-ġad-nwerriwhom-lu-š ġedda.	We're not going to show them to him tomorrow.

II. Grammatical Notes.

A. Future time is indicated by substituting *ġad-* for *ka-* of the durative tense, e.g. *ka-nekteb* 'I write, I am writing' and *ġad-nekteb* 'I will write, I am going to write', etc. In rapid speech *ġad-* is often abbreviated to *ġa-*, e.g. *ġad-iži* or *ġa-iži* 'he will come, he's going to come'.

---

* Note Moroccan *-hom* 'them' and English 'it', since Moroccan *flus* is plural while English 'money' is singular.

B. The following set of endings are exemplified in this lesson:

-li	'to me, for me'
-lek	'to you, for you' (sg.)
-lu	'to him, for him'
-lha	'to her, for her'
-lna	'to us, for us'
-lkom	'to you, for you' (pl.)
-lhom	'to them, for them'

These are the same endings which were learned with *dyal* (*dyali* 'my, mine', *dyalek* 'you, yours', etc.) in Lessons 21-23 combined with the preposition *l-, le-* 'to' (cf. the Grammatical Note, Lesson 34). Note that with the ending *-na,* the form *-nna* sometimes occurs instead of *-lna* in rapid speech, e.g. *kteb-nna* or *kteb-lna* 'he wrote to us'. Whether the translation is 'to' or 'for' is purely a function of English context, e.g. *werraha-li* 'he showed it to me' but *šraha-li* 'he bought it for me'.

As meaning requires, these endings are added directly to any and all verb forms which already have the endings for 'him (it)', 'her (it)', or 'them', e.g. *qeddemtihom* 'you introduced them' and *qeddemtihom-lna* 'you introduced them to us'. They are also added to verb forms, as meaning requires, when there is no previous pronoun ending, e.g. *žabu* 'they brought' and *žabu-li s-sarut* 'they brought me the key'.

The two verbs *ɛṭa* 'to give' and *werra* 'to show' are exceptions. They take the simple pronoun endings learned in Lessons 53-57. For example, compare *ɛṭani* 'he gave (to) me' and *werrini* 'he showed (to) me' with *žab-li* 'he brought (to) me'. But both *ɛṭa* and *werra* are completely regular if the ending for 'him (it)', 'her (it)', or 'them' is already present, e.g. *werrini l-xedma* 'show me the work' but *werriha-li* 'show it to me'.

C. The endings discussed above are integral parts of the verb forms, and negation follows the regular pattern of prefixing *ma-* and suffixing *-š,* e.g. *qeddemtihom-lna* 'you introduced them to us' and *ma-qeddemtihom-lna-š* 'you didn't introduce them to us'.

III. Exercises.

A. Go through the text of this lesson and make all the verb forms encountered negative. In the sentences, make any other changes which may be necessary to make good sense.

B. In the following sentences, supply the Moroccan for the English in parentheses and read the sentence aloud. Then omit the underlined noun and replace it with a pronoun ending on the verb. Once again read the resulting sentence aloud. Note the following illustration.

rfed (to him) *had l-bakit.*
rfed-lu had l-bakit.
refdu-lu.

1. *rfedt* (for them) *l-xenša le-ḍ-ḍaṛ.*
2. *žabu* (to me) *le-flus l-bareƐ.*
3. *ġselna* (for you) *ṭ-ṭumubil dyalek.*
4. *teṛžemti* (for her) *ž-žwab?*
5. *ġad-neqṛa* (to you, pl.) *le-bṛa dyalha.*
6. *ketbet* (for me) *l-Ɛonwan.*
7. *baƐu* (to him) *l-biškliṭat.*
8. *žebti* (to us) *le-ktab?*
9. *ṣifṭu* (to us) *l-xedma wel-l-bareƐ.*
10. *ġad-nsiyyeb* (to you, sg.) *s-sarut.*
11. *ġad-išriw* (for him) *dak ṭ-ṭumubil.*
12. *xellaw* (for me) *t-teṣwiṛa?*
13. *ġad-nekteb* (to them) *l-Ɛanawin.*
14. *žib* (for us) *had l-bakitat le-ḍ-ḍaṛ.*
15. *ġad-ileffu* (for you, sg.) *le-Ɛwayež.*
16. *šedditi* (for her) *l-bab?*
17. *kobb* (for him) *atay fe-l-kas dyalu.*
18. *ġad-nteṛžmu* (for you, pl.) *duk le-bṛawat ġedda.*
19. *Ɛăllitiw* (for her) *ṣ-ṣnaḍeq?*
20. *ġad-nžib* (to you, pl.) *ž-žwab ġedda.*
21. *qṛat* (to them) *le-ktab.*

C. Repeat Exercise **B** above making each of the verb forms negative.

IV. Vocabulary.

ġedda fe-ṣ-ṣbaɛ	tomorrow morning
mṛatek	your wife
ɛad	just, just now

LESSON SIXTY-ONE

I. Text.

mša mɛakom le-s-sinima?	Did he go to the movies with you?
ḅḅak mša mɛakom l-ṭanža?	Did your father go to Tangier with you?
ka-imši l-l-xedma fe-ž-žuž.	He goes to work at two o'clock.
ka-nemši l-lmeḍṛaṣa xemsa de-l-meṛṛat fe-l-ʔusbuɛ.	I go to school five times a week.
bġit nemši mɛakom le-ḍ-ḍaṛ l-biḍa.	I want to go to Casablanca with you.
bġiti temši mɛana?	Do you want to go with us?
la, ma-bġit-š nemši mɛakom l-yum.	No, I don't want to go with you today.
bġa imši l-l-xedma bekri ġedda.	He wants to go to work early tomorrow.
weldu bġa imši mɛah.	His son wants to go with him.
bġat teġsel šɛăṛha daba.	She wants to wash her hair now.
ṃṃi bġat teġsel had le-ḥwayež l-yum.	My mother wants to wash these clothes today.
ṃṃhom ma-bġat-š teġsel le-ḥwayež l-yum.	Their mother doesn't want to wash the clothes today.
ṃṃha bġat temši mɛaha l-l-meḍṛaṣa.	Her mother wants to go to school with her.
bġat temši l-l-ḥanut mɛa ṃṃha.	She wants to go to the store with her mother.

bġaw igelsu ɛla had š-šelyat hadu.	They want to sit on these chairs here.
l-xeddama ma-bġaw-š igelsu ɛăl l-leṛḍ.	The workers don't want to sit on the ground.
bġina neɛṭiweh had le-ktub.	We want to give him these books.
bġina neɛtiwhom-lu qbel ġedda.	We want to give them to him before tomorrow.
ɛlaš bġitiw tbiɛu ḍaṛkom l-had n-nas?	Why do you want to sell your house to these people?
ɛlaš bġitiw tbiɛuha l-had n-nas?	Why do you want to sell it to these people?
ɛlaš bġitiw tbiɛu-lhom ḍaṛkom?	Why do you want to sell them your house?
ɛlaš bġitiw tbiɛuha-lhom?	Why do you want to sell it to them?

II. Grammatical Notes.

A. The imperfect tense is identical with the durative tense except for the prefix *ka-*. Thus in addition to such forms as *ka-nekteb* 'I write, I am writing', etc., such forms as *nekteb,* etc., without a preceding *ka-* occur.

Unlike the durative tense, the imperfect tense has no direct and simple translation into English. Imperfect tense forms are translated in a variety of manners, depending on context and use. One of the most common uses of imperfect verb forms is in verb phrases such as *bġit nemši* 'I want to go', *bġaw igelsu* 'they want to sit', etc., where the imperfect is translated as the English infinitive 'to go', 'to sit', etc. Note that the specific imperfect form used always corresponds with the doer of the action, 'I', 'you', 'he', 'she', etc.

B. In Lessons 21-23 the student was introduced to such expressions as *le-ktab dyali* 'my book', etc. The form *dyal* with its various endings is re-listed here for reference.

dyali	my, mine	*dyalna*	our, ours
dyalek	your, yours (sg.)	*dyalkom*	your, yours (pl.)
dyalu	his	*dyalhom*	their, theirs
dyalha	her, hers		

In addition to such uses as *ṭ-ṭumubil dyali* 'my car', possession can be expressed by adding these endings directly to a limited number of nouns. Summarized below are two examples which have already been learned individually in preceding lessons.

ḍaṛi	my house	*ṃṃi*	my mother
ḍaṛek	your (sg.) house	*ṃṃek*	your (sg.) mother
ḍaṛu	his house	*ṃṃu*	his mother
ḍaṛha	her house	*ṃṃha*	her mother
ḍaṛna	our house	*ṃṃna*	our mother
ḍaṛkom	your (pl.) house	*ṃṃkom*	your (pl.) mother
ḍaṛhom	their house	*ṃṃhom*	their mother

Only a limited number of nouns can take these endings. For the great majority of nouns, possession is expressed only by the use of *dyal*. Most importantly, nouns of family relationship ('mother', 'father', 'brother', 'sister', etc.) should not be used with *dyal*. Usually the direct possessive endings are the only acceptable usage. Note in passing that the forms *xay* 'my brother and *ḅḅa* 'my father' are irregular in terms of the ending for 'my'. Note also the inversion, as is to be expected, in *xti* 'my sister' as opposed to *xetha* 'her sister'.

Other than nouns of family relation, usually only very short nouns which end in consonants take the possessive endings. Which nouns take these endings directly must be learned gradually by experience, and further comments will be made on them in following lessons. When in doubt, the student should always use a form of *dyal*. Summarized below are the other noun forms which have occurred so far with possessive endings.

ḅḅa	my father	*xay*	my brother
ḅḅak	your (sg.) father	*xak*	your (sg.) brother
ḅḅah	his father	*xah*	his brother
ḅḅaha	her father	*xaha*	her brother
ḅḅana	our father	*xana*	our brother
ḅḅakom	your (pl.) father	*xakom*	your (pl.) brother
ḅḅahom	their father	*xahom*	their brother
xwatati	'my sisters'	*xti*	my sister
xwatatek	your (sg.) sisters	*xtek*	your (sg.) sister
xwatatu	his sisters	*xtu*	his sister

xwatatha	her sisters	*xetha*	her sister
weldi	my son	*benti*	my daughter
weldek	your (sg.) son	*bentek*	your (sg.) daughter
weldu	his son	*bentu*	his daughter
mṛatek	your wife	*bentha*	her daughter
xutek	your (sg.) brothers	*bentna*	our daughter
šƐăṛha	her hair		

III. Exercises.

A. Go through the forms listed above at the end of Grammatical Note **B.** Where the lists are not complete (e.g. the form *weldhom* 'their son' is not given), supply the missing forms by using the proper ending. Note that an inverted form *šăƐr-* 'hair' will be found before *-i* 'my', *-ek* 'your' (sg.), and *-u* 'his', as opposed to *šƐăṛha* 'her hair'.

B. Go through the texts of Lessons 41-46 and form new sentences by eliminating the *ka-* prefix from durative forms and using a form of the verb *bġa* 'to want'. For example, the sentence *ka-iweqqfu ṭ-ṭumubil dyalhom qeddam ḍ-ḍaṛ* 'They park their car in front of the house' should be changed to *bġaw iweqqfu ṭ-ṭumubil dyalhom qeddam ḍ-ḍar* 'They want to park their car in front of the house'. In cases where such a change would lead to a nonsensical sentence, further changes should be made to produce an acceptable sentence.

IV. Vocabulary.

ṃṃha	her mother
ṃṃhom	their mother
mša	to go
mƐakom	with you (pl.)
weldu	his son

LESSON SIXTY-TWO

I. Text.

tebġi dži le-s-sinima mɛaya?	Would you like to come to the movies with me?
la, ma-nebġi-š.	No, I wouldn't care to.
nebġi nemši ġedda f-le-ɛšiya.	I'd like to go tomorrow evening.
tebġini nžib-lek l-qehwa?	Would you like (for) me to bring you some coffee?
tebġini ndir-lek fiha ši-šwiya d-le-ḥlib?	Would you like for me to put a little milk in it for you?
nebġi negles ḥdak.	I'd like to sit beside you.
tebġini negles ḥdak f-le-ġda?	Would you like for me to sit beside you at dinner?
nebġik tegles hna ḥdaya.	I'd like for you to sit here beside me.
nebġik tegles hna ḥda had s-siyyed.	I'd like for you to sit here beside this gentleman.
ḅḅa ibġini negles ḥdak f-le-ġda.	My father would like for me to sit beside you at dinner.
ḅḅak ibġik tegles ḥdaya.	Your father would like for you to sit beside me.
had s-siyyed ibġina nemšiw mɛah le-ṣ-ṣuq.	This gentleman would like for us to go to the market with him.
ḅḅana ibġina nemšiw mɛa had s-siyyed.	Our father would like for us to go with this gentleman.
ma-nebġiweh-š iži mɛana.	We wouldn't like for him to come with us.
ma-nebġiweh-š igles ḥdana f-le-ġda.	We wouldn't like for him to sit beside us at dinner.
ṃṃi tebġi had s-siyyed ihḍeṛ mɛana.	My mother would like for this gentleman to talk with us.
tebġih ihḍeṛ mɛana.	She'd like for him to talk with us.

tebġiwna nžiw mƐakom le-ṣ-ṣuq?	Would you like for us to come with you to the market?
nebġiw nemšiw mƐakom.	We'd like to go with you.
nebġiwkom džiw mƐana.	We'd like for you to come with us.
ḅḅa u-ṃṃi ibġiw had s-siyyed iẓuṛ ḍaṛna.	My father and mother would like for this gentleman to visit our house.
ibġiweh iẓuṛ ḍaṛna.	They'd like for him to visit our house.

II. Grammatical Notes.

A. The imperfect tense of *bġa* is translated into English as 'would like', e.g. *nebġi* 'I would like', etc.

B. Note the absence of a Moroccan equivalent for English 'to' in such an expression as *ma-nebġi-š* 'I wouldn't care (like) to'.

C. Note the pattern of such English expressions as 'he'd like (for) us to go' or 'she'd like (for) this gentleman to speak'. The Moroccan pattern is almost identical. The only differences are the lack of a Moroccan equivalent for English 'for' in such sentences and the fact that the Moroccan imperfect is used as the equivalent for English 'to go', 'to speak', etc.; e.g. *ibġina nemšiw* and *tebġi had s-siyyed ihḍeṛ.*

D. Note the pattern of endings on the preposition *mƐa* 'with' in the forms summarized below. Note that except for the form *mƐaya* 'with me', the endings are identical with those discussed in Grammatical Note **B** of Lesson 61.

mƐa	with		
mƐaya	with me	*mƐana*	with us
mƐak	with you (sg.)	*mƐakom*	with you (pl.)
mƐah	with him	*mƐahom*	with them
mƐaha	with her		

III. Exercises.

A. Go through the text of this lesson and make all positive verb forms negative. Make any other changes, if any, which are required to make good sense. Read each new sentence so formed aloud.

B. Go through the text of this lesson and turn all statements into questions, first positive and then negative. Read each new sentence so formed out loud and focus attention on the exact shades of meaning involved.

C. Go through the sentences in the text of this lesson and change the various imperfect forms of ***bġa*** in the following manner: Of the seven possible forms ('I', 'you' (sg.), 'he', 'she', 'we', 'you' (pl.), and 'they'), whichever one is encountered, change it successively to the other six. Make whatever additional changes may be necessary to achieve good sense in the sentences as a consequence of the original change.

For example, the first sentence *tebġi dži le-s-sinima mɛaya?* would logically be first changed to *nebġi nži le-s-sinima mɛak,* then to *ibġi iži le-s-sinima mɛaya?,* etc.

IV. Vocabulary.

fiha	in her, in it
siyyed	gentleman, man
ɛdak	next to you (sg.), beside you
ɛdana	next to us, beside us
ɛdaya	next to me, beside me

LESSON SIXTY-THREE

I. Text.

dak s-siyyed gales ɛda xti.	That man is sitting beside my sister.
huwa gales ɛdaha daba.	He's sitting beside her now.
kont gales ɛdaha f-le-ġda.	I (m.) was sitting beside her at dinner.
xti galsa ɛda dak s-siyyed.	My sister is sitting beside that gentleman.
kanet galsa ɛdah f-le-ġda.	She was sitting beside him at dinner.
ma-kanet-š galsa ɛdah qbel le-ġda.	She wasn't sitting beside him before dinner.

imken-li negles hna ħdakom?	Can I sit here beside you?
imken-li ndir had š-šelya ħdakom?	Can I put this chair beside you?
imken-lek tegles ħdahom.	You can sit beside them.
imken-lek ddir š-šelya dyalek ħdahom.	You can put your chair next to them.
dir ṣ-ṣnadeq fe-l-qent.	Put the boxes in the corner.
dir l-bakitat ħdahom.	Put the packages beside them.
dir d-dheb ɛăl ṭ-ṭebla.	Put the gold on the table.
dir l-feḍḍa ħdah.	Put the silver beside it.
ġa-ndir-lek l-berrad ɛăl ṣ-ṣiniya.	I'm going to put the teapot on the tray for you (sg.)
ġa-ndir l-kisan ħdah.	I'll put the glasses beside it.
xay thelḷa fiya.	My brother took care of me.
benti ka-tthelḷa fiya.	My daughter takes care of me.
d-drari dyali ka-ithelḷaw fiya.	My children take care of me.
waš ma-thelḷat-š fik?	Didn't she take care of you?
ġad-nthelḷaw fik.	We'll take care of you.
waš d-drari dyalek ka-ithelḷaw fik?	Do your children take care of you?
thelḷiti fih mezyan?	Did you (sg.) take good care of him?
dir had le-ħwayež fe-ṣ-ṣenduq.	Put these clothes in the box.
dirhom fih.	Put them in it.
d-drari dyalna ġad-ithelḷaw fina.	Our children are going to take care of us.
huwa le-kbir fina.	He's the biggest one among us.
škun le-kbir fikom?	Which one of you is the biggest? (Who is the biggest among you?)
ṃṃkom ma-ġad-tthelḷa-š fikom.	Your mother isn't going to take care of you.
d-drari dyalkom ġad-ithelḷaw fikom.	Your children are going to take care of you.

ma-nebġi-š nthella fihom.	I wouldn't like to take care of them.
ma-bġit-š nthella fihom.	I don't want to take care of them.
l-kisan fe-ṣ-ṣiniya.	The glasses are on the tray.
kobb l-qehwa fihom.	Pour the coffee in them.
dir s-sokkaṛ fihom.	Put some sugar in them.

II. Grammatical Notes.

A. With prepositions ending in vowels, the form for 'me' is *-ya,* e.g. *ɛdaya* 'beside me'. Otherwise the endings are the same as for *dyal* (see Grammatical Note **D** of Lesson 61 and Grammatical Note **B** of Lesson 62). Note that the familiar preposition *f-* 'in, on' has the form *fi-* before pronoun endings.

A summary of forms:

ɛdaya	beside me	*fiya*	in me
ɛdak	beside you (sg.)	*fik*	in you (sg.)
ɛdah	beside him, it	*fih*	in him, it
ɛdaha	beside her, it	*fiha*	in her, it
ɛdana	beside us	*fina*	in us
ɛdakom	beside you (pl.)	*fikom*	in you (pl.)
ɛdahom	beside them	*fihom*	in them

B. Note that differing contexts bring about the three different translations 'in', 'of' and 'among' for *f-* in this lesson.

C. The translation of *škun le-kbir fikom?* as 'Which one of you is the biggest?' illustrates an important point: Word for word translations are sometimes impossible, and the most natural way of expressing an idea in English often differs greatly from the usual way of expression in Moroccan.

III. Exercises.

Change all singular pronoun endings to the corresponding plural ones (e.g. 'me' to 'us', 'him' to 'them', etc.) and vice versa in the sentences in the text of these lessons. Make any other changes necessary to achieve good sense. Read the resulting new sentences out loud.

IV. Vocabulary.

gales	sitting
galsa (f.)	
imken	it is possible
imken-li	I can
imken-lek	you (sg.) can
škun	who
thel̤l̤a (*ka-ithel̤l̤a*) *f-*	to take care of

LESSON SIXTY-FOUR

I. Text.

ža f-weqt le-ġda.	He came at dinner time.
dima ka-neġsel yeddiya qbel weqt le-ġda.	I always wash my hands before dinner time.
ʕmelt l-bakit ʕla ḍheṛ l-weld.	I put the package on the boy's back.
ġad-nʕămlu had ṣ-ṣnadeq f-ṭ-ṭumubil.	We're going to load these boxes in the car.
ʕayyednah men ḍheṛ l-weld.	We took it off the boy's back.
ġad-nʕăyyduhom men ṭ-ṭumubil.	We're going to take them out of the car.
m̤m̤i ʕăllet bab ḍ-ḍaṛ.	My mother opened the door of the house.
šeddit bab l-bit dyali.	I closed the door of my room.
bent xti mšat l-l-medṛaṣa bekri l-yum.	My sister's daughter went to school early today.
bent xti nsatna l-bareʕ.	My sister's daughter forgot us yesterday.
weld dak ṛ-ṛažel ma-ka-imši-š l-l-medṛaṣa.	That man's son does not go to school.
šeft weld dak ṛ-ṛažel hna l-bareʕ.	I saw that man's son here yesterday.

II. Grammatical Notes.

A. Review the discussion of *d-, de-* and *dyal* in the Grammatical Notes of Lessons 47, 48, and 49.

B. A different way of expressing the same meanings of *d-, de-* and *dyal* as discussed in Lessons 47, 48, and 49 is by placing two nouns side by side. This construction is called 'the construct state'. Note that, regardless of the English translation, the first noun in a construct state never takes the definite article. Summarized below are the examples introduced in the text of this lesson.

weqt le-ġda	dinner-time
ḍheṛ l-weld	the boy's back
bab ḍ-ḍaṛ	the (main, front) door of the house
bab l-bit	the door of the room
bent xti	my sister's daughter, niece
weld dak ṛ-ṛažel	that man's son

Note: The construct state is used with only a limited number of nouns. It is limited in much the same way as the possessive endings discussed in Grammatical Note **B** of Lesson 61. Further details of the use of the construct state are discussed in following lessons.

III. Exercises.

Make construct states out of the phases below by omitting *d-, de-* or *dyal* and by dropping the definite article of the first word. For example, such a phrase as *l-bent dyal xti* 'my sister's daughter' would be changed to *bent xti.*

1. *l-ɛanut dyal n-nežžaṛ.*
2. *le-ɛwayež de-n-nas.*
3. *le-ɛwayež de-d-drari.*
4. *l-lun de-l-kuṛa.*
5. *l-lun d-le-mdad.*
6. *l-bab de-l-buṣṭa.*
7. *ḍ-ḍaṛ dyal le-fqi.*
8. *l-bab de-l-ɛanut.*
9. *l-ɛanut dyal l-gezzar.*
10. *ḍ-ḍaṛ d-benti.*

IV. Vocabulary.

ḍheṛ	back
weqt	time
yeddiya	my hands
ḥăyyed	to take off, to take away, to remove
εmel	to load, to put

LESSON SIXTY-FIVE

I. Text.

mṛat xay ka-texdem hna.	My brother's wife works here.
šefti mṛat xay l-yum?	Have you (sg.) seen my brother's wife today?
ma-bġit-š nbiε maganti.	I don't want to sell my watch.
dert magant ḅḅa εăl ṭ-ṭebla.	I put my father's watch on the table.
daret škaṛt le-fqi fe-ṭ-ṭumubil dyalu.	She put the teacher's briefcase in his car.
š-derti be-škaṛtek?	What did you (sg.) do with your briefcase?
š-εăndu f-yeddu?	What does he have in his hand?
yedd l-bent ḍḍeṛṛet.	The girl's hand got hurt.
yeddi ḍḍeṛṛet fe-l-ḥadita.	My hand got hurt in the accident.
yedd ṃ̂ṃ̂i ḍḍeṛṛet fe-l-ḥad̉ita.	My mother's hand got hurt in the accident.
waš ḍḍeṛṛet εămmtek f-dak l-ḥadita?	Did your aunt get hurt in that accident?
fayn ka-texdem εămmtek?	Where does your aunt work?
εămmt had l-bent ma-ḍḍeṛṛet-š.	This girl's aunt didn't get hurt.
εămmt had l-bent ka-texdem fe-l-măεmel de-l-biškliṭat.	This girl's aunt works at the bicycle factory.
dert yeddi f-žibi.	I put my hand in my pocket.
daretha f-yeddi.	She put it in my hand.

II. Grammatical Notes.

A. Parts of the body regularly take possessive endings directly rather than the construction with *dyal* (cf. Grammatical Note **B,** Lesson 61), e.g. *yedd* 'hand', *yeddi* 'my hand', *yeddu* 'his hand', etc.

B. For possession with nouns, the construct state (cf. Grammatical Note **B,** Lesson 64) rather than the construction with *dyal* is used regularly for parts of the body and terms of kinship and family relation, e.g. *yedd m̤m̤i* 'my mother's hand', *bent xti* 'my sister's daughter', *mṛat xay* 'my brother's wife'.

C. Feminine nouns ending in *-a* regularly change the *-a* to *-t* before taking possessive endings or occurring as the first noun of a construct state, e.g. *magana* 'watch', *maganti* 'my watch', *magant ḅḅa* 'my father's watch'. The word *mṛa* 'woman, wife' adds a *-t, e.g. mṛatek* 'your (sg.) wife', *mṛat xay* 'my brother's wife'.

D. Note that *yedd* 'hand' is feminine, even though ending in a consonant, e.g. *yeddi ḍḍeṛṛet* 'my hand got hurt', etc.

III. Exercises.

Go through the text of this lesson and change all statements to questions and all questions to statements. Simultaneously change all forms for 'I', 'me', and 'my' to the forms for 'you', and 'your' (sg.) and vice versa. Read the resulting new sentences out loud.

IV. Vocabulary.

ḍḍeṛṛ	to get hurt
škaṛa	satchel, briefcase
yedd (f.)	hand (of body only, not of clock)
ɛadita	accident, wreck
ɛămma	paternal aunt (i.e. father's sister)

LESSON SIXTY-SIX

I. Text.

ɛṭani waɛed le-ktab.	He gave me a book.
ɛṭah-li.	He gave it (m.) to me.
ɛṭitu ṭ-ṭumubil dyali.	I gave him my car.
ɛṭitha-lu	I gave it (f.) to him.
werritih t-tṣaweṛ?	Did you show him the pictures?
werritihom-lu?	Did you show them to him?
ɛlaš werrak l-konnaš dyali?	Why did he show you my notebook?
ɛlaš werrah-lek?	Why did he show it (m.) to you?
ɛṭawha le-bṛa dyali.	They gave her my letter.
ɛṭawha-lha.	They gave it (f.) to her.
ɛṭathom l-ɛonwan dyalha.	She gave them her address.
ɛṭatu-lhom.	She gave it (m.) to them.
ɛṭinah le-hdiya dyalek.	We gave him your (sg.) present.
ɛṭinaha-lu.	We gave it (f.) to him.
ɛṭana le-hdiya dyalek.	He gave us your present.
ɛṭaha-lna.	He gave it (f.) to us.
ɛṭitiwhom l-qešwaša ž-ždida?	Did you (pl.) give them the new toy?
ɛṭitiwha-lhom?	Did you give it to them?
ɛṭawkom atay?	Did they give you (pl.) tea?
ɛṭaweh-lkom?	Did they give it to you?
werritu ṭ-ṭiyyaṛa ž-ždida.	I showed him the new airplane.
werritha-lu.	I showed it (f.) to him.
werrani ṭ-ṭiyyaṛa dyalu.	He showed me his airplane.
werraha-li.	He showed it (f.) to me.
ɛṭawna ẓ-ẓṛabi dyalhom.	They gave us their rugs.
ɛṭawhom-lna.	They gave them to us.
werrinahom ẓ-ẓṛabi ž-ždad dyalna.	We showed them our new rugs.
werrinahom-lhom.	We showed them to them.

ʕṭatkom le-ḥwayež?	Did she give you (pl.) the clothes?
ʕṭathom-lkom?	Did she give them to you?
ʕṭitiwha le-ḥwayež?	Did you (pl.) give her the clothes?
ʕṭitiwhom-lha?	Did you give them to her?

II. Grammatical Notes.

A. Reread Grammatical Note **B** of Lesson 60.

B. The verb *ʕṭa* 'to give' is different from most other verbs with respect to pronoun endings. When 'to me', 'to you', 'to him', etc. are expressed with this verb, the forms with *l-* 'to, for' (as given in Lesson 60) are used only if the verb already has 'him (it)', 'her (it)', or 'them' as an object, e.g. *ʕṭahom-lha* 'he gave them to her'. If the object to be given is a noun, the equivalent of 'to me', 'to you' etc. is expressed by the ordinary pronoun endings without the use of *l-* 'to, for', e.g. *ʕṭani le-ktab* 'he gave me the book'. The same pattern is usually followed with *werra,* e.g. *werrinaha-lu* 'we showed it (f.) to him', *werrawna t-tṣaweṛ* 'they showed us the pictures'.

III. Exercises.

Note: As the exercises are done, read the resulting new sentences out loud.

A. Go through the text and make all the sentences negative, e.g. change *ʕṭahom-lha* to *ma-ʕṭahom-lha-š.*

B. Go through the text and change all the perfect tense forms to future forms. Make all the future forms both positive and negative, e.g. change *werrawna t-tṣaweṛ* first to *ġad-iwerriwna t-tṣaweṛ* and then to *ma-ġad-iwerriwna-š t-tṣaweṛ.*

IV. Vocabulary.

hdiya	gift, present
ṭiyyaṛa	airplane

LESSON SIXTY-SEVEN

I. Text.

ḅḅa kan ka-itkellem mɛaha.	My father was talking with her.
kan ka-itkellem mɛaha mnin dxelt.	He was talking with her when I came in.
ma-kan-š ka-itkellem mɛaha mnin dxelt.	He wasn't talking with her when I came in.
konti ka-ttkellem mnin dxelna?	Were you talking when we came in?
d-drari dexlu mnin kont ka-nexdem.	The children came in when I was working.
ma-kont-š ka-nexdem mnin dexlu d-drari.	I wasn't working when the children came in.
kanet ka-tekteb le-bṛawat.	She was writing letters.
ma-mšat-š mɛahom ɛla ḥăqq-aš kanet ka-tekteb le-bṛawat.	She didn't go with them because she was writing letters.
ɛṭitu-lu mnin ṭeḷbu menni.	I gave it to him when he asked me for it.
ɛṭitu-lu ɛla ḥăqq-aš ṭeḷbu menni.	I gave it to him because he asked me for it.
ṭḷebt mennu le-flus.	I asked him for some money.
kont ḥaẓeq.	I was broke.
ṭḷebt mennu le-flus ɛla ḥăqq-aš kont ḥaẓeq.	I asked him for some money because I was broke.
ṭḷebt le-flus men ḅḅa.	I asked my father for some money.
ma-ɛṭahom-li-š.	He didn't give me any [literally 'them to me', since *flus 'money'* is pl.].

II. Grammatical Notes.

A. The Moroccan equivalent for the English past progressive ('was doing', 'were going', etc.) is the perfect of *kan* 'to be' followed by the durative tense.

Summarized below are the examples of this construction which occur in this lesson.

kan ka-itkellem	he was talking
ma-kan-š ka-itkellem	He wasn't talking
konti ka-ttkellem	you (sg.) were talking
ma-kont-š ka-nexdem	I wasn't working
kanet ka-tekteb	she was writing

Note that this construction is made negative by using the regular negative form of *kan* 'to be', e.g. *ma-kont-š ka-nexdem.*

B. The syntax of Moroccan *ṭḷeb* 'to ask for' is different from its English equivalent. The thing asked for is placed as the immediate object of *ṭḷeb,* e.g. *ṭḷebt le-flus* 'I asked for some money'. The person or source asked is introduced by *men* 'of, from', as in *ṭḷebt le-flus men ḅḅa* 'I asked my father for some money'. Note that the somewhat more formal English word 'request' functions exactly like Moroccan *ṭḷeb,* e.g. 'I requested some money from my father'.

C. The preposition *men* 'from' doubles the final *n* before pronoun endings, e.g. *menni* 'from me', *mennu* 'from him', etc.

III. Exercises.

Change the verb in the sentences below to the past progressive form, both positive and negative, e.g. change *qṛa l-žarida* first to *kan ka-iqṛa l-žarida* and then to *ma-kan-š ka-iqṛa l-žarida.* Read the resulting sentences out loud.

1. *qṛit l-žarida.*
2. *ġeslet le-ɛwayež.*
3. *xdemna fe-l-keššina.*
4. *ġad-yeɛmel l-xedma bekri.*
5. *ɛawenti xak f-le-ɛsab?*
6. *ddaw d-drari le-ṣ-ṣbiṭaṛ?*
7. *ġad-nteṛžem had le-bṛawat.*
8. *ɛămmṛet l-kisan b-atay.*
9. *dar bezzaf de-n-năɛnaɛ fe-l-berrad.*
10. *lbest l-kebbuṭ ž-ždid dyali.*

IV. Vocabulary.

dxel	to come in, to go in, to enter
mnin	when (conjunction only, not used as 'when?' in questions)

tkellem	to talk, to converse
ṭḷeb	to ask for (see Grammatical Note **B**)
ḥaẓeq	broke, without money
ɛla ḥăqq-aš	because

LESSON SIXTY-EIGHT

I. Text.

kont ka-nbiɛ	I used to sell, I sold (habitually)
kont ka-nbiɛ ṭ-ṭumubilat.	I used to sell cars.
ɛam luwwel kont ka-nbiɛ ṭ-ṭumubilat.	Last year I sold automobiles.
be-l-ḥăqq daba ka-nbiɛ l-biškliṭat.	But now I sell bicycles.
kan ka-imši	he used to go, he went (habitually)
kan ka-imši l-l-xedma fe-t-tesɛud.	He used to go to work at nine o'clock.
daba ka-imši fe-s-setta.	Now he goes at six.
š-šheṛ lli daz kan ka-imši l-lxedma fe-l-ɛăšṛa.	Last month he went to work at ten o'clock.
had š-šheṛ ka-imši fe-s-sebɛa.	This month he goes at seven.
kanet ka-tɛawen ṃṃha fe-l-xedma.	She used to help her mother at work.
kanet ka-tɛawen xaha f-le-ḥsab mnin kan ṣġiṛ.	She helped her brother in arithmetic when he was little.
konti ka-teddiha le-s-sinima koll nhaṛ?	Did you use to take her to the movies every day?
konti ka-teddiha le-s-sinima koll nhaṛ ɛam luwwel?	Did you take her to the movies every day last year?
ka-teɛṭihom š-šekḷaṭ.	She is giving them some chocolate.
dima ka-teɛṭihom š-šekḷaṭ mnin ka-iṭeḷḅuh mennha.	She always gives them some chocolate when they ask her for it.

kanet ka-teƐṭi š-šekḷaṭ le-d-drari mnin šeftha.	She was giving the children some chocolate when I saw her.
kanet ka-teƐṭihom ši-šwiya d-le-flus koll nhaṛ.	She used to give them a little money every day.
Ɛam luwwel kanet ka-teƐṭihom le-flus dyalhom nhaṛ s-sebt.	Last year she gave them their money on Saturday.
xeḷḷeṣ	to pay
had š-šheṛ ka-ixeḷḷṣu l-xeddama nhaṛ s-sebt.	This month they're paying the workers on Saturday.
š-šheṛ lli daz kanu ka-ixeḷḷṣuhom nhaṛ le-xmis.	Last month they paid them on Thursday.
kanu ka-ixeḷḷṣuhom meṛṛtayn fe-š-šheṛ	They used to pay them twice a month.

II. Grammatical Notes.

Lesson 67 showed the Moroccan construction *kan* plus the durative tense as equivalent to the English past progressive, e.g. *kan ka-itkellem mƐaha* 'He was talking with her'. The text sentences of this lesson show that this Moroccan construction also translates the English 'used to' construction, e.g. *kont ka-nbiƐ ṭ-ṭumubilat* 'I used to sell cars'. Whether a given occurrence of this Moroccan construction is to be translated as equivalent to the English past progressive or the English 'used to' construction depends on context.

There is a third important usage for the Moroccan construction in question. It is used to translate the English past tense when a repetitive or habitual situation is referred to. Note that it is incorrect to use the Moroccan perfect for the English past tense in such cases. For clarity, the examples given in the text are cited together below:

Ɛam luwwel kont ka-nbiƐ ṭ-ṭumubilat.	Last year I sold automobiles.
š-šheṛ lli daz kan ka-imši l-l-xedma fe-l-Ɛăšṛa.	Last month he went to work at ten o'clock.
kanet ka-tƐawen xaha f-le-ḥsab mnin kan ṣġiṛ.	She helped her brother in arithmetic when he was little.

konti ka-teddiha le-s-sinima koll nhaṛ ɛam luwwel?	Did you take her to the movies every day last year?
ɛam luwwel kanet ka-teɛṭihom le-flus dyalhom nhaṛ s-sebt.	Last year she gave them their money on Saturday.
š-šheṛ lli daz kanu ka-ixeḷḷṣuhom nhaṛ le-xmis.	Last month they paid them on Thursday.

III. Exercises.

A. Go through the text and make all the verb forms negative. Read the resulting forms and sentences out loud.

B. Go through the six sentences listed in the Grammatical Notes above and apply the following changes to them, reading each resulting new sentence out loud as it is formed:

1. Change all 'he' forms to 'she' forms.
2. Change all 'she' forms to 'he' forms.
3. Change all 'I' forms to 'you (sg.)' forms. Make these sentences questions.
4. Change all 'you (sg.)' forms to 'I' forms.
5. Change all 'he' and 'she' forms to 'they' forms.

IV. Vocabulary.

lli daz	which passed, last (m.)
š-šheṛ lli daz	last month
mennha	from her
xeḷḷeṣ	to pay

LESSON SIXTY-NINE

I. Text.

ḥsen	better
l-kebbuṭ dyalek ḥsen men dyali.	Your coat is better than mine.
ka-ixdem ḥsen menni.	He works better than I do.
l-xedma dyalu mezyana ɛla dyali.	His work is better than mine.

ṭwil	tall, long
ṭwel	taller, longer
xay ṭwel menni.	My brother is taller than I am.
xtu ṭwila ɛlih.	His sister is taller than he is.
nqa	cleaner
had l-bit nqa men l-axoṛ.	This room is cleaner than the other one.
ḥla	sweeter
l-qehwa de-l-yum ḥla men de-l-bareḥ.	Today's coffee is sweeter than yesterday's.
wsăɛ	broader, wider
had ẓ-ẓenqa wsăɛ men hadik.	This street is wider than that one.
sxun	hot
sxen	hotter
dak l-lḥăm sxun bezzaf.	That meat is very hot.
l-makla kanet sxuna bezzaf.	The food was too hot.
l-yum sxen men l-bareḥ.	Today is hotter than yesterday.
ḍyeq	narrower
had l-bab ḍyeq men l-oẋṛa.	This door is narrower than the other one.
š-šeṛžem de-l-bit dyali ḍyeq men dyalu.	The window of my room is narrower than his.
had le-ḥwayež mwessxin ɛla haduk.	These clothes are dirtier than those.
ana kbeṛ mennu.	I'm bigger than he is.
xay feṛḥan kteṛ menni l-had š-ši.	My brother is happier than I am about this.

II. Grammatical Notes.

A. The comparative form of the adjective in Moroccan has the pattern *CCeC* (sometimes *CCăC* when a ɛ is present), e.g. *sxen* 'hotter'. However, this comparative is usually formed only from adjectives which have the pattern

CCiC, CaCeC, or *CiyyeC,* although there are a few examples from other types of adjectives. Six such forms are given in this lesson:

ḍyeq	(from *ḍiyyeq* 'narrow')	narrower
kbeṛ	(from *kbir* 'big')	bigger
sxen	(from *sxun* 'hot')	hotter
ṭwel	(from *ṭwil* 'long, tall')	longer, taller
wsăɛ	(from *waseɛ* 'wide')	wider
ḥsen	(from *mezyan* 'good')	better

B. There are a few comparatives with the pattern *CCa,* e.g. *nqa* 'cleaner' and *ḥla* 'sweeter'.

C. A common way of expressing comparison is with the simple adjective followed by *ɛla* 'on, with respect to', e.g. *xtu ṭwila ɛlih* 'His sister is taller than he is'. Comparison is occasionally expressed with *kteṛ* 'more', as in *xay feṛḥan kteṛ menni l-had š-ši* 'My brother is happier about this than I am'. This use of *kteṛ* in comparisons is, however, much rarer than the corresponding use of 'more' in English.

III. Exercises.

Cover the left-hand column of comparative forms in Grammatical Note **A** above and try to recall or reconstruct them from looking at the adjectival forms in the parentheses to the right of them.

IV. Vocabulary.

ḍyeq	narrower
kbeṛ	bigger
kteṛ	more
nqa	cleaner
sxen	hotter
sxun	hot
ṭwel	longer, taller
wsăɛ	wider
ḥla	sweeter
ḥsen	better

LESSON SEVENTY

I. Text.

had ẓ-ẓeṛbiya kḥăl men l-oxṛin.	This rug is blacker than the others.
had l-buḷa ṣfeṛ men hadik.	This light-bulb is yellower than that one.
hada huwa le-kbir.	This is the biggest one.
ma-kayen-š weld fe-l-meḍṛaṣa mwessex bḥalu.	He's the dirtiest boy in school.
š-men	which, what
š-men fqi qal-lek dak š-ši?	Which teacher told you that?
š-men ktub bġiti?	Which books do you want?
aš-en huwa, šnuwa, šnu	what, which (m.)
aš-en hiya, šniya, šni	what, which (f.)
aš-en huma, šnuma	what, which (pl.)
šnuma had le-ḥwayež?	What are these things?
šniya l-mezyana fihom?	Which one of them is the best?

II. Grammatical Notes.

A. There is a small group of adjectives with the characteristic pattern *CCeC* for the masculine singular, *CeCCa* for the feminine singular, and *CuCeC* for the plural. Most of these adjectives share the semantic characteristic of referring to color or some sort of physical characteristic, often a defect. They are conventionally referred to as 'adjectives of color and defect'. Adjectives of this sort so far encountered are:

byeḍ, biḍa, buyeḍ	white	*xḍeṛ, xeḍṛa, xuḍeṛ*	green
kḥăl, keḥla, kuḥel	black	*ẓṛeq, ẓeṛqa, ẓuṛeq*	blue
ṣfeṛ, ṣefṛa, ṣufeṛ	yellow	*ḥmeṛ, ḥămṛa, ḥumeṛ*	red

Note the appearance of *i* instead of *ey* in the feminine *biḍa* 'white' as well as a couple of cases of *ă* instead of *e* next to the *consonant* ḥ. The adjectives of color and defect serve as their own comparative forms, e.g. *kḥăl* means both 'black' and 'blacker'.

B. There is no specific Moroccan form corresponding to English superlatives in '-est' as in 'biggest', 'dirtiest', etc. Equivalent meanings are expressed in a variety of ways. The most common is the simple adjective with the definite article, as in *hada huwa le-kbir* 'This one is the biggest', 'This is the big one'. Likewise compare two possible translations of *my-kayen-š weld fe-l-meḍṛaṣa lli mwessexx bƐalu* 'He's the dirtiest boy in the school' or 'There isn't a boy in the school (who's) as dirty as he is'.

C. The simplest Moroccan equivalent for 'which' before a noun is *š-men,* e.g. *š-men ktub bġiti?* 'Which books do you want?' Equally common are paraphrases on the pattern of 'Who is the (man, woman, boy, etc.) that . . .' and 'What is (are) the (book, shirt, things, etc.) that . . .', e.g. *škun huwa s-siyyed lli džuwwež* 'Which man got married?' and *šmen ṭ-ṭubis iweṣṣeḷni l-b-ḅenk?* 'Which bus will get me to the bank?'

Several equivalents must be distinguished for English 'which one(s)'. Referring to people, *škun* is used, and masculine, feminine, or plural is signaled by an immediately following *huwa* 'he', *hiya* 'she', or *huma* 'they', as in *škun hiya lli džuwwẓet?* 'Which one (f.) got married?' Referring to things, the form *aš-en* (*aš* 'what' plus a linking *-en*) is used, with masculine, feminine, and plural once again being signaled by a following *huwa, hiya,* or *huma.* In conversation, the masculine is usually shortened to *šnuwa* or *šnu,* the feminine to *šniya* or *šni,* and the plural to *šnuma,* e.g. *šnuma lli ġad-tăƐṭih?* 'Which ones are you going to give him?'

III. Exercises.

For the statements in the text, construct pertinent questions. For the questions in the text, construct pertinent answers.

IV. Vocabulary.

aš-en huwa, šnuwa, šnu	what, which
aš-en hiya, šniya, šni (f.)	
aš-en huma, šnuma (pl.)	
š-men	which, what
Ɛwayež	things

LESSON SEVENTY-ONE

I. Text.

ka-neġsel šăεṛi meṛṛtayn fe-š-šher.	I wash my hair twice a month.
šăεṛi ḥmeṛ.	My hair is red.
ma-εăndu-š bezzaf de-š-šεăṛ.	He doesn't have much hair.
ṭaḥet waḥed š-šăεṛa f-le-ḥrira dyali.	A hair fell in my soup.
žbeṛt waḥed š-šăεṛa ḥămṛa fe-l-kebbuṭ dyali.	I found a red hair on my coat.
ḥăyyed had š-šăεṛa men εăyni.	Take this hair out of my eye.
mša le-ṣ-ṣuq u-šra l-biḍ.	He went to the market and bought some eggs.
ma-tensa-š l-biḍ l-yum.	Don't forget the eggs today.
had l-biḍ mezyan bezzaf.	These eggs are very good.
klit l-biḍ l-yum.	I ate eggs today.
ka-yakol l-biḍ bezzaf.	He eats eggs a lot.
had l-biḍa ma-ši mezyana.	This egg isn't good.
bġit žuž de-l-biḍat.	I want two eggs.
ka-yakol tlata de-l-biḍat koll ṣbaḥ.	He eats three eggs every morning.
dima ka-ddir le-bṣel fe-le-ḥrira.	She always puts onion(s) in the soup.
šrina bezzaf d-le-bṣel.	We bought a lot of onions.
dima ka-nakol le-bṣel f-le-ḥrira dyali.	I always eat onion(s) in my soup.
žbeṛt waḥed l-beṣla fe-z-zlafa dyali.	I found an onion in my bowl.
εămlet tlata de-l-beṣlat fe-le-ḥrira.	She put three onions in the soup.

II. Grammatical Notes.

There are a number of nouns in Moroccan which are masculine singular in form but which have a collective meaning. Quite often these nouns are only translatable into English as plurals, e.g. *biḍ* 'eggs'. Sometimes the corresponding English word is also a collective, e.g. *šεăṛ* 'hair'. An important difference is that English 'hair' is either collective (e.g. 'she washed her hair') or a singular (e.g. 'I found a hair in my soup'), depending on use. Moroccan collectives cannot be used as singulars.

Singulars, called 'nouns of unity', are derived from collective nouns by adding the feminine ending *-a,* e.g. collective *biḍ* 'eggs', noun of unity *biḍa* '(an) egg'. If the structure of the noun calls for it, inversion occurs with the addition of the *-a* to form nouns of unity, e.g. collective *bṣeḷ* 'onions', noun of unity *beṣḷa* '(an) onion'; collective *šεăṛ* 'hair', noun of unity *šăεṛa* '(a) hair'.

Nouns of unity form plurals by adding *-t,* e.g. noun of unity *biḍa* pl. *biḍat.* These plurals are used only in counting, e.g. *žuž d-l-biḍat* 'two eggs'. Except in counting, the Moroccan collective is used in those cases where English uses the plural, e.g. *šra l-biḍ* 'he bought some eggs'. Three collective nouns are introduced in this lesson:

biḍ	eggs	*bṣeḷ*	onions	*šεăṛ*	hair
biḍa	(an) egg	*beṣḷa*	(an) onion	*šăεṛa*	(a) hair

III. Exercises.

Take the following five words and use each one of them successively in forming phrases with the collective words *biḍ, bṣeḷ,* and *šεăṛ*.

1. *bezzaf.*
2. *ši-šwiya.*
3. *tlata.*
4. *tmenya.*
5. *εăšṛa.*

IV. Vocabulary.

biḍ (collective)	eggs
bṣeḷ (collective)	onions
kla (*ka-yakol*)	to eat

šεăṛ (collective) — hair
noun of unity *šăεṛa*
εăyni — my eye.

Note: In future lessons 'collective' will be abbreviated as 'coll.' and 'noun of unity' as 'n.u'.

LESSON SEVENTY-TWO

I. Text.

bġit ntkellem mεak qbel-ma iži. — I want to talk to you (sg.) before he comes.

ṣifeṭna-lu l-bakit qbel-ma iži. — We sent him the package before he came.

werrih le-bṛa qbel-ma tṣifeṭha. — Show him the letter before you send it.

werritih le-bṛa qbel-ma tṣifeṭha? — Did you show him the letter before you sent it?

kemmel — to finish, complete

dima ka-ikemmel l-xedma dyalu qbel-ma imši le-ḍ-ḍaṛ. — He always finishes his work before he goes home.

dima kan ka-ikemmel l-xedma dyalu qbel-ma imši le-ḍ-ḍaṛ. — He always used to finish his work before he went home.

xeṣṣni — I have to, I must

xeṣṣni nkemmel had l-xedma qbel-ma nemši. — I have to finish this work before I go.

xeṣṣni nkemmel qbel-ma iži ḅḅa. — I have to finish before my father comes.

xeṣṣni nšuf ḅḅak qbel-ma ikemmel l-xedma. — I have to see your father before he finishes the work.

šeftu qbel-ma ikemmel l-xedma. — I saw him before he finished the work.

ġad-teġsel yeddik qbel-ma takol? — Are you going to wash your hands before you eat?

ġselti yeddik qbel-ma takol?	Did you wash your hands before you ate?
xeṣṣna	we have to, we must
xeṣṣna nġeslu yeddina qbel-ma naklu.	We have to wash our hands before we eat.
xeṣṣna nkemmlu l-xedma qbel-ma naklu.	We have to finish the work before we eat.
xeṣṣna nkemmlu l-xedma qbel-ma nṭeḷbu mennha le-flus.	We have to finish the work before we ask her for the money.
kemmelna l-xedma qbel-ma nṭeḷbu le-flus mennha.	We finished the work before we asked her for the money.
xeṣṣu	he has to, he must
xeṣṣu ikemmel qbel-ma nxeḷḷṣuh.	He has to finish before we pay him.
xeṣṣu ixeḷḷeṣ l-xeddama qbel-ma imši.	He has to pay the workers before he goes.

II. Grammatical Notes.

A. The word *xeṣṣ* takes the pronoun endings usually associated with verbs (These endings are discussed in the Grammatical Notes of Lessons 53-57), and renders English 'have to, must', e.g. *xeṣṣni* 'I have to, I must', *xeṣṣu* 'he has to, he must', *xeṣṣna* 'we have to, we must', etc. The verb form following *xeṣṣ* is always in the imperfect, e.g. *xeṣṣna naklu* 'we have to eat', etc.

B. The conjunction *qbel-ma* is regularly used before imperfect verb forms, regardless of whether English usage calls for a past tense or a present tense, e.g. *qbel-ma takol* is translated either as 'before you eat' or 'before you ate.'

C. The remaining durative forms of *ka-yakol* 'he eats' are totally predictable. The prefixes are regular, e.g. *ka-nakol 'I eat', ka-takol* 'you (sg.) eat'. The plural suffixes are regular, and the *o* of the singular is elided, e.g. *ka-naklu* 'we eat', etc.

III. Exercises.

A. Below are a number of short sentence pairs. Turn them into one longer sentence by joining them with *qbel-ma*. Be sure always to use the imperfect tense after *qbel-ma*. As an illustration, the two short sentences *kemmelt l-xedma* 'I finished the work' and *mšit le-ḍ-ḍaṛ* 'I went home' can be combined into *kemmelt l-xedma qbel-ma nemši le-ḍ-ḍaṛ* 'I finished the work before I went home'. Read the resulting longer sentences out loud.

1. *xeṣṣna nemšiw.*
   ġad-išufuna.
2. *bġina nšufu d-drari.*
   ġad-imšiw l-l-meḍṛaṣa.
3. *waš tebġi takol daba?*
   ġad-nemšiw le-s-sinima.
4. *lbest le-ʕwayež ž-ždad dyali.*
   tkellemt mʕa dak l-bent.
5. *xeṣṣu iʕăyyed duk le-ʕwayež le-mwessxin.*
   ġad-temši mʕah le-s-sinima.
6. *qṛit l-žarida.*
   klit le-ġda.
7. *ġeslet le-ʕwayež.*
   klat.
8. *ʕămmṛet l-kisan b-atay.*
   žaw n-nas.
9. *ddaw d-drari le-ṣ-ṣbiṭaṛ?*
   ḍḍeṛṛu.
10. *dar bezzaf de-n-năʕnaʕ fe-l-berrad.*
    kebbu atay fe-l-kisan.

B. Take each one of the twenty sentences above and use the proper form of *xeṣṣ* with the verb, changing the verb to the imperfect. For example, change *qṛit* 'I read' to *xeṣṣni neqṛa* 'I have to read', etc. Read each resulting new sentence out loud.

IV. Vocabulary.

kemmel	to finish
qbel-ma	before (conjunction; see Grammatical Note **B**)
xeṣṣ	have to, must, (see Grammatical Note **A**)
yeddik	your (sg.) hands
yeddina	our hands

LESSON SEVENTY-THREE

I. Text.

kont bġit nemši le-s-sinima, be-l-ɛăqq ma-kanu-š ɛăndi le-flus.	I wanted to go to the movies, but I didn't have the money.
kan bġa išufha qbel-ma temši.	He wanted to see her before she left.
ma-kanet-š bġat tɛawenni, waxxa kanu ɛăndha le-flus.	She didn't want to help me, even though she had the money.
ḅḅa ma-bġa-š ixellini nemši mɛahom.	My father wouldn't let me go with them.
ṭḷebna mennhom iɛawnuna, be-l-ɛăqq ma-bġaw-š.	We asked them to help us, but they wouldn't.
ɛlaš ma-bġat-š tqulha-lek?	Why wouldn't she tell you?
ɛlaš ma-bġat-š?	Why did she refuse?
ɛlaš ma-bġiti-š dži mɛaya dak n-nhaṛ?	Why wouldn't you come with me the other day?
ɛlaš l-xeddama ma-bġaw-š ixedmu l-bareɛ?	Why did the workers refuse to work yesterday?
ka-ikmi.	he smokes
ka-nebġi nekmi.	I like to smoke.
ma-ka-nebġiha-š bezzaf.	I don't like her very much.
had ṛ-ražel ka-ibġiweh n-nas bezzaf.	People like this man a lot.
had l-makla ka-teɛžebni bezzaf.	I like this food a lot.
ma-ka-tɛežbek-š l-xedma dyalek?	Don't you like your work?
ma-ɛžebha-š dak atay.	She didn't like that tea.
ma-ɛežbuni-š.	I didn't like them.
ma-kanet-š ka-teɛžebni s-sinima.	I didn't use to like the movies.
bġaw idexlu men š-šeṛžem.	They tried to get in through the window.
had ṭ-ṭumubil ka-tebġi z-zit bezzaf.	This car needs (uses) a lot of oil.

II. Grammatical Notes.

A. Lessons 48 and 62 pointed out some details of the meaning and use of the verb *bġa*. The past tense of English 'to want' is rendered by the perfect of *kan* 'to be' followed by the perfect of *bġa*. Compare *bġit nemši* 'I want to go' and *kont bġit nemši* 'I wanted to go'.

In addition to its basic meanings of 'to want' and 'would like', *bġa* has a variety of other meanings and uses. In the negative perfect it is usually best translated as 'wouldn't' or 'refused', e.g. *ḅḅa ma-bġa-š ixellini nemši* 'My father wouldn't let me go', or *ɛlaš l-xeddama ma-bġaw-š ixedmu l-bareɛ?* 'Why did the workers refuse to work yesterday?' In this negative meaning, usually only context distinguishes between a reference to present or past time. For example, *ɛlaš ma-bġat-š tqulha-lek?* can be translated either as 'Why wouldn't she tell you?' or 'Why won't she (doesn't she want to) tell you?'.

Another important meaning is 'to like, to be fond of', as in *ma-ka-nebġiha-š bezzaf* 'I don't like her very much'. In this sense, the perfect tense of *bġa* is not used as equivalent to the English present tense. The last two sentences of the text of this lesson illustrate uses of *bġa* in the sense of 'to try' and 'to need, to use'.

B. The use of *bġa* as an equivalent for English 'to like' is less common than *ɛžeb* 'to please', as in *ma-ɛežbuni-š* 'I didn't like them'.

III. Exercises.

Go through the sentences in the exercise section of Lesson 40 and change them as follows: Form new sentences by beginning with *ɛlaš* 'why' and a negative perfect tense form of *bġa* according to the verb at the beginning of each sentence. In the process, the verb following *bġa* must be changed to the imperfect. For example, change *ɛṭat le-bṛa l-l-qaḍi* 'She gave the letter to the judge' to *ɛlaš ma-bġat-š teɛṭi le-bṛa l-l-qaḍi?* 'Why did she refuse to give the letter to the judge?' As each new sentence is formed, read it aloud.

IV. Vocabulary.

dak n-nhaṛ	the other day
kma (*ka-ikmi*)	to smoke
waxxa	even though, although
ɛetta	until
ɛžeb	to please

LESSON SEVENTY-FOUR

I. Text.

dima ka-idxol fe-l-xemsa.	He always comes in at five o'clock.
dima ka-idxol žwayeh l-xemsa.	He always comes in around five o'clock.
ɛlaš dima ka-ddxol bekri?	Why do you always come in early?
xeṣṣek ddxol bekri l-yum.	You have to come in early today.
ka-ddxol žwayeh t-tlata nhaṛ le-xmis.	She comes in around three on Thursdays.
xeṣṣha ddxol fe-ṛ-ṛebɛa l-yum.	She has to go in at four today.
d-drari dima ka-idexlu fe-t-tlata.	The children always go in at three.
l-xeddama dima ka-idexlu žwayeh s-setta.	The workers always come in around six.
had ṛ-ṛažel dima ka-idxol mɛăṭṭel.	This man always comes in late.
had le-mṛa dima ka-ddxol mɛăṭṭla.	This woman always comes in late.
had n-nas dima ka-idexlu mɛăṭṭḷin.	These people always come in late.
waš ġad-ddexlu bekri ġedda?	Are you going to come in early tomorrow?
xeṣṣkom ddexlu bekri ġedda.	You have to come in early tomorrow.
xeṣṣhom idexlu daba.	They have to go in now.
xeṣṣhom idexlu qbel-ma iži ḅḅahom.	They have to go in before their father comes.

II. Grammatical Notes.

A. The durative of *dxel* 'to enter' has an *o* in it, i.e. *ka-idxol* 'he enters'. This *o* drops with inversion in the plural forms, e.g. *ka-idexlu* 'they enter'.

B. Note the form *ka-ddxol* 'you (sg.) enter, she enters'. Instead of the expected durative prefix *te-* (as in *ka-tekteb* 'you write, she writes') a *d* appears. This is the usual pattern if the following consonant is *d,* as in the case with the verb *dxel.*

C. Note the masculine, feminine, and plural forms for 'late', m. *mɛăṭṭel,* f. *mɛăṭṭla,* and pl. *mɛăṭṭlin.* They are used in agreement with the thing or person referred to, e.g. m. *huwa mɛăṭṭel* 'he's late', f. *hiya mɛăṭṭla* 'she's late' pl. *huma mɛăṭṭlin* 'they're late'.

III. Exercises.

Go through the twenty-five sentences of the exercise section of Lesson 40. Make new sentences out of them by using an appropriate form of *xeṣṣ* 'have to, must' with the necessary changes of the verb forms. For example, *ɛṭat le-bṛa l-l-qaḍi* should be changed to *xeṣṣha teɛṭi le-bra l-l-qaḍi.* Any further changes needed to make good sense should also be made, e.g. the adverb *l-bareɛ* 'yesterday' must be dropped from some of the sentences. Read each new sentence out loud as it is formed.

IV. Vocabulary.

mɛăṭṭel	late
mɛăṭṭla (f.)	
mɛăṭṭlin (pl.)	
žwayeh	about, around (with reference to time of day)

LESSON SEVENTY-FIVE

I. Text.

kif-aš ka-texdem had l-makina?	How does this machine work?
werrini kif-aš ka-texdem had l-makina?	Show me how this machine works.
kif-aš xeṣṣni nxeddem had l-makina?	How am I supposed to operate this machine?

ġad-nwerrik kif-aš xeṣṣek txeddemha.	I'll show you how you have to use it.
kif-aš nxeddem had l-makina?	How do I work this machine?
ġad-nwerriwek kif-aš txeddemha.	We'll show you how to work it.
kif-aš nkemmlu l-xedma dyalna fe-l-weqt?	How can we finish our work on time?
iwerriwkom kif-aš tkemmluha.	They'll show you (pl.) how to finish it.
kif-aš ka-ixedmu had l-makinat?	How do these machines work?
qul-li kif-aš ka-ixedmu had l-makinat?	Tell me how these machines work?
nqul-lek ġedda.	I'll tell you tomorrow.
nqul-lek ġedda kif-aš ka-ixedmu.	I'll tell you how they work tomorrow.
qal-li kif-aš nxeddem ṭ-ṭumubil dyalu.	He told me how to operate his car.
qul-li kif-aš nxeddem ṭ-ṭumubil dyalek.	Tell me how to operate your car.
qolt-lek l-bareḥ kif-aš txeddemha.	I told you how to operate it yesterday.

II. Grammatical Notes.

A. This lesson shows some additional examples of the imperfect as equivalent to the English infinitive, e.g. *qolt-lek l-bareḥ kif-aš txeddemha* 'I told you how to operate it yesterday'.

In addition to this common use, the imperfect is often used to express a potential or immediately future action, e.g. *nqul-lek ġedda* 'I'll tell you tomorrow'. In questions especially this use of the imperfect shows a variety of different translations, all with the implications of immediately potential or future action. In such a question as *kif-aš nxeddem had l-makina?* 'How do I work this machine?', the Moroccan imperfect is translated by the English present tense which has a future potential reference. Or note the translation with 'can' in *kif-aš nkemmlu l-xedma dyalna fe-l-weqt?* 'How can we finish our work on time?'

B. Note the translation of *xeṣṣ* as 'supposed to' in ***kif-aš xeṣṣni nxeddem had l-makina?*** 'How am I supposed to operate this machine?'

III. Exercises.

Repeat the exercise of Lesson 74 making all the sentences into questions instead of statements.

IV. Vocabulary.

kif-aš	how
makina	machine
makinat (pl.)	
nqul-lek	I'll tell you (sg.)
xeddem	to operate, to work, to use
qal-li	he told me
qolt-lek	I told you (sg.)
qul-li	tell (sg.) me

LESSON SEVENTY-SIX

I. Text.

qal	he said, he told
qal-lek	he told me, he said that
xah mṛiḍ.	His brother is sick.
xeṣṣek dži ġedda.	You (sg.) have to come tomorrow.
qal-lek xah mṛiḍ.	He said (that) his brother was sick.
qal-lek xeṣṣek dži ġedda.	He said (that) you'd have to come tomorrow.
dima ka-iqul l-ɛăqq.	He always tells the truth.
waš had ṛ-ṛažel ka-iqul l-ɛăqq?	Is this man telling the truth?
ma-ndiru-š had l-xedma.	We won't do this work.
qolna ma-ndiru-š dak l-xedma.	We said (that) we wouldn't do that work.

ma-ġad-nemšiw-š le-s-sinima l-yum.	We aren't going to the movies today.
qolna-lha l-bareε ma-ġad-nemšiw-š le-s-sinima l-yum.	We told her yesterday that we weren't going to the movies today.
kayen l-biḍ fe-l-keššina?	Are there any eggs in the kitchen?
qolti kayen l-biḍ fe-l-keššina?	Did you say (that) there were some eggs in the kitchen?
ma-qolti-š kayen l-biḍ?	Didn't you say (that) there were some eggs?
kayna bezzaf de-l-xedma.	There's a lot of work.
qolti-lu kayna bezzaf de-l-xedma.	Did you tell him there was a lot of work?
ma-qolt-lu-š kayna bezzaf de-l-xedma.	I didn't tell him there was very much work.
kaynin bezzaf de-n-nas hna l-yum.	There are a lot of people here today.
škun lli qal-lek?	Who told you?
škun lli qal-lek kaynin bezzaf de-n-nas hna l-yum?	Who told you there were a lot of people here today?
huwa hna.	He's here.
škun lli qal-lek huwa hna?	Who told you he was here?
kan hna.	He was here.
škun lli qal-lek kan hna?	Who told you he'd been here?

II. Grammatical Notes.

A. The verb *qal* 'to say, to tell' (present tense *ka-iqul*) has *o* instead of *e* in the forms of 'I', 'we', and 'you' (sg. and pl.) in the perfect tense, e.g. *qolt* 'I said', etc.; cf. the comments on *kan* 'to be' in the Grammatical Notes of Lesson 31. As an equivalent to English 'tell', *qal* always takes the preposition *l-* 'to' before the person told, e.g. *qal-li* 'he told me', etc.

B. Notice the change of tense in such English sentence pairs as 'His brother is sick' and 'He told me his brother was sick'. After 'he told me', 'was' is used even though the implication is that the brother is still sick. As an additional example, note 'was' in 'Who told you he was (i.e., he is still at this moment) here?' Such changes of tense do not take place in Moroccan. Compare such a pair of examples as *huwa hna* 'He's here' and ***škun lli qal-lek huwa hna?*** 'Who told you he was ('and he still is at this moment I'm speaking') here?' The use of the Moroccan perfect implies previous time, as is shown in such a pair as *kan hna* 'He was here' and *škun lli qal-lek kan hna?* 'Who told you he had been ('he no longer is at this moment') here?'

C. The form *škun* 'who', as in *škun had ṛ-ṛažel?* 'Who is this man?' is almost always expanded to *škun lli* before a verb, as in *škun lli qal-lek?* 'Who told you?'

D. Note that there is no equivalent for English 'that' in such sentences as *qal-lek xah mṛiḍ* 'He said (that) his brother was sick.'

E. On the use of the imperfect in *ma-ndiru-š had l-xedma* 'We won't do this work', cf. Grammatical Note **A** of Lesson 75.

III. Exercises.

Go through the sentences of the exercise in Lesson 40 and prefix a form of 'told me' to each one of them, thus making a longer sentence. For example, from *ع ṭa l-biškliṭa l-l-bent* 'He gave the bicycle to the girl', form the sentence *qal-li ع ṭa l-biškliṭa l-l-bent* 'He told me he'd given the bicycle to the girl.'

In those cases where the subject of the verb is 'I' or 'we', use a form of 'told him'. For example, when the verb *šrina* 'we bought' is encountered in one of the sentences, it should be expanded to *qolna-lu šrina* 'we told him we bought . . .' Read the resulting sentences out loud.

IV. Vocabulary.

dar (*ka-idir*)	to do
kayen	there is
kayna (f.)	
kaynin (pl.)	there are
škun lli	who (before verbs; see Grammatical Note **C**)
(*l-*) *ح ăqq*	(the) truth

LESSON SEVENTY-SEVEN

I. Text.

ka-iġsel yeddih.	He's washing his hands.
ṃ̂ṃ̂u qalet-lu iġsel yeddih.	His mother told him to wash his hands.
ka-ikemmlu l-xedma dyalhom.	They're finishing their work.
qolna-lhom ikemmlu l-xedma dyalhom.	We told them to finish their work.
qalu-li ma-ndxol-š qbel s-setta.	They told me not to come in before six.
ma-qalu-li-š ndxol f-had s-saƐa.	They didn't tell me to come in right now.
dxel l-l-bit dyalu.	He went into his room.
ġad-idxol l-l-bit dyalu?	Is he going to go into his room?
qoltiw l-l-weld?	Did you (pl.) tell the boy?
qoltiw-lu idxol l-l-bit dyalu?	Did you tell him to go into his room?
ġad-teġsel yeddiha.	She's going to wash her hands.
škun lli qal-lha teġsel yeddiha?	Who told her to wash her hands?
d-drari ka-iġeslu yeddihom.	The children are washing their hands.
ma-ġad-tqul-š le-d-drari iġeslu yeddihom?	Aren't you going to tell the children to wash their hands?
bda	to begin ('he began')
bda ka-iġsel yeddih.	He began washing (to wash) his hands.
d-drari bdaw ka-iġeslu yeddihom.	The children began washing (to wash) their hands.

II. Grammatical Notes.

A. The imperfect tense is further used as the equivalent of the English infinitive (cf. Grammatical Note A of Lesson 61, Grammatical Note C of Lesson 62, and Grammatical Note A of Lesson 75) after forms of 'tell', as in *qalet-lu iġsel yeddih* 'She told him to wash his hands'.

B. The plural of *yedd* 'hand' is *yeddin* (this plural has not been used so far in the lessons). An irregularity is that the final *-n* is dropped before the possessive endings. The form for 'my' is *-ya,* i.e. *yeddiya* 'my hands'. The other endings are regular, e.g. *yeddik* 'your (sg.) hands', *yeddih* 'his hands', etc.

C. Note the use of the durative tense after *bda* 'to begin', as in *bda ka-iġsel yeddih* 'He began washing (to wash) his hands', *d-drari bdaw ka-iġeslu yeddihom* 'The children began washing (to wash) their hands',

D. The preposition *l-* 'to' must be used with *dxel* 'to enter', go in, come in' when a place entered is mentioned, e.g. *dxelt le-ḍ-ḍaṛ* 'I entered the house, I went into the house'.

III. Exercises.

Go through the sentences in the exercise of Lesson 40 and make the following changes. Read the resulting new sentences out loud.

1. Where the subject of the verb is 'we', prefix *qal-lna* 'he told us' to the sentence and change the verb to the imperfect, thus forming a new complex sentence. For example, change *ɛṭina le-flus l-l-xeddam* 'We gave the money to the worker' to *qal-lna neɛṭiw le-flus l-l-xeddam* 'He told us to give the money to the workers.'

2. In the other sentences, prefix *qolt-l-* 'I told' with an appropriate object ('you', 'him', 'her', 'them') and change the verb to the imperfect. For example, *xella ṣ-ṣenḍuq meɛlul* 'he left the box open' is to be changed to *qolt-lu ixelli ṣ-ṣenḍuq meɛlul* 'I told him to leave the box open'.

IV. Vocabulary.

bda (*ka-ibda*)	to begin

LESSON SEVENTY-EIGHT

I. Text.

kayen l-uqid?	Are there any matches?
la, ma-kayen wqid.	No, there aren't any matches.
la, ma-kayen-š.	No, there aren't any.
ɛlaš ma-qolti-li-š ma-kayen wqid?	Why didn't you tell me there weren't any matches?
ɛlaš ma-qolti-li-š ma-kayen-š?	Why didn't you tell me there weren't any?

kayna sinima f-had le-blad?	Is there a movie in this town?
la, ma-kayna sinima f-had le-blad.	No, there isn't a movie in this town.
la, ma-kayna-š f-had le-blad.	No, there isn't any in this town.
qolt-lu l-bareᴤ ma-kayna sinima hna.	I told him yesterday there isn't a movie here.
qolt-lu l-bareᴤ ma-kayna-š hna.	I told him yesterday there isn't any here.
kaynin bezzaf de-ṭ-ṭumubilat f-had le-blad?	Are there many cars in this town?
la, ma-kaynin-š bezzaf de-ṭ-ṭumubilat.	No, there aren't many cars.
qalu-lna ma-kaynin-š bezzaf.	They told us there weren't many.
men qbel	already, previously, beforehand
kaynin le-flus?	Is there any money?
la, ma-kaynin flus.	No, there isn't any money.
la, ma-kaynin-š.	No, there isn't any.
qolt-lek men qbel ma-kaynin-š.	I told you beforehand that there wasn't any.
kaynin l-uṛaq?	Are there any tickets?
la, ma-kaynin wṛaq.	No, there aren't any tickets.
qalet-lna men qbel ma-kaynin-š.	She told us beforehand that there weren't any.

II. Grammatical Notes.

A. The negative of the forms *kayen* (m.), *kayna* (f.) 'there is' and *kaynin* (pl.) 'there are' is made without the final *-š* when a following noun is used without the definite article. In the negative the noun is regularly without the definite article when the meaning 'any' is implied. Compare the positive *kayen l-uqid* 'there are some matches' and the negative *ma-kayen wqid* 'there aren't any matches'. There is no equivalent for English 'any', even when no noun occurs, e.g. *ma-kaynin-š* 'there aren't any'.

B. Another collective noun is introduced in this lesson, *wqid* 'matches'. The noun of unity is regular, *wqida* '(a) match' (Cf. the Grammatical Notes of Lesson 71).

III. Exercises.

Go through the text of Lesson 76. In every sentence where ***kayen, kayna,*** or ***kaynin*** occurs, form a new sentence by negating these forms. Remember that a noun following such negative forms does not take the definite article. Note that other negatives in the sentence do not need to be changed. In Moroccan, as in English, sentence types such as 'Didn't you say there were some?' and 'Didn't you say there weren't any?' are equally valid.

IV. Vocabulary.

blad (f.)	town, city
men qbel	already, previously, beforehand
wqid (coll.)	matches

LESSON SEVENTY-NINE

I. Text.

šʕal men kas?	How many glasses?
šʕal men kas d-atay?	How many glasses of tea?
šʕal men kas d-atay šṛeb?	How many glasses of tea did he drink?
šʕal šṛeb?	How many did he drink?
šṛebna ʕḍašel kas d-atay.	We drank eleven glasses of tea.
šṛebna ʕḍaš.	We drank eleven.
šʕal kayen men šeṛžem f-had ḍ-ḍaṛ?	How many windows are there in this house?
kayen ṭnašel šeṛžem.	There are twelve windows.
šʕal kayen?	How many are there?
kayen ṭnaš.	There are twelve.
šʕal kayna men makina?	How many machines are there?
šʕal ʕăndkom?	How many do you have?
ʕăndna telṭašel makina.	We have thirteen machines.
šʕăl	to light, to strike
šʕal ʕăndu men wqida f-žibu?	How many matches does he have in his pocket?
ʕăndu ṛbăʕṭaš.	He has fourteen.
šʕal šʕăl men wqida?	How many matches did he strike?
šʕăl ṛbăʕṭašel wqida.	He struck fourteen matches.

II. Grammatical Notes.

A. Numerals from eleven up are followed by singular rather than plural nouns, e.g. *ʕḍašel kas* 'eleven glasses'. For collectives (cf. the Grammatical Notes of Lesson 71), the singular noun following such numerals is the noun of unity, e.g. *ṛbăʕṭašel wqida* 'fourteen matches'.

B. The numerals from eleven through nineteen take the ending *-el* when used directly before nouns, e.g. *ʕḍaš* 'eleven' and *ʕḍašel kas* 'eleven glasses'.

C. Just as in English, the form *šʕal* 'how many' can occur without an accompanying noun, e.g. *šʕal ʕăndkom?* 'how many do you (pl.) have?' When a count noun (cf. Grammatical Note A of Lesson 40) is used with *šʕal,* it remains singular and is preceded by the preposition *men* 'of, from', *e.g. šʕal men kas?* 'how many glasses?' With collective nouns, it is the noun of unity which follows *men,* e.g. *šʕal men wqida?* 'how many matches?'

An interesting feature of sentence structure is that such forms as *kayen* 'there is' and *ʕăndi* 'I have', etc. usually come between *šʕal* and *men,* e.g. *šʕal ʕăndu men wqida?* 'How many matches does he have?' or *šʕal šʕăl men wqida?* 'How many matches did he strike?'

III. Exercises.

Go through the text of this lesson and form new phrases and sentences by substituting *bezzaf* 'a lot' for every occurrence of *šʕal* 'how many'. Bear in mind that other appropriate changes will have to be made to accompany the substitution. The substitution will turn questions into statements, and *bezzaf* requires plural rather than singular count nouns. To illustrate: the sentence *šʕal men kas d-atay šṛeb?* 'How many glasses of tea did he drink?' will become *šṛeb bezzaf de-l-kisan d-atay* 'He drank a lot of glasses of tea.'

IV. Vocabulary.

ṛbăʕṭaš (-el)	fourteen
šʕal	how many (see Grammatical Note C.)
šʕăl	to light, to strike
telṭaš (-el)	thirteen
ṭnaš (-el)	twelve
ʕḍaš (-el)	eleven

LESSON EIGHTY

I. Text.

šɛal de-n-năɛnaɛ?	How much mint?
šɛal de-n-năɛnaɛ dar f-atay?	How much mint did he put in the tea?
šɛal dar de-n-năɛnaɛ f-atay?	How much mint did he put in the tea?
šɛal d-le-flus?	How much money?
šɛal ɛăndu d-le-flus?	How much money does he have?
šɛal ɛăndu d-le-flus f-žibu?	How much money does he have in his pocket?
had ṛ-ṛažel šɛal ɛăndu d-le-flus?	How much money does this man have?
šɛal kayen d-atay?	How much tea is there?
šɛal fiha d-atay?	How much tea is there in it?
had l-berrad šɛal fih d-atay?	How much tea is there in this teapot?
šɛal kayna de-l-makla?	How much food is there?
šɛal fiha de-l-makla?	How much food is there in it?
had t-tellaža šɛal fiha de-l-makla?	How much food is there in this refrigerator?
šɛal kayen d-le-qṭen?	How much cotton is there?
šɛal fih d-le-qṭen?	How much cotton is there in it?
had ṣ-ṣenḍuq šɛal fih d-le-qṭen?	How much cotton is there in this box?
had l-xenša šɛal fiha de-ṣ-ṣuf?	How much wool is there in this bag?
had ṣ-ṣnaḍeq šɛal fihom de-l-feḍḍa?	How much silver is there in these boxes?

II. Grammatical Notes.

A. Before mass nouns (cf. Grammatical Note **A** of Lesson 40), *šɛal* is translated as 'how much'. It is joined to mass nouns by *d-, de-,* in the same way count nouns are preceded by *men*. (Cf. Grammatical Note **C** of Lesson 79), e.g. *šɛal de-l-makla?* 'How much food?'

B. The preposition *f-,* 'in' is often used with pronoun endings with the sense of 'there is, there are' understood, e.g. *šɛal fih d-le-qṭen?* 'How much cotton is there in it?' Notice the pattern whereby a noun is placed at the beginning of such a sentence with a form of *f-*, as in ***had ṣ-ṣenduq šεal fih d-le-qṭen?*** 'How much cotton is there in this box?' Such a straightforward construction as ***šεal d-le-qṭen f-had ṣ-ṣenduq?*** is also possible of course, with approximately the same meaning.

III. Exercises.

A. Form new phrases and sentences by substituting ***bezzaf*** for ***šεal*** in the text of this lesson, in a manner paralleling the instructions given for the exercises in Lesson 79.

B. Make a question out of each of the twenty-five sentences in the exercises of Lesson 40 by using ***šεal*** and making the appropriate changes. For example, the sentence ***šra žuž de-l-bulat*** 'He bought two light-bulbs' should be changed to ***šεal šra men bula?*** 'How many light-bulbs did he buy?'

IV. Vocabulary.

tellaža	refrigerator

LESSON EIGHTY-ONE

I. Text.

had ṛ-ṛažel šεal εăndu men dāṛ?	How many houses does this man have?
εăndu xemsṭaš.	He has fifteen.
had ṛ-ṛažel εăndu xemsṭašel dāṛ.	This man has fifteen houses.
šεal εăndha men weṛqa?	How many tickets does she have?
εăndha seṭṭaš.	She has sixteen.
had l-bent εăndha seṭṭašel weṛqa.	This girl has sixteen tickets.
had n-nas šεal εăndhom men ṭumubil?	How many cars do these people have?
had n-nas εăndhom sbăεṭašel ṭumubil.	These people have seventeen cars.

ɛăndhom sbăɛṭaš.	They have seventeen.
šɛal fih men makina?	How many machines does it have (in it)?
fih tmenṭaš.	It has eighteen.
had l-măɛmel šɛal fih men makina?	How many machines does this factory have?
had l-măɛmel fih tmenṭašel makina.	This factory has eighteen machines.
šɛal kayen men bit fe-ḍ-ḍaṛ dyalkom?	How many rooms are there in your house?
ḍ-ḍaṛ dyalkom šɛal fiha men bit?	How many rooms does your house have in it?
kayen tsăɛṭašel bit fe-ḍ-ḍar dyalna.	There are nineteen rooms in our house.
ḍ-ḍaṛ dyalna fiha tsăɛṭašel bit.	Our house has nineteen rooms in it.
fiha tsăɛṭaš.	It has nineteen.

II. Grammatical Notes.

A. This lesson shows a number of additional examples of *f-* 'in' plus pronoun endings with the sense of 'there is, there are' (cf. Grammatical Note **B** of Lesson 80). It is often convenient to translate such uses of *f-* 'in' with a form of 'to have', as in *šɛal fih men makina?* 'How many machines does it have in it?'

B. Such forms as *ɛăndi* 'I have', *ɛăndek* 'you (sg.) have', etc. usually render English 'have' only in the sense of possession. Compare the other equivalent of English 'have' mentioned in Grammatical Note **A** above.

C. To render 'have' or 'has' with a noun, the noun is first stated and then *ɛăndu* 'he has', *ɛăndha* 'she has', or *ɛăndhom* 'they have' is repeated after it, e.g. *had l-bent ɛăndha seṭṭašel weṛqa* 'This girl has sixteen tickets.' The construction is as if we said 'This girl, she has sixteen tickets' in English.

III. Exercises.

Parallel to the exercises of Lessons 79 and 80, make statements out of questions by substituting *bezzaf* for every occurrence of *šɛal* in the text of this lesson. Read the resulting new formations out loud.

IV. Vocabulary.

sbăɛṭaš (*-el*)	seventeen
seṭṭaš (*-el*)	sixteen
tmenṭaš (*-el*)	eighteen
tsăɛṭaš (*-el*)	nineteen
xemsṭaš (*-el*)	fifteen

LESSON EIGHTY-TWO

I. Text.

le-ɛrira fiha le-mleɛ?	Does the soup have any salt in it?
le-ɛrira šɛal fiha d-le-mleɛ?	How much salt is there in the soup?
ma-fiha ġir šwiya d-le-mleɛ.	It's only got a little bit of salt in it.
ma-fiha mleɛ.	There isn't any salt in it.
šraw ṭ-ṭɛin?	Did they buy any flour?
šɛal šraw de-ṭ-ṭɛin?	How much flour did they buy?
ma-šraw ṭɛin.	They didn't buy any (flour).
kliti l-xux?	Did you eat any peaches?
šɛal kliti men xuxa?	How many peaches did you eat?
ma-klit ġir šwiya de-l-xux.	I only ate a few peaches.
Ɛăndek ši-flus?	Do you (sg.) have any money?
šɛal Ɛăndek d-le-flus?	How much money do you have?
ma-Ɛăndi ġir šwiya d-le-flus.	I only have a little bit of money.
ma-Ɛăndi flus.	I don't have any money.
ma-Ɛăndi-š.	I don't have any.
Ɛăndu waɛed š-šelya?	Does he have a chair?
la, ma-Ɛăndu šelya.	No, he doesn't have a chair.
Ɛăndu ši-šelyat?	Does he have any chairs?
la, ma-Ɛăndu šelyat.	No, he doesn't have any chairs.
la, ma-Ɛăndu-š.	No, he doesn't have any.
šɛal Ɛăndu men šelya?	How many chairs does he have?
ma-Ɛăndu ġir šwiya de-š-šelyat.	He only has a few chairs.

had le-blad fiha ši-sinimat?	Does this town have any movies in it?
ġir šwiya.	Only a few.
la, ma-fiha sinimat.	No, it doesn't have any movies.
šςal fiha men sinima?	How many movies does it have?
ma-fiha-š.	It doesn't have any.

II. Grammatical Notes.

A. The student is already familiar with such negations as *ma-ςăndi-š* 'I don't have', etc. The use of *ġir* 'only, just, (nothing) other than' usually calls for a preceding negative, but without the final *-š* (cf. the comment on *baqi,* Grammatical Note **C**, Lesson 52), e.g. *ma-ςăndi ġir šwiya d-le-flus* 'I only have a little bit of money.'

B. Note the pattern of *ma-ςăndi flus* 'I don't have any money' and *ma-šraw ṭςin* 'They didn't buy any flour', where the final *-š* of the negative is omitted and the noun occurs without the definite article and without *ši-* 'some, any'. This is the regular Moroccan equivalent for English expressions with 'not any'.

C. A very common pattern in English is a negative use of 'any', without a noun, e.g. 'I don't have any', 'I didn't eat any', etc. For forms of 'to have' and cases of *f-* 'in' with pronoun endings, the Moroccan equivalent is a simple negative, with final *-š* and no translation equivalent for English 'any', e.g. *ma-ςăndi-š* 'I don't have any'. In the case of verb forms, there is usually no equivalent for 'any', and the noun is repeated, e.g. *ma-klit xux* 'I didn't eat any peaches'.

Such English expressions with 'any' usually have two different meanings, depending on stress. In 'I don't have any', the 'have' is stressed in answer to 'Do you have any money?', while the 'any' is stressed in answer to 'How much money do you have?' Moroccan makes no such distinction, and *ma-ςăndi-š* is used in both cases. The pattern is true generally, e.g. *ma-klit xux* 'I didn't eat any (peaches)', *ma-fiha-š* 'There isn't any in it', etc.

III. Exercises.

A. In the texts of Lessons 80 and 81, form answers to questions with *šςal* by substituting *ġir šwiya* for *šςal,* e.g. change *šςal ςăndha men weṛqa?* 'How many tickets does she have?' to *ma-ςăndha ġir šwiya de-l-uṛaq* 'She only has a few tickets'. Read the resulting new sentences out loud.

B. In the texts of Lessons 80 and 81, form categorical negative answers of the 'not any' type in response to the sentences with *šḥal,* e.g. answer *šḥal dar de-n-năɛnaɛ f-atay?* 'How much mint did he put in the tea?' with *ma-dar năɛnaɛ f-atay* 'He didn't put any mint in the tea.' Read each resulting new sentence out loud.

IV. Vocabulary.

ṭḥin	flour
xux (coll.)	peaches

LESSON EIGHTY-THREE

I. Text.

tleffet	to turn around
tleffet išuf škun lli muṛah.	He turned around to see who was behind him.
tleffet išuf ṭ-ṭumubil.	He turned around to look at the car.
tleffett nehḍeṛ mɛah.	I turned around to talk to him.
tleffetna nhedṛu mɛahom.	We turned around to talk to them.
wqef	to (come to a) stop, to stand
wqef yakol le-ġda.	He stopped to eat dinner.
wqefna nšufuhom fe-l-medṛaṣa.	We stopped to see them at school.
dxelt neqṛa ḍ-ḍeṛṣ ž-ždid.	I went in to study the new lesson.
glesna nhedṛu ɛăl ḍ-ḍeṛṣ ž-ždid.	We sat down to talk about the new lesson.
ma-mšit-š nšufu.	I didn't go see him.
ɛlaš ma-mšiti-š dzuṛ xak?	Why didn't you (sg.) go visit your brother?
mšit nešri l-uqid, be-l-ḥăqq žbeṛt l-ḥanut mešduda.	I went to buy some matches but I found the shop closed.
žat teġsel le-ḥwayež u-ma-žebṛet ṣabun.	She came to wash the clothes but she couldn't find any soap.

ža iṭleb menni le-flus u-ma-žberni-š fe-ḍ-ḍaṛ.	He came to ask me for some money and didn't find me at home.
ka-nemši nẓuṛ xay meṛṛa fe-š-šheṛ.	I go visit my brother once a month.
ka-iži iddina l-l-meḍṛaṣa fe-t-tmenya.	He comes to take us to school at eight o'clock.
ma-ġad-iži-š iƐawenna.	He's not going to come help us.

II. Grammatical Notes.

A. The text of the present lesson shows examples of the Moroccan imperfect corresponding to the English infinitive after verbs of motion, as in *mšit nešri l-uqid* 'I went to buy some matches'. For previous similar uses of the imperfect, see Grammatical Note **A** of Lesson 61, Grammatical Note **C** of Lesson 62, Grammatical Note **A** of Lesson 75, and Grammatical Note **A** of Lesson 77.

B. Note the idiomatic use of English 'couldn't' corresponding to the Moroccan perfect in *ma-žebṛet ṣabun* 'she couldn't find any soap'.

III. Exercises.

Go through the text of this lesson and make all the sentences negative, on the pattern of *ma-mšit-š nšufu* 'I didn't go see him.'

IV. Vocabulary.

ḍeṛṣ	lesson
ṣabun	soap
tleffet	to turn around
wqef	to (come to a) stop, to stand

LESSON EIGHTY-FOUR

I. Text.

mšat qṛat ḍ-ḍuṛuṣ dyalha.	She went and studied her lessons.
ma-mšat-š teqṛa ḍ-ḍuṛuṣ.	She didn't go study the lessons.
mšit šrit z-zit.	I went and bought some oil.
mšiti ẓeṛti xak?	Did you (sg.) go visit your brother?
žat ġeslet le-Ɛwayež u-mšat.	She came and washed the clothes and left.
aži šufni ġedda.	Come (sg.) see me tomorrow.
ma-dži-š tšufni ġedda.	Don't come (sg.) see me tomorrow.
ma-dži-š ttkellem mƐah.	Don't come (sg.) talk to him.
siru diru l-xedma dyalkom.	Go (pl.) do your work.
ma-temšiw-š taklu f-had s-saƐa.	Don't go (pl.) eat right now.

II. Grammatical Notes.

A. To indicate purpose and completed action, the perfect tense of a verb of motion is followed immediately by another verb in the perfect tense, as in *mšat qṛat ḍ-ḍuṛuṣ dyalha.* 'She went and studied her lessons'. Note that there is no Moroccan equivalent for 'and' in such expressions as *mšat qṛat* 'she went and studied'. Compare the difference in meaning of the pattern studied in Lesson 83, e.g. *ža iṭleb menni le-flus* 'He came to ask me for some money.'

B. The imperative of a verb of motion is immediately followed by another imperative to indicate purpose. Note the similarity to English structure of such patterns as *aži!* 'come!', *šufni!* 'see me!' and *aži šufni!* 'come see me!'

C. The comments of Notes **A** and **B** above apply only to positive sentences. In negatives, only the imperfect is used in such verb phrases, following the pattern studied in Lesson 83. Compare such positive and negative pairs as *ža qṛa ḍ-ḍuṛuṣ* 'He came and studied the lessons' and *ma-ža-š iqṛa ḍ-ḍuṛuṣ* 'He didn't come study the lessons', or further, *aži šufni ġedda!'* and *ma-dži-š tšufni ġedda!* 'Don't come (sg.) see me tomorrow!'

III. Exercises.

Go through the text of this lesson and make all sentences negative. In accordance with Grammatical Note C above, note that as the verb of motion is negated, the following verb must be changed from the perfect to the imperfect. For example, the negative of *mšit šrit z-zit* is *ma-mšit-š nešri z-zit.*

IV. Vocabulary.

ḍuṛuṣ (pl. of *ḍeṛṣ*)	lessons

Note: *mša* 'to go' is also used in the sense of 'to go away, to leave', as in *žat ġeslet le-Ꜫwayež u-mšat* 'She came and washed the clothes and (then) left.'

LESSON EIGHTY-FIVE

I. Text.

šꜪal hadi fe-s-saꜪa?	What time is it?
hadi ž-žuž.	It's two o'clock.
hadi t-tmenya.	It's eight o'clock.
hadi l-weꜪda.	It's one o'clock.
mšit l-l-xedma fe-l-weꜪda.	I went to work at one o'clock.
hadi l-weꜪda u-qṣem.	It's five past one.
mša fe-l-weꜪda u-qṣem.	He went at five past one.
hadi ṛ-ṛebꜪa ġir qṣem.	It's five till four.
mšat fe-l-xemsa ġir qṣem.	She left at five till five.
hadi s-setta u-qeṣmayn.	It's ten past six.
ṭ-ṭiyyaṛa ġad-temši fe-s-setta u-qeṣmayn.	The airplane's going to leave at ten past six.
hadi s-sebꜪa ġir qeṣmayn.	It's ten minutes till seven.
qolt-lu iži fe-t-tesꜪud ġir qeṣmayn.	I told him to come at ten till nine.

II. Grammatical Notes.

The equivalent of 'it is' in expressions of time is *hadi,* as in *hadi l-weɛda* 'It's one o'clock'. Time after the hour is expressed by *u* 'and' plus a period of time, as in *l-weɛda u-qṣem* 'five past one'. Time before the hour is expressed by the word *ġir* plus a period of time, as in *fe-t-tesɛud ġir qeṣmayn* 'at ten till nine'.

III. Exercises.

Go through the text of the lesson and substitute *ġir* for *u-* and vice versa in all expressions of time. Read the resulting sentences out loud.

IV. Vocabulary.

qṣem	(period of) five minutes
qeṣmayn	(period of) ten minutes
(*l-*) *weɛda*	one (o'clock)

LESSON EIGHTY-SIX

I. Text.

hadi l-weɛda u-ṛbăɛ.	It's a quarter past one.
ġad-iɛollu l-ɛanut fe-l-ɛăšṛa u-ṛbăɛ.	They're going to open the shop at ten fifteen (10:15).
hadi t-tlata llaṛeb.	It's a quarter till three.
šefnah l-bareɛ fe-ṭ-ṭnaš llaṛeb.	We saw him yesterday at a quarter till twelve.
hadi ṛ-ṛebɛa u-tulut.	It's four twenty (4:20).
ṭḷebt mennu iži fe-s-sebɛa u-tulut.	I asked him to come at twenty past seven.
hadi t-tmenya ġir tulut.	It's twenty till eight.
bda ka-iqṛa ḍ-ḍuṛuṣ dyalu fe-l-weɛda ġir tulut.	He began studying his lessons at twenty till one.

wṣel	to arrive
hadi l-weƐda u-xems qṣam.	It's twenty-five past one.
ġad-iweṣlu fe-t-tlata u-xems qṣam.	They're going to arrive at three twenty-five (3:25).
hadi ṭ-ṭnaš u-sbăƐ qṣam.	It's twelve thirty-five (12:35).
wṣelt f-le-Ɛḍaš u-sbăƐ qṣam.	I arrived at eleven thirty-five (11:35).
weṣlet t-tlata.	Three o'clock has come.
weṣlet t-tlata?	Is it three o'clock yet?
baqi ma-weṣlet t-tlata.	It isn't three o'clock yet.

II. Grammatical Notes.

As in English, time of day in Moroccan is expressed by various amounts of time before and after the hour. The principal patterns are shown in the texts of this and the preceding lesson. Time after the hour is expressed by *u* 'and', time before the hour is expressed by *ġir* 'except'. Fifteen minutes before the hour is expressed by the special form *llaṛeb.*

In English only the terms 'quarter' and 'half' ('half past six', 'quarter till seven') exist in addition to statements of a specific number of minutes ('it's ten twenty', 'it's eleven thirty-four'). Moroccan has in addition the terms *qṣem* 'five minutes', *qeṣmayn* 'ten minutes', *tulut* 'twenty minutes', *xems qṣam* 'twenty-five minutes', and *sbăƐ qṣam* 'thirty-five minutes'.

III. Exercises.

A. In the text of Lesson 85, replace the terms *u-qṣem* and *ġir qṣem* with *u-ṛbăƐ* and *llaṛeb.* Read the resulting new sentences out loud.

B. According to the instructions of **A** above, substitute *u-tulut* and *ġir tulut* for *u-qeṣmayn* and *ġir qeṣmayn.*

IV. Vocabulary.

llaṛeb	minus a quarter
ṛbăƐ	quarter
sbăƐ qṣam	thirty-five minutes
tulut	(period of) twenty minutes
xems qṣam	twenty-five minutes
wṣel	to arrive

Note: Until further information is given, the student is to use the expressions of time above only in the patterns illustrated in this lesson.

LESSON EIGHTY-SEVEN

I. Text.

xeṣṣek temši men daba saƐa.	You have to go in an hour.
ġad-ibda men daba saƐa.	He's going to begin in an hour.
weqt-aš ġad-nweṣlu?	What time are we going to arrive?
nweṣlu men daba saƐa.	We'll arrive in an hour.
ġad-yewṣel men daba saƐtayn.	He'll arrive two hours from now.
xeṣṣna nešeddu l-Ɛanut men daba saƐtayn.	We have to close the shop in two hours.
weṣlu fe-l-xemsa u-neṣṣ.	They arrived at five thirty.
xeṣṣek dži fe-ṭ-ṭnaš u-neṣṣ.	You (sg.) have to come at twelve thirty.
nṣifeṭ-lek ṭ-ṭumubil men daba ṛbăƐ saƐa.	I'll send you the car in a quarter of an hour.
kemmel l-xedma fe-ṛbăƐ saƐa.	He finished the work in fifteen minutes.
ġad-iweṣlu men daba tulut saƐa.	They're going to arrive twenty minutes from now.
kemmelt l-xedma f-tulut saƐa.	I finished the work in twenty minutes.
kla le-ġda dyalu f-neṣṣ saƐa.	He ate his dinner in half an hour.
weqt-aš ġad-naklu?	What time are we going to eat?
ġad-naklu men daba neṣṣ saƐa.	We're going to eat in half an hour.
weqt-aš xeṣṣna nƐollu l-biban?	What time are we supposed to open the doors?
xeṣṣna nƐolluhom men daba neṣṣ saƐa.	We have to open them in half an hour.

II. Grammatical Notes.

A. In expressions of time, *ṛbăƐ* 'quarter', *tulut* 'twenty minutes' ('third'), and *neṣṣ* 'half' must be followed by *saƐa* 'hour' unless used immediately in telling the time of day. Compare *fe-l-weƐda u-tulut* 'at one twenty (1:20)' and *men daba tulut saƐa* 'twenty minutes from now'.

B. Such an English expression as 'in a quarter of an hour' is unclear. It can refer to the duration of an action ('He finished the work in fifteen minutes.') or to the fact that an action is supposed to occur at the end of a period of time ('I'll send you the car in a quarter of an hour.'). Moroccan *f-* 'in' with an expression of time refers only to the duration of an action, as in *kemmelt l-xedma f-tulut saɛa* 'I finished the work in twenty minutes'. English 'in' when referring to end of a period of waiting is rendered by Moroccan *men daba* 'from now', as in *nebda men daba tulut saɛa* 'I'll begin twenty minutes from now'.

III. Exercises.

Go through the sentences of the text of this lesson and

1. Substitute *tulut saɛa* for all other expressions of time.
2. Substitute *saɛtayn* for all other expressions of time.
3. Substitute *ṛbăɛ saɛa* for all other expressions of time.

IV. Vocabulary.

neṣṣ	half
saɛa	hour
saɛtayn	two hours
weqt-aš	when, (at) what time

LESSON EIGHTY-EIGHT

I. Text.

nžib-lek ṣ-ṣabun men daba qṣem.	I'll bring you the soap in five minutes.
men daba qṣem ġad-ibda.	It begins in five minutes.
kemmel l-xedma dyalu f-qeṣmayn.	He finished his work in ten minutes.
tkellemna xems qṣam.	We talked (for) twenty-five minutes.
glesna mɛahom sbăɛ qṣam.	We sat with them (for) thirty-five minutes.

ġad-ikemmelha men daba saɛtayn.	He'll finish it in two hours
qal-li ġad-ikemmelha men băɛd saɛtayn.	He told me he was going to finish it in two hours.
nweṣlu men daba neṣṣ saɛa.	We'll arrive half an hour from now.
wṣelna men băɛd neṣṣ saɛa.	We arrived after (in) half an hour.
xdemt ɛešrin ɛam f-dak l-măɛmel.	I worked in that factory for twenty years.
ɛešna ɛešrin ɛam fe-l-meġṛib.	We lived in Morocco for twenty years.
šɛăl ɛešrin wqida.	He struck twenty matches.
qṛit waḥed u-ɛešrin ktab š-šheṛ lli daz.	I read twenty-one books last month.
ɛăndhom waḥed u-ɛešrin biškliṭa.	They have twenty-one bicycles.
ɛaš tlatin ɛam fe-ḍ-ḍaṛ l-biḍa.	He lived in Casablanca for thirty years.
had ḍ-aṛ fiha tlatin bit.	This house has thirty rooms in it.
ktebt waḥed u-tlatin bṛa l-yum.	I wrote thirty-one letters today.
had l-medṛaṣa fiha waḥed u-tlatin fqi.	This school has thirty-one teachers.
qal-li la xemsa u-tlatin meṛṛa.	He told me 'no' thirty-five times.
ɛṭinah xemsa u-tlatin teṣwiṛa.	We gave him thirty-five pictures.

II. Grammatical Notes.

A. The term *qṣem* 'five minutes' can be used independently of telling time (cf. the comments on *ṛbăɛ* and *tulut* in Grammatical Note A of Lesson 87), e.g. *nžib-lek ṣ-ṣabun men daba qṣem* 'I'll bring you the soap in five minutes.' The same is true of *qeṣmayn, xems qṣam,* and *sbăɛ qṣam,* which are multiples of *qṣem,* e.g. *tkellemna xems qṣam* 'We talked twenty-five minutes.'

B. The phrase *men băɛd* 'after' is used with expressions of time in the past similarly to the use of *men daba* 'from now' in reference to the future. Compare the two sentences *ġad-ikemmelha men daba saɛtayn* 'He'll finish it in two hours' and *qal-li ġad-ikemmelha men băɛd saɛtayn* 'He told me he was going to finish it in two hours.'

C. As was mentioned in Grammatical Note **A** of Lesson 79, numerals from eleven on are followed by singular rather than plural nouns, e.g., *ɛešrin ɛam* 'twenty years', *waḥed u-tlatin fqi* 'thirty-one teachers'.

III. Exercise.

Insofar as makes good sense, go through the text of Lesson 87 and replace all occurrences of *men daba* with *men băɛd,* changing the time involved from present or future to past. Read the resulting new sentences out loud.

IV. Vocabulary.

men băɛd	(see Grammatical Note **B**)
tlatin	thirty
waḥed u-tlatin	thirty-one
xemsa u-tlatin	thirty-five
waḥed	one
ɛam	year
ɛešrin	twenty
waḥed u-ɛešrin	twenty-one

LESSON EIGHTY-NINE

I. Text.

hadi t-tesɛud u-waḥed u-ɛešrin (dqiqa).	It's twenty-one (minutes) past nine.
hadi t-tmenya ġir waḥed u-ɛešrin (dqiqa).	It's twenty-one (minutes) till eight.
hadi l-xemsa ġir dqiqa.	It's one minute till five.
wṣel fe-l-weḥda u-tnayn u-ɛešrin.	He arrived at twenty-two past one.
had l-măɛmel ka-ixedmu fih tnayn u-ɛešrin ṛažel.	This factory has twenty-two men working in it.

mša fe-ṭ-ṭnaš u-tnayn u-tlatin.	He left at twelve thirty-two.
hadi le-εḍaš u-sebεa de-d-dqayeq.	It's seven minutes past eleven.
hadi l-xemsa ġir tlata de-d-dqayeq.	It's three minutes till five.
ġad-ibda men daba setta de-d-dqayeq.	It's going to begin in six minutes.
šεal baqi le-t-tesεud?	How long is it till nine o'clock?
šεal baqi le-ṛ-ṛebεa?	How long is it till four o'clock?
šεal baqi le-ž-žuž?	How long is it till two o'clock?
ṭḷebt le-flus mennha ṛebεin meṛṛa.	I asked her for the money forty times.
šra ṛebεin ṣenḍuq d-l-uqid.	He bought forty boxes of matches.
žaw men băεd ṛebεin dqiqa.	They came after forty minutes.

II. Grammatical Notes.

A. For periods of time before and after the hour not expressable in terms of the vocabulary given in Lessons 85-87 (e.g. *qṣem* 'five minutes'), the word dqiqa 'minute', pl. *dqayeq* is used with a numeral, as in *hadi l-xemsa ġir tlata de-d-dqayeq* 'It's three minutes till five.'

B. Note the pattern exemplified in *šεal baqi le-t-tesεud?* 'How long is it till nine o'clock?'

C. Above twenty, compound numerals are formed by combining the simple numerals from one to nine with the numerals *εešrin* 'twenty', *tlatin* 'thirty', *ṛebεin* 'forty', etc. The smaller numeral is placed first and joined to the following by *u* 'and', as in *sebεa u-ṛebεin* 'forty-seven'. Note that there is a special word for two, *tnayn,* used only in compound numerals, *tnayn u-εešrin, tnayn u-tlatin, tnayn u-ṛebεin,* etc.

D. The patterns of *xemsa d-le-ktub* and *εešrin ktab,* showing the use of singular and plural nouns with numerals, are familiar from previous lessons. Occasionally there are nouns which have no singulars (the only one given so far is *nas* 'people'). Such nouns are used with numbers above ten in the same manner as with numbers from ten on down. Compare *ṛebεin de-n-nas* 'forty people' with *ṛebεin ṣenḍuq* 'forty boxes'.

III. Exercises.

Go through the texts of Lessons 85-87 and subtract one minute from each expression of time given, giving the Moroccan equivalent. For example, change *hadi l-weɛda u-qṣem* to *hadi l-weɛda u-ṛebɛa de-d-dqayeq.*

IV. Vocabulary.

dqiqa	minute
dqayeq (pl.)	
ṛebɛin	forty
tnayn	two (used only in compound numbers)

LESSON NINETY

I. Text.

tsenna	to wait, to wait for
tsennahom ši-saɛtayn.	He waited about two hours for them.
ma-tsennit ġir ši-qṣem.	I only waited about five minutes.
ma-ġad-imken-li ntsennak ġir ši-neṣṣ saɛa.	I'll only be able to wait about half an hour for you.
šɛal hadi u-nta ka-ttsennahom?	How long have you (sg.) been waiting for them?
hadi saɛa w-ana ka-ntsennahom.	I've been waiting for them for an hour.
šɛal hadi u-nta ka-temši l-had l-meḍṛaṣa?	How long have you (sg.) been going to this school?
hadi ɛam w-ana ka-nemši l-had l-meḍṛaṣa.	I've been going to this school for a year.
šɛal hadi u-ḅḅak fe-ṣ-ṣbiṭaṛ?	How long has your father been in the hospital?
šɛal hadi baš šeftih?	How long has it been since you saw him?
hadi saɛa baš šeftu.	I saw him an hour ago.
šɛal hadi baš ḍḍeṛṛu yeddik?	How long has it been since your (sg.) hands got hurt?
hadi ši-ɛam baš ḍḍeṛṛu.	They got hurt about a year ago.

II. Grammatical Notes.

Note the sentence pattern of 'How long have you been waiting for them?' The Moroccan equivalent of 'how long' in such sentences is *šɛal hadi.* The Moroccan pattern is completed by *u-* 'and' followed by the durative tense. Thus the Moroccan equivalent of the total sentence 'How long have you been waiting for them?' is *šɛal hadi u-nta ka-ttsennahom?* A closely similar pattern is where *u-* 'and' is followed by an equational sentence, as in *šɛal hadi u-ḅḅak fe-ṣ-ṣbiṭaṛ?* 'How long has your father been in the hospital?'

The phrase *šɛal hadi baš* is equivalent in meaning to 'how long has it been since' or 'how long ago was it that', as in *šɛal hadi baš šeftih?* 'How long has it been since you saw him?

Answers to the two different types of questions discussed in the paragraphs above are formed by dropping *šɛal* and placing an expression of length of time after *hadi,* with an appropriate following sentence. Thus a possible answer to *šɛal hadi u-nta ke-ttsennah?* 'How long have you been waiting for him?' is *hadi saɛa w-ana ka-ntsennah* 'I've been waiting for him for an hour'. Note the similarly constructed reply to *šɛal hadi u-ḅḅak fe-ṣ-ṣbiṭaṛ?* 'How long has your father been in the hospital?', to which a possible answer is *hadi ʔusbuɛ u-huwa fe-ṣ-ṣbiṭaṛ* 'He's been in the hospital for a week'. A special point of these constructions where the termination is a durative tense is that the subject pronoun (*ana, nta,* etc.) must always be included, even if the person is clear from the verb form. Thus *ɛna* 'we' cannot be omitted from *hadi ši-telt snin u-ɛna ka-nxedmu hna* 'We've been working here about three years,' even though the verb form *ka-nxedmu* necessarily implies *ɛna.*

An example of this kind of substitution with *šɛal hadi baš* is such a question as *šɛal hadi baš ḍ-ḍeṛṛu yeddik?* 'How long has it been since your hands got hurt?', to which a possible answer is *hadi ši-ɛam baš ḍḍeṛṛu* 'They got hurt about a year ago' or 'It's been about a year since they got hurt.' An interesting feature of this past tense pattern is that it is possible to place the verb before *hadi,* in which case *baš* is dropped. Thus one can say either *hadi ši-ʔusbuɛ baš šefnah* or *šefnah hadi ši-ʔusbuɛ,* both with the same meaning, 'We saw him about a week ago'.

III. Exercises.

A. Put the following sentences and expressions of time together on the pattern of *hadi saɛa w-ana ka-ntsennahom.* Read the resulting sentences out loud.

1. *saɛa.*	*ka-itsennani.*
2. *ʔusbuɛ.*	*ka-nemšiw l-had l-meḍḍrasa.*

3. *ɛam.* *ka-nbiɛ ṭ-ṭumubilat.*
4. *tulut saɛa.* *ḥna fe-d-ḍaṛ.*
5. *ɛešrin ɛam.* *ka-teɛṭih le-flus.*
6. *tnayn u-tlatin ɛam.* *ka-ixeddem had l-makina.*
7. *ši-telt snin.* *ka-ikteb-lna meṛṛa fe-š-šheṛ.*
8. *ɛamayn.* *ka-imšiw le-s-sinima nhaṛ le-xmis.*
9. *ši-šheṛ u-neṣṣ.* *ka-nxedmu mɛahom.*
10. *telṭṭaš ɛam.* *ka-tnuḍ fe-s-setta.*

B. With the sentences of Exercise **A** above form questions on the pattern of *šḥal hadi u-ntuma ka-txedmu hna?* Change statements with *ana* and *ḥna* into questions with *nta* and *ntuma.*

C. Take the expressions of time in Exercise **A** above and combine them with the following to form sentences on the pattern of *hadi saɛa baš šeftu.*

1. *bdit l-xedma.*
2. *kemmel ḍ-ḍuṛuṣ.*
3. *beɛna ḍ-ḍaṛ dyalna.*
4. *žabet-li le-ḥwayež.*
5. *šeddu dak l-ḥanut.*
6. *mšaw l-l-meġṛib.*
7. *xedmet mɛana.*
8. *šrit had l-biškliṭa.*
9. *wṣelna men fas.*
10. *siyyeb duk le-bṛawat.*

D. Take the sentences of Exercise **C** above and form questions on the pattern of *šḥal hadi baš šeftih?* Change statements referring to *ana* and *ḥna* to questions with *nta* and *ntuma.*

IV. Vocabulary.

baš	since, ago (with certain expressions of time)
ši	about, around (with reference to duration of time)
tsenna	to wait, to wait for

LESSON NINETY-ONE

I. Text.

waš ʕăndek t-tilifun fe-ḍ-ḍaṛ?	Do you have a telephone at home?
ma-ʕăndi-š t-tilifun fe-ḍ-ḍaṛ.	I don't have a telephone at home.
ḍṛeb-li t-tilifun.	He telephoned me.
ḍṛebt-lu t-tilifun.	I phoned him.
ʕlaš ma-ḍḍṛeb-lha-š t-tilifun?	Why don't you give her a phone call?
šʕal hadi baš ḍṛebti t-tilifun le-ḅḅak?	How long has it been since you telephoned your father.
hadi ṛebʕ snin ma-šeftu.	I haven't seen him for four years.
hadi ʔusbuʕ ma-tkellemt mʕah.	I haven't talked with him for a week.
ma-šefnah-š hadi xems snin.	We haven't seen him for five years.
ma-ḍṛebt-lha-š t-tilifun hadi šheṛ.	I haven't phoned her for a month.
hadi ši-ʕamayn baš kont ka-nexdem temma.	I used to work there about two years ago.
hadi xems snin baš konna ka-nemšiw l-dak l-meḍṛaṣṣa.	We used to go to that school five years ago.
kanet ka-teqṛa ḍ-ḍuṛuṣ dyalha hadi saʕtayn.	She was studying her lessons two hours ago.
konna ka-ntkellmu fe-t-tilifun hadi ġir qṣem.	We were talking on the phone only about five minutes ago.
kan ka-yakol le-ġda hadi ši-neṣṣ saʕa.	He was eating dinner about half an hour ago.

II. Grammatical Notes.

A. Note the pattern of *hadi saʕa baš šeftu* 'I saw him an hour ago, it's been an hour since I saw him'. The negation of this pattern drops the ***baš*** and uses only *ma-* without final *-š* for the negative verb form, i.e. ***hadi saʕa ma-šeftu*** 'I haven't seen him for an hour'. Notice that the nature of the English translation differs from the positive to the negative.

It is also possible, without change of meaning, to place the verb before the expression of time with *hadi.* In this pattern the negative *-š* must be used in the verb form, e.g. one may say either *hadi saƐa ma-šeftu or ma-šeftu-š hadi saƐa* 'I haven't seen him for an hour.'

B. Note the indication of past progressive and habitual action (cf. Grammatical Note A, Lesson 67 and the Grammatical Notes of Lesson 68) in such sentences as *hadi ši-Ɛamayn baš kont ka-nexdem temma* 'I used to work there about two years ago' and *konna ka-ntkellmu fe-t-tilifun hadi ġir qṣem* 'We were talking on the phone only about five minutes ago.'

III. Exercise.

Go through the text of this lesson and make all negative verb forms positive. Make other grammatical changes necessary as a consequence of changing the verb form from negative to positive.

IV. Vocabulary.

ṛebƐ snin	four years
tilifun	telephone
ḍṛeb t-tilifun l-	to telephone (someone)
temma	there
xems snin	five years

LESSON NINETY-TWO

I. Text.

Ɛămmṛu ma-ka-ikemmel l-xedma dyalu fe-l-weqt.	He never finishes his work on time.
Ɛămmeṛ weldi ma-mša l-l-meġṛib.	My son has never been to Morocco.
Ɛămmeṛha ma-ka-takol l-lƐăm?	Doesn't she ever eat meat?
Ɛămmeṛ bentu ma-theḷḷat fih.	His daughter never took (good) care of him.

ɛămmeṛhom ma-šraw ši-ɛwayež ždad.	They never bought any new clothes.
ɛămmeṛ duk n-nas ma-ɛawnuna.	Those people have never helped us.
ɛămmeṛni ma-ka-nexdem.	I never work.
ɛămmeṛni ma-šeft dak ṛ-ṛažel men qbel.	I've never seen that man before.
waš ɛămmṛek ma-ka-dži fe-l-weqt?	Don't you ever come on time?
ɛămmṛek ma-ṣifeṭṭi-lu le-flus dyalu?	Didn't you ever send him his money?
ɛămmeṛna ma-derna had l-xedma men qbel.	We've never done this (kind of) work before.
ɛămmeṛna ma-ka-nnuḍu bekri.	We never get up early.
ɛămmeṛkom ma-ka-tɛollu had š-šṛažem?	Don't you ever open these windows?
ɛămmeṛkom ma-ka-teqṛaw l-žarida?	Don't you ever read the newspaper?

II. Grammatical Notes.

This lesson shows the use of the particle *ɛămmeṛ* 'never, not ever'. This particle regularly takes the same pronoun endings as verbs (cf. the Grammatical Notes of Lessons 53-57), e.g. *ɛămmeṛni* 'I never', etc. Negative verbs used with *ɛămmeṛ* omit the final negative *-š,* as in *ɛămmeṛni ma-ka-nexdem* 'I never work', etc.

When verbs used with *ɛămmeṛ* have noun subjects, there are two possible patterns, with no difference in meaning. One pattern is for the noun to come before *ɛămmeṛ,* in which case *ɛămmeṛ* takes the appropriate pronoun ending, as in *had le-mṛa ɛămmeṛha ma-ka-tešṛeb atay?* 'Doesn't this woman ever drink tea?' The other possibility is for *ɛămmeṛ* to come before the noun, in which case it takes no pronoun ending, as in *ɛămmeṛ weldi ma-mša l-l-meġṛib* 'My son has never been to Morocco.'

III. Exercises.

A. In the text of this lesson, take the sentences with ***ana*** 'I' and ***ḥna*** 'we' as subjects and change them into questions with ***nta*** 'you' (sg.) and ***ntuma*** 'you' (pl.). For example, *ʕămmeṛni ma-ka-nexdem* 'I never work' should be changed to *ʕămmṛek ma-ka-texdem?* 'Don't you ever work?' Read the resulting new sentences out loud.

B. Reverse the procedure of Exercise **A** above by changing the questions in the text with *nta* 'you' (sg.) and *ntuma* 'you' (pl.) to statements with *ana* 'I' and *ḥna* 'we'. For example such a sentence as *ʕămmeṛkom ma-ka-teqṛaw l-žarida?* 'Don't you ever read the newspaper?' should be changed to *ʕămmeṛna ma-ka-neqṛaw l-žarida* 'We never read the newspaper'. Read the resulting new sentences out loud.

IV. Vocabulary.

ʕămmeṛ	never, not ever (cf. the Grammatical Notes)

LESSON NINETY-THREE

I. Text.

ḅḅak žab-lek ši-ḥaža?	Did your father bring you anything?
ma-žab-li ḥetta ḥaža.	He didn't bring me anything.
žbeṛti ši-ḥaža mezyana?	Did you find anything good?
ma-žbeṛt ḥetta ḥaža.	I didn't find anything.
kayna ši-ḥaža f-had ṣ-ṣenḍuq?	Is there anything in this box?
ma-fih ḥetta ḥaža.	It doesn't have anything in it.
waš daru ši-ḥaža f-had l-xenša?	Did they put anything in this bag?
ma-daru fiha ḥetta ḥaža.	They didn't put anything in it.
had l-xenša š-kayen fiha?	What does this bag have in it?
had l-xenša ma-fiha ḥetta ḥaža.	This bag doesn't have anything in it.
š-qal-lek le-fqi?	What did the teacher tell you?
ma-qal-li walu.	He didn't tell me anything.

nfăƐ	to be of use to, to help
nfăƐni bezzaf.	It helped me a lot.
dak l-xedma nefƐătni bezzaf.	That work helped me a lot.
nefƐătkom ši-ƹaža?	Was anything of use to you (pl.)?
ma-nefƐătna ƹetta ƹaža.	Nothing helped us.
ma-ġad-infăƐhom walu.	Nothing will help them.
šnu ġad-ddir ġedda?	What are you going to do tomorrow?
ma-ġad-tenfăƐna ƹetta ƹaža?	Won't anything help us?
ƹetta ƹaža!	Not a thing!
walu!	Nothing!

II. Grammatical Notes.

The two forms *ƹetta ƹaža* 'nothing' and *walu* 'nothing' are equivalent in meaning and are interchangeable, except for a difference in gender. Such sentences as *ma-nefƐătna ƹetta ƹaža* 'Nothing helped us' and *ma-ġad-infăƐhom walu* 'Nothing will help them' illustrate that *ƹetta ƹaža* is feminine and *walu* is masculine. The sentences also illustrate the fact that, although the *ma-* is retained elsewhere in the sentence, the final *-š* of the usual negative pattern is dropped when *ƹetta ƹaža* and *walu* are used.

III. Exercise.

Go through the sentences of the text and substitute *walu* for the occurrences of *ƹetta ƹaža.*

IV. Vocabulary.

nfăƐ	to be of use to, to help
ši-ƹaža	something, anything
walu	nothing
ƹetta ƹaža	nothing

LESSON NINETY-FOUR

I. Text.

ža ši-ḥădd?	Did anyone come?
škun lli ža?	Who came?
ma-ža ḥetta ḥădd.	Nobody came.
šafek ši-ḥădd?	Did anybody see you?
škun lli šafek?	Who saw you?
ma-šafni ḥetta ḥădd.	Nobody saw me.
ža ši-waḥed išufkom?	Did anybody come to see you?
Ɛămmeṛ ḥetta waḥed ma-ka-iži išufna.	Nobody ever comes to see us.
ka-yeɛṭikom ši-waḥed le-flus?	Is there anyone giving you money?
Ɛămmeṛ ḥetta waḥed ma-ka-yeɛṭina le-flus.	Nobody ever gives us any money.
ma-ɛṭak ḥetta waḥed ši-flus?	Didn't anybody give you any money?
la, ḥetta waḥed.	No, nobody.
Ɛămmeṛ ḥetta waḥed ma-xdem kteṛ men had š-ši.	Nobody ever worked more than this.
Ɛămmeṛni ma-šeft ḥetta ḥădd feṛḥana bḥalha.	I've never seen anyone as happy as she is.
Ɛămmeṛna ma-šefna ḥetta waḥed kbeṛ mennu.	We've never seen anyone bigger than he is.

II. Grammatical Notes.

A. The forms *ši-ḥădd* and *ši-waḥed* are equivalent in meaning and interchangeable, in the same way as English 'someone' and 'somebody'. Note that Moroccan has no distinction parallel to English 'someone' and 'somebody' as opposed to 'anyone' and 'anybody'. The negatives *ḥetta ḥădd* and *ḥetta waḥed* are likewise interchangeable and equivalent in meaning, just as are English 'no one' and 'nobody'.

B. When the negative forms *ḥetta ḥădd* and *ḥetta waḥed* are used, the regular final *-š* of negation is dropped, but the familiar *ma-* is retained. Compare *ma-ža-š* 'He didn't come' and *ma-ža ḥetta ḥădd* 'nobody came'.

C. The negative forms *ɛetta waɛed* and *ɛetta ɛădd* can be used independently. Just as it is possible in English to say, for example, 'No, nobody!' instead of a full sentence, one can say in Moroccan *la, ɛetta ɛădd!*

D. The Moroccan equivalent of the English superlative was first mentioned in Grammatical Note **B** of Lesson 70. Various expressions with *ɛămmeṛ* 'ever, never' also often serve as equivalents for English superlatives. For example, the translation 'I've never seen anyone as happy as she is' was given in the text for the sentence *ɛămmeṛni ma-šeft ɛetta ɛădd feṛɛana bɛalha.* An equally good translation would be 'She's the happiest person I've ever seen'. Also note the logical equivalence of two such sentences as 'We've never seen anyone bigger than he is' and 'He's the biggest man (boy, person, etc.) we've ever seen'. Both sentences are equally good translations for *ɛămmeṛna ma-šefna ɛetta waɛed kbeṛ mennu.*

III. Exercises.

A. Go through the text of this lesson and substitute *ši-waɛed* for every occurrence of *ši-ɛădd* and vice versa. Do the same with *ɛetta ɛădd* and *ɛetta waɛed.*

B. Go through the text of this lesson and change all the perfect tenses to futures. For example, *ma-ža mɛah ɛetta ɛădd* 'Nobody came with him' should be changed to *ma-ġad-iži mɛah ɛetta ɛădd* 'Nobody is going to come with him'.

IV. Vocabulary.

ši-waɛed	someone, somebody, anyone, anybody
ši-ɛădd	someone, somebody, anyone, anybody
ɛetta waɛed	no one, nobody, not anybody
ɛetta ɛădd	no one, nobody, not anybody

LESSON NINETY-FIVE

I. Text.

šɛal ɛăndek men ktab?	How many books do you have?
ma-ɛăndi ġir ktab waḥed.	I've only got a single book.
ma-ɛăndi ġir waḥed.	I've only got one.
ma-ɛăndi ḥetta ktab.	I don't have a single book.
ma-ɛăndi ḥetta waḥed.	I don't have a single one.
šɛal kliti men biḍa?	How many eggs did you eat?
ma-klit ġir biḍa weḥda.	I only ate one egg.
ma-klit ġir weḥda.	I just ate one.
ma-klit ḥetta biḍa.	I didn't eat a single egg.
ma-klit ḥetta weḥda.	I didn't eat a single one.
šɛal beɛtiw men stilu?	How many fountain pens did you (pl.) sell?
ma-beɛna ḥetta stilu.	We didn't sell a single fountain pen.
ma-beɛna-š ḥetta qlam.	We didn't even sell a pencil.
šra mennek bezzaf de-l-makla?	Did he buy much food from you?
ḥetta l-xobz.	Not even any bread.
ɛăndna atay?	Do we have any tea?
ma-ɛăndna atay, ma-ɛăndna-š ḥetta l-ma.	We don't have any tea, we don't even have any water.
kayen l-lḥăm?	Is there any meat?
ma-kayen lḥăm, ma-kayen-š ḥetta l-xobz.	There isn't any meat, there isn't even any bread.
ma-mša-š l-fas, ma-mša-š ḥetta le-ḍ-ḍaṛ l-biḍa.	He didn't go to Fez, he didn't even go to Casablanca.

II. Grammatical Notes.

A. The Moroccan equivalent for English 'one' is an adjective and has both masculine and feminine forms. As is true of all adjectives, it follows the noun, as in *ktab waḥed* 'one book', *biḍa weḥda* 'one egg'.

B. The two different meanings of *ɛetta* 'not a single' and 'not even a, not even (any)' entail differences in the use of the negative ending *-š*. The meaning 'not a single' regularly calls for the negative *ma-* without *-š,* as in *ma-ɛăndi ɛetta ktab* 'I don't have a single book'. In the sense of 'not even (a, any)', a full negation is called for elsewhere in the sentence, as in *ma-kayen-š ɛetta l-xobz* 'There isn't even any bread', *ma-mša-š ɛetta le-ḍ-ḍaṛ l-biḍa* 'He didn't even go to Casablanca'.

C. In English one would be more likely to say 'Not a one!' instead of 'He didn't take a single ticket' in answer to 'How many tickets did he take?' Similarly in Moroccan one may say simply *ɛetta weɛda!* instead of a full sentence such as, for example, *ma-ɛăndu ɛetta weṛqa* 'He doesn't have a single ticket'.

III. Exercises.

Go through the text and change all the perfect tense verb forms to futures.

IV. Vocabulary.

qlam	pencil
stilu	fountain pen
waɛed	one
weɛda (f.)	
ɛetta	not a single; not even (a, any)

LESSON NINETY-SIX

I. Text.

weqt-aš mšiti l-ɛănd ṭ-ṭbib?	What time did you go to the doctor's?
iži mɛak le-ḍ-ḍaṛ men ɛănd ṭ-ṭbib.	He'll come home with you from the doctor's.
men t-tlata u-huwa ɛănd ṭ-ṭbib.	He's been at the doctor's since three o'clock.
waš huwa ɛănd l-ɛăžžam?	Is he at the barber's?

šcal hadi u-huwa cănd l-căžžam?	How long has he been at the barber's?
men l-wecda u-huwa cănd l-căžžam.	He's been at the barber's since one o'clock.
bqa	to remain, stay
šcal bqa căndkom?	How long did he stay with you (at your home)?
bqa căndna ši-šheṛ.	He stayed with us about a month.
ma-căndhom la-flus wa-la-makla.	They have neither food nor money.
ma-mšit la-l-fas wa-la-le-ṛ-ṛbaṭ.	I didn't go to either Fez or Rabat.
ažiw l-căndna nhaṛ le-xmis u-šufu d-drari.	Come over to our place Thursday and see the children.
mšina men căndha žwayeh t-tescud.	We left her place at around nine o'clock.
kan căndi l-weqt bezzaf.	I had a lot of time.
ma-kan căndi weqt bezzaf.	I didn't have much time.
kanet căndu wacd l-biškliṭa ždida.	He had a new bicycle.
ma-kanet căndu la-ṭumubil wa-la-biškliṭa.	He didn't have either a car or a bicycle.
kanu căndkom ši-flus?	Did you have any money?
ma-kanu căndna ġir šwiya d-le-flus.	We only had a little bit of money.

II. Grammatical Notes.

A. Reread the Grammatical Notes of Lesson 8.

B. In Lesson 24 the student began learning the forms *căndi* 'I have', *căndek* 'you (sg.) have', etc. Actually *cănd* is a preposition with a range of meaning not covered by any single English word. The core meaning roughly includes 'at, with, in the possession of, at the house of, at the place of'. Strictly speaking, therefore, such sentences as *căndi waced ṭ-ṭumubil* 'I have a car' must be interpreted as equational sentences. A forced literal translation of *căndi waced ṭ-ṭumubil* might be 'A car is in my possession'.

The past tense of English 'to have' is rendered by ***kan*** 'he (it) was', ***kanet*** 'she (it) was', or ***kanu*** 'they were' placed before a form of ***Ɛănd***. The use of ***kan, kanet,*** or ***kanu*** depends on whether the thing possessed is masculine, feminine, or plural. For example, since ***ṭumubil*** 'car' is feminine, 'I had a car' is rendered as ***kanet Ɛăndi waƐed ṭ-ṭumubil,*** and since ***flus*** 'money' is plural, 'I had some money' is rendered as ***kanu Ɛăndi ši-flus.***

III. Exercises.

Go through the texts of Lessons 24, 27, and 40 and put all sentences with ***Ɛăndi*** 'I have', etc. into the perfect tense. For example, in Lesson 40 change ***š-Ɛăndkom f-had l-bakit?*** 'What do you have in this package?' to ***š-kan Ɛăndkom f-had l-bakit?*** 'What did you have in this package?'

IV. Vocabulary.

bqa	to remain, to stay
la . . . wa-la	neither . . . nor
Ɛăžžam	barber
Ɛănd	(see Grammatical Note **B**)

LESSON NINETY-SEVEN

I. Text.

le-fqi fe-l-mekteb dyalu daba.	The teacher is in his office now.
le-fqi ka-ikun fe-l-mekteb dyalu koll nhaṛ fe-ṣ-ṣbaƐ.	The teacher is in his office every day in the morning.
dima ka-ikunu Ɛăndhom le-flus.	They always have money.
ġad-ikunu Ɛăndna men t-tesƐud.	They'll be with us from nine o'clock on.
men t-tesƐud u-huma Ɛăndna.	They've been with us since nine o'clock.
škun lli qal-lek dak š-ši?	Who told you that?
had š-ši ma-ġad-ikun-š mezyan.	This isn't going to be good.
xeṣṣek ddir had š-ši deġya.	You have to do this quickly.

ʕlaš bġiti ddir dak š-ši?	What do you want to do that for?
ma-ka-ndiru-š dak š-ši ʕăndna.	We don't do that in our country.
ʕăndna fe-l-meġṛib ka-nšeṛbu atay bezzaf.	In Morocco we drink tea a lot.
ma-bqit-š nexdem temma.	I don't work there any more.
ma-bqa-š išufha.	He doesn't see her any more.
ma-bqina-š nemšiw l-ʕănd dak l-ḥăžžam.	We don't go to that barber any more.

II. Grammatical Notes.

A. The student is already familiar with the lack of a Moroccan equivalent for 'is' or 'are' in such sentences as *huwa fe-ḍ-ḍaṛ,* 'He's in the house', etc. When English 'is' or 'are' however refer to something habitual or repetitive, then the durative tense of *kan* 'to be' must be used, as in such a sentence as *le-fqi ka-ikun fe-l-mekteb dyalu koll nhaṛ fe-ṣ-ṣbaḥ* 'The teacher is in his office every day in the morning'. Or compare *huma mʕăṭṭlin* 'They're late' (on a specific occasion) and *dima ka-ikunu mʕăṭṭlin* 'They're always late.'

B. Grammatical Note **B** of Lesson 96 revealed that uses of *ʕănd* in the sense of 'to have' are actually equational sentences. The durative and future of *kan* 'to be' are used with *ʕănd* to signal habitual or future meanings of 'to have', as in *dima ka-ikunu ʕăndhom le-flus* 'They always have money' and *ʕămmeṛhom ma-ġad-ikunu ʕăndhom le-flus.* 'They'll never have any money.'

C. The forms *had* 'this' and *dak* 'that' are always used immediately with nouns, as in *had le-bṛa* 'this letter' or *dak l-ḥăžžam* 'that barber'. The expressions *had š-ši* 'this' and *dak š-ši* 'that' are used with reference to general situations, as in *škun lli qal-lek dak š-ši* 'Who told you that?'

D. The negative perfect tense of *bqa* 'to stay, to remain' is used with a following imperfect as equivalent to English 'no longer, not any more', as in *ma-bqit-š nexdem temma* 'I don't work there any more.'

E. The word *ʕăndna* 'we have, at our place' also has the idiomatic meaning of 'in our country', as for example a Moroccan contrasting differences between Morocco and the United States.

III. Exercise.

Repeat the exercise of Lesson 96 but using the future rather than the perfect tense of ***kan*** 'to be'.

IV. Vocabulary.

dak š-ši	that (see Grammatical Note **C**)
had š-ši	this (see Grammatical Note **C**)
mekteb	office
ɛăndna	in our country (see Grammatical Note **E**)

LESSON NINETY-EIGHT

I. Text.

ila	if (introducing possible conditions only)
ila ža ġedda, qul-lu iḍṛeb-li t-tilifun.	If he comes tomorrow, tell him to phone me.
ila ma-ža-š fe-l-weqt, nḍṛeb-lek t-tilifun.	If he doesn't come on time, I'll phone you.
ila ṭlebtiha mennha, teɛṭiha-lek.	If you ask her for it, she'll give it to you.
ila ma-žit-š fe-l-weqt, sir bla biya.	If I don't come on time, go without me.
ila ma-derti-š had š-ši, xeṣṣek temši bla biya.	If you don't do this, you'll have to go without me.
ila ṭelbu mennek le-flus, sir mɛahom l-l-ḅenk.	If they ask you for money, go to the bank with them.
ila beɛtiw ṭ-ṭumubil b-taman mezyan, imken-lkom džiw mɛana.	If you sell the car for a good price, you'll be able to come with us.
ila kemmlet l-xedma fe-l-weqt, neɛṭiwha le-flus.	If she finishes the work on time, we'll give her some money.

ila nsaw, siru bla bihom.	If they forget, go without them.
ila ma-žbeṛtiwhom-š fe-ḍ-ḍaṛ, siru le-s-sinima bla bihom.	If you don't find them at home, go to the movies without them.
ila ḍṛeb-li t-tilifun, ma-ižbeṛni-š fe-ḍ-ḍaṛ.	If he phoned me, he wouldn't find me at home.
ila šraw mennek ḍ-ḍaṛ dyalek, tkun feṛƐan?	If they bought your house from you, would you be happy?
Ɛawel	to try
xfeq	to fail
ila Ɛawelti ddir dak š-ši, ġad-texfeq.	If you tried to do that, you would fail.
ila ḍḍeṛṛiti, nƐawlu nthelḷaw fik.	If you got hurt, we'd try to take care of you.
ila xefqet, ma-imken-li-š nṣifeṭ-lha le-flus.	If she failed, I wouldn't be able to send her the money.
ila šeftu, nqulha-lu.	If I saw him, I'd tell (it to) him.

II. Grammatical Notes.

A. In English such pairs of sentences as 'if you ask her for it, she will give it to you' and 'if you asked her for it, she would give it to you' are quite common. They show the pattern of 'if' followed by the present tense in one case ('if you ask') and by the past tense in the other case ('if you asked'). The difference of meaning is slight, primarily a matter of attitude on the part of the speaker. The use of the past tense after 'if' ('if you asked') generally indicates doubt on the part of the speaker as to whether an event will actually occur ('if you asked', implying 'I don't imagine you will'). The use of the present tense after 'if' indicates the likelihood or possibility of an event actually occurring ('if you ask', implying 'it's entirely possible you will ask, I don't know whether you will or not').

Moroccan shows no equivalent for such English pairs as 'if you ask—if you asked', 'if he goes—if he went', etc. In Moroccan, *ila* 'if' is always followed by the perfect tense. If more than one English translation is possible in any given case, context determines which is appropriate. For example, *ila ža* can be translated either as 'if he comes' or 'if he came', but in such a context as *ila ža ġedda, qul-lu idṛeb-li t-tilifun,* only 'if he comes' is possible.

B. Note the forms *bla biya* 'without me', *bla bihom* 'without them'. The form for 'without' is regularly *bla bi-* before pronoun endings. The endings are added regularly, e.g. *bla bik* 'without you' (sg.), *bla bih* 'without him', *bla biha* 'without her', etc.

C. Note that *mša* 'to go' has irregular imperatives, sg. *sir* and pl. *siru.*

D. Note the form *nqulha-lu* in *ila šeftu nqulha-lu* 'if I saw him I'd tell (it to) him'. It is usual for the pronoun ending *-ha* 'it' (f.) to be used in Moroccan equivalents of 'tell' when a specific thing or situation is implied but not expressed in English.

III. Exercises.

Go through the text of this lesson and make all positive forms negative and all negative forms positive.

IV. Vocabulary.

bla bi- (before pronoun endings only)	without
ila	if
sir (sg.), *siru* (pl.)	go (see Grammatical Note C)
xfeq	to fail
ɛawel	to try

LESSON NINETY-NINE

I. Text.

kun	if (introducing impossible conditions)
kun kan ka-ixdem hna, kun qoltha-lek.	If he were working here, I would have told you.
kun konna ka-nxedmú ɛăndhom, kun qaluha-lek.	If we had been working at their place, they would have told you.
kun qalha-li ši-waɛed, kun žit nšufek.	If someone had told me, I would have come to see you.
kun žitiw l-ɛăndi, kun ɛṭitkom t-tṣaweṛ.	If you had come to my place, I would've given you the pictures.

kteṛ men had š-ši	more (than this)
kun xdemna kteṛ men had š-ši, kun ma-xfeqna-š.	If we had worked more, we wouldn't have failed.
kun ktebti-lna men qbel, kun ṣifeṭna-lek l-bakit qbel-ma iži.	If you had written us beforehand, we would have sent you the package before he arrived.
kun qṛat kteṛ men had š-ši, kun ma-xefqet-š.	If she had studied more, she wouldn't have failed.
kun kanu ɛăndi le-flus, kun mšit mɛakom.	If I had the money, I'd go with you.
kun ma-konti-š kbeṛ menni, kun ma-dditi-š l-biškliṭa dyali.	If you weren't bigger than me, you wouldn't have taken my bicycle.
ṭaṛ	to fly
kun kanu ɛăndi ž-žnaweḥ, kun ṭeṛt.	If I had wings, I would fly.
kun kanu ɛăndha ž-žwaneḥ, kun ṭaṛet.	If she had had wings, she would have flown.
kun ma-kan-š kbeṛ menni, kun ḍṛebtu.	If he hadn't been bigger than me, I would have hit him.
kun kont ġani, kun šritha-lek.	If I were rich, I would buy it for you.
kun kanet ġanya, kun šrathom-li.	If she had been rich, she would have bought them for me.
kun ma-kanu-š aġniya, kun ma-ṭlebt mennhom walu.	If they weren't rich, I wouldn't ask them for anything.
mat	to die
ġṛeq	to drown
kun ma-kont-š ana, kun ġṛeq.	If it hadn't been for me, he would have drowned.
kun ma-kan-š ḅḅa, kun mett.	If it weren't for my father, I would die.
kun ma-kanu-š huma, ġṛeqna.	If it hadn't been for them, we would have drowned.
kun ma-kanet-š hiya, kun ma-konna-š ka-naklu.	If it weren't for her, we wouldn't be eating.

II. Grammatical Notes.

A. Such phrases as 'if we had worked' and 'if I were rich' indicate two different kinds of contrary-to-fact conditions in English. The first kind refers to past circumstances which did not occur, i.e. 'if we had worked' implies 'we did not work'. The second kind refers to present but unreal circumstances, i.e. 'if I were rich' implies 'I am not rich'.

Moroccan makes no distinction between present and past contrary-to-fact conditions. Both are translated by ***kun*** 'if' followed by the perfect tense. In most cases there is no ambiguity as to the English equivalent, e.g. ***kun xdemna*** can be translated only 'if we had worked'. The only ambiguity is with forms of ***kan*** 'to be'. Thus, ***kun kont*** is equivalent to both 'if I were' (present contrary-to-fact) and 'if I had been' (past contrary-to-fact), ***kun kanet*** translates both 'if she were' and 'if she had been', etc. General context is the decisive factor in determining whether present or past contrary-to-fact conditions are referred to.

A similar ambiguity exists when ***kan*** is used in verb phrases or in idiomatic expressions, e.g. *kun kan ka-ixdem hna,* where the English translation might be either 'if he were working here' or 'if he had been working here', depending on whether a present or past contrary-to-fact condition is involved. Note the use with ***Eănd*** in the sense of 'to have', e.g. ***kun kanu Eăndi le-flus*** 'if I had money' or 'if I had had money', depending on present or past contextual circumstances.

B. A special use of ***kan*** in its basic meaning of 'to exist', 'to be' must be noted, as illustrated in ***kun ma-kont-š ana*** 'if it weren't for me' (literally, 'if I didn't exist') or 'if it hadn't been for me'. In this usage a subject must always be expressed for ***kan,*** either a pronoun, as ***ana*** in the example above, or a noun, as in ***kun ma-kan-š ḅḅa*** 'if it weren't for my father'. As with other conditional uses of ***kan*** 'to be' after ***kun*** 'if', the double translational possibility exists in English.

C. In English, contrary-to-fact conditions with 'if' are almost always followed by 'would' or 'would have', as in 'If someone had told me, I would have come to see you'. The equivalent of English 'would' or 'would have' in such cases is rendered by Moroccan ***kun*** followed by the perfect tense, exactly the same structure as for the conditions themselves. Note the construction as illustrated in the text by such sentences as ***kun kont ġani, kun šritha-lek*** 'If I were rich, I would buy it for you', etc.

D. Lessons 98 and 99 show the contrast between two different Moroccan words for 'if': *ila* for possible conditions and ***kun*** for contrary-to-fact conditions. The different types of constructions associated with *ila* and ***kun*** should not be confused with one another despite the fact that both words are translated as 'if'.

III. Exercises.

A. Take the possible conditions with *ila* in the text of Lesson 99 and form parallel contrary-to-fact conditions. Note that changes other than substituting ***kun*** for *ila* are necessary, e.g. such a reference to future time as *ġedda* 'tomorrow' must be replaced by some reference to present or past time, e.g. *l-bareƹ* 'yesterday'. Read the resulting new sentences out loud.

B. Reverse the instructions of Exercise A above and change the contrary-to-fact conditions of Lesson 99 to possible conditions, e.g. change ***kun qṛat kteṛ men had š-ši kun ma-xefqet-š*** 'If she had studied more, she wouldn't have failed' to ***ila qṛat kteṛ men had š-ši, ma-texfeq-š*** 'If she studies more, she won't fail.'

IV. Vocabulary.

ġani	rich
ġanya (f.)	
aġniya (pl.)	
ġṛeq	to drown
kun	if
mat	to die
men	than
ṭaṛ	to fly
žnaweƹ	wings

LESSON ONE HUNDRED

I. Text.

hada huwa ṛ-ṛažel.	This is the man.
hadi hiya le-mṛa.	This is the woman.
hadu huma n-nas.	There are the people.

lli	who, which, that
ɛlih	on him, about him
hada huwa ṛ-ṛažel lli ṭaɛ.	This is the man that fell.
hada huwa ṛ-ṛažel lli ɛawen ḅḅa.	This is the man that helped my father.
hada huwa ṛ-ṛažel lli ɛawen ḅḅa.	This is the man (that) my father helped.
hada huwa ṛ-ṛažel lli ḍeṛbet ṭ-ṭumubil.	This is the man (that) the car hit.
hada huwa ṛ-ṛažel lli qolna-lek ɛlih.	This is the man (that) we told you about.
hada huwa ṛ-ṛažel lli kanu ɛăndu le-flus.	This is the man that had the money.
hada huwa ṛ-ṛažel lli ḍehṛu ḍḍeṛṛ.	This is the man whose back got hurt.
hada huwa ṛ-ṛažel lli š-škaṛa dyalu fiha le-bṛawat.	This is the man whose briefcase has the letters in it.
hada huwa ṛ-ṛažel lli f-žibu l-uṛaq.	This is the man that's got the tickets in his pocket.
hadik hiya l-bent lli ḍeṛbet xti.	That's the girl that hit my sister.
hadik hiya l-bent lli ḍeṛbet xti.	That's the girl my sister hit.
hadik hiya l-bent lli bġit ntkellem mɛaha.	That's the girl that I want to talk with.
hadik hiya l-bent lli ɛăndha le-ɛwayež ž-ždad.	That's the girl that has the new clothes.
hadik hiya l-bent lli ṃṃha matet.	That's the girl whose mother died.
hadik hiya l-bent lli šra-lha ḅḅaha biškliṭa ždida.	That's the girl whose father bought her a new bicycle.
fayn d-drari lli ɛṭitihom š-šekḷat?	Where are the children (that) you gave the chocolate to?
waš haduk huma n-nas lli ġad-nwerriwhom t-tṣaweṛ?	Are those the people we're going to show the pictures to?

II. Grammatical Notes.

A. When Moroccan *lli* 'who, which, that' is the subject of a following verb, the usage is exactly like English. Cf. such sentences as *hada huwa ṛ-ṛažel lli ṭaɛ* 'This is the man that fell.'

B. Compare the word order of *lli ḍeṛbet ṭ-ṭumubil* and 'that the car hit' in the sentence *hada huwa ṛ-ṛažel lli ḍeṛbet ṭ-ṭumubil* 'this is the man that the car hit'. The Moroccan word order in such sentences is fixed. In the case of two different nouns which would take the same verb form, this fixed word order is ambiguous. English has such differences as 'the man that helped my father' and 'the man that my father helped'. In Moroccan the only possible word order is *lli ɛawen ḅḅa,* and the question of who helped whom can only be inferred from context. A similar example is *hadik hiya l-bent lli ḍeṛbet xti,* which can mean either 'That's the girl that hit my sister' or 'that's the girl (that) my sister hit.'

C. Unlike English, a preposition referring back to *lli* must have a pronoun object. Compare English 'the girl that I want to talk with' and Moroccan *l-bent lli bġit ntkellem mɛaha.* The structure is as if one said 'the girl that I want to talk with her'. Note that phrases with *ɛănd* 'to have' technically fall into this category, e.g. *hada huwa ṛ-ṛažel lli kanu ɛăndu le-flus* 'This is the man that had the money'.

D. English 'whose' is translated by Moroccan *lli* followed by a possessive. Note the way *hadik hiya l-bent* 'that's the girl' and *ṃṃha matet* 'her mother died' are joined by *lli* into the sentence *hadik hiya l-bent lli ṃṃha matet* 'That's the girl whose mother died'. Sentences of this sort can be somewhat complex, but the basic structure is simple if the material following *lli* is taken as a separate unit which, as a whole, refers back to the material preceding *lli.*

E. In cases where English 'that' is not the subject of a following verb it can be omitted, as in 'This is the man (that) we told you about'. The corresponding *lli* can never be omitted in such cases, e.g. *hada huwa ṛ-ṛažel lli qolna-lek ɛlih.*

F. In the case of *ɛṭa* 'to give' and *werra* 'to show', the person to whom something is given or shown appears as a pronoun ending on the verb, e.g. *fayn d-drari lli ɛṭitihom š-šekḷaṭ?* 'Where are the children that you gave the chocolate to?'

G. The forms *hada* 'this' and *hadak* 'that' require *huwa* 'he' before a following noun with the definite article, e.g. *hadak huwa l-weld* 'That's the boy'.

The feminine and plural forms of these demonstratives similarly require ***hiya*** 'she' and ***huma*** 'they', e.g. ***hadik hiya l-bent*** 'that's the girl' and ***hadu huma n-nas*** 'these are the people'.

III. Exercises.

Change each of the sentences below into a sentence using *lli* by taking the underlined noun and using it in a phrase on the order of 'This is . . .', 'These are . . .', or 'That is . . .', 'Those are . . .', followed by *lli*. For example, the sentence *šrit had ṭ-ṭumubil l-bareḥ* 'I bought this car yesterday' should be changed to *hadi hiya ṭ-ṭumubil lli šrit l-bareḥ* 'This is the car (that) I bought yesterday'.

A. Sentences where *lli* is the subject of a following verb.

1. *had l-bent ka-tɛawen xay.*
2. *dak l-weld dima ka-iweqqef l-biškliṭa dyalu muṛa ḍ-ḍaṛ.*
3. *duk n-nas ɛămmeṛhom ma-ka-ixedmu.*
4. *dak l-metɛăllma ddat le-flus dyalna.*
5. *had l-xeddama baqi ma-žebṛu xedma.*
6. *dak t-tellaža ma-ši mezyana.*
7. *had l-magana meṣnuɛa men d-dheb.*
8. *had l-ġoṛṛaf meṣnuɛ men l-feḍḍa.*
9. *dak ḍ-ḍaṛ kanet ġalya bezzaf men qbel.*
10. *dak l-weld xfeq fe-l-xedma dyalu.*

B. Sentences where *lli* is the object of a following verb.

1. *žebt-lu had le-bṛawat.*
2. *waš baqi ma-qṛaw had ḍ-ḍuṛuṣ?*
3. *ṭ-ṭumubil ḍeṛbet had s-siyyed.*
4. *šrit l-biḍ.*
5. *ɛṭawna hdiya.*
6. *šrina had ẓ-ẓeṛbiya fe-l-ḥanut dyalu.*
7. *žbeṛt waḥed l-mešṭa.*
8. *ɛmelna bezzaf d-le-ḥwayež fe-ṭ-ṭumubil.*
9. *derna dak l-xedma wel-l-bareḥ.*
10. *ġad-idiru had l-xedma băɛd ġedda.*

C. Sentences where a preposition refers back to *lli*.

1. *kont ka-nexdem f-had l-măƐmel.*
2. *ġad-nebqaw Ɛănd duk n-nas ši-šheṛ.*
3. *kteb le-bṛa b-had s-stilu.*
4. *konti gales Ɛda had l-bent?*
5. *weqqef ṭ-ṭumubil muṛa dak ḍ-ḍaṛ.*
6. *ġad-ṭṭleb le-flus men duk n-nas?*
7. *dar l-feḍḍa f-had ṣ-ṣenduq.*
8. *Ɛṭatha le-d-drari.*
9. *kanet ka-tthelḷa f-dak l-bent.*
10. *ġad-iddi le-flus dyalu l-lḅenk.*

D. Sentences where *lli* is followed by a possessive.

1. *ġad-nešriw ḍ-ḍaṛ dyal duk n-nas.*
2. *had l-xeddam ma-Ɛăndu flus bezzaf.*
3. *had l-bent ḅḅaha mat.*
4. *mšit l-Ɛănd dak l-Ɛăžžam.*
5. *had s-siyyed ḍḍeṛṛ ḍehṛu fe-l-Ɛadita.*

IV. Vocabulary.

lli	who, which, that (see the Grammatical Notes)

LESSON ONE HUNDRED ONE

I. Text.

škun huwa had l-weld?	Who is this boy?
škun hiya had l-bent?	Who is this girl?
škun huma had n-nas?	Who are these people?
Ɛliha	on (about) her, on it (f.)
Ɛliya	on me, about me.
Ɛṭitu š-šelya lli kont gales Ɛliha.	I gave him the chair that I was sitting on.
Ɛăyydu ṭ-ṭebla lli konna ka-ndiru Ɛliha le-ktub dyalna.	They took away the table that we used to put our books on.

l-bent lli qolt-lek ɛliha ġad-dži ġedda.	The girl (that) I told you about is coming tomorrow.
škun lli qal-lek ɛliya?	Who told you about me?
ɛlihom	on them, about them
škun hiya l-bent lli qalet-lkom ɛla duk ẓ-ẓṛabi?	Who is the girl that told you about those rugs.
ma-ġad-nešriw-š duk ẓ-ẓṛabi lli qalet-lna ɛlihom.	We're not going to buy those rugs (that) she told us about.
fayn derti l-xemsin weṛqa lli ɛṭitek?	Where did you put the fifty tickets I gave you?
daret l-xemsin stilu lli šrina f-had ṣ-ṣenḍuq.	She put the fifty fountain pens (that) we bought in this box.
kaynin settin tilifun fe-l-mekteb lli ka-nexdem fih.	There are sixty telephones in the office (that) I work in.
had le-ktab ž-ždid lli ɛṭana, fih settin ḍeṛs.	This new book (that) he gave us has sixty lessons in it.
dak s-siyyed l-ġani lli qolt-lek ɛlih ɛăndu sebɛin ḍaṛ.	That rich man (that) I told you about has seventy houses.
škun huma duk s-sebɛin de-n-nas lli žaw mɛak?	Who are those seventy people that came with you.
žab-li tmanin teṣwiṛa ždida.	He brought me eighty new pictures.
ɛašet setta u-tamanin ɛam.	She lived eighty-six years.
baɛ tesɛin xenša de-ṣ-ṣuf.	He sold ninety bags of wool.
le-xnaši lli baɛ š-kan fihom?	What was in the bags that he sold?
had l-măɛmel ka-ixedmu fih tesɛud u-xemsin de-n-nas.	There are fifty-nine people working in this factory.
had ḍ-ḍaṛ le-kbira fiha waḥed u-xemsin bit.	This big house has fifty-one rooms in it.
weṣlet ṛebɛa u-settin bṛa l-yum.	Sixty-four letters arrived today.
ṣifeṭna tmenya u-sebɛin bakit l-l-buṣta.	We sent seventy-eight packages to the post office.
ẓaṛ tnayn u-tmanin blad ṣġiṛa fe-l-meġrib.	He visited eighty-two small towns in Morocco.
had le-blad ṣ-ṣġiṛa ma-fiha ġir tlata u-tesɛin ḍaṛ.	This little town only has ninety-three houses in it.

II. Grammatical Notes.

A. The pronoun *škun?* 'who?' is regularly used with *huwa* 'he', *hiya* 'she', or *huma* 'they' before a following noun, as in *škun hiya had l-bent?* 'Who is this girl?'.

B. The preposition *εla* 'on, about' has the form *εli-* before pronoun endings.

III. Exercises.

Go through the exercises of Lesson 40 and, in so far as makes sense, form new sentences according to the following pattern: Using *fayn* 'where' form a question with the underlined material in the sentence and join it to the remainder of the sentence with *lli*. For example, from *εṭa le-ktab le-ṛ-ṛažel* form the sentence *fayn le-ktab lli εṭa le-ṛ-ṛažel?*

IV. Vocabulary.

sebεin	seventy
settin	sixty
tmanin	eighty
tesεin	ninety
xemsin	fifty

LESSON ONE HUNDRED TWO

I. Text.

εṭani ši-dwa nfăεni bezzaf.	She gave me some medicine that helped me a lot.
εṭitu qlam kan εăndi.	I gave him a pencil that I had.
šrina ṭumubil ma-ka-temši-š mezyan.	We bought a car that doesn't run well.
fe-l-ʔaxir	finally, at last
fe-l-ʔaxir žbeṛt ši-waḥed qal-li l-ḥăqq.	I finally found someone that told me the truth.
fe-l-ʔaxir žbeṛna xeddam ka-iži fe-l-weqt.	At last we've found a worker who comes on time.

ṭleb menni le-flus waḥed l-weld ka-ixdem ɛăndi.	A boy that works for me asked me for some money.
ṭelbu menni le-flus ši-nas kanu ka-ixedmu ɛăndi.	Some people that used to work at my place asked me for some money.
waḥed l-bent ṣġiṛa ḅḅaha mṛiḍ ṭelbet menni nɛawenha.	A little girl whose father is sick asked me to help her.
waḥed l-weld ṃṃu mṛiḍa ṭleb menni nɛawnu.	A boy whose mother was sick asked me to help him.
waḥed s-siyyed kanet mṛatu mṛiḍa ṭleb mennna nɛawnuh.	A man whose wife had been sick asked us to help him.
bġit ši-dwa infăɛni.	I want a medicine that will do me good.
xeṣṣni nežbeṛ š-waḥed iqul-li l-ḥăqq.	I have to find someone who'll tell me the truth.
ḍuwweṛ ɛla	to look for, to hunt for,
ka-iḍuwwṛu ɛla ši-xnaši irefdu fihom l-makla dyalhom.	They're looking for some bags to carry their food in.
ka-ḍḍuwweṛ ɛla ši-ṛažel ikunu ɛăndu le-flus bezzaf.	She's looking for a man with a lot of money.
ka-nḍuwweṛ ɛla ḍaṛ kbira ikunu fiha ɛăšṛa d-le-byut.	I'm looking for a big house with ten rooms in it.
bġat ši-ḥaža teqṛaha.	She wants something to read.
bġina ši-ḥaža nakluha.	We want something to eat.
ka-nḍuwwṛu ɛla ši-ẓeṛbiya mezyana neɛṭiwha-lhom.	We are looking for a good rug to give them.
ka-iḍuwweṛ ɛla ši-bent ikun ḅḅaha ġani.	He's looking for some girl with a rich father.
bġina ši-metɛăllma tkun l-xedma dyalha mezyana.	We want a maid whose work will be good.

II. Grammatical Notes.

A. The use of *lli* as studied in Lessons 100 and 101 was to join two phrases or sentences together into a larger sentence. There was always a specific noun to which *lli* referred, e.g. in *l-bent lli qolt-lek ɛliha ġad-dži ġedda* 'The girl I told you about is coming tomorrow', *lli* refers to *l-bent*. In all the examples given in Lessons 100 and 101, all the nouns to which *lli* referred had the definite article. In the case of indefinite nouns, e.g. those with 'some' or 'a' in English, *lli* cannot be used. Sentences are put together according to the same patterns as shown in Lessons 100 and 101, but with no equivalent for English 'who', 'which' or 'that', e.g. *šrina ṭumubil ma-ka-temši-š mezyan* 'We bought a car that doesn't run well.'

B. A small difference in pattern is where *lli* serves as the object of the verb, as in *hada hiya l-bent lli šeft* 'This is the girl I saw'. In the constructions where *lli* does not occur, the object must be supplied by a pronoun ending, as in *bġina ši-ḥaža nakluha* 'We want something to eat'.

C. In constructions of the sort discussed in this lesson, future possibilities are always indicated in Moroccan by the imperfect tense. This consistent use of the imperfect contrasts to a variety of different constructions in English, e.g. 'with' in *ka ḍḍuwweṛ ɛla ši-ṛažel ikunu ɛăndu le-flus bezzaf* 'She's looking for a man with a lot of money', or note the 'will' in *xeṣṣni nežbeṛ ši-waḥed iqul-li l-ḥăqq* 'I have to find someone who'll tell me the truth'. The English infinitive, as is often the case elsewhere (cf. Grammatical Note **A**, Lesson 77), also occurs as the translation of the Moroccan imperfect in such sentences, e.g. *ġad-ižib-li ṣenduq ndir fih le-ḥwayež* 'He's going to bring me a box to put the clothes in'. Another possible translation for this last sentence would be 'He's going to bring me a box for me to put the clothes in'.

D. Reread Grammatical Note **B**, Lesson 76. In constructions of the sort discussed above, a Moroccan equational sentence can be translated as an English present or an English past, depending on circumstances or the tense of another verb in the sentence, e.g. in *waḥed l-bent ṣġiṛa ḅḅaha mṛiḍ ṭelbet menni nɛawenha,* the phrase *ḅḅaha mṛiḍ* can be translated either as 'whose (her) father is sick' or 'whose father was sick'. If the perfect of the Moroccan *kan* 'to be' is used, the meaning can only be 'had been', indicating the condition no longer exists at the time one is speaking of, e.g. *waḥed s-siyyed kanet mṛatu mṛiḍa ṭleb mennna nɛawnuh* 'A gentleman whose wife had been sick asked us to help him', implying that the wife was no longer sick at the time of the request.

III. Exercises.

Review the exercises of Lessons 100-101.

IV. Vocabulary.

ḍuwweṛ ع*la*	to look for, to hunt for
*fe-l-*ʔ*axir*	finally, at last

LESSON ONE HUNDRED THREE

I. Text.

qḍeṛ	can, to be able
*ka-iqḍeṛ ixeddem had l-makina b-yedd we*ح*da.*	He can operate this machine with one hand.
*ma-ka-iqḍeṛ-š itkellem n-negliza, be-l-*ح*ăqq ka-iktebha.*	He can't speak English, but he writes it.
ka-neqḍeṛ neqṛa mezyan b-had n-nḍaḍeṛ ž-ždad.	I can read well with these new glasses.
*ma-neqḍeṛ-š nemši m*ع*ak, ana mešġul.*	I can't go with you, I'm busy.
*waš teqḍeṛ te*ع*mel-li had l-xedma?*	Can you do this work for me?
ma-neqḍeṛ-š nšufu men hna.	I can't see him from here.
*ma-kont-š ka-neqḍeṛ ntkellem l-*ع*ăṛbiya mnin wṣelt l-lmeġṛib.*	I wasn't able to speak Arabic when I arrived in Morocco.
ma-kanet-š ka-teqḍeṛ teqṛa mezyan b-had n-nḍaḍeṛ.	She wasn't able to read well with these glasses.
*kan ka-iqḍeṛ ye*ع*mel had l-xedma qbel l-*ح*adita.*	He was able to do this work before the accident.
*fe-l-*ʔ*axir qḍeṛ išedd l-bab.*	He finally succeeded in getting the door shut.
*bġit nerfed ṣ-ṣnaḍeq, be-l-*ح*ăqq ma-qḍeṛt-š.*	I tried to lift the boxes, but I couldn't.
ma-qedṛet-š tkemmel l-xedma dyalha fe-l-weqt.	She didn't manage to get her work done on time. (She wasn't able to finish her work on time; she failed to finish her work on time.)

ma-qedṛet-š teqṛa mezyan b-had n-nḍaḍeṛ.	She wasn't able to read well with these glasses. (She failed to read well with these glasses, it turned out that she couldn't read well with these glasses.)
qḍeṛ ɛla	to be able to afford, to be able to do
ma-iqḍeṛ-š ɛla had l-xedma.	He's not up to this work, he's not able to do this work.
kif-aš qḍeṛti ɛla had ḍ-ḍaṛ?	How were you able to afford this house?
luwwel	first
had l-weld huwa l-luwwel.	This boy is (the) first.
waš hadi l-meṛṛa l-luwwla?	Is this the first time?
tani	second
hada huwa t-tani.	This is the second one.
hadi ˀusbuɛ baš weṣlet le-bṛa t-tanya.	The second letter arrived a week ago.
talet	third
ṣ-ṣenḍuq t-talet kan ɛameṛ b-le-ɛwayež.	The third box was full of clothes.
dxol men l-bab t-talta.	Go in through the third door.
ṛabeɛ	fourth
hada huwa ṛ-ṛabeɛ.	This is the fourth one.
hadi l-meṛṛa ṛ-ṛabɛa u-huwa ka-iḍṛeb-li t-tilifun l-yum.	This is the fourth time he's telephoned me today.

II. Grammatical Notes.

The durative of *qḍeṛ* is used only to refer to general and enduring situations as in *ka-iqḍeṛ ixeddem had l-makina b-yedd weɛda* 'He can operate this machine with one hand'. As is usual with other verbs, general and enduring situations in past time are indicated with the perfect tense of *kan* 'to be' before the durative of *qḍeṛ*, as in *ma-kanet-š ka-teqḍeṛ mezyan b-had n-nḍaḍeṛ* 'She wasn't able to read well with these glasses'. This last sentence implies repeated, habitual, or extended use of the glasses in question. The sentence *ma-qeḍṛet-š teqṛa mezyan b-had n-nḍaḍeṛ* (with the same translation as the preceding one, 'She wasn't able to read well with these glasses') implies a specific experimental trial of a pair of glasses, with unsatisfactory results.

When a specific event in the present or near future is referred to, the imperfect of *qḍeṛ* is used, as in *ma-neqḍeṛ-š nšufu men hna* 'I can't see him from here' or *teqḍeṛ teƐmel-li had l-xedma?* 'Can you (will you be able) to do this work for me?'

The perfect tense of *qḍeṛ* almost always refers to one specific event or period and is often equivalent to the past tense of English 'succeed' or 'manage to' as in *fe-l-ˀaxir qḍeṛ išedd l-bab* 'He finally succeeded in getting the door shut', 'he finally managed to shut the door'. The negative of the perfect tense is even sometimes conveniently translated as 'failed to', e.g. a possible idiomatic translation of *ma-qeḍṛet-š teqṛa mezyan b-had n-nḍaḍeṛ* is 'She failed to read well with these glasses'.

III. Exercises.

For every sentence in the text having *ana* 'I' as the subject, form a pertinent question having *nta* 'you' as the subject. Read the questions out loud.

IV. Vocabulary.

luwwel	first
nḍaḍeṛ (pl.)	(eye) glasses
qḍeṛ	can, be able
ṛabeƐ	fourth
talet	third
tani	second

LESSON ONE HUNDRED FOUR

I. Text.

ṣnăع	to make, to manufacture
meṣnuع	made, manufactured
had l-xeddam ka-iṣnăع ṣ-ṣwani men l-feḍḍa.	This worker makes trays out of silver.
had ṣ-ṣwani meṣnuعin men l-feḍḍa.	These trays are made of silver.
ka-iṣenعu l-buḷat f-had l-măعmel.	They manufacture light-bulbs in this factory.
l-buḷat ka-ikunu meṣnuعin men z-zaž.	Light bulbs are made out of glass.
daba bdaw ka-iṣenعu t-tellažat fe-l-meġṛib.	They have begun to manufacture refrigerators in Morocco now.
t-tellaža dyali meṣnuعa f-ᵓamirika.	My refrigerator was made in America.
had le-bṛa mektuba b-le-mdad.	This letter was written with ink.
had ṣ-ṣnadeq mektuba عlihom ši-ḥaža.	These boxes have something written on them.
xneq	to stop up, to block up
xneqt l-mežṛa b-le-qṭen.	I stopped up the drain with cotton.
l-mežṛa kanet mexnuqa b-le-ḥwayež le-mwessxin.	The drain was stopped up with dirty clothes.
qleb	to turn over, turn upside down, backwards.
ḍeṛbet ṭ-ṭebla u-qelbetha.	She hit the table and turned it over.
šeft waḥed ṭ-ṭumubil meqluba qeddam l-ḅenk.	I saw a car upside down in front of the bank.
mnin dxelt, žbeṛt le-qṛaعi kollhom meqlubin.	When I went in I found all the bottles turned upside down.
عlaš had ṭ-ṭbaṣel meqlubin?	Why are these dishes upside down?
ketbet l-عonwan meqlub.	She wrote the address backwards.
lbes s-serwal meqlub.	He put his pants on backwards.

II. Grammatical Notes.

A. Many Moroccan verbs have a derived form called the 'passive participle'. For verbs on the pattern of *CCeC,* e.g. ***kteb*** 'to write', the pattern is to prefix ***me*** and insert *-u-* between the last two consonants. Note the following pairs of verbs and passive participles:

kteb	to write
mektub	(having been) written
qleb	to turn upside down, backwards
meqlub	(having been turned) upside down, backwards
ṣnăƐ	to make, to manufacture
meṣnuƐ	(having been) made, manufactured.
xneq	to stop up, block (up)
mexnuq	(having been) stopped up, blocked (up)

These participles are regularly made feminine by adding *-a* and plural by adding *-in.* Note the masculine, feminine, and plural participles in:
žab-li waḥed l-ġoṛṛaf meṣnuƐ men d-dheb.
l-mežṛa kanet mexnuqa.
žbeṛt le-qṛaƐi kollhom meqlubin.

B. The Moroccan passive participle can be used only in referring to states, never to actions. Compare the difference in English between 'The drain was stopped up' and 'The drain got stopped up'. The Moroccan ***l-mežṛa kanet mexnuqa*** means only 'The drain was stopped up', signaling a condition, not an action.

C. For the use of ***ka-ikunu*** 'they are' instead of an equational sentence in ***l-buḷat ka-ikunu meṣnuƐin men z-zaž*** 'Light bulbs are made out of glass', see Grammatical Note A, Lesson 97.

D. Note the English past tense for a Moroccan equational sentence in ***t-tellaža dyali meṣnuƐa f-ˀamirika*** 'My refrigerator was made in America', with the time factor irrelevant. The insertion of ***kanet*** 'was' into the sentence above would give the absurd and impossible implication that the refrigerator in question used to have the characteristic of having been made in America but no longer does now.

III. Exercises.

In the sentences below, supply the proper form—masculine, feminine, or plural—of the passive participle of the verb written in parentheses. Read the resulting sentences out loud.

1. *had ṣ-ṣiniya (ṣnăɛ) men d-dheb.*
2. *had l-buḷa (ṣnăɛ) fe-l-meġrib.*
3. *žabet-li ši-ġṛaṛef (ṣnăɛ) men l-feḍḍa.*
4. *šrit waḥed ṣ-ṣenduq ṣġiṛ (ṣnăɛ) men l-feḍḍa.*
5. *had t-tellažat kollhom (ṣnăɛ) f-ʔamirika.*
6. *le-bṛawat dyalu kollhom (kteb) b-le-mdad.*
7. *žabet-li waḥed l-kas (kteb) ɛlih ši-ḥaža.*
8. *žbeṛt l-mežṛa (xneq) b-le-ḥwayež le-mwessxin.*
9. *ɛlaš had l-mežṛa (xneq)?*
10. *ɛlaš had ṭ-ṭebṣil (qleb)?*
11. *xay lbes l-kebbuṭ (qleb).*
12. *žbeṛt l-qeṛɛa (qleb) mnin dxelt.*

IV. Vocabulary.

ʔamirika	America
kollhom	all of them
mektub	written
meqlub	turned over, upside down, backward(s)
mexnuq	stopped up, blocked
mežṛa	drain
qleb	to turn over, turn upside down, backwards
ṣnăɛ	to make, to manufacture
tellaža	refrigerator
xneq	to stop up, block (up)

LESSON ONE HUNDRED FIVE

I. Text.

smăε	to hear, listen (to)
smăεti had l-ʔoğniya men qbel?	Have you heard this song before?
εămmeṛni ma-smăεt dak l-ʔoğniya men qbel.	I'd never heard that song before.
smăεtiha?	Did you hear her?
ġenna	to sing
ġenna-lna l-ʔoğniya ž-ždida dyalu.	He sang his new song for us.
ka-tğenni le-d-drari fe-l-meḍṛaṣa.	She sings to the children at school.
εlaš ma-ġenniti-š kteṛ men had š-ši?	Why don't you sing more?
smăεtu ka-iğenni.	I heard him singing.
semεuna ka-ntkellmu.	They heard us talking.
ma-smăεtiha-š ka-tğenni?	Didn't you hear her singing?
εămmeṛkom ma-smăεtiwha ka-tğenni men qbel?	Haven't you ever heard her sing before?
ma-ġad-iži-š mεana tesmăεhom ka-iğenniw?	Aren't you going to come with us to hear them sing?
ṣuwweb	to fix, to repair
šafetni ka-nešεăl l-εafya.	She saw me lighting the fire.
bğat tšufni ka-nešεăl l-εafya.	She wants to watch me light the fire.
ġad-nšuf l-xeddama ka-iṣuwwbu ṭ-ṭumubil.	I'm going to watch the workers fix(ing) the car.
žbeṛt xay ka-iṣuwweb l-biškliṭa dyalu.	I found my brother fixing his bicycle.

II. Grammatical Notes.

The text of this lesson illustrates the use of the Moroccan durative as equivalent to English forms ending in '-ing', as in *smăεtu ka-iğenni* 'I heard him singing'.

III. Exercises.

From *semƐu* 'they heard' and *ka-ntkellmu* 'we talk, we are talking', it is possible to form a compound sentence *semƐuna ka-ntkellmu* 'They heard us talking'. Combine the following sentence pairs into compound sentences according to this pattern. Read the resulting compound sentences out loud.

1. *smăƐtiʔ*	Did you hear?
ka-tġenni.	She is singing.
2. *semƐet.*	She heard.
ka-itkellem.	He is talking.
3. *ma-Ɛămmeṛkom smăƐtiwehʔ*	Haven't you ever heard him?
ka-iġenni.	He sings.
4. *ma-smăƐthom-š.*	I didn't hear them.
ka-iġenniw.	They are singing.
5. *ma-šeftu-š.*	I didn't see him.
ka-ikteb waƐed le-bṛa.	He's writing a letter.
6. *šeftihaʔ*	Did you see her?
ka-ḍḍuwweṛ Ɛăl l-kebbuṭ dyalha.	She's looking for her coat.
7. *koll nhaṛ ka-nšuf dak l-bent.*	Every day I see that girl.
ka-ttsenna xaha.	She's waiting for her brother.
8. *šeftha.*	I saw her.
ka-tešƐăl l-Ɛafya.	She's lighting the fire.
9. *žebṛet l-weld dyalha.*	She found her son.
ka-isiyyeb ṭ-ṭbaṣel men š-šeṛžem.	He's throwing the plates out the window.
10. *žbeṛni.*	He found me.
ana gales fe-l-mekteb dyali ka-nešṛeb atay.	I'm sitting in my office drinking tea.

IV. Vocabulary.

ʔoġniya	song
ġenna (ka-iġenni)	to sing
smăƐ	to hear
ṣuwweb	to fix, to repair
Ɛafya	fire

LESSON ONE HUNDRED SIX

I. Text.

mnin	when, as, while
le-xbaṛ	the news (item)
smăƐnaha ka-tweṣṣel-lu le-xbaṛ.	We heard her tell(ing) him the news.
(l-bareɛ) smăƐnaha weṣṣlet-lu le-xbaṛ.	(1) (Yesterday) we heard her tell him the news.
	(2) (Yesterday) we heard that she had told him the news.
smăƐnaha weṣṣlet-lu le-xbaṛ.	(1) We heard her tell him the news.
	(2) We hear that she's told him the news.
smăƐnaha mnin weṣṣlet-lu le-xbaṛ.	We heard her tell him (as she told him) the news.
mnin kont f-fas smăƐt ḅḅaha Ɛṭaha bezzaf d-le-flus.	When I was in Fez I heard that her father gave (had given) her a lot of money.
smăƐt ḅḅaha Ɛṭaha bezzaf d-le-flus.	I hear (heard) that her father gave (had given) her a lot of money.
smăƐti ḅḅaha Ɛṭaha bezzaf de-le-flus?	Have you heard that her father gave her a lot of money?
smăƐthom ma-mšaw-š.	I hear (heard) that they didn't go.
smăƐtiha ka-tġenni?	(1) Did you hear her sing(ing)?
	(2) Did you hear that she was singing?
ma-smăƐtiha-š ġad-tġenni?	Haven't you heard that she's going to sing?
smăƐtiha ġennat temma?	(1) Did you hear her sing there?
	(2) Did you hear that she sang there?
smăƐtiha ma-ġennat-š?	Have you heard that she didn't sing?
smăƐtiha mnin ġennat l-ᵉoġniya ž-ždida dyalha?	Did you hear her sing (when she sang) her new song?
šefti l-bent mnin ṭaɛet fe-l-wad u-ġeṛqet?	Did you see the girl fall (when she fell) into the river and drown (drowned)?

ma-šefnaha-š mnin ġeṛqet fe-l-wad.	We didn't see her drown (as she drowned) in the river.
(*l-bareḥ*) *smăƐt l-weld dyalu kan mṛiḍ.*	(Yesterday) I heard that his son had been sick.
smăƐtu kan mṛiḍ.	I hear that he was sick.
(*l-bareḥ*) *smăƐna d-drari dyalhom mṛaḍ.*	(Yesterday) we heard that their children were sick.
smăƐnahom mṛaḍ.	We hear that they are sick.

II. Grammatical Notes.

A. An important aspect of English sentence structure is illustrated by the difference between 'fix' and 'fixing' in such sentence pairs as 'I saw him fix the car' and 'I saw him fixing the car'. The use of 'fix' indicates that the speaker witnessed the completion of the action. The use of 'fixing' indicates that the speaker witnessed at least part of the action but not necessarily the completion of it. For example, the sentence with 'fix' might be followed by 'and then I drove it home', whereas the sentence with 'fixing' might be followed by some such statement as 'but I left before he finished'.

In Lesson 105 illustrations were given of the Moroccan durative used as equivalent to English verb forms in '-ing' in such sentences as *šeftu ka-iṣuwweb ṭ-ṭumubil* 'I saw him fixing the car'. Moroccan structure does not provide the rigorous distinction between completed and incompleted action as does English with such pairs as 'fix' and 'fixing' in the sentence types illustrated above. Where a process rather than a result is the prime focus of attention, the Moroccan durative is used in contexts of past time even in those cases where English does not use the '-ing' form, e.g. *Ɛămmeṛkom ma-smăƐtiwha ka-tġenni men qbel?* 'Haven't you ever heard her sing before?' In references to future time, the Moroccan durative must be used regardless of whether English usage would call for an '-ing' form or not, e.g. *ma-ġad-dži-š mƐana tesmăƐhom ka-iġenniw?* 'Aren't you going to come with us to hear them sing?'

The Moroccan structure for signaling definitely completed action calls for the conjunction *mnin* 'when, as, while'. For example, the Moroccan sentence *smăƐnaha mnin weṣṣlet-lu le-xbaṛ* can be translated into English either as 'We heard her tell him the news' or 'We heard her when she told him the news'. Situation and context decide which translation is more appropriate in any given case. As a further example, note the contrasting sentence pairs *šeftu ka-išɛăl l-ɛafya* 'I saw him light(ing) the fire' and *šeftu mnin sɛăl l-ɛăfya* 'I saw him light (when he lit) the fire'.

B. The use of the verb *smăɛ* 'to hear' poses special problems for the English speaker. In English, 'to hear that (such and such has happened)' means to know something by second hand report. Moroccan *smăɛ* is used in the same way, but there is no equivalent for 'that'. Instead of an equivalent for 'that', Moroccan structure has the subject of a following verb as the object of *smăɛ*. Observe how *smăɛthom* 'I heard them' and *ma-mšaw-š* combine in *smăɛthom ma-mšaw-š* 'I heard that they didn't go'.

An ambiguity is encountered in such sentences when the action involved is actually susceptible of being heard as well as being reported about. Thus such a sentence as *smăɛnaha weṣṣlet-lu le-xbaṛ* is ambiguous. It can mean either 'We heard that she told him the news' or 'we heard her tell him the news'. To be completely clear, such other constructions as *smăɛnaha mnin weṣṣlet-lu le-xbaṛ* 'We heard her when she told him the news' or *ši-waḥed qal-lna weṣṣlet-lu le-xbaṛ* 'Someone told us that she'd told him the news' must be used.

A final ambiguity is the use of the English present tense in such expressions as 'I hear that they didn't go'. In such cases, the English present tense actually refers to past time, and the Moroccan durative form cannot be used to translate it. Such uses of the English present tense refer to very recent past actions and are regularly translated by the Moroccan perfect. In such a sentence as *smăɛt bḅaha ɛṭaha bezzaf d-le-flus,* only external knowledge of the recentness of the act of hearing determines whether 'I hear' or 'I heard' is the appropriate English translation. Thus both ' I hear her father gave (has given) her a lot of money' or 'I heard her father gave (had given) her a lot of money' are possible translations. If some such phrase as *mnin kont f-fas* 'when I was in Fez' is added, the past time of the situation is completely clear and only 'I heard' is possible as translation.

C. As has been pointed out before (cf. Grammatical Note **D**, Lesson 102) a Moroccan equational sentence in a context of past time is translated with 'was' or 'were'. The use of the perfect of *kan* 'to be' in such contexts usually signals time previous to the time signalled by the main verb of the sentence. In *smăɛtu kan mṛiḍ'* I heard that he had been sick', the implication is that he was no longer sick at the time, i.e. the state of being sick preceded the act of hearing. In *smăɛnahom mṛaḍ* on the other hand, the state of sickness is still in existence at the time of hearing, and the translation is either 'we hear that they are sick' or 'we heard that they were (are) sick'.

D. The sentence patterns described above apply to verbs other than *smăɛ* 'to hear' and *šaf* 'to see', e.g. *žbeṛna l-xeddam ṣuwweb l-mežṛa* 'We found that the worker had fixed the drain', etc.

III. Exercises.

Go through the text of this lesson and change all statements to questions and all questions to statements. For statements which have 'I' or 'we' as the subject, use the appropriate form of 'you' (singular for 'I' and plural for 'we') as the subject in the question. Likewise change 'you' (sg.) into 'I' in forming statements from questions. Read the new sentences resulting from these changes out loud.

IV. Vocabulary.

mnin	when, as, while
wad	river
weṣṣel	(literally 'to take, to cause to arrive'; 'to tell' only when used in connection with words such as *xbaṛ* 'news', etc.)
xbaṛ	item of news, news

LESSON ONE HUNDRED SEVEN

I. Text.

ɛṛef	to know
ka-yeɛṛef xay.	He knows my brother.
aš ka-teɛṛef fe-ṭ-ṭumubilat?	What do you know about cars?
ma-ka-neɛṛef-š (kif-aš) nxeddem had l-makina.	I don't know how to operate this machine.
kont ka-neɛṛef ḅḅak mnin kan mɛăllem fe-l-măɛmel.	I knew your father when he was a foreman at the factory.
ma-kan-š ka-yeɛṛef (kif-aš) ixeddem l-makina.	He didn't know how to operate the machine.

ma-kanet-š ka-teʕṛef ttkellem n-negliza mnin žat l-ˀamirika.	She didn't know how to speak English when she came to America.
ma-ʕṛeft kif-aš nkemmel l-xedma.	I don't know how to finish the work.
ma-ʕăṛfet fayn temši.	She doesn't know where to go.
daba ʕṛefna škun ġad-iʕawenna.	Now we know who's going to help us.
ma-ʕṛeftha-š ʕlaš mšat.	I didn't know why she left.
ma-ʕṛefnahom-š weqt-aš kanu ġad-iweṣlu.	We didn't know when they were going to arrive.
ʕăṛfetni kont ġad-nemši fe-ṭ-ṭiyyaṛa.	She knew that I was going to go by plane.
ʕăṛfuha ġad-dži ġedda.	They know she's coming tomorrow.
škun had ṛ-ṛažel?	Who is this man?
ma-ʕṛeft.	I don't know.
ma-ʕṛeft had ṛ-ṛažel škun huwa.	I don't know who this man is.
dak le-mṛa šʕal ʕăndha d-le-flus?	How much money does that woman have?
ma-ʕṛefna.	We don't know.
ma-ʕṛefna dak le-mṛa šʕal ʕăndha d-le-flus.	We don't know how much money that woman has.
men băʕd-ma qal dak š-ši, ʕad ʕṛefnah ma-bġa-š iʕawenna.	After he said that we realized he wouldn't help us.
men băʕd ši-šwiya, ʕṛeftu ma-kan-š ġad-ikemmel fe-l-weqt.	After a little while, I realized he wasn't going to finish on time.

II. Grammatical Notes.

A. The durative and perfect tenses of the verb *ʕṛef* 'to know' do not correspond directly to the English present and past tenses. In cases where a general and more or less enduring situation is referred to, the durative of *ʕṛef* corresponds to the English present tense, and the durative preceded by the perfect tense of *kan* 'to be' corresponds to the English past tense, as in *ka-yeʕṛef* *xay* 'He knows my brother' and *kont ka-neƐṛef ḅḅak mnin kan mƐăllem fe-l-măƐmel* 'I knew (used to know) your father when he was a foreman at the factory'.

B. When a specific occasion is referred to, the perfect tense of *Ɛṛef* is used as the equivalent of both the English past and present tenses. In statements, only the context indicates whether present or past time is referred to. Compare the two sentences *Ɛăṛfetni kont ġad-nemši fe-ṭ-ṭiyyaṛa* 'She knew that I was going to go by plane' and *Ɛăṛfuha ġad-dži ġedda* 'They know she's coming tomorrow'.

In the negative, the perfect tense of *Ɛṛef* takes a preceding *ma-* but never a final *-š* when present time is meant, as in *ma-Ɛăṛfet fayn temši* 'She doesn't know where to go' or *ma-Ɛṛeft* 'I don't know'. The final *-š* of the negative is usually included when past time is meant, as in *ma-Ɛṛefnahom-š weqt-aš kanu ġad-iweṣlu* 'We didn't know when they were going to arrive.'

C. In Grammatical Note **B** of Lesson 106, it was pointed out how *smăƐthom* 'I heard them' and *ma-mšaw-š* 'they didn't go' can combine to form a sentence *smăƐthom ma-mšaw-š* 'I heard that they didn't go'. A similar pattern is followed with *Ɛṛef* 'to know'. In English such a pair of sentences as 'I don't know' and 'Who is this man?' combine to form 'I don't know who this man is'. In Moroccan, the usual pattern is for the subject of the second sentence (noun or pronoun) to show up as the object of *Ɛṛef* in the longer combined sentence. Observe the combination of *ma-Ɛṛeft* 'I don't know' and *škun had ṛ-ṛažel?* 'Who is this man?' into *ma-Ɛṛeft had ṛ-ṛažel škun huwa* 'I don't know who this man is'. Observe the addition of the pronoun *huwa* 'he' in the combined sentence. The second part of such a combined sentence must always have a pronoun reference to the object of *Ɛṛef*. In the sentence *ma-Ɛṛefna dak le-mṛa šƐal Ɛăndha d-le-flus* 'We don't know how much money that woman has', the pronoun reference is the *-ha* at the end of *Ɛăndha*. In *ma-Ɛṛeftha-š Ɛlaš mšat* 'I didn't know why she left', the pronoun is implicit in the verb form *mšat*.

D. The perfect tense of *Ɛṛef* often has the implications of 'to realize, to learn, to come to know, to figure out'. Observe such a sentence as *daba Ɛṛefna škun ġad-iƐawenna* 'Now we (have finally figured out, come to know) know who's going to help us'.

E. The use of Moroccan *kif-aš* 'how' as equivalent for English 'how to' after 'know' is not necessary, although it is possible. Thus both *ma-ka-neƐṛef-š nxeddem had l-makina* and *ma-ka-neƐṛef-š kif-aš nxeddem had l-makina* are acceptable translations for 'I don't know how to operate this machine.'

III. Exercises.

Combine each of the following pairs of sentences into one longer sentence according to the pattern discussed in Grammatical Note C above.

1.	*ma-ɛṛeft-š.*	I didn't know.
	ɛlaš mšat?	Why did she go?
2.	*ma-ɛṛefna-š.*	We didn't know.
	weqt-aš kanu ġad-iweṣlu?	What time were they going to arrive?
3.	*ɛăṛfet.*	She knew.
	kont ġad-nemši fe-ṭ-ṭiyyaṛa.	I was going to go by plane.
4.	*ɛăṛfu.*	They know.
	ġad-dži ġedda.	She's coming tomorrow.
5.	*ma-ɛṛefna.*	We don't know.
	dak le-mṛa šḥal ɛăndha d-le-flus?	How much money does that woman have?
6.	*ɛad ɛṛefna.*	Then we realized.
	ma-bġa-š iɛawenna.	He wouldn't help us.
7.	*ɛṛeft.*	I realized.
	ma-kan-š ġad-ikemmel fe-l-weqt.	He wasn't going to finish on time.
8.	*ma-ɛṛefti?*	Don't you know?
	xak wṣel.	Your brother has arrived.
9.	*waš ɛăṛfet?*	Does she know?
	š-ka-teɛmel bentha?	What is her daughter doing?
10.	*ma-ɛṛefti?*	Don't you know?
	ɛlaš ḅḅak ma-bġa-š yăɛṭik le-flus?	Why won't your father give you the money?

IV. Vocabulary.

mɛăllem	foreman
ɛṛef	to know

LESSON ONE HUNDRED EIGHT

I. Text.

ḅḅaha ɛṭaha ši-flus baš tešri ṭumubil.	Her father gave her some money to (so she could) buy a car.
ḍṛebt-lha t-tilifun baš ma-tensa-š dži fe-l-weqt.	I phoned her so she wouldn't forget to come on time.
xeṣṣhom iqṛaw bezzaf baš ma-ixefqu-š.	They have to study hard (in order) not to (so they won't) fail.
qbeḍ	to seize, grab, hold (on to)
qebḍet l-weld baš ma-iṭiḥ-š.	She grabbed the boy so he wouldn't fall.
qbeḍ-li had t-teṣwiṛa baš nšufha mezyan.	Hold this picture for me so I can get a good look at it.
ṭfa	to turn out, turn off, put out
nɛăs	to sleep, go to sleep, go to bed
ṭfit ḍ-ḍuw baš nnɛăs.	I turned out the light so I could go to sleep.
ġad-nṭfiw ḍ-ḍuw baš ma-išufuna-š.	We're going to put out the light so they won't see us.
qalet-lna ma-nheḍṛu-š baš tenɛăs.	She told us not to talk so she could go to sleep.
ṣuwweṛ	to photograph, take a picture of
wqeft ḥda l-bab baš iṣuwweṛni ḅḅa.	I stood next to the door so my father could take a picture of me.
ṣuwweṛ ḍ-ḍaṛ baš nṣifṭu-lha t-teṣwiṛa.	Photograph the house so we can send her the picture.
rtaḥ	to rest
ḥăyydet ḍ-ḍuw baš nertaḥu ši-šwiya.	She took away the light so we could rest a a little.
bqa fe-ḍ-ḍaṛ baš irtaḥ.	He stayed at home to rest.
šɛălna ḍ-ḍuw baš inuḍu.	We turned on the light so they'd get up.
xellina ḍ-ḍuw mešɛul baš ma-inăɛsu-š.	We left the light turned on so they wouldn't go to sleep.

II. Grammatical Notes.

A. The word *baš* is used to indicate purpose. It is regularly followed by the imperfect. A variety of English translations correspond to the use of *baš* plus an imperfect. The translations usually involve 'to', 'in order to' 'will' 'would', 'can', or 'could'. The particular translation is determined by English context, and often several English translations are interchangeable with no particular difference in meaning. For example, the sentences 'They have to study hard in order not to fail', 'They have to study hard not to fail', and 'They have to study hard so that they won't fail' are all equivalent and adequate translations of the Moroccan *xeṣṣhom iqṛaw bezzaf baš ma-ixefqu-š.*

B. A proper understanding of Moroccan grammer is not possible without an understanding of the concepts 'root' and 'pattern'. Most Moroccan words are built upon a basic consonantal skeleton called the 'root'. This root occurs in 'patterns' with various vowels and additional, non-root consonants. The two concepts of root and pattern are fundamental to the structure of Moroccan words. The root usually has some fundamental kernel of meaning which is expanded or modified by the pattern. An example of a root is the consonant sequence *KTB,* which always has something to do with the concept of 'writing'. For example:

KTeB	he wrote
KTaB	book
meKTeB	office (i.e. a place where writing is done)

There are three basic root types, 'triliteral', 'quadriliteral', and 'atypical'. Roots having three constituent elements are called triliteral, e.g. the *KTB* of *kteb* 'to write' and *ktab* 'book'. Roots with four constituent elements are called quadriliteral, e.g. the *TṚŽM* of *teṛžem* 'to translate'. Roots with fewer than three or more than four constituent elements are called atypical, as in such a word as *ma* 'water'.

III. Exercises.

The sentence pairs below each consist of a question and a statement. Make a compound sentence out of each pair by changing the question to a statement and joining it to the following statement with *baš* 'in order to, so that'. Keep in mind that *baš* must be followed by an imperfect verb form. In changing the questions to statements, replace 'you' (sg.) with 'I' and 'you' (pl.) with 'we'.

Illustration:

Question: *ɛlaš šritiw-lha ṭumubil?*
Statement: *kanet ferɛana.*
Compound: *šrina-lha ṭumubil baš tkun ferɛana.*

1. *ɛlaš ṃṃu ɛṭatu le-flus?*
   šra magana ždida.

2. *ɛlaš ḍrebti-lu t-tilifun?*
   qolt-lu iži bekri.

3. *ɛlaš xeṣṣhom iqraw bezzaf?*
   ma-xefqu-š.

4. *ɛlaš qbeḍ l-bent?*
   ma-ṭaɛet-š.

5. *teqbeḍ-li had t-teṣwiṛa?*
   šeftha mezyan.

6. *ɛlaš ṭfitiw ḍ-ḍuw?*
   nɛăsna.

7. *ɛlaš qbeḍtiweh?*
   ma-ḍḍeṛṛ-š.

8. *ɛlaš năɛsu mɛăṭṭlin?*
   kemmlu ḍ-ḍuṛuṣ dyalhom.

9. *ɛlaš ġad-ṭṭfi ḍ-ḍuw?*
   ma-šafetni-š.

10. *ɛlaš qal-lkom ma-theḍṛu-š?*
    nɛăs.

11. *ɛlaš wqefti ɛda l-bab?*
    ḅḅa ṣuwweṛni.

12. *ɛlaš ġad-tṣuwweṛ d-drari?*
    kanu ferɛanin.

13. *ɛlaš ṣuwwṛet ḍ-ḍar?*
    ṣifṭet-lu t-teṣwiṛa.

14. *ɛlaš ɛăyydu ḍ-ḍuw?*
    ġad-nertaɛ ši-šwiya.

15. *ɛlaš bqitiw fe-ḍ-ḍaṛ?*
    nertaɛu ši-šwiya.

IV. Vocabulary.

baš	to, in order to, so that
ḍuw	light
nɛăs	to sleep, go to sleep, go to bed
qbeḍ	to sieze, grab, hold (on to)
rtaɛ	to rest
ṣuwweṛ	to photograph, take a picture of
šɛăl	to turn on
ṭfa (ka-iṭfi)	to turn out, turn off, put out

LESSON ONE HUNDRED NINE

I. Text.

šḥal εăndek?	How many do you have?
εăndi mya.	I have a hundred.
šḥal εăndha men stilu?	How many fountain pens does she have?
εăndha ši-mya.	She has around a hundred.
žaw mya de-n-nas.	A hundred people came.
myat ktab	a hundred books
baε-li myat ktab.	He sold me a hundred books.
fayn le-myat ktab lli baε-lek?	Where are the hundred books he sold you?
ṭlebt mennu mya u-xemsin ḍuḷaṛ.	I asked him for a hundred and fifty dollars.
ma-εṭani ġir myat ḍuḷaṛ.	He only gave me a hundred dollars.
xeṣṣha txeḷḷeṣ mya u-sebεa u-tlatin ḍuḷaṛ.	She has to pay a hundred and thirty-seven dollars.
sellef (l-)	to lend (to)
sellfu-li myatayn ḍuḷaṛ.	They lent me two hundred dollars.
nsellef-lu myatayn u-xemsin ḍuḷaṛ.	I'll lend him two hundred and fifty dollars.
kanu myatayn de-n-nas temma.	There were two hundred people there.
žaw mεah telt-emya de-n-nas.	Three hundred people came with him.
εlaš sellefti-lha duk t-telt-emyat ḍuḷaṛ?	Why did you lend her that three hundred dollars?
hadi telt-emya u-waḥed u-sebεin εam baš mat.	He died three hundred and seventy-one years ago.
εăndu f-žibu ṛbăε-myat ḍuḷaṛ.	He has four hundred dollars in his pocket.
žbeṛt kteṛ men rbăε-myat ḍuḷaṛ.	I found more than four hundred dollars.
š-derti b-duk ṛ-ṛbăε-myat ḍuḷaṛ lli žbeṛti?	What did you do with that four hundred dollars you found?

sellfet-li xems-emyat derhem.	She lent me five hundred dirhams.
ġad-nṭleb mennhom isellfu-li xems-emyat derhem.	I'm going to ask them to lend me five hundred dirhams.
bġit xems-emyat derhem baš nešri ši-ɛwayež ždad.	I want five hundred dirhams so I can buy some new clothes.
fayn mšaw l-xems-emya de-n-nas lli weṣlu l-bareɛ?	Where did the five hundred people go that arrived yesterday?
šɛal ɛăndek d-le-flus?	How much money do you have?
ɛăndi xems-emya u-ɛḍašel ḍuḷaṛ.	I have five hundred and eleven dollars.

II. Grammatical Notes.

A. As is true for all numerals above ten, the hundreds are followed by singular rather than plural nouns, e.g. *myat ktab* 'a hundred books'. Except for the special form *myatayn* 'two hundred' there is a variation between *mya* and *myat* for the other hundreds. The form *myat* occurs directly before nouns, e.g. *myat ḍuḷaṛ* 'a hundred dollars', *xems-emyat derhem* 'five hundred dirhams'. The forms without the final *-t* are used in all cases where a noun does not directly follow, e.g. *ɛăndi mya* 'I have a hundred' *xems-emya u-ɛḍašel ḍuḷaṛ* 'five hundred and eleven dollars'.

The hundreds are compounded with smaller numbers by *u* 'and' e.g. *myatayn u-xemsin ḍuḷaṛ* 'two hundred and fifty dollars,' *telt-emya u-waɛed u-sebɛin ɛam* 'three hundred and seventy-one years'. As with the numerals from eleven through ninety-nine, plural nouns which have no singular are counted on the same pattern as *xemsa d-le-ktub* 'five books', e.g. *xems-emya de-n-nas* 'five hundred people' (cf. Grammatical Note **D**, Lesson 89.)

B. Roots are classified not only according to the number of constituent elements (cf. Grammatical Note **B**, Lesson 108). They are further classified as 'strong' if all constituent elements are consonants and 'weak' if one or more of the constituent elements is a vowel. Examples of strong roots are the verbs *xfeq* 'to fall', *šedd* 'to close', and *tṛžem* 'to translate'. The *e* of each of these examples is a part of the pattern, which will be discussed later. Examples of weak roots are the verbs *šaf* 'to see', *šra* 'to buy', *suger* 'to insure' and *ṣifeṭ* 'to send'. The *a, u,* and *i* in the forms cited are part of the root.

The question of deciding whether a vowel is to be considered a part of a root is somewhat complex and will be discussed later.

III. Exercises.

Supply the Moroccan form for the numeral in parentheses and read the resulting phrase out loud.

1. (115) *derhem.*
2. *ši-*(200) *de-n-nas.*
3. (300) *ktab.*
4. (117) *šelya.*
5. (583) *tellaža.*
6. (400) *ʔoġniya.*
7. (100) *mekteb.*
8. (500) *ḥăžžam.*
9. *ši-*(100) *qlam.*
10. (298) *stilu.*
11. (321) *tilifun.*
12. (450) *ɛam.*
13. (575) *saɛa.*
14. (218) *ḍeṛṣ.*
15. (214) *ḍeṛṣ.*
16. *ši-*(400) *xuxa.*
17. (319) *tellaža.*
18. *ši-*(300) *wqida.*
19. (411) *makina ždida.*
20. *ši-*(500) *makina kbira.*
21. (112) *biḍa.*
22. (516) *hdiya.*
23. (534) *ṭiyyaṛa.*
24. (213) *ḥadita.*
25. (367) *škaṛa.*
26. (446) *weld.*
27. (399) *mṛa.*
28. (186) *bent.*
29. *ši-*(500) *kas d-atay.*
30. *ši-*(200) *ḍaṛ ždida.*

IV. Vocabulary.

derhem	dirham (basic unit of Moroccan currency, equivalent to twenty cents.)
ḍuḷaṛ	dollar
mya, -t	hundred
myatayn	two hundred
ṛbăɛ-mya, -t	four hundred
sellef (*l-*)	to lend (to)
telt-emya, -t	three hundred
xems-emya, -t	five hundred

LESSON ONE HUNDRED TEN

I. Text.

had le-ktab fih sett-emyat ṣefḥa.	This book is six hundred pages long.
qṛiti had s-sett-emya u-xemsin ṣefḥa?	Have you read these six hundred and fifty pages?
had ṣ-ṣbiṭaṛ fih daba sett-emya u-tesɛud u-ṛebɛin de-n-nas.	This hospital has six hundred and forty-nine people in it now.

had l-žarida ma-fiha ġir ṛebƹa de-ṣ-ṣefḥat.	This newspaper only has four pages in it.
ƹlaš ḥăyydet tesƹud de-ṣ-ṣefḥat men l-konnaš dyalek?	Why did she take nine pages out of your notebook?
šraw sbăƹ-myat kilu d-le-qṭen.	They bought seven hundred kilograms of cotton.
had ṣ-ṣenduq fih sbăƹ-mya u-xemsa u-ƹešrin kilu de-d-dheb.	This box has seven hundred and twenty-five kilograms of gold in it.
ƹăndi sbăƹ-myat ḍuḷaṛ u-ḍuḷaṛ.	I have seven hundred and one dollars.
qṛa temn-emyat ṣefḥa.	He read eight hundred pages.
qṛat temn-emya u-xemsa de-ṣ-ṣefḥat.	She read eight hundred and five pages.
ƹṭaha ḅḅaha temn-emya u-tnayn u-tesƹin derhem.	Her father gave her eight hundred and ninety-two dirhams.
šrina tlata de-l-kilu de-s-sokkaṛ.	We bought three kilograms of sugar.
žbeṛna tsăƹ-mya u-tlata de-l-kilu de-ṣ-ṣuf ž-ždid f-le-xnaši.	We found nine hundred and three kilograms of new wool in the bags.
baƹu tsăƹ-myat teṣwiṛa.	They sold nine hundred pictures.
ƹam luwwel beƹna tsăƹ-mya u-tmenya de-ẓ-ẓṛabi.	Last year we sold nine hundred and eight rugs.
bġina tsăƹ-mya u-tesƹud u-tesƹin šelya.	We want nine hundred and ninety-nine chairs.
sellfu-li tsăƹ-myat derhem u-derhem.	They lent me nine hundred and one dirhams.
žaw tsăƹ-mya u-waḥed de-n-nas.	Nine hundred and one people came.
kanu myat šelya u-šelya u-mya u-waḥed de-n-nas.	There were a hundred and one chairs and a hundred and one people.

II. Grammatical Notes.

A. When the numerals two through ten are used with a preceding hundred, a following noun is joined to them in the same way as for the numbers two through ten alone, e.g. *temn-emya u-xemsa de-ṣ-ṣefḥat* 'eight hundred and five pages'.

The usual pattern for one is to give the round figure and then repeat the noun with *u* 'and', *myat šelya u-šelya* 'a hundred and one chairs'. The words which occur only in the plural have a somewhat different pattern, e.g. *mya u-waƹed de-n-nas* 'a hundred and one people'.

B. The word *kilu* 'kilogram' has no plural, e.g. *tlata de-l-kilu de-s-sokkaṛ* 'three kilograms of sugar'.

C. In Lesson 108, Grammatical Note **B**, the difference between triliteral, quadriliteral, and atypical roots was discussed. In Lesson 109, Grammatical Note **B**, the difference between strong and weak roots was discussed. To summarize, triliteral roots have three constituent elements (*KTB* in *kteb* 'to write') quadriliteral roots have four constituent elements (the *TṚŽM* in *teṛžem* 'to translate'), atypical roots have fewer than three or more than four constituent elements (*ma* 'water'), strong roots are those in which all the root elements are consonants (*ŠDD* in *šedd* 'to close'), and weak roots are those in which at least one root element is a vowel (*A* in *šra*).

Strong triliteral roots are further classified as 'sound' when all three consonants are different (*KTB* of *kteb*) and 'doubled' when the last two consonants are the same (*ŠDD* of *šedd*).

III. Exercises.

A. Supply the Moroccan form for the numeral in parentheses and read the resulting phrase out loud.

1. (601) *kas.*
2. (602) *de-ḍ-ḍyuṛ.*
3. (909) *d-le-ktub.*
4. (708) *de-n-nas.*
5. (501) *ˀoġniya.*
6. (804) *de-ṭ-ṭumubilat.*
7. (903) *de-r-ržal.*
8. (705) *de-t-tellažat.*
9. (806) *de-d-drari.*
10. (107) *de-l-kilu.*

B. Repeat the exercise of Lesson 109 but increase the numeral in parentheses by 400 for each phrase. That is, instead of '(115) derhem' read '(515) derhem', etc.

IV. Vocabulary.

kilu (no pl.)	kilogram
sbăɛ-mya, -t	seven hundred
sett-emya, -t	six hundred
ṣefḥa pl. *ṣefḥat*	page
temn-emya, -t	eight hundred
tsăɛ-mya, -t	nine hundred

LESSON ONE HUNDRED ELEVEN

I. Text.

mat hadi ˀalef ɛam.	He died a thousand years ago.
kaynin ˀalef u-xems-emyat xeddam f-dak l-măɛmel.	There are one thousand five hundred workers in that factory.
xeḷḷeṣt had ṭ-ṭumubil b-ˀalef u-temn-emyat u-xemsa u-sebɛin ḍuḷaṛ.	I paid one thousand eight hundred and seventy-five dollars for this car.
šrinaha b-ˀalfayn derhem.	We bought it for two thousand dirhams.
kan t-taman dyalha ˀalfayn u-sbăɛ-mya u-tnayn u-ṛebɛin ḍuḷaṛ.	Its price was two thousand seven hundred and forty-two dollars.
ṭlebt mennhom isellfu-li telt-alaf derhem.	I asked them to lend me three thousand dirhams.
had l-medṛaṣa fiha telt-alaf u-mya u-tesɛud u-ɛešrin de-d-drari.	This school has three thousand one hundred and twenty-nine children in it.
žaw ši-ṛebɛ-alaf de-n-nas.	About four thousand people came.
had le-ktab fih ṛebɛ-alaf ṣefḥa u-ṣefḥa.	This book is four thousand and one pages long.
baɛu ṛebɛ-alaf u-myatayn u-teltašel weṛqa.	They sold four thousand two hundred and thirteen tickets.

wzen	to weigh.
had l-kamiyu ka-iwzen rebƐ-alaf kilu.	This truck weighs four thousand kilograms.
ṭ-ṭumubil dyali ka-tewzen ši-ˀalef kilu.	My car weighs around a thousand kilograms.
xeḷḷeṣna had l-kamiyu b-ṛebƐ-alaf ḍuḷaṛ.	We paid four thousand dollars for this truck.
ṣenƐu kteṛ men ˀalfayn tellaža f-dak l-măƐmel Ɛam luwwel.	They manufactured more than two thousand refrigerators in that factory last year.
wzen-li kilu de-ḷ-lƐăm.	Weigh me a kilogram of meat.
ġad-iṣenƐu xems-alaf kamiyu had l-Ɛam.	They're going to make five thousand trucks this year.
kaynin xems-alaf u-tsăƐ-mya u-ṛebƐa u-settin ḍaṛ f-had le-blad.	There are five thousand nine hundred and sixty-four houses in this town..
fayn l-xems-alaf ḍuḷaṛ lli selleft-lek?	Where's the five thousand dollars I lent you?
baƐha b-xems-alaf u-xems-emyat ḍuḷaṛ.	He sold it for five thousand five hundred dollars.

II. Grammatical Notes.

A. With reference to sums of money, 'for' is rendered by *b-*, as in *šrinaha b-ˀalfayn derhem* 'We bought it for two thousand dirhams'. The use of *xeḷḷeṣ* 'to pay' is slightly different from the pattern in English. The thing paid for occurs as the direct object of *xeḷḷeṣ* and the amount paid is introduced by *b-*, as in *xeḷḷeṣna had l-kamiyu b-ṛebƐ-alaf ḍuḷaṛ* 'We paid four thousand dollars for this truck.'

B. The classification of roots into the types discussed in Lessons 108, 109, and 110 is especially important to an understanding of the Moroccan verb system. In English a verb may be of almost any shape or size. On the one hand, English has verbs as long as 'institutionalize' and on the other hand, it has verbs as short as 'go'. In Moroccan, verbs have only a limited number of clearly defined shapes. These verb forms are built up on the basic root consonants combined with a small number of patterns. If we use the *F*, *Ɛ*, and *L* as a shorthand to symbolize the first, second, and third consonants of a root, the three most common patterns of Moroccan verbs with sound triliteral roots are:

(I)	$F\varepsilon\binom{e}{\breve{a}}L$	for example, *kteb,* 'to write'
(II)	$F\binom{e}{\breve{a}}\varepsilon\varepsilon\binom{e}{\breve{a}}L$	for example, *kemmel* 'to finish'
(III)	*Faɛel*	for example, *ɛaqeb* 'to punish'

These various shapes of the Moroccan verb are called 'Measures'. Measure I is characterized by the short vowel between the second and third consonants of the root. Familiar examples of Measure I are:

ḍṛeb	to hit	*ṭleb*	to ask (for)
ġsel	to wash	*xdem*	to work
kteb	to write	*žbeṛ*	to find
šṛeb	to drink	*wṣel*	to arrive
šɛăl	to light	*nfăɛ*	to help, be of use to

Measure II is characterized by having the middle consonant of the root doubled, with a short vowel both before and after it. Familiar examples of Measure II are:

ṛežžăɛ	to return, take back, send back	*xeḷḷeṣ*	to pay (for)
weqqef	to stop, park	*ɛămmeṛ*	to fill
xeddem	to work, operate	*sellef*	to lend

The vowel in the patterns of Measures I and II is always *e* unless an adjoining root consonant is ɛ. (The student must distinguish between the specific consonant ɛ and the formulaic use of the symbol ɛ to symbolize the second consonant of a root.) When a neighboring consonant is ɛ, the vowel is *ă*. Compare the presence of *e* and *ă* as opposed to each other in *kteb* 'to write' and *šɛăl* 'to light' or in *xeḷḷeṣ* 'to pay' and *ṛežžăɛ* 'to return, send back, take back'.

Measure III is of much rarer occurrence than Measures I and II. The only example with a strong root so far encountered in the Lessons is *ɛaqeb* 'to punish'. Measure III is characterized by an *a* between the first and second consonants of the root and a short vowel between the second and third consonants of the root.

III. Exercises.

Supply the Moroccan form for the numeral in parentheses and read the resulting phrase out loud.

1. (1125) *derhem.*
2. (2872) *qlam.*
3. (4790) *de-n-nas.*
4. (1476) *stilu.*
5. (5964) *ktab.*
6. (5636) *tilifun.*
7. (2624) *šelya.*
8. (1417) *kamiyu.*
9. (2819) *ɛam.*
10. (2668) *tellaža.*
11. (3080) *ˀoǧniya.*
12. (5429) *makina.*
13. (3778) *ṭiyyaṛa.*
14. (5461) *škaṛa.*
15. (1982) *kas.*
16. (3814) *hdiya.*
17. (4143) *weld.*
18. (4071) *bent.*
19. (3065) *ḍaṛ.*
20. (4950) *ṛažel.*

IV. Vocabulary.

ˀalef	(one) thousand
ˀalfayn	two thousand
kamiyu	truck
ṛebɛ-alaf	four thousand
telt-alaf	three thousand
wzen	to weigh
xems-alaf	five thousand

LESSON ONE HUNDRED TWELVE

I. Text.

weṣlet l-yum kteṛ men sett-alaf bṛa.	More than six thousand letters arrived today.
kanu ɛaḍṛin sett-alaf u-temn-emya u-tlata u-tmanin de-n-nas.	There were six thousand eight hundred and eighty-three people present.

had l-mektaba fiha kteṛ men sebƐ-alaf ktab.	This library has more than seven thousand books in it.
Ɛăndi f-žibi temn-alaf u-myatayn u-ṭnašel ḍuḷaṛ.	I have eight thousand two hundred and twelve dollars in my pocket.
hadi ši-telt snin baš beƐna-lhom tesƐ-alaf ṣenḍuq d-l-uqid.	Some three years ago we sold them nine thousand boxes of matches.
konna ka-nṣifṭu-lhom kteṛ men Ɛăšṛ-alaf mkoƐla koll šheṛ.	We were sending them more than ten thousand rifles every month.
kayna ši-Ɛešrin alef biškliṭa f-had le-blad.	There are about twenty thousand bicycles in this town.
xeḷḷṣet dak ḍ-ḍaṛ le-kbira b-ši-myat alef ḍuḷaṛ.	She paid some hundred thousand dollars for that big house.
had le-blad fiha myatayn u-tlata u-ṛebƐin alef u-xems-emya u-tnayn u-tesƐin de-n-nas.	This city has two hundred and forty-three thousand, five hundred and ninety-two people in it.
had l-ḅenk fih tsăƐ-myat alef ḍuḷaṛ.	This bank has nine hundred thousand dollars in it.
sellef-li tlata de-d-drahem.	He lent me three dirhams.
sir l-Ɛăndu u-ṭleb mennu xemsa de-ḍ-ḍuḷaṛat.	Go to him and ask him for five dollars.
ka-iṣenƐu kteṛ men xems-emyat alef stilu fe-l-Ɛam f-had l-măƐmel.	They make more than five hundred thousand fountain pens a year in this factory.
had le-fluka ka-tewzen ši-tlata u-Ɛešrin alef kilu.	This boat weighs about twenty-three thousand kilograms.
ṣnăƐ xemsṭašel alef sarut fe-š-šheṛ lli daz.	He made fifteen thousand keys last month.
Ɛṭani melyun ḍuḷaṛ.	He gave me a million dollars.
žabu ši-žuž d-le-mlayen de-d-drahem l-l-ḅenk.	They brought about two million dirhams to the bank.
had le-blad ka-iƐišu fiha ši-xemsa d-le-mlayen de-n-nas.	About five million people live in this city.
ṣenƐu ṭnašel melyun buḷa Ɛam luwwel.	They manufactured twelve million light bulbs last year.
šraw myat ṭiyyaṛa b-ši-xems-emyat melyun ḍuḷaṛ.	They bought a hundred airplanes for about five hundred million dollars.

II. Grammatical Notes.

A. Above ten thousand, *ʔalef* 'thousand' is counted as an ordinary noun. It sometimes loses the initial *ʔ* when preceded by another numeral, e.g. *xemsṭašel alef* 'fifteen thousand', *myatayn u-tlata u-ṛebɛin alef* 'two hundred and forty-three thousand.'

B. The numerals *melyun* 'million' and *mlayen* 'millions' are simple nouns and are counted accordingly, cf. *žuž d-le-ktub* 'two books' and *žuž d-le-mlayen* 'two million', etc.

C. In Lesson 109 a weak root was defined as one which had a vowel element as a basic part of the root. Weak roots are further classified as 'middle-weak' when the vowel element occurs medially (as in the verb *šaf* 'to see') and 'final weak' when the vowel element occurs finally (as in the verb *šra* 'to buy'). In verbs, this vowel element is always variable, as in the forms *šaf* 'he saw', *ka-išuf* 'he sees', *šeft'* I saw', *šra* 'he bought', *ka-išri* 'he buys', and *šrit* 'I bought'. The weak element of a root is given the shorthand symbolization (*V*). Thus while we say that the root of *kteb* is *KTB,* we say that the root of *šaf* is *Š*(*V*)*F* and the root of *šra* is *ŠR*(*V*). The specific pattern of *kteb* is represented formulaically by *FɛeL,* while those of *šaf* and *šra* are respectively *F*(*V*)*L* and *Fɛ*(*V*).

III. Exercises.

A. Repeat the exercise of Lesson 111 adding 5000 to each numeral in parentheses. That is, instead of '(3778) *ṭiyyaṛa*' read '(8778) *ṭiyyaṛa*', etc.

B. Read out loud the Moroccan for the following numerals.

1. 44,403.
2. 81,316.
3. 28,804.
4. 61,497.
5. 66,536.
6. 12,638.
7. 19,004.
8. 86,845.
9. 52,267.
10. 48,340.
11. 29,360.
12. 89,308.
13. 68,864.
14. 61,497.
15. 88,656.
16. 84,763.
17. 16,674.
18. 69,262.
19. 69,236.
20. 39,481.

IV. Vocabulary.

drahem	pl. of *derhem*
ḍuḷaṛat	pl. of *ḍuḷaṛ*
melyun	million
pl. *mlayen*	
sebƐ-alaf	seven thousand
sett-alaf	six thousand
temn-alaf	eight thousand
tesƐ-alaf	nine thousand
ḥaḍeṛ	present, in attendance
Ɛăšṛ-alaf	ten thousand

LESSON ONE HUNDRED THIRTEEN

I. Text.

ḥădded	to press, iron
xeṣṣek tḥădded l-kebbuṭ qbel-ma tlebsu.	You should iron the coat before you put it on.
ḥădddet-li s-serwal dyali.	She ironed my trousers for me.
ḥămmem	to give a bath to, to bathe
lebbes	to dress (someone)
ḥămmettu m̄m̄u qbel-ma tlebbsu.	His mother bathed him before she dressed him.
ka-tḥămmem d-drari koll nhaṛ.	She bathes the children every day.
xemmem	to think
f-aš ka-txemmem?	What are you thinking about?
ka-nxemmem fe-ḍ-ḍuṛuṣ dyali.	I'm thinking about my lessons.
xemmmu bezzaf qbel-ma isellfu-li le-flus.	They did a lot of thinking before they lent me the money.
ṣaff	to line up, put in a line
ṣaffithom ḥda l-bab.	I lined them up next to the door.
ṣaffu d-drari qeddam l-medṛaṣa.	They lined the children up in front of the school.

ġad-nƐămmṛu l-kisan be-l-ma qbel-ma nṣaffuhom Ɛăl ṭ-ṭebla.	We're going to fill the glasses with water before we line them up on the table.
Ɛayen	to wait, to wait for
Ɛayentu ši-saƐa qbel-ma nemši.	I waited for him about an hour before I left.
žbeṛtu ka-iƐayen xah.	I found him waiting for his brother.
Ɛlaš ma-tƐayenhom-š hna?	Why don't you wait for them here?
qaḍa	to finish
qaḍaw l-xedma dyalhom qbel mennna.	They finished their work before us.
mnin nqaḍi b-had l-makina, ġad-nbiƐha.	When I finish with this machine, I'm going to sell it.
qaḍiti?	Have you finished?

II. Grammatical Notes.

Grammatical Note **B** of Lesson 111 explained the concept of the Measures of the Moroccan verb and gave the pattern for Measures I, II, and III of the sound triliteral verb. Measures I, II, and III for doubled roots, middle-weak roots, and final-weak roots are similar in pattern.

Measure I for doubled roots usually has the pattern *FeƐƐ*, e.g. *šedd* 'to close'. When there is a ح or a Ɛ in the root, the vowel is usually *ă* instead of *e*, as in *ḥăll* 'to open'. For middle-weak and final-weak roots, the patterns for Measure I are *FaL* (e.g. *šaf* 'to see') and *FƐa* (e.g. bda 'to begin') respectively. Familiar examples of Measure I for doubled, middle-weak, and final-weak roots are:

kebb	to pour	*baƐ*	to sell	*mša*	to go
leff	to wrap (up)	*kan*	to be	*nsa*	to forget
medd	to hand	*qal*	to say	*šra*	to buy
šedd	to close	*ṭaḥ*	to fall	*Ɛṭa*	to give
ḥăll	to open	*žab*	to bring	*ṭfa*	to put out

Measure II for doubled roots has the same pattern as for sound roots, but observe *ă* instead of *e* next to the consonant ḥ. Examples given in this lesson are *xemmem* 'to think', *حămmen* 'to bathe', and *حădded* 'to iron'. Measure III for doubled roots usually lacks the *e* between the last two consonants, e.g. *ṣaff* 'to line up, put in a line'. Otherwise, the pattern is the same as for sound roots.

Measures II and III of middle-weak roots follow essentially the same pattern as Measures II and III from sound roots. A *w* or *y* is used for the missing second consonant of the root. A given root is always consistent in taking a *w* or *y*, but there is no way of predicting and each case must be separately memorized. A medial *-yy-* is usually preceded by *i* and a medial *-ww-* by *-u-*, e.g. *siyyeb* 'to throw' and *ṣuwweṛ* 'to photograph'. An initial ح or ع takes *ă* in the pattern, e.g. *حăyyed* 'to remove, take away'. Measure III is completely regular, e.g. *عawen* 'to help', *حawel* 'to try', and *عayen* 'to wait, wait for'.

Final weak roots follow the pattern of sound roots with a final *-a* substituting for the final *-eL* or *-ăL* of the sound root pattern. Examples of Measure II are *werra* 'to show', *xella* 'to leave', and *ġenna* 'to sing'. An example of Measure III is *qaḍa* 'to finish'.

III. Exercises.

Identify each of the verbs below as to type of root (that is, as triliteral, quadriliteral, or atypical, and as sound, doubled, or weak) and as to whether its pattern is Measure I, II, or III.

1. *عawen.*
2. *weqqef.*
3. *šaf.*
4. *žbeṛ.*
5. *xella.*
6. *nsa.*
7. *عaqeb.*
8. *ẓaṛ.*
9. *lbes.*
10. *baع.*
11. *dar.*
12. *žab.*
13. *qṛa.*
14. *ḍṛeb.*
15. *gḷes.*
16. *ġsel.*
17. *kteb.*
18. *rfed.*
19. *kan.*
20. *šra.*
21. *ža.*
22. *عṭa.*
23. *kebb.*
24. *šedd.*
25. *leff.*
26. *siyyeb.*
27. *teṛžem.*
28. *medd.*
29. *qeddem.*
30. *werra.*
31. *mša.*
32. *bġa.*
33. *hḍeṛ.*
34. *عmel.*
35. *حăyyed.*
36. *حăll*
37. *xdem.*
38. *dxel.*
39. *ṭleb.*
40. *xeḷḷeṣ.*
41. *kla.*
42. *kemmel.*
43. *xeddem.*
44. *qal.*
45. *bda.*
46. *šعăl.*
47. *wqef.*
48. *wṣel.*
49. *nfăع.*
50. *bqa.*

IV. Vocabulary.

lebbes	to dress (someone)
qaḍa	to finish
ṣaff	to line up, put in line
xemmem	to think
ɛăddeḍ	to iron, press
ɛămmem	to give a bath to, bathe
ɛayen	to wait, wait for

LESSON ONE HUNDRED FOURTEEN

I. Text.

žedded	to renew
ma-žedddu-lu-š t-tesriɛ dyalu.	They didn't renew his permit.
ma-nžeddedhom-lek-š.	I won't renew them for you.
xda	to take (for oneself), to get
ka-yaxod	to get, to take
ka-naxdu ši-xems-emyat derhem fe-l-ᵓusbuɛ.	We get about five hundred dirhams a week.
fayn xditi had le-flus?	Where did you get this money?
waš fik ma dži mɛaya?	Would you like to come with me?
la, ma-fiya ma nemši.	No, I don't feel like going.
waš fiha ma tešṛeb ši-ɛaža?	Does she feel like drinking something?
la, ma-fiha ma-tešṛeb ɛetta ɛaža.	No, she doesn't feel like drinking anything.
ṭuwwel	to lengthen, make longer
had ṭ-ṭebla ma-ši ṭwila bezzaf.	This table isn't very long.
xeṣṣkom ṭṭuwwluha šwiya.	You should lengthen it a little.
ṭuwwlet-lu l-kebbuṭ.	She lengthened the coat for him.
ṛžăɛ	to return, come back, go back
weqt-aš ġad-iṛžăɛ?	What time is he going to come back?

II. Grammatical Notes.

A. Review the discussion of root types and verb measures in the Grammatical Notes of Lessons 108-113.

B. The preposition *f-* 'in' with pronoun endings is used idiomatically as an approximate equivalent of English 'to feel like, to wish to', as in *waš fik ma dži?* 'Would you like to come? As the sentence just quoted illustrates, the construction regularly requires the word *ma* (which has nothing to do with the word *ma* meaning 'not') followed by the imperfect. Negatives are formed by prefixing *ma-* 'not' to the preposition, e.g. *ma-fiya ma nemši* 'I don't feel like going'. The construction is used only in questions and in negative statements.

C. The word *xda* 'to take (for oneself), to get' must be distinguished from *dda* 'to take (from one place to another)'. Note that the forms for *xda,* durative *ka-yaxod,* are exactly similar to the forms for *kla* 'to eat', durative *ka-yakol.*

III. Exercises.

Identify each of the verbs below according to type of root and as to measure.

1. *ḥawel.*
2. *xfeq.*
3. *ṭaṛ.*
4. *mat.*
5. *ġṛeq.*
6. *ḍuwweṛ* (*ɛla*).
7. *ṣnăɛ.*
8. *xneq.*
9. *qleb.*
10. *smăɛ.*
11. *ġenna.*
12. *ṣuwweb.*
13. *qbeḍ.*
14. *ṭfa.*
15. *nɛăs.*
16. *ṣuwweṛ.*
17. *šɛăl.*
18. *sellef.*
19. *ḥădded.*
20. *ḥămmem.*
21. *lebbes.*
22. *xemmem.*
23. *ṣaff.*
24. *ɛayen.*
25. *qaḍa.*
26. *žedded.*
27. *xda.*
28. *ṭuwwel.*
29. *ṛžăɛ.*
30. *ža.*

IV. Vocabulary.

ṛžăɛ	to return, come back, go back
tesriḥ	permission, permit, license
ṭwil	long
ṭuwwel	to lengthen, make longer
xda (*ka-yaxod*)	to take (for oneself), to get
žedded	to renew

LESSON ONE HUNDRED FIFTEEN

I. Text.

xrež	to go out, leave
xrež fe-s-setta.	He left at six o'clock.
dima ka-ixrož fe-ṭ-ṭnaš.	He always goes out at twelve.
qalet-lha ṃ̂ṃ̂ha texrož men l-bit.	Her mother told her to leave the room.
xerrež	to take out, get out, send out, expel
xerržuh men l-meḍṛaṣa.	They expelled him from school.
ġad-nxerrež-lek ṣ-ṣnadeq men ḍ-ḍaṛ.	I'll take the boxes out of the house for you.
nsit ma-xerrežt-š le-ḥwayež men ṭ-ṭumubil.	I forgot to take the clothes out of the car.
εṭini ši-ḥaža tkun ḥluwa.	Give me something (that'll be) sweet.
ma-fiya ma nakol ḥetta-ḥaža ḥluwa f-had s-saεa.	I don't feel like eating anything sweet right now.
had atay ḥlu bezzaf.	This tea is very sweet.
ḥălla	to sweeten, make sweet
ḥăllat l-makla bezzaf.	She's made the food too sweet.
ṭleb mennha tḥălli atay kteṛ men had š-ši.	Ask her to make the tea sweeter.
wessăε	to widen, make wide, make wider
had ẓ-ẓenqa xeṣṣhom iwessεuha.	They ought to widen this street.
žbeṛ l-wad waseε bezzaf.	He found that the river was very wide.

kanet had ẓ-ẓenqa ḍiyyqa bezzaf qbel-ma iwessεuha.	This street was very narrow before they widened it.
š-šeṛžem dyal had l-bit ḍiyyeq bezzaf.	The window of this room is too narrow.

II. Grammatical Notes.

A. In Grammatical Note C of Lesson 45 it was pointed out that some verbs which show a final *-a* in the perfect have *-i* in the durative (e.g. *šra* 'he bought', *ka-išri* 'he buys') while others retain the final *-a* in the durative (e.g. *nsa* 'he forgot', *ka-insa* 'he forgets'). This is true only of Measure I verbs. Verbs of Measures II and III with final *-a* in the perfect always change the *-a* to *-i* in the durative, (e.g. *ḥălla* 'he sweetened', *ka-iḥălli* 'he sweetens').

B. There is no direct Moroccan equivalent for English 'too' in such expressions as 'too narrow', 'too sweet', etc. The same meaning is often expressed by *bezzaf* 'very' e.g. *ḥăllat l-makla bezzaf* 'She's made the food too sweet.'

III. Exercises.

Review the exercises of Lessons 113 and 114.

IV. Vocabulary.

ḍiyyeq	narrow
waseɛ	wide, broad
wessăɛ	to widen, make wide, make wider
xerrež	to take out, get out, send out, expel
xrež	to go out, leave
ḥălla	to sweeten
ḥlu	sweet
ḥluwa (f.)	

LESSON ONE HUNDRED SIXTEEN

I. Text.

xud	take
xud ṭaksi!	Take a taxi!
ɛlaš ma-taxod-š ṭaksi?	Why don't you take a taxi?
ila ma-bġitiw-š tweṣlu mɛăṭṭlin, xudu ṭaksi.	If you don't want to arrive late, take a taxi.
xud had d-dwa meṛṛtayn fe-n-naṛ.	Take this medicine twice a day.
weṣṣel	to take, cause to arrive, get (someone) there.

weṣṣelthom l-bareɛ fe-l-lil le-ḍ-daṛ be-ṭ-ṭumubil dyali.	I took them home in my car last night.
weṣṣel-lha had le-bṛa.	Take this letter to her.
ṭ-ṭaksi weṣṣelni fe-l-weqt.	The taxi got me there on time.
faq	to wake up
weqt-aš feqti l-yum?	What time did you wake up today?
ka-nfiq koll nhaṛ fe-s-setta.	I wake up every day at six o'clock.
fiyyeq	to wake (someone) up
qolt-lha tfiyyeqni fe-t-tmenya.	I told her to wake me up at eight o'clock.
bdaw ka-iheḍṛu u-fiyyquni.	They began to talk and woke me up.
tɛămmem	to take a bath, bathe oneself
tɛămmmet tlata de-l-meṛṛat l-bareɛ.	She took three baths yesterday.
bġit ntɛămmem qbel-ma nakol.	I want to take a bath before I eat.
ṭiyyeɛ	to drop, knock down, knock over
ṭiyyɛet ṣiniya ɛamṛa be-l-kisan.	She dropped a tray full of glasses.
ṭiyyeɛ l-berrad men ɛăl ṭ-ṭebla.	He knocked the teapot off the table.

II. Grammatical Notes.

A. Measure II verbs usually have a causative meaning. They are derived widely from the roots of Measure I verbs, nouns, adjectives, and occasionally other parts of speech. Measure II is an open form in the sense that new words of this pattern are invented freely to fit new situations. It is often possible to guess the meaning of a previously unfamiliar Measure II verb if one is familiar with the basic meaning of the root, e.g. *ždid* 'new' and *žedded* 'to renew, make new', or *ṭwil* 'long' and *ṭuwwel* 'to lengthen'.

To illustrate this relationship, a number of Measure II verbs are listed below, each compared with a related word having the same root.

Measure II		*Related Word*	
fiyyeq	to wake (someone) up	*faq*	to wake up
lebbes	to dress (someone)	*lbes*	to put on, wear
ṛežžăɛ	to return, send back, take back	*ṛžăɛ*	to return, go back, come back

ṭiyyeḥ	to drop, knock down	*ṭaḥ*	to fall
ṭuwwel	to lengthen	*ṭwil*	long
weqqef	to stop, stand, park	*wqef*	to (come to a) stop, stand
wessăɛ	to widen	*waseɛ*	wide
weṣṣel	to take, cause to arrive	*wṣel*	to arrive
xeddem	to operate, make work	*xdem*	to work
xerrež	to take out, get out, send out, expel	*xrež*	to go out, leave
žedded	to renew	*ždid*	new
ḥălla	to sweeten	*ḥlu*	sweet
ɛămmeṛ	to fill	*ɛameṛ*	full

B. The verb *xda* 'to take' has an irregular imperative *xud,* pl. *xudu.*

III. Exercises.

In **A** of the Grammatical Notes above, cover the left-hand column of Measure II verbs with a piece of paper. Work down the right-hand column of related words and read aloud, from memory, the corresponding Measure II verb. If your memory fails you on any given item, attempt to construct the Measure II verb according to the patterns learned in the last few lessons. Check your work by sliding the covering piece of paper down the page after each attempt.

IV. Vocabulary.

faq	to wake up
fiyyeq	to wake (someone) up
tḥămmem	to take a bath
ṭaksi	taxi
ṭiyyeḥ	to drop, knock down
weṣṣel	to take, cause to arrive, get (someone) there
xud, pl. *xudu*	(imperative of *xda* 'to take')

LESSON ONE HUNDRED SEVENTEEN

I. Text.

ɛăllem	to teach
ɛăllemni (kif-aš) ntkellem l-ɛăṛbiya.	He taught me (how) to speak Arabic.
le-fqi ġad-iɛăllemha teqṛa.	The teacher is going to teach her to read.
ṭelbu menni nɛăllemhom kif-aš iġenniw.	They asked me to teach them how to sing.
tɛăllem	to learn
fayn tɛăllemti ttkellem l-ɛăṛbiya?	Where did you learn to speak Arabic?
ma-imken-lu itɛăllem walu menni.	He can't learn anything from me.
ḍeṛṛ	to hurt (someone, something)
ṛaṣi ka-iḍeṛṛni.	I have a headache. (My head is hurting me.)
ṭaɛ u-ḍeṛṛ ṛaṣu.	He fell and hurt his head.
ḍeṛbettu u-ḍeṛṛet-lu ɛăynu.	She hit him and hurt his eye.
tṣuwweb	to get (be) repaired, get (be) fixed
xeṣṣu itṣuwweb.	It needs to be fixed.
ġad-nddi ṭ-ṭumubil dyali ttṣuwweb.	I'm going to take my car to get fixed.
tqaḍa	to run out, come to an end, be finished
tqaḍat-lna l-makla.	We've run out of food.
tqaḍa s-sokkaṛ l-bareɛ.	The sugar ran out yesterday.
le-ɛlib ġad-itqaḍa-lna ġedda.	The milk's going to run out on us tomorrow.
mšaw-li flusi.	I've lost my money.
šɛal xdaw-lek d-le-flus?	How much money did they take from you?

II. Grammatical Notes.

A. Review Grammatical Note **B** of Lesson 60.

B. The endings *-li, -lek, -lu* etc., discussed in Grammatical Note **B** of Lesson 60 are often used in the general sense of indicating the person with respect to whom a given action takes place. Several examples of such usage are given in this lesson. They are repeated below for reference.

ḍeṛbettu u-ḍeṛṛet-lu ɛăynu.	She hit him and hurt his eye.
tqaḍat-lna l-makla.	We've run out of food.
le-ḥlib ġad-itqaḍa-lna ġedda.	The milk's going to run out on us tomorrow.
mšaw-li flusi.	I've lost my money.
šḥal xdaw-lek d-le-flus?	How much money did they take from you?

III. Exercises.

Go through the text of the lesson and devise a pertinent question for each statement and a pertinent statement for each question. For example, *fayn tɛăllemti ttkellem l-ɛăṛbiya?* might pertinently be answered by *tɛăllemt ntkellem l-ɛăṛbiya fe-l-meġrib.* Note that it is possible to construct more than one question to correspond to a given statement, and vice versa. For example, two possible pertinent questions for *tqaḍat-lna l-makla* are *weqt-aš tqaḍat-lna l-makla?* and *waš tqaḍat-lna l-makla?* Still further pertinent questions are possible for this one statement of course.

IV. Vocabulary.

ḍeṛṛ	to hurt (someone, something)
ṛaṣ	head
tqaḍa	to run out, come to and end, be finished
tṣuwweb	to get (be) repaired, get (be) fixed
tɛăllem	to learn
ɛăllem	to teach

LESSON ONE HUNDRED EIGHTEEN

I. Text.

fešš	to let air out of, deflate
ɛlaš feššiti ṛ-ṛwiḍa?	Why did you let the air out of the tire?
xeṣṣek tfešš ṛ-ṛwiḍa qbel-ma tɛăyyedha.	You should let the air out of the tire before you take it off.
ttfešš	to go flat, deflate
ṛ-ṛwiḍa ġad-ttfešš.	The tire's going to go flat.
xeṣṣek tewqef qbel-ma ttfešš.	You should stop before it goes flat.
baqi ma-ttfeššet-š.	It still hasn't gone flat.
ttfekk	to get loose, get free, get out of a difficult situation, come untied
fe-l-l?axir ttfekkit mennu.	I finally got free from him.
ṭlebt mennhom iɛawnuni baš nttfekk.	I asked them to help me get loose.
kif-aš ġad-ttfekk men had š-ši?	How are you going to get out of this?
lli	the one(s) who, the one(s) that
fekk	to untie, release, rescue (from a difficult situation)
huwa lli fekkni.	He's the one that saved me.
ɛlaš fekkiti l-kelb?	Why did you untie the dog?
huma lli ṭlebna mennhom ifekkuna men dak l-xedma.	They're the ones we asked to rescue us from that job.
ttexneq	to get stopped up
l-mežṛa ttxenqet.	The drain has gotten stopped up.
šɛal hadi baš ttxenqet l-mežṛa?	How long has it been since the drain got stopped up?
ila derti had š-ši fiha, ma-ġad-ttexneq-š.	If you put this in it, it won't get stopped up.

kra	to rent
kra-li ḍ-ḍaṛ dyalu b-ʔalef derhem fe-š-šheṛ.	He rented me his house for a thousand dirhams a month.
krina mennhom žuž de-ḍ-ḍyuṛ.	We rented two houses from them.
waš hadi hiya lli ġad-tekriw mennhom?	Is this the one you're going to rent from them?
ttekra	to be rented (out), to rent, be for rent
had ḍ-ḍaṛ ttekrat wella baqi?	Has this house been rented yet?
be-šɛal ka-ttekra had ḍ-ḍaṛ?	How much does this house rent for?
waš had l-kamiyu ka-ittekra?	Is this truck for rent?

II. Grammatical Notes.

A. If the base form of a verb begins with *tt-*, the usual *t-* or *te-* prefix in the durative is dropped, cf. the forms *ka-ttekra* in *be-šɛal ka-ttekra had ḍ-ḍaṛ?* and *ġad-ttfekk in kif-aš ġad-ttfekk?* Compare the *t* in such forms as *ka-tšuf* 'you see, she sees'.

B. Note the construction with *wella* 'or' in *had ḍ-ḍaṛ ttekrat wella baqi?* 'Has this house been rented yet?' The construction is regular and can be extended indefinitely, e.g. *waš mša wella baqi?* 'Has he gone yet (or not)?'

C. Note the use of *lli* (cf. Lessons 100 and 101) in the sense of 'the one(s) who', e.g. *huwa lli fekkni* 'He's the one that saved me.' The usage is regular and can be extended indefinitely, e.g. *hiya lli qaletha-li* 'She's the one who told me'.

III. Exercises.

Apply the instructions of the exercise of Lesson 117 to this lesson.

IV. Vocabulary.

fekk	to untie, release, rescue (from a difficult situation)
fešš	to let the air out of, deflate
kra (*ka-ikri*)	to rent

ṛwiḍa	wheel, tire
ttfekk	to get loose, get free, get out (of a difficult situation)
ttfešš	to go flat, deflate
ttekra	to be rented (out), be for rent, rent
ttexneq	to get stopped up
wella	or

LESSON ONE HUNDRED NINETEEN

I. Text.

ddabez	to quarrel, to have a quarrel
huwa u-mṛatu dima ka-iddabzu.	He and his wife are always quarreling.
qalu-li ddabezti mɛaha.	They told me you quarreled with her.
ma-bǧina-š nddabzu.	We don't want to quarrel.
tfahem	to come to an understanding, to understand (each other)
xeṣṣek ttfahem mɛah.	You have to come to an understanding with him.
ntfahmu men băɛd ši-šwiya.	We'll come to an agreement after a little while.
waš ttfahemtiw wella baqi?	Have you come to an understanding yet (or not)?
herres	to break
ṭaḥet u-herrset ṭ-ṭbaṣel kollhom.	She fell and broke all the dishes.
ṭiyyeḥt l-qeṛɛa u-herrestha.	I knocked the bottle over and broke it.
xeṣṣna nherrsu š-šeṛžem baš ndexlu.	We have to break the window to get in.
herres l-makina lli kan ka-ixeddem.	He broke the machine that he was operating.
therres	to get broken, break
t-tellaža ṭaḥet men l-kamiyu u-therrset.	The refrigerator fell out of the truck and broke.
mnin ɛămmṛet l-kisan b-atay, therrsu.	When she filled the glasses with tea, they broke.

tṣaff	to get in line, to form a line, to line up
tṣaffit qeddam l-bab.	I got in line in front of the door.
qolt le-d-drari itṣaffu fe-ẓ-ẓenqa.	I told the children to line up in the street.
tṣaffina mƐahom.	We got in line with them.
džuwwež	to get married
Ɛămmeṛni ma-ġad-ndžuwwež.	I'm never going to get married.
smăƐtek džuwwežti Ɛam luwwel.	I hear you got married last year.
ttexlăƐ	to get scared, to be scared, afraid
ttexlăƐt mennu.	I got scared of him.
qolt-lu ma-ittexlăƐ-š.	I told him not to be afraid.

II. Grammatical Notes.

A. Measures Ia, IIa(V), and IIIa(VI) are formed from Measures I, II, and III respectively. Measure Ia has the form of Measure I prefixed with *tt-* (*tte-* if two consonants follow), e.g., *ttfekk* 'to get loose', *ttexlăƐ* 'to get scared'. Measures IIa(V) and IIIa(VI) usually have the form of Measures II and III prefixed with *t-*, e.g., *tƐămmem* 'to take a bath', *tqaḍa* 'to run out, to come to an end'.

Instead of *tt-* and *t-* the prefixes *ḍ-*, *d-*, and *ṭ-* also occur, depending on the initial consonant of the Measure I, II, or III form to which they are prefixed. An initial *ḍ* always requires a *ḍ* prefix, e.g., Measure I *ḍeṛṛ* 'to hurt' and Measure Ia *ḍḍeṛṛ* 'to get hurt'. A *d, ž,* or *z* requires a *d* prefix, e.g., *džuwwež* 'to get married'. No examples with *ṭ-* have been given so far.

B. Measures Ia and IIa(V) almost always have a passive or an intransitive meaning with respect to the corresponding Measure I or II. Compare Measure II *Ɛămmem* 'to bathe, to give a bath to' and Measure IIa(V) *tƐămmem* 'to take a bath, to bathe'. Measure IIIa(VI) sometimes has a passive or intransitive meaning, e.g. *tqaḍa* 'to run out, to be finished', but more often a reciprocal meaning involving action between two or more people, e.g., *ddabez* 'to quarrel', *tfahem* 'to come to an understanding (with each other)'.

For reference, all Measure Ia, IIa(V), and IIIa(VI) verbs which have occurred in the lessons so far are listed below. Insofar as they have occurred in the lessons, the corresponding Measure I, II, and III verbs are listed next to them.

Measure Ia		Measure I	
ḍḍeṛṛ	to get hurt	*ḍeṛṛ*	to hurt
ttfekk	to get loose	*fekk*	to untie, to release
ttfešš	to go flat, to deflate	*fešš*	to let the air out of, to deflate
ttekra	to be rented, to be for rent	*kra*	to rent
ttexneq	to get stopped up	*xneq*	to stop up, to block
ttexlăɛ	to get scared, to be scared, afraid		

Measure IIa(V)		Measure II	
džuwwež	to get married		
thella (f-)	to take care of		
therres	to get broken, break	*herres*	to break
tkellem	to talk		
tleffet	turn around		
tsenna	to wait (for)		
tṣuwweb	to get (be) repaired, fixed	*ṣuwweb*	to fix, to repair
tɛăllem	to learn	*ɛăllem*	to teach
tḥămmem	to take a bath	*ḥămmem*	to give a bath to

Measure IIIa(VI)		Measure III	
ddabez	to quarrel		
tfahem	to come to an understanding		
tqaḍa	to run out, to come to an end	*qaḍa*	to finish
tṣaff	to get in line, to form a line, to line up	*ṣaff*	to line up, to put in line

C. For the student who wishes to progress from the study of Moroccan to the study of Modern Standard (Literary) Arabic, correspondences between the verb Measures of these two forms of Arabic should be noted. The form and numbering of Measures I, II, and III in Moroccan correspond to Measures I, II, and III of Modern Standard Arabic. Moroccan Measures IIa and IIIa correspond to Modern Standard Arabic's Measures V and VI, which is indicated by writing 'IIa(V)' and 'IIIa(VI)'. Moroccan has no equivalent for Modern Standard Arabic's Measure IV, and Modern Standard Arabic has nothing corresponding to Moroccan Measure Ia.

III. Exercises.

A. Apply the instructions of the exercise of Lesson 117 to this lesson.

B. In Grammatical Note **B** above, cover the left-hand column of verbs with a piece of paper. Work down the right-hand column of related verbs and read aloud, from memory, the corresponding Measure Ia, IIa(V), and IIIa(VI) verbs. Check your work by sliding the covering piece of paper down the page and uncovering each test form in turn.

IV. Vocabulary.

ddabez	to quarrel, to have a quarrel
džuwwež	to get married
herres	to break
tfahem	to come to an understanding, to understand (each other)
therres	to get broken, to break
tṣaff	to get in line, to form a line, to line up
ttexlăع	to get scared, to be scared, afraid

LESSON ONE HUNDRED TWENTY

I. Text.

qal-li ṭ-ṭbib xeṣṣni nertaح bezzaf.	The doctor told me I need to rest a lot.
rtaحiti mezyan wella la?	Did you get a good rest or not?
ع̆ămmeṛhom ma-ع̆ăndhom l-weqt baš irtaحu.	They never have time to rest.
htemm (b-)	to be interested (in), to be concerned (about)

ka-ihtemm bezzaf be-s-siyasa.	He's very interested in politics.
ɛămmṛek ma-htemmiti be-s-siyasa?	Haven't you ever been interested in politics?
ma-htemmina-š b-le-flus.	We weren't concerned about money.
ḥtaṛem	to respect
ma-bqa ḥetta ḥădd ka-yeḥtaṛmu.	No one respects him anymore.
n-nas kollhom ka-yeḥtaṛmuha bezzaf.	All the people respect her very much.
ntaxeb	to elect
škun lli ġad-intaxbu ṛaʔis?	Whom are they going to elect president?
ntaxebnah ṛaʔis ɛam luwwel.	We elected him president last year.
stexbeṛ	to inquire, to make inquiries
stexbeṛna ɛliha qbel-ma nekriwha.	We inquired about it before we rented it.
ma-štexbeṛti-š qbel-ma tebda?	Didn't you inquire before you began?
kollu	all of it (m.)
kollha	all of it (f.)
kla l-xobz kollu.	He ate all the bread.
xerržet z-zit kollha men l-qeṛɛa.	She took all the oil out of the bottle.
mšaw-li flusi kollhom.	I've lost all my money.
xlaq	to be born
xlaqiti fe-ḍ-ḍaṛ l-biḍa?	Were you born in Casablanca?
xlaqit f-ʔamirika.	I was born in America.
ṣlaḥ	to be of use, to be fit
ma-ṣlaḥ-li-š.	It wasn't of any use to me.
werrini l-aš islaḥ.	Show me what it's fit for.

II. Grammatical Notes.

A. As was mentioned in Lesson 119, Moroccan has no equivalent for Modern Standard Arabic Measure IV. There is likewise no Moroccan equivalent for Measure VII. The remaining Measures—VIII, IX, and X—

are of relatively rare occurrence. Measure VIII is characterized by *-te-* inserted after the first consonant of the root in the case of doubled roots, e.g. *htemm* (*b-*) 'to be interested (in)'. For other kinds of roots, *-ta-* is inserted after the first consonant of the root, e.g. *rtaḥ* 'to rest' and *ḥtaṛem* 'to respect'.

Measure IX has the pattern *FɛaL*, e.g., *xlaq* 'to be born', *ṣlaḥ* 'to be of use, to be fit'. Measure X consists of *ste-* prefixed to the form of Measure I, e.g. *stexbeṛ* 'to inquire, to make inquiries'.

Most Moroccan verbs follow the patterns of Measures I, Ia, II, and IIa(V). There are a moderate number of verbs which have the patterns of Measures III and IIIa(VI). There are fewer than fifty verbs which have the pattern of Measure IX, and there are even fewer examples of Measures VIII and X.

B. Note that the perfect tense endings for Measure IX, Measure VIII from middle-weak roots, and Measure VIII from doubled roots have the same perfect tense patterns as Measure I doubled roots (cf. Grammatical Note **A**, Lesson 37); that is, an *-i-* is added with the forms for 'I', 'you', and 'we', e.g. *rtaḥit* 'I rested' *xlaqiti* 'you were born', *ma-htemmina-š* 'we weren't concerned, we didn't care'.

C. Note the use of *kollu* 'all of it (m.)', *kollha* 'all of it (f.)' *kollhom* 'all of them'. Used immediately after a noun these forms translate English 'all', e.g., *l-xobz kollu* 'all the bread', *z-zit kollha* 'all the oil', *flusi kollhom* 'all my money'.

III. Exercises.

Apply the instructions of the exercise of Lesson 117 to this lesson.

IV. Vocabulary.

htemm (*b-*)	to be interested (in), to be concerned (about)
kollha	all of it (f.)
kollu (m.)	
ntaxeb	to elect
ṛaʔis	president

siyasa	politics
stexbeṛ	to inquire, to make inquiries
ṣlaε	to be of use, to be fit.
xlaq	to be born
εtaṛem	to respect

LESSON ONE HUNDRED TWENTY-ONE

I. Text.

feṛgăε	to blow up, to cause to explode
εlaš ġad-ifeṛgεu l-qenṭṛa?	Why are they going to blow up the bridge?
εăyydu n-nas qbel-ma ifeṛgεu l-qenṭṛa.	They got the people out of the way before they blew up the bridge.
tfeṛgăε	to explode, to blow up, to be blown up
l-buḷa tfeṛgεet f-yeddi.	The light bulb blew up in my hand.
mat mnin tfeṛgεet ṛ-ṛwiḍa.	He died when the tire exploded.
seqṣa	to ask
seqṣitu fayn xlaq.	I asked him where he was born
εlaš ma-tseqṣih-š kif-aš txeddem l-makina?	Why don't you ask him how to operate the machine?
seqṣatna fayn mša ṛ-ṛaʔis.	She asked us where the president had gone.
kaynin xemsa d-le-qnaṭeṛ f-had le-blad.	There are five bridges in this town.
le-qnaṭeṛ kollhom tfeṛgεu.	All the bridges have been blown up.
had ṭ-ṭumubil εăyyed mennha ši-waεed žuž de-ṛ-ṛwayeḍ.	Somebody has taken off two of this car's wheels.
xeṣṣni nešri ṛebεa de-ṛ-ṛwayeḍ ždad.	I have to buy four new tires.
ṭ-ṭumubilat εăndhom ṛebεa de-ṛ-ṛwayeḍ, l-biškliṭat ġir žuž.	Cars have four wheels, bicycles only two.
ḍ-ḍuṛuṣ kanu ṭwal bezzaf.	The lessons were too long.

had ẓ-ẓṛabi kollhom ṭwal u-ḍiyyqin.	All of these rugs are long and narrow.
le-qnaṭeṛ kollhom ṭwal, ɛla ḥăqq-aš l-wad waseɛ.	All the bridges are long, because the river is wide.
ṣuwwbu le-mžaṛi ḍiyyqin bezzaf.	They made the drains too narrow.
le-mžaṛi lli ḍiyyqin bezzaf ka-ittxenqu.	Drains that are too narrow get stopped up.
l-aš ka-iṣlaḥu had le-mžaṛi?	What are these drains (good) for?

II. Grammatical Notes.

Verbs from quadriliteral roots regularly have the pattern shown by *teṛžem* 'to translate' and *feṛgăɛ* 'to blow up, to make explode'. There are some weak (i.e., having a vowel element as a part of the root) quadriliteral verbs. The weak part of the root is always the second or the fourth constituent element. When the second element of a quadriliteral verb is weak, it is always either *i,* as in *ṣifeṭ* 'to send', or *u,* as in *suger* 'to insure'. When the fourth element of a quadriliteral verb is weak, it is *a* in the perfect and *i* in the durative, e.g. *seqṣa* 'to ask', durative *ka-iseqṣi* 'he asks'.

Intransitive and passive quadriliteral verbs are formed by prefixing *t-,* exactly as for Measures IIa(V) and IIIa(VI) (cf. the Grammatical Notes of Lesson 119). An illustrative pair is *feṛgăɛ* 'to blow up, to cause to explode', and *tfeṛgăɛ* 'to blow up, to explode, to get blown up'.

III. Exercises.

Identify each of the verbs below according to type of root and as to Measure.

1. *ža.*
2. *wessăɛ.*
3. *xerrež.*
4. *xrež.*
5. *ḥălla.*
6. *fiyyeq.*
7. *tḥămmem.*
8. *ṛežžăɛ.*
9. *ṭiyyeḥ.*
10. *faq.*
11. *weṣṣel.*
12. *ṛžăɛ.*
13. *ṭaḥ.*
14. *tsenna.*
15. *ḍeṛṛ.*
16. *ḍḍeṛṛ.*
17. *tqaḍa.*
18. *theḷḷa.*
19. *tṣuwweb.*
20. *tɛăllem.*
21. *ɛăllem.*
22. *tleffet.*
23. *tkellem.*
24. *fekk.*
25. *fešš.*
26. *kra.*
27. *ttfekk.*
28. *ttfešš.*

29. *ttekra.*
30. *ttexneq.*
31. *ddabez.*
32. *džuwwež.*
33. *herres.*
34. *tfahem.*
35. *therres.*
36. *tṣaff.*
37. *ttexlăɛ.*
38. *rtaḥ*
39. *htemm.*
40. *ntaxeb.*
41. *stexber.*
42. *ṣlaḥ.*
43. *xlaq.*
44. *ḥtaṛem.*
45. *feṛgăɛ.*
46. *seqṣa.*
47. *tfeṛgăɛ.*
48. *ṣifeṭ.*
49. *kteb.*
50. *dda.*

IV. Vocabulary.

ḍiyyqin (pl.)	narrow
feṛgăɛ	to blow up, to cause to explode
mžaṛi	drains
qenṭṛa	bridge
qnaṭeṛ (pl.)	
ṛwayeḍ	wheels, tires
seqṣa	to ask
tfeṛgăɛ	to explode, to blow up, to be blown up
ṭwal (pl.)	long

LESSON ONE HUNDRED TWENTY-TWO

I. Text.

ma-imken-li-š nemši mɛakom bla flus.	I can't go with you without (any) money.
qolt-lu imši bla biya.	I told him to go to work without me.
nemši bla biha.	I'm going to go without her.
ža bla kebbuṭ.	He came without a coat.
ṣifeṭ le-bṛa bla tenber.	He sent the letter without a stamp.
xeṣṣni nemši l-l-buṣṭa nešri ši-tnaber.	I have to go to the post office and buy some stamps.
be-šḥal had t-tnaber?	How much are these stamps?
men	who
mɛa men mšiti?	Whom did you go with?
bent men hadi?	Whose daughter is this?
dyal men had ṭ-ṭumubil?	Whose car is this?
de-mmen had le-flus?	Whose money is this?

le-mmen xeṣṣni neɛṭi had le-bṛawat?	Whom should I give these letters to?
bqa gales bla-ma yeɛmel ḥetta ḥaža.	He just sat there without doing anything.
šedd l-bab bla-ma nsemɛu.	He closed the door without my hearing him.
ma-temši-š bla-ma txeḷḷeṣ l-xedma.	Don't leave without paying for the work.
ma-žbeṛt fe-l-xenša ġir waḥed ṭ-ṭebṣil mherres.	All I found in the bag was a broken plate.
žab-li waḥed ṭ-ṭebṣil ɛameṛ be-l-lḥăm.	He brought me a plate full of meat.
l-magana dyali mherrsa.	My watch is broken.
siyyeb had ṭ-ṭbaṣel le-mherrsin.	Throw out these broken dishes.
waš l-xedma mkemmla wella baqi?	Is the work done yet?
dak š-ši mkemmel daba.	That's finished now.

II. Grammatical Notes.

A. The preposition ***bla*** 'without' usually takes nouns directly, without any equivalent for English 'some', 'any' or 'a', e.g., ***bla kebbuṭ*** 'without a coat', ***bla flus*** 'without any money'. Pronoun endings are not used directly with ***bla***. Instead, the preposition ***b-*** with pronoun endings is used after ***bla***, e.g. ***bla biya*** 'without me', ***bla bik*** 'without you', ***bla bih*** 'without him', etc. The form ***bla-ma*** is used before the imperfect as the equivalent of English '-ing' forms after 'without', e.g., ***bla-ma yeɛmel ḥetta ḥaža*** 'without (his) doing anything'.

B. The form ***men*** 'who' is used only in expressions of possession, e.g., ***bent men hadi?*** 'Whose daughter is this?', and after prepositions, e.g. ***mɛa men mšiti?*** 'Whom did you go with?' Note the form ***-mmen*** after ***d(e)-*** 'of' and ***l(e)-*** 'to', as in ***de-mmen had le-flus?*** 'Whose money is this?' and ***le-mmen xeṣṣni neɛṭi had le-bṛawat?*** 'Whom should I give these letters to?'

III. Exercises.

A. Replace *mƐa* 'with' and *b-* 'with' with *bla* 'without' in the following sentences. Read each new sentence with *bla* out loud.

1. *ma-imken-li-š nemši mƐakom.*
2. *bġat teġsel had l-kebbuṭ be-ṣ-ṣabun.*
3. *ġad-itṣaff mƐakom?*
4. *ma-tebġi-š dži mƐana.*
5. *ka-yakol l-lƐăm b-le-mleƐ.*

B. Re-do Exercise **A** above, and in addition to replacing *mƐa* and *b-* with *bla,* change questions into statements, statements into questions, positive sentences into negative sentences, and negative sentences into positive sentences.

C. Join each of the sentence pairs below into a longer compound sentence using *bla-ma.* For example, *šedd l-bab* 'He closed the door' and *ma-smăƐnah-š* 'We didn't hear him' can be combined to form *šedd l-bab bla-ma nsemƐuh* 'He closed the door without our hearing him'.

1. *mša le-ḍ-ḍaṛ.*
   ma-kemmel-š l-xedma dyalu.
2. *Ɛămmṛet l-kisan.*
   ma-daret-š fihom sokkaṛ.
3. *bqina ka-nhedṛu.*
   ma-xemmemna-š fe-l-weqt.
4. *feqt u-neḍt u-mšit.*
   ma-fiyyeqt Ɛetta waƐed.
5. *Ɛlaš ma-werritihom-š t-tṣaweṛ?*
   ma-ttsennani-š!
6. *xdaw ṭ-ṭumubil.*
   ma-xeḷḷṣuha-š.
7. *ma-temšiw-š!*
   qulu-lha l-Ɛonwan dyalu!
8. *dxel.*
   ma-šeftu-š.
9. *džuwwžet.*
   ma-Ɛăṛfu-š n-nas.
10. *hḍeṛ.*
    le-fqi ma-semƐu-š.

IV. Vocabulary.

bla	without (see Grammatical Note **A**)
bla bi- (before pronoun endings)	
bla-ma (before imperfect verb forms)	
mherres	broken
mkemmel	finished, done
men	who (see Grammatical Note **B**)
tenber	(postage) stamp
pl. *tnaber*	
ṭebṣil	dish, plate

LESSON ONE HUNDRED TWENTY-THREE

I. Text.

le-ktab dyali mṣaff εăl ṭ-ṭebla mεa l-oẋṛin.	My book is lined up on the table with the others.
šeft bezzaf de-n-nas mṣaffin qeddam s-sinima.	I saw a lot of people lined up in front of the movie.
wessex	to get dirty, to make dirty
ṭeḥt u-wessext l-kebbuṭ ž-ždid dyali.	I fell down and got my new coat dirty.
d-drari dima ka-iwessxu le-ḥwayež dyalhom.	Children always get their clothes dirty.
twessex	to get dirty, to become dirty
d-drari dima ka-itwessxu.	Children always get dirty.
ḥwayži twessxu.	My clothes have gotten dirty.
εäṭṭel	to delay, to hold up, to make late
ġad-nεäṭṭlu ṭ-ṭiyyaṛa ḥetta iwṣel ṛ-ṛaʔis.	We're going to delay the plane until the president arrives.
ddit mṛati le-ṭ-ṭbib, dak š-ši lli εäṭṭelni.	I took my wife to the doctor, that's what made me late.
tεäṭṭel	to be late, to be delayed
ṭ-ṭiyyaṛa tεäṭṭlet.	The airplane has been delayed.
ma-bġina-š ntεäṭṭlu fe-l-xedma dyalna.	We don't want to fall behind in our work.
xelli ḍ-ḍuw meṭfi ḥetta nertaḥ šwiya.	Leave the light off until I rest a little while.
mnin ṛžäεt, žbeṛt l-εafya meṭfiya.	I found the fire out when I came back.
le-εwafi kollhom meṭfiyin daba.	All the fires are out now.
ṭ-ṭiyyaṛa tεäṭṭlet, be-l-ḥäqq tsennitha ḥetta weṣlet.	The plane was delayed, but I waited for it till it arrived.
tsenninah ḥetta ža.	We waited for him till he came.

II. Grammatical Notes.

A. When referring to future time, *ḥetta* 'until' is always followed by the imperfect, e.g. *ḥetta iwṣel* 'until he arrives'.

B. The plurals of Moroccan nouns are usually irregular and have to be memorized, cf. Grammatical Note **C**, Lesson 3. However, there are some regular patterns which can be noted. Three of them are listed below.

(**1**) Many nouns ending in *-a* form their plural by adding *-t*, e.g., *buḷa* 'light bulb', pl. *buḷat*. For shorter nouns especially this pattern is not consistent, e.g. *ɛafya* 'fire', pl. *ɛwafi*. There are, however, several types of nouns in *-a* for which the plural in *-t* is fully consistent. One type is words which have five or more consonants, e.g. *biškliṭa* pl. *biškliṭat* and *metɛăllma* pl. *metɛăllmat*. Another type is words for which there is a corresponding masculine noun not ending in *-a*, e.g., *fqiha* 'woman schoolteacher' pl. *fqihat*, with corresponding masculine *fqi* 'man schoolteacher'.

(**2**) Almost all nouns of the pattern *Feɛɛal* which refer to professional or habitual activity form a masculine plural by adding *-a*. This ending must not be confused with the feminine singular ending *-a*. Five such words have occurred in the lessons so far. They are:

gezzar	pl. *gezzara*	butcher
nežžaṛ,	pl. *nežžaṛa*	carpenter
ṣeṛṛaq,	pl. *ṣeṛṛaqa*	thief
ṭebbax,	pl. *ṭebbaxa*	male cook
xeddam,	pl. *xeddama*	worker

(**3**) If we take the letters *F-ɛ-L-L* as a shorthand way of referring to any sequence of four consonants, an extremely common plural pattern can be symbolized as *FɛaLeL*. This is the most common and regular noun plural pattern in Moroccan. Almost all singular nouns which have exactly four consonants in them, regardless of vowel pattern or vowel ending, form their plural according to this pattern. A specific exception is the singular pattern *Feɛɛal,* discussed immediately above, and feminines in *-a* derived from it (e.g., *tellaža* 'refrigerator' pl. *tellažat*). Otherwise the pattern is almost completely consistent. Listed below are plurals of this sort which have been encountered in the lessons so far. Note the variety of different singular patterns, all having the common factor of four consonants.

drahem, pl. of *derhem*	'dirham'
ġṛaṛef, pl. of *ġoṛṛaf*	'pitcher'
kbabeṭ, pl. of *kebbuṭ*	'coat'
knaneš, pl. of *konnaš*	'notebook'
mḍaṛeṣ, pl. of *meḍṛaṣa*	'school'
mkaḥel, pl. of *mkoḥla*	'rifle'
mlayen, pl. of *melyun*	'million'
qnaṭeṛ, pl. of *qenṭṛa*	'bridge'
ṣnadeq, pl. of *ṣenduq*	'box'
šṛažem, pl. of *šeṛžem*	'window'
tnaber, pl. of *tenber*	'(postage) stamp'
tṣaweṛ, pl. of *teṣwiṛa*	'picture'
ṭbaṣel, pl. of *ṭebṣil*	'dish, plate'

III. Exercises.

A. Part (3) of Grammatical Note **B** above contains a list of quadriliteral plural nouns with their corresponding singulars. Cover the plurals in the left-hand part of the list, then work down the list of singulars and attempt to read out loud from memory the corresponding plurals. Check your work by moving the cover sheet down the column one line at a time.

B. In the text of this lesson construct a pertinent question for every statement and a pertinent statement for every question. For example a simple pertinent question for *ḥwayži twessxu* 'My clothes have gotten dirty' might be *kif-aš twessxu ḥwayži?* 'How did my clothes get dirty?

IV. Vocabulary.

mṣaff	lined up, in line
meṭfi	out, extinguished, (turned) off
twessex	to get dirty, to become dirty
tɛăṭṭel	to be late, to be delayed
wessex	to get dirty, to make dirty
ḥetta	until
ɛăṭṭel	to delay, to hold up, to make late
ɛwafi	fires

LESSON ONE HUNDRED TWENTY-FOUR

I. Text.

ɛăndna waḥed ṭ-ṭebbaxa mezyana bezzaf.	We have a very good (woman) cook.
ɛam luwwel kanu ka-ixedmu ɛăndi tlata de-ṭ-ṭebbaxat.	I had three cooks working for me last year.
ġeṭṭa	to cover, cover up
qolt-lha tġeṭṭi l-makla b-ši-ḥaža.	I told her to cover the food with something.
ġeṭṭitha be-l-kebbuṭ dyali.	I covered her with my coat.
fayn le-ġṭa dyal had ṣ-ṣenduq?	Where's the lid to this box?
xebba	to hide (something)
xebba le-flus.	He hid the money.
ġad-nxebbiw had le-bṛawat.	We're going to hide these letters.
txebba	to hide (oneself)
l-bent txebbat muṛa l-bab.	The girl hid behind the door.
txebbina ɛla ḥăqq-aš ttexlăɛna.	We hid because we were scared.
kan mxebbi muṛa l-bab.	He was hidden behind the door.
žbeṛt le-bṛa mxebbya fe-l-konnaš dyalu.	I found the letter hidden in his notebook.
kanu bezzaf d-le-flus mxebbyin fe-l-mežṛa.	There was a lot of money hidden in the drain.
ana metfahem mɛah.	I'm in agreement with him.
huwa u-mṛatu metfahmin.	He and his wife understand each other.

II. Grammatical Notes.

A. In Grammatical Note A of Lesson 104, the form of passive participles of Measure I sound verbs was discussed, e.g. *kteb* 'to write' with passive participle *mektub* 'written'. The passive participle of Measure I verbs with doubled roots is exactly the same, e.g. *šedd,* 'to close' with passive participle *mešdud* 'closed', *ḥăll* 'to open' with passive participle *meḥlul* 'open, opened'. The passive participle of Measure I verbs with final-weak roots is *meFɛi,* with the prefix *me-* and with *-i* substituted for the final *-a,* e.g. *ṭfa* 'to put out, to turn off' with passive participle *meṭfi* 'out, extinguished, (turned) off'.

B. Measure IIa(V) and IIIa(VI) verbs ending in *-a* always keep the-*a* in the durative, e.g. *tsenna* 'to wait', *ka-itsenna* 'he waits'.

C. Plurals on the pattern of *FƐaLeL* (e.g., *kbabeṭ* 'coats') are called 'quadriliteral broken plurals'. A number of nouns with only three consonants in the singular form quadriliteral broken plurals. One common pattern is for nouns with *a* after the first consonant of the singular to form a quadriliteral broken plural by inserting *w* as the second consonant of the plural pattern. Examples so far encountered in the lessons are:

mwagen, sg. *magana*	'clock, watch'
swaret, sg. *ṣarut*	'key'
ḥwanet, sg. *ḥanut*	'shop, store'

Another common pattern is for singulars with *a, u,* or *i* after the second consonant to insert *y* as the third consonant of the plural pattern. Examples encountered so far are:

dqayeq, sg. *dqiqa*	'minute'
flayek, sg. *fluka*	'boat'
ṛwayeḍ, s.g. *ṛwiḍa*	'wheel, tire'
zlayef, sg. *zlafa*	'bowl'

Quadriliteral broken plurals which would be expected to end in *-y* if the pattern *FƐaLeL* were strictly followed actually end in *-i,* e.g.

ṣwani, sg. *ṣiniya*	'tray'
ẓṛabi, sg. *ẓeṛbiya*	'rug, carpet'
Ɛwafi, sg. *Ɛafya*	'fire'

D. In Lesson 123 it was pointed out that nouns of the pattern *FeƐƐaL* which refer to professional or habitual activity form a regular masculine plural by adding *-a,* e.g. *gezzar* 'butcher', pl. *gezzara.* Almost all corresponding feminine singulars of the pattern *FeƐƐaLa* form their plural by adding *-t,* regardless of meaning, e.g. *ṭebbaxa* '(woman) cook' with pl. *ṭebbaxat,* or *tellaža* 'refrigerator' with pl. *tellažat.*

III. Exercises.

Read out loud from memory the plural of each of the nouns below. If your memory fails on any given item, attempt to construct the plural on the basis of the patterns discussed in Lessons 123 and 124.

1. *derhem.*
2. *ġoṛṛaf.*
3. *kebbuṭ.*
4. *konnaš.*
5. *ṣenduq.*
6. *šeṛžem.*
7. *tenber.*
8. *ṭebṣil.*
9. *meḍṛaṣa.*
10. *mkoεla.*
11. *qenṭṛa.*
12. *teṣwiṛa.*
13. *fluka.*
14. *ṛwiḍa.*
15. *zlafa.*
16. *magana.*
17. *sarut.*
18. *εanut.*
19. *ṣiniya.*
20. *ẓeṛbiya.*
21. *Ɛafya.*
22. *gezzar.*
23. *nežžaṛ.*
24. *seṛṛaq.*
25. *ṭebbax.*
26. *xeddam.*
27. *εežžam.*
28. *buḷa.*
29. *fqiha.*
30. *kuṛa.*
31. *makina.*
32. *sella.*
33. *ṣefεa.*
34. *šelya.*
35. *tellaža.*

IV. Vocabulary.

ġṭa	lid, top
ġeṭṭa	to cover
metfahem	understanding (each other), in agreement (with)
mxebbi	hidden
mxebbya (f.)	
mxebbyin (pl.)	
txebba	to hide (oneself)
ṭebbaxa	(woman) cook
xebba	to hide (homething)

LESSON ONE HUNDRED TWENTY-FIVE

I. Text.

xay ma-ši mžuwwež.	My brother isn't married.
waš hiya mžuwwža wella baqi?	Is she married yet?
xwatatu kollhom mžuwwžin.	All his sisters are married.
škun lli qal-lek ana ṣġeṛ mennu?	Who told you that I was smaller than him?

bġit zeṛbiya (tkun) ṣġeṛ men hadi šwiya.	I want a rug (that will be) a little smaller than this one.
had ṭ-ṭbaṣel ṣġeṛ men haduk lli šrit ɛam luwwel.	These dishes are smaller than the ones that I bought last year.
had s-serwal qṣiṛ bezzaf ɛliya.	This pair of trousers is too short for me.
ḍ-ḍuṛuṣ f-had le-ktab kollhom qṣaṛ bezzaf.	All the lessons in this book are quite short.
ana qṣeṛ men xay.	I'm shorter than my brother.
le-bṛa lli ktebt-lu ana qṣeṛ men hadik lli ktebti-lu nta.	The letter that I wrote him is shorter than the one you wrote him.
had t-tqašeṛ ž-ždad qṣeṛ men duk l-balyin lli siyyebt.	These new socks are shorter than those worn-out ones that I threw away.
hadi hiya benti le-kbira.	This is my oldest daughter.
weldi ṣ-ṣġiṛ ɛad ɛṭinah biškliṭa.	We've just given my youngest son a bicycle.
škun huwa le-kbir fihom?	Who is the oldest one of them?
škun huwa ṣ-ṣġiṛ fikom?	Which one of you is the youngest?
ana kbeṛ mennu b-ɛamayn.	I'm two years older than he.
waš nta ṣġeṛ mennha?	Are you younger than she is?
hiya kbeṛ mennu šwiya.	She's a little bit older than he.
ṃṃi ṣġeṛ men ḅḅa b-ši-telt snin.	My mother is younger than my father by about three years.

II. Grammatical Notes.

A. A large number (but not all) singular nouns on the pattern of *FeɛLa* form their plural on the pattern of *FɛaLi*. Examples encountered in the lessons so far are:

mšaṭi, sg. *mešṭa*	comb
mžaṛi, sg. *mežṛa*	drain
qṛaɛi, sg. *qeṛɛa*	bottle
ṭbali, sg. *ṭebla*	table
xnaši, sg. *xenša*	bag

Plurals which are made by adding an ending are called 'sound plurals', e.g., *ṣefʕa,* 'page' pl. *ṣefʕat.* Plurals which involve an internal change in the singular are called 'broken plurals', e.g. those listed immediately above. There are a large variety of broken plural patterns, but beyond the patterns *FʕaLeL* and *FʕaLi* discussed in Lessons 123-125 there is little predictability.

Two additional fairly frequent plural patterns are *FʕaL* and *FʕuL,* exemplified by the plurals *ržal* and *ktub* from *ṛažel* 'man' and *ktab* 'book' respectively. Whether a given noun has one of these plural patterns is, however, unpredictable from a knowledge of the singular. The same is true of less frequently occurring patterns. The only practical procedure for the student is to memorize noun plurals as he encounters them.

B. When a degree of comparison is indicated, the amount of difference is introduced by the preposition *be-,* as in ana *kbeṛ mennu b-ʕamayn* 'I'm (by) two years older than he is'. Similar constructions with 'by' can be found in English, e.g. *ṃṃi ṣġeṛ men ḅḅa b-ši-telt snin* 'My mother is younger than my father by about three years'.

C. Comparatives such as *kbeṛ* 'bigger' have only the one form, regardless of masculine, feminine, or plural reference.

III. Exercises.

Go through the text of this lesson and construct pertinent questions for all statements and pertinent statements for all questions. For example, a pertinent statement corresponding to *waš hiya mžuwwža wella baqi?* 'Is she married yet?' might be *hadi telt snin u-hiya mžuwwža* 'She's been married for three years'.

IV. Vocabulary.

kbir	old
kbeṛ	bigger; older
mžuwwež	married
qṣiṛ	short
qṣaṛ (pl.)	
qṣeṛ	shorter
ṣġiṛ	young
ṣġeṛ	smaller; younger

LESSON ONE HUNDRED TWENTY-SIX

I. Text.

had s-siyyed meحtaṛem bezzaf.	This man is very much respected.
ḅḅaha u-ṃṃha meحtaṛmin bezzaf f-le-blad.	Her father and mother are very much respected in the town.
ddi had ṛ-ṛwiḍa l-mefšuša ttṣuwweb.	Take this flat tire to be fixed.
mnin xrežt men s-sinima žbeṛt ṛ-ṛwayeḍ de-ṭ-ṭumubil dyali mefšušin kollhom.	When I came out of the movie, I found all the tires of my car flat.
l-kuṛa mefšuša.	The ball has the air let out of it.
xay xḷaq ṭṛeš.	My brother was born deaf.
hadi telt snin u-hiya ṭeṛša.	She's been deaf for three years.
ma-kayna meḍṛaṣa le-ṭ-ṭuṛeš f-had le-blad.	There isn't any school for the deaf in this city.
žbeṛtu naعes mnin dxelt.	I found him asleep when I came in.
hadi saعtayn u-hiya naعsa.	She's been asleep for two hours.
hadi saعtayn baš neعset.	She went to sleep two hours ago.
qalet-li kanu naعsin.	She told me that they were asleep.
qal-li neعsu.	He told me they had gone to sleep.
rkeb (عla, f-)	to ride, to mount, to get on board
rkeb عăl l-biškliṭa dyalu u-mša.	He got on his bicycle and left.
عămmeṛni ma-rkebt عăl l-biškliṭa men qbel.	I've never ridden a bicycle before.
rkeb f-had le-fluka hadi.	Get on board this boat here.
xud ṭ-ṭubis lli ka-iwqef حda l-meḍṛaṣa.	Take the bus that stops beside the school.
xudu ṭ-ṭubis le-حmeṛ u-tweṣlu fe-l-weqt.	Take the red bus and you'll arrive on time.
xeṣṣek terkeb fe-ṭ-ṭubis daba, qbel-ma imši.	You should get on the bus now, before it leaves.
عămmeṛha ma-ka-terkeb fe-ṭ-ṭubis.	She never rides the bus.

II. Grammatical Notes.

A. The verb *xda* 'to take' has the irregular imperative *xud,* pl. *xudu*.

B. The formation of the passive participle of Measure I has been discussed in Grammatical Note A of Lesson 104 and Grammatical Note A of Lesson 124. The passive participle of Measure Ia is always the participle of the corresponding Measure I verb. Thus such a pair as *xneq* 'to stop up' and *ttexneq* 'to get stopped up' have a common passive participle, *mexnuq* 'stopped up'. A further example is *mefšuš* 'flat, deflated', which is the passive participle of both Measure I *fešš* 'to let the air out of, to deflate' and Measure Ia *ttfešš* 'to go flat, to become deflated'.

For Measures other than I and Ia, the passive participle is formed simply by prefixing *m-* (*me-* before two consonants), without any internal change in the verb, e.g., Measure II *herres* 'to break' with passive participle *mherres* 'broken', Measure VIII *ɛtaṛem* 'to respect' with passive participle *maɛtaṛem* 'respected'. Verbs ending in *-a* change it to *-i* e.g., *xebba* 'to hide', passive participle *mxebbi* 'hidden'.

Just as Measures I and Ia usually have a common passive participle so also do Measures II and IIa(V). The common participle is formed from the Measure II verb, e.g., *mwessex* 'dirty' serves as passive participle for Measure II *wessex* 'to make dirty' and Measure IIa(V) *twessex* 'to get dirty, to become dirty'. A similar example is *mherres* 'broken', which is the passive participle of both Measure II *herres* 'to break (something)' and Measure IIa(V) *therres* 'to break, to get broken'.

In the cases where a Measure III verb and a Measure IIIa(VI) verb stand in a strict active-passive or transitive-intransitive relationship, they also share a common passive participle, formed from the Measure III verb, e.g. *mṣaff* 'lined up, in line' is the passive participle of both Measure III *ṣaff* 'to put in line' and Measure IIIa(VI) *tṣaff* 'to get in line'. However, in those cases where a Measure IIIa(VI) verb has a reciprocal meaning, a separate participle with no particular implications of passivity is formed, e.g. IIIa(VI) *tfahem* 'to come to a mutual understanding, to understand (each other)' with participle *metfahem* '(mutually) understanding'.

Participles are never formed from Measure IX verbs, and Measure X verbs are so rare as to be of little importance for the patterns of participle formation.

Listed below are all passive participles (other than from Measure I verbs) which have occurred in the lessons so far.

Passive Participle	Related Verb	Passive Participle	Related Verb
mherres	*herres, therres*	*mxebbi*	*xebba, txebba*
mkemmel	*kemmel*	*mžuwwež*	*džuwwež*
mṣaff	*ṣaff, tṣaff*	*meḥtaṛem*	*ḥtaṛem*
metfahem	*tfahem*	*mɛăṭṭel*	*ɛăṭṭel, tɛăṭṭel*
mwessex	*wessex, twessex*		

C. Participles are sometimes encountered which have acquired a meaning independent of the verb they are formally derived from, e.g. *metɛăllma* 'maid', which is formally the feminine participle of Measure IIIa(VI) *tɛăllem* 'to learn'. Such exceptions must be memorized as vocabulary items.

III. Exercises.

In Grammatical Note **B** above, cover the left-hand column of passive participles with a piece of paper and attempt to reproduce them from the related verbs given in the right-hand column. Check your work by sliding the cover sheet down the left-hand column line by line after each attempt.

IV. Vocabulary.

mefšuš	flat, deflated
meḥtaṛem	respected
naɛes	sleeping, asleep
rkeb ɛla, rkeb f-	to ride, to mount, to get on board
ṭṛeš	deaf
ṭeṛša (f.)	
ṭuṛeš (pl.)	
ṭubis	(local) bus
xud	take (imperative of *xda* 'to take')
xudu (pl.)	

LESSON ONE HUNDRED TWENTY SEVEN

I. Text.

žbeṛtu waqef fe-l-bab.	I found him standing at the door.
kanet waqfa qeddam le-mraya mnin dxelt.	She was standing in front of the mirror when I came in.
d-drari xeṣṣhom ibqaw waqfin ʕetta igles le-fqi.	The children have to remain standing till the teacher sits down.
huwa labes qamižža ždida l-yum.	He's wearing a new shirt today.
šeftha labsa kebbuṭ xḍeṛ.	I saw her wearing a green coat.
duk n-nas labsin mezyan l-yum.	Those people are well-dressed today.
waš nta ṛažeʕ daba?	Are you on your way back now?
ka-tkun ṛažʕa men l-xedma koll nhaṛ fe-s-setta.	Every day at six o'clock she's on her way back from work.
waš ntuma ṛažʕin daba wella men băʕd?	Are you going back now or later?
šefthom ṛažʕin men l-xedma.	I saw them on their way back from work.
žbeṛtu xarež men ḍ-ḍaṛ mnin wṣelt.	I found him coming out of the house when I arrived.
mnin wṣelt le-ḍ-ḍaṛ žbeṛtu xrež.	When I arrived at the house I found he had gone out.
ma-šeftiha-š xarža men ṭ-ṭumubil?	Didn't you see her getting out of the car?
ġad-ikunu xaržin fe-žwayeh s-setta.	They'll be coming out around six.
ġad-ikunu xeržu qbel-ma nweṣlu.	They'll (already) have gone out before we arrive.
koll nhaṛ ka-nšufu maši f-had ẓ-ẓenqa.	Every day I see him walking on this street.
škun dak l-weld lli kan maši mʕak l-l-meḍṛaṣa l-bareʕ?	Who's that boy that was walking to school with you yesterday?

škun dak l-weld lli kan ka-imši mɛak l-l-meḍṛaṣa ɛam luwwel?	Who's that boy that used to walk to school with you last year?
kanet mašya l-l-ḅenk u-wqefna ntkellmu šwiya mɛaha.	She was on the way to the bank and we stopped to talk with her a little.
duk t-tlata de-d-drari kanu mašyin fe-ẓ-ẓenqa mnin ḍeṛbethom ṭ-ṭumubil.	Those three children were walking in the street when the car hit them.

II. Grammatical Notes.

A. The passive participle has been discussed in Grammatical Note **A** of Lesson 104, Grammatical Note **A** of Lesson 124, and Grammatical Note **B** of Lesson 126. Some Moroccan verbs also have an 'active participle'. For Measure I the form is generally *FaɛeL,* e.g. *waqef* 'standing'. Measure I verbs with final-weak roots have the pattern *Faɛi,* e.g. *maši* 'going'.

B. All participles, active and passive, are regularly made feminine by adding *-a* and plural by adding *-in,* e.g. *ṭebṣil mherres* 'a broken plate', *šelya mherrsa* 'a broken chair', *buḷat mherrsin* 'broken light bulbs'. For the dropping out of the *e* before the final *s* of *mherres* in the feminine and plural forms, see the discussion of elision and inversion in Grammatical Note **D** of Lesson 25 and Grammatical Note **C** of Lesson 42.

Participles ending in *i* have a special sub-pattern. Passive participles of Measure I add *y* to the final *i* before the feminine and plural endings, e.g. *meṭfi* 'out, extinguished, turned off', with feminine *meṭfiya* and plural *meṭfiyin.* All participles other than the passive of Measure I change the final *i* to *y,* e.g. *maši* 'going', f. *mašya,* pl. *mašyin,* or *mxebbi* 'hidden', f. *mxebbya,* pl. *mxebbyin.*

C. Adjectives with the singular pattern *FɛiL* usually have the plural pattern *FɛaL.* Examples encountered so far are:

kbir, pl. *kbaṛ*	big	*ṣġiṛ,* pl. *ṣġaṛ*	small, little
mṛiḍ, pl. *mṛaḍ*	sick	*ṭwil,* pl. *ṭwal*	long
qṣiṛ, pl. *qṣaṛ*	short	*ždid,* pl. *ždad*	new

III. Exercises.

A. In Grammatical Note **C** above, cover the right-hand column of plurals and reconstruct them from the list of singulars in the left-hand column.

B. Recite aloud the active participles for the verbs *lbes, mša, ržăƐ, wqef,* and *xrež.*

C. Go through the list of participles in Grammatical Note B of Lesson 126 and construct the feminine and plural forms for each, reciting them out loud.

IV. Vocabulary.

labes	wearing, (having) dressed (oneself)
maši	going, walking, on the way
qamižža	shirt
ṛažeƐ	returning, on the way back
waqef	standing
xarež	(in the process of) leaving, coming out, going out

LESSON ONE HUNDRED TWENTY-EIGHT

I. Text.

ha	here (is, are)!
maži	coming
ha-huwa maži daba!	Here he comes now!
dima ka-iži fe-žwayeh had s-saƐa.	He always comes around this time.
ha-hiya mažya daba!	Here she comes now!
ka-dži koll nhaṛ fe-l-xemsa.	She comes at five o'clock every day.
ha-huma mažyin!	Here they come!
ka-ižiw bezzaf.	They come quite often.
ha le-flus dyaḷek!	Here's your money!
ha šelya u-ha ṭebla!	Here's a table and a chair.
ha l-uṛaq lli ṭlebti.	Here are the tickets you asked for.
huwa maši l-l-medṛaṣa.	He's going to school.
kan maši l-l-medṛaṣa.	He was going to school.
ka-imši l-l-medṛaṣa.	He goes to school.
kan ka-imši l-l-medṛaṣa.	He used to go to school.

ha-huwa žayeb l-xobz.	Here he is bringing the bread.
waš žaybahom mɛaha?	Is she bringing them with her?
aš dak š-ši lli žaybin?	What is it that they're bringing?
dxel rafed waḥed ṣ-ṣiniya f-yeddih.	He came in carrying a tray in his hands.
aš dak š-ši lli rafda ɛla ṛaṣha?	What is that thing she's carrying on her head?
žaw r-ržal de-le-blad kollhom rafdin le-mkaḥel dyalhom.	All the men of the town came, carrying their rifles.

II. Grammatical Notes.

A. The active participle of middle-weak Measure I verbs has the form *FayeL,* e.g. ***žab*** 'to bring', active participle ***žayeb*** 'bringing'.

B. The use and meaning of the Moroccan active participle causes considerable difficulty for the English speaker. In Grammatical Note **C** of Lesson 47, it was pointed out that the Moroccan durative translates both the English present and progressive tenses, e.g. ***ka-ixdem*** 'he works' or 'he is working, ***ka-ikteb*** 'he writes' or 'he is writing'. This is so for most verbs, but not for verbs which refer to motions or states.

For Moroccan verbs which refer to motions or states, the durative tense has only a habitual or repetitive meaning; it never refers to an immediate state or single progressive action. The student is already familiar with a similar pattern of meaning in the contrast between equational sentences and sentences using the durative of ***kan*** 'to be' (cf. Grammatical Note **C,** Lesson 104, and Grammatical Note **A,** Lesson 97); i.e., the durative of ***kan*** refers only to habitual or repetitive events, as in ***ka-ikun fe-l-mekteb dyalu koll nhaṛ*** 'He's in his office every day'.

C. Subject pronouns are often not expressed for active participles and must be inferred from context, e.g. ***aš dak š-ši lli žaybin?*** 'What is it that they're bringing?' The pronoun ***huma*** 'they' would be placed before ***žaybin*** only in a context where some ambiguity might occur, e.g. where possibly the pl. ***žaybin*** 'bringing' might incorrectly be interpreted as tacitly having ***ḥna*** 'we' or ***ntuma*** 'you' (pl.) as subject.

D. The active participle takes object pronoun endings just as verbs do, e.g. *waš žaybahom mƐaha?* 'Is she bringing them with her?'

E. As is true with English '-ing' forms, the Moroccan active participle is sometimes used to refer to an immediate future, e.g. *waš ntuma ṛažƐ in daba wella men băƐd?* 'Are you going back now or later?'

F. The verb *ža* 'to come' has an irregular active participle, *maži* 'coming'.

III. Exercises.

In the text of this lesson, form new sentences according to the instructions below. Read each new sentence out loud.

(1) For sentences with *huwa* 'he' (either expressed or implied) as subject, substitute first *hiya* 'she' and then *huma* 'they'.

(2) For sentences with *hiya* 'she' as subject, substitute first *huwa* 'he' and then *huma* 'they'.

(3) For sentences with *huma* 'they' as subject, substitute first *huwa* 'he' and then *hiya* 'she'.

IV. Vocabulary.

ha	here (is, are)
maži	coming
rafed	carrying
žayeb	bringing

LESSON ONE HUNDRED TWENTY-NINE

I. Text.

Ɛamel	having put
ha ṣ-ṣenḍuq lli Ɛamel fih le-flus.	Here's the box that I've put the money in.
ha ṣ-ṣenḍuq lli Ɛmelt fih le-flus.	Here's the box that I put the money in.
žabet-li waḥed ṣ-ṣiniya, Ɛamla fiha berrad u-žuž de-l-kisan.	She brought me a tray on which she had put a teapot and two glasses.

žabet-li waḥed ṣ-ṣiniya u-εămlet fiha berrad u-žuž de-l-kisan.	She brought me a tray and put a teapot and two glasses on it.
ha t-tellaža lli εamlin fiha l-makla.	This is the refrigerator that they've put the food in.
ha t-tellaža lli εămlu fiha l-makla.	This is the refrigerator that they put the food in.
mġeṭṭi	having covered; covered
werrana ši-ṭbaṣel de-l-makla, mġeṭṭihom b-waḥed l-mendil byeḍ.	He showed us some dishes of food which he had covered with a white cloth.
ṭ-ṭbaṣel kanu mġeṭṭyin b-waḥed l-mendil.	The dishes were covered with a cloth.
šeftha mġeṭṭya ṛaṣha b-waḥed l-mendil ḥmeṛ.	I saw that she had covered her head with a red scarf.
šeftha ka-tġeṭṭi ṛaṣha.	I saw her covering her head.
mnin wṣelt žberthom mġeṭṭyin l-makla b-waḥed l-mendil kbir.	When I arrived I found that they had covered the food with a large cloth.
huwa labes l-keswa ž-ždida dyalu.	He's wearing his new suit.
ka-ilbes l-keswa ž-ždida dyalu daba.	He's putting on his new suit now.
ka-ilbes l-keswa ž-ždida dyalu koll nhaṛ.	He wears his new suit every day.
kanet galsa fe-š-šelya dyali mnin dxelt.	She was sitting in my chair when I came in.
kanet ka-tegles fe-š-šelya dyali koll nhaṛ.	She used to sit in my chair every day.
εam luwwel ma-kont ka-nnεăs ġir ši-setta de-s-saεat fe-l-lila.	Last year I only slept about six hours a night.
kont naεes mnin dexlu ka-iheḍṛu.	I was sleeping when they came in talking.
kont naεes be-l-ḥăqq xay fiyyeqni.	I was sleeping, but my brother woke me up.

II. Grammatical Notes.

A. There is a difference in form between active and passive participle only for Measure I verbs. For all other verbs there is but a single participle, the form of which was discussed in Grammatical Note B of Lesson 126. This single participle functions either as active or passive depending on context. For example, *mġeṭṭi* serves both as the active and passive participle of *ġeṭṭa* 'to cover'.

B. With verbs of motion, the Moroccan active participle is approximately equivalent to the English verb form in '-ing', e.g. *maši* 'going', *žayeb* 'bringing', etc. For most other verbs the active participle indicates a current state or situation brought about by some previous action. Isolated translations are not fully accurate, e.g. to translate *ɛamel,* the active participle of *ɛmel* 'to put, to do', as 'having put' is not fully revealing. Active participles of this sort are used more rarely than the active participles of verbs of motion. They occur only in context and with the specific implication that the state of affairs brought about by a previous action is still in effect at some later time. Compare the pair of sentences:

ha ṣ-ṣenḍuq lli ɛamel fih le-flus.	Here's the box I've put the money in.
ha ṣ-ṣenḍuq lli ɛmelt fih le-flus.	Here's the box I put the money in.

In the first sentence, the use of *ɛamel* means that the speaker put the money in the box at some previous time and that it is still there at the time he is speaking. In the second sentence the use of *ɛmelt* 'I put' simply refers to a past action with no implication as to whether or not the money is still in the box at the time the person is speaking. The various sentences with *ɛamel* 'having put' and *mġeṭṭi* 'having covered' in the text of this lesson further illustrate the use of the active participle as a form signalling a current situation brought about and enduring from some previous action.

C. There is a small group of Moroccan verbs which refer both to the beginning of an action or the process or state arising from the beginning of an action, e.g., *nɛăs* means both 'to sleep' and 'to go to sleep', *lbes* means both 'to put on' and 'to wear'. There are not many verbs of this sort, and only five of them have been encountered in the lessons so far.

gles	to take a seat (beginning action) to sit (resulting action)
lbes	to put on (beginning action) to wear (resulting process)

nɛăs	to go to sleep (beginning action) to sleep (resulting process)
rkeb	to mount, to get on board (beginning action) to ride (resulting process)
wqef	to stand up, to get up; to come to a stop (beginning action) in a state of having stopped (resulting state)

When these verbs refer to the beginning of an action, their durative tense often has the kind of double translation pointed out in Grammatical Note C of Lesson 44. Thus, in the sense of 'to put on', ***ka-ilbes*** is sometimes equivalent to English 'he puts on' (repetitive habit) and sometimes to 'he is putting on' (progressive action), similar to such familiar double translations as 'he writes, he is writing' for ***ka-ikteb,*** etc.

When a resulting state or process is referred to, however, these verbs behave similarly to the verbs of motion. That is, the durative tense refers only to repetitive or habitual action and the active participle is used to refer to an immediate state or single progressive action. This difference can be illustrated by contrastive sets:

ka-igles	he takes a seat, he is taking a seat
ka-igles	he sits
huwa gales	he is sitting
ka-ilbes	he puts on, he is putting on
ka-ilbes	he wears
huwa labes	he is wearing
ka-inɛăs	he goes to sleep, he is going to sleep
ka-inɛăs	he sleeps
huwa naɛes	he is asleep, sleeping
ka-irkeb	he mounts, he is mounting
ka-irkeb	he rides
huwa rakeb	he is riding

ka-iwqef	he stands up, he is standing up; he stops, he is stopping.
ka-iwqef	he stands (still)
huwa waqef	he is standing (still, stopped)

III. Exercises.

All of the sentences in the text of this lesson are statements. For each sentence, construct a question to which the statement might serve as an answer.

IV. Vocabulary.

fe-l-lila	per night, a night
keswa	suit (of clothes)
mġeṭṭi	having covered; covered
mendil	napkin, cloth, scarf, handkerchief
saɛat	hours
ɛamel	having put

LESSON ONE HUNDRED THIRTY

I. Text.

šṛib	(act of) drinking
šṛib l-qehwa bezzaf ma-ši mezyan.	Drinking a lot of coffee is not good (for you).
băɛɛăd men	to avoid, keep away from
kont ka-nbăɛɛăd men l-gezzar ɛla ḥăqq-aš ma-kanu ɛăndi flus.	I was avoiding the butcher because I didn't have any money.
tekmal	completion, (act of) completing
ka-ntsennaw tekmal de-l-xedma.	We are waiting for the completion of the work.

tuwsaɛ	(act of) enlarging
tuwsaɛ had ḍ-ḍaṛ ka-iṭeḷḷeb flus bezzaf.	Enlarging this house takes a lot of money.
mdabza	quarrel
baqi ma-nsaw dak le-mdabza dyalhom.	They still haven't forgotten that quarrel of theirs.
fe-š-men yum wṣel?	What day did he arrive?
bqa mɛana sett iyyam.	He stayed with us six days.
ma-bqat ġir sebɛ iyyam.	There are only seven days left.
ɛămmeṛni ma-šeft weld fḍuli bɛalu.	He's the nosiest boy I've ever seen.
ma-kayna-š mṛa fḍuliya kteṛ mennha.	She's the nosiest woman in existence.
nas fḍuliyin bezzaf haduk!	Those people are too nosy.
huwa ḅumbi.	He's a fireman.
žaw bezzaf de-l-ḅumbiya.	A lot of firemen came.

II. Grammatical Notes.

A. Most Arabic verbs have accompanying verbal nouns. The meaning of the verbal noun is related to the meaning of the verb in the same way that such an English verbal noun as 'completion' is related to the verb 'to complete'. There is no specific consistent pattern for the verbal noun of Measure I and Ia verbs, and they must be learned individually as vocabulary items. A very frequent pattern is, however, *FɛiL,* e.g. *šṛib* '(act of) drinking'.

The verbal noun pattern for Measures II and IIa(V) is almost always *teFɛaL,* e.g. *tekmal* 'completion, act of completing', the verbal noun of *kemmel* 'to complete'. A very common verbal noun pattern for Measures III and IIIa(VI) is *mFaɛLa, e.g. mdabza* 'quarrel' the verbal noun of *ddabez* 'to quarrel'.

Note that verbal nouns occur freely in the construct state (cf. Grammatical Note B of Lesson 64) with other nouns, as in *tekmal ḍ-ḍaṛ* 'the completion of the house'.

B. From Lessons 111 and 112 the student is familiar with the forms for 'three thousand' through 'ten thousand'. These forms consist of a plural *alaf* 'thousands' and special short forms of the numerals from 'three' through 'ten'. Recapitulated, these short forms are:

telt	three	*sebƐ*	seven
ṛebƐ	four	*temn*	eight
xems	five	*tesƐ*	nine
sett	six	*Ɛăšṛ*	ten

These short numerals are used only before a limited number of plural nouns, as opposed to the usual pattern in such a phrase as *xemsa d-le-ktub* 'five books'. Other than *alaf* 'thousands', the only two nouns so far presented which take these numerals are *snin* 'years' and *iyyam* 'days'.

C. Moroccan has a number of nouns and adjectives ending in *-i,* usually with a relational meaning of some sort (cf. English 'wind' and 'windy', 'sun' and 'sunny', etc.) Such words are called 'nisbas'. The feminine of such nouns is regularly formed by adding *-ya,* e.g. *mṛa fḍuliya* 'a nosy woman'. With nouns indicating professional activity the plural is formed by adding *-ya,* e.g. *ḅumbi* 'fireman', pl. *ḅumbiya.* Otherwise the plural is formed by adding *-yin,* e.g. *nas fḍuliyin* 'nosy people'.

III. Exercises.

Construct appropriate questions and answers for the statements and questions in the text.

IV. Vocabulary.

ḅumbi, pl. *-ya*	fireman
băƐƐăd men	to avoid, to keep away from
fḍuli	nosy, impolitely inquisitive
mdabza	quarrel
šṛib	(act) of drinking
tekmal	completion, (act of) completing
yum	day (period of 24 hours)
iyyam (pl.)	

PART TWO

THE DIALOGS

DIALOG ONE

A: *ʔahlen wa sahlen.*[1]	Hello.
B: *ʔahlen.*	Hello to you.
A: *še-xbaṛek?*[2]	How are you (sg)?
B: *l-ḥămdu l-llah.*[3]	I'm fine.
u-nta?[4]	And you (sg.)?
A: *ana bi-xir, l-ḥămdu l-llah.*[5]	I'm fine, thank God.
B: *še-xbaṛ ṣ-ṣḥiḥa?*	How's your health?
A: *ka-nɛăddi. u-nta, še-xbaṛ ṣ-ṣḥiḥa?*	Not bad. And you, how's your health?
B: *l-ḥămdu l-llah.*	Fine.

Notes

1. The greeting *ʔahlen wa sahlen* and its reply, *ʔahlen* are slightly formal or serious in tone. They are used, for example, when two people are introduced to each other for the first time. There are various other greetings which are used among friends on casual encounters and informal occasions.

2. The form *še-xbaṛek?* 'How are you' is used only in speaking to one person. Moroccan has different forms for 'you' depending on whether one person or several people are being spoken to.

3. The expression *l-ḥămdu l-llah* 'the praise be to God' is the first of many conversational references to God that the student will encounter. In English the word 'God' is usually restricted to either oaths, both profane and serious, or to formally serious situations. Arabic on the other hand employs references to God, and to religion in general, in a wide variety of everyday situations.

4. The form *nta* 'you' is used only in speaking to a man. There are separate forms for 'you' which are used in speaking to a woman or to several people. The student will learn them later. Learning the proper use of these forms is important. A masculine form spoken to a woman or a feminine form

spoken to a man is at best comically ridiculous, and in some circumstances such an error could lead to offensive misunderstandings.

5. The English here is simply a reflection of the Moroccan phraseology. The English speaker would be more likely to say 'thank you' rather than 'thank God' in this context in a casual conversation.

DIALOG TWO

A: *s-salamu ɛalikom.*[1]	Hello.
B: *wa ɛalikom s-salam.*	Hello.
A: *še-xbaṛek?*	How are you?
B: *bi-xir, l-ḥămdu l-llah.*	Fine.
A: *še-xbaṛ mwalin ḍ-ḍaṛ?*	How's the family?
B: *la-bas*[2] *l-ḥămdu l-llah.*	Fine, thank you.
u-ka-isellmu ɛlik.	And they greet you.
A: *še-xbaṛ ṣ-ṣḥiḥa?*	How's your health?
B: *fi ʔaman llah, l-ḥămdu l-llah.*	Fine, thank you.

Notes

1. The greeting *s-salamu ɛalikom* 'peace be upon you' and its answer, *wa ɛalikom s-salam* 'and upon you be peace' is another example of a conversational religious reference (cf. the comments on *l-ḥămdu l-llah* in note 3 of Dialog One). This expression is a set phrase which can be addressed to a man, a woman, or to several people simultaneously without different forms for 'you' (cf. notes 2 and 4 of Dialog One). Like *ʔahlen wa sahlen* (cf. note 1 of Dialog One) this greeting is somewhat formal and is not used casually among friends.

2. The expression *la-bas* is less formal than *bi-xir*. With the rising intonation of a question, *la-bas?*, this phrase is the most common casual greeting among friends, roughly equivalent to such an informal English greeting as 'Hi!' or 'Hi there!'

DIALOG THREE

A: *ʔahlen.*	Hello.
B: *ʔahlen wa sahlen, še-xbaṛek?*	Hello to you. How are you?
A: *la-bas, l-ḥămdu l-llah. u-nta še-xbaṛek?*	Fine, thank God, and how are you?
B: *iwa ka-nɛăddi. še-xbaṛ l-ɛaʔila?* [1]	Not bad. How's your family?
A: *la-bas, l-ḥămdu l-llah.*	Fine, thanks.
ka-isellmu ɛlik. kif ṣ-ṣḥiḥa?	They greet you. How's your health?
B: *la-bas, l-ḥămdu l-llah.*	Fine, thank God.
A: *be-s-slama.*	Good-bye.
B: *ḷḷah isellmek.* [2]	Good-bye.

Notes

1. The word *iwa* is a common exclamation with no set translatable meaning. It is often equivalent to 'oh' or 'well'.

2. Cf. note 3, Dialog One. Note that *ḷḷah isellmek* is the routine answer to *be-s-slama.*

DIALOG FOUR

A: *s-salamu ɛalikom.*	Hello.
B: *wa ɛalikom s-salam.*	Hello.
A: *še-xbaṛek?*	How are you?
B: *la-bas, l-ḥămdu l-llah.*	Fine, thanks.
še-xbaṛ l-ɛaʔila?	How's the family?
A: *la-bas l-ḥămdu l-llah.*	Fine, thanks.
ka-isellmu ɛlik.	They greet you.
B: *sellem-li ɛlihom.*	Say hello to them for me.
A: *slam mbelleġ.* [1]	I will.
B: *be-s-slama.*	Good-bye.
A: *ḷḷah isellmek.*	Good-bye.

Notes

1. Literally 'greeting reported'. The structure is similar to such English expressions as 'mission accomplished'.

DIALOG FIVE

A: *ṣbaح l-xir.*[1]	Good morning.
B: *ṣbaح l-xir.*	Good morning.
A: *še-xbaṛek?*	How are you?
B: *la-bas, l-ح ămdu l-llah.*	Fine, thanks.
A: (*šnu*) *smiytek men feḍlek?*[2]	What's your name, please?
B: *smiyti muح ămmed.*	My name is Mohammed.
u-nta šnu smiytek?	And you, what's your name?
A: *ana smiyti žamal d-din.*	My name is Jamal Eddine.
B: *metšeṛṛfin, a s-si žamal d-din.*[3]	I'm glad to meet you, Mr. Jamal Eddine.
A: *w-ana metšeṛṛef حett-ana, a s-si muح ămmed.*	And I'm glad to meet you too, Mr. Mohammed.

Notes

1. Many speakers say *ṣbăح* instead of *ṣbaح* for 'morning', especially at ordinary conversational speed. Compare such an English word as 'greasy', which is pronounced by some people to rhyme with 'easy' and by others to rhyme with 'fleecy'. Both *ṣbăح* and *ṣbaح* are acceptable pronunciations, but the writing *ṣbaح* has been used throughout this book for the sake of consistency.

2. Not all occurrences of English 'please' may be translated by *men feḍlek,* which is used only in making requests. In the sense of offering something (as in 'please have a seat'), 'please' is translated quite differently, as will be learned in later lessons. Note also that *men feḍlek* is singular and used only in speaking to one person. The form for addressing several people will be covered later.

3. There is no exact English equivalent for Moroccan *a.* The use of 'hey' in such expressions as 'Hey, John!' or 'Hey kids, get off the grass!' is somewhat similar, but English 'hey' is used only for hailing people at a distance or for the expression of surprise or anger. Moroccan *a* is used regularly before all names, titles, and common nouns when they are used in speaking directly to someone.

DIALOG SIX

A: *ʔahlen.*	Hello.
B: *ʔahlen wa sahlen.*	Hello to you.
A: *tfeḍḍel.*[1]	Come in.
B: *baṛak ḷḷahu fik.*[2]	Thank you (sg.).
A: *še-xbaṛek?*	How are you?
B: *la-bas, l-ḥămdu l-llah.*	Fine, thanks.
u-nta še-xbaṛek?	And how are you?
A: *la-bas, l-ḥămdu l-llah.*	Fine, thank God.
tfeḍḍel gles.	Please have a seat.
B: *baṛak ḷḷahu fik.*	Thank you.
A: *kif ṣ-ṣḥiḥa?*	How's your health?
B: *ka-nεăddi.*	Not bad.
A: *tfeḍḍel, εmel ši-gaṛṛu.*	Please have a cigarette.
B: *baṛak ḷḷahu fik.*	Thank you.
A: *bla žmil.*	You're welcome.

Notes

1. This is the opposite to *men feḍlek* (cf. note 3, Dialog Five). It has the general implications of proposing to someone that he satisfy his own pleasure with respect to some situation or thing. As such, it has a wide variety of different contextual translations in English. A very common use is that of inviting someone to enter a room or building of some sort. As such, it is translatable 'please come in' or 'please go in'. The student will observe various contextual translations in subsequent material. Note also that *tfeḍḍel* is singular. The form appropriate to two or more people is given later.

2. This expression, which literally means 'God bless you' (cf. note 3, Dialog One), is exceedingly common. It is used not only as an equivalent for English 'thank you' but also very often instead of *men feḍlek* 'please' (cf. note 3, Dialog Five) in making a request or asking a favor. The form given is singular only. The form used in speaking to two or more people at once is given later.

DIALOG SEVEN

A: *ṣbaḥ l-xir.*	Good morning.
B: *ṣbaḥ l-xir.*	Good morning.
A: *tfeḍḍel.*	Come in.
B: *baṛak ḷḷahu fik.*	Thank you.
A: *tfeḍḍel gles.*	Please sit down.
tešṛob ši-kwiyes d-atay?[1]	Would you like a glass of tea?
B: *waxxa, baṛak ḷḷahu fik.*	Yes, thank you.
A: *kif tebġi atay dyalek? ḥlu aw messus?*	How would you like your tea, sweet or slightly sweet?
B: *messus, ḷḷah ixellik.*[2]	Slightly sweet, please.
A: *tfeḍḍel.*[3]	(Here you are.)

Notes

1. Diminutives are common in Moroccan Arabic. Although the basic meaning is to indicate a smaller size or lesser quantity than is indicated by the base noun (*kas 'glass', kwiyes* 'small glass'), the diminutives have a wide variety of stylistic and metaphorical implications which must be learned by gradual experience. The use of diminutive *kwiyes* 'small glass' does not necessarily imply either a small glass or a small quantity of tea. Rather it gives a tone of friendliness to the invitation. Compare such an English invitation as 'How about a drop of tea?', where the use of 'drop' has nothing to do with any specific quantity of tea. The text sentence is the student's first encounter with a reference to tea. Tea drinking is a very important custom in Morocco, and tea is consumed in large quantities, both informally and individually as well as in a variety of different social circumstances. Typically tea is brewed with a pot stuffed full of mint and is served very hot and heavily sugared. It is always served in glasses, never cups. The drinking of cold tea is unknown in Morocco.

2. This phrase is equivalent in meaning to *men feḍlek* (cf. Note 3, Dialog Five), never to *tfeḍḍel.* The original literal meaning is 'God bless you', (cf. note 3, Dialog One).

3. Cf. Note 1, Dialog Six concerning the various contextual uses and translations of *tfeḍḍel.* The English translation 'Here you are' has been placed in parentheses in this context since the situation involved (handing a glass

of tea to someone) is one where it would be perfectly polite for the English speaker to remain silent.

DIALOG EIGHT

A: *mse-l-xir.*	Good evening.
B: *mse-l-xir.*	Good evening.
A: (*šnu*) *smiytek, men feḍlek?*	What's your name, please?
B: *smiyti ع̆ăzzuz.*	My name is Azzuz.
A: *tfeḍḍel.*	Come in.
B: *baṛak ḷḷahu fik a sidi.*	Thank you, sir.
A: *tfeḍḍel, gles عla had š-šelya.*	Please, take this chair.
B: *baṛak ḷḷahu fik.*	Thank you.
A: *tfeḍḍel, عmel ši-gaṛṛu.*	Please, have a cigarette.
B: *la, baṛak ḷḷahu fik.*	No, thanks.
A: *tebġi l-qehwa?* [1]	Would you like some coffee?
B: *iyeh, b-koll faṛaح.*	Yes, I'd love some.

Notes

1. Coffee is drunk less commonly in Morocco than is tea. It is usually drunk from small cups and is brewed stronger and more heavily sugared than American coffee.

DIALOG NINE

A: *ˀahlen.*	Hello.
B: *ˀahlen wa sahlen.*	Hello.
A: *še-xbaṛek?*	How are you?
B: *la-bas, l-ح̆ămdu l-llah, u-nta še-xbaṛek?*	Fine, thank God, and how are you?
A: *la-bas, l-ح̆ămdu l-llah, še-xbaṛ l-عaˀila?*	Fine, thank God. How's your family?
B: *la-bas, l-ح̆ămdu l-llah.*	Fine, thank God.
ka-isellmu عlik.	They greet you.
A: *sellem-li عlihom.*	Say hello to them for me.
B: *slam mbelleġ.*	I will.
A: *be-s-slama.*	Good-bye.
B: *ḷḷah isellmek.*	Good-bye.

DIALOG TEN

A: *tfeḍḍel.*	Come in.
B: *baṛak ḷḷahu fik.*	Thanks.
A: *tebġi l-qehwa?*	Would you like some coffee?
B: *waxxa, b-koll faṛaح.*	Yes, with pleasure.
A: *tkun حluwa, ḷḷah ixellik.*	Sweet, please.
B: *be-s-slama.*	Good-bye.
A: *ḷḷah isellmek.*	Good-bye.

DIALOG ELEVEN

A: *s-salamu عalikom.*	Hello.
B: *wa عalikom s-salam.*	Hello.
A: *smiytek men feḍlek?*	What's your name please?
B: *smiyti l-bašir.*	My name is El-Bashir.
A: *ʔahlen be-s-si l-bašir.*	Welcome, Mr. El-Bashir.
tfeḍḍel, gles.	Please sit down.
B: *baṛak ḷḷahu fik.*	Thank you.
A: *عmel ši-gaṛṛu.*	Have a cigarette.
B: *baṛak ḷḷahu fik.*	Thank you.
A: *ḷḷah ihennik.*	Good-bye.
B: *ḷḷah ihennik, a sidi.*	Good-bye.

DIALOG TWELVE

A: *ṣbaح l-xir a sidi.*	Good morning, sir.
B: *ṣbaح l-xir.*	Good morning.
A: *smeح-li, bġit nṣeqṣik.*	Excuse me. I want to ask you a question.
B: *عla ṛaṣi u-عăyniya.*	At your service.
A: *ka-tăعṛef fayn žat kolliyat l-عulum?*[1]	Do you know where the College of Sciences is?
B: *iyeh, bġiti temši l-temma?*	Yes, do you want to go there?
A: *iyeh, qul-li ḷḷah ixellik, kif-aš nemši-lha.*	Yes, please tell me how to get there.

B: *b-koll(i) faṛaḥ.*	Certainly ('with all pleasure')
ṭlăɛ mɛa šariɛ muḥămmed l-xamis ḥetta tuwṣel qeddam tanawiyt mulay yusef.[2]	Go up Mohammed the Fifth Avenue till you come to Moulay Youssef High School.
A: *iyeh, u-men băɛd?*	Yes, and then?
B: *men băɛd, lwi ɛăl l-imin u-dxol ɛăl l-qăws. ɛla yeddek de-š-šmal ġa-telqa wiẓaṛat t-teɛlim.*	Then you turn right and go through the archway. On your left you'll find the Ministry of Education.
A: *ka-năɛṛef l-wiẓaṛa fayn žat.*	I know where the ministry is.
B: *iwa ḥdaha be-d-dat kayna kolliyat l-ʔadab, u-ḥdaha l-xizana l-ɛamma. ġad-dzid ġir ši-xlifat u-telqa kolliyat l-ɛulum.*	Well, right near it you have the College of Arts, and next to it the general library. You just go a few more steps and you'll find the College of Sciences.
A: *daba ɛad ɛṛeft, baṛak ḷḷahu fik.*	Now I know, thank you.
B: *bla žmil.*	You're welcome.
A: *ḷḷah ihennik a sidi.*	Good-bye, sir.
B: *be-s-slama sidi.*	Good-bye.

Notes

1. The scene is in Rabat, the capital of Morocco.

2. Mohammed the Fifth, who died in February of 1961, was the king of Morocco. He was a great popular hero, and many public places are named after him.

DIALOG THIRTEEN

A: *mse-l-xir a sidi.*	Good evening, sir.
B: *mse-l-xir.*	Good evening.
A: *smeḥ-li ḷḷah ixellik, ka-tăɛṛef l-metḥef fayn ža?*	Excuse me, do you know where the museum is?
B: *maɛḷum. ɛṛefti fayn ža l-ʔutil l-malaki?*	Of course, do you know where the Royal Hotel is?

A: *iyeh.*	Yes.
B: *sir ṭul l-l-ˀutil l-malaki, u-men băƐd Ɛla yeddek d-l-imin.*	Go straight ahead to the Royal Hotel and then to your right.
A: *fe-ẓ-ẓenqa l-luwwla?*	At the first street?
B: *iyeh.*	Yes.
A: *waš l-metḥef ža f-dak ẓ-ẓenqa?*	Is the museum on that street?
B: *iyeh, Ɛăl š-šmal.*	Yes, on your left.
A: *baṛak ḷḷahu fik a sidi.*	Thank you very much.
B: *bla žmil.*	You're welcome.
A: *be-s-slama.*	Good-bye.
B: *ḷḷah isellmek.*	Good-bye.

DIALOG FOURTEEN

A: *ˀahlen.*	Hello.
B: *ˀahlen (wa sahlen)*	Hello.
A: *bġit nsuwwlek.*	I want to ask you a question.
B: *Ɛla ṛaṣi u-Ɛăyniya.*	At your service.
A: *ka-tăƐṛef fayn kayen ši-meṭƐăm mezyan ma-ikun-š bƐid men hna?*	Do you know where there is a good restaurant not far from here?
B: *iyeh, l-meṭƐăm l-waṭani ṛah qoddam l-metḥef.*	Yes, the National Restaurant is near the Museum.
A: *u-l-metḥef qṛib men hna?*	And is the museum near here?
B: *la, bƐid šwiya, ka-tăƐṛef saḥt muḥămmed l-xamis fayn žat?*	No, fairly far. Do you know where Mohammed V Square is?
A: *la, ma-ka-năƐṛefha-š.*	No, I don't know.
B: *saḥt muḥămmed l-xamis žat ḥda l-ˀutil l-malaki.*	Mohammed V Square is near the Royal Hotel.
A: *iyeh, daba Ɛad Ɛṛeft.*	Ah, now I understand.
baṛak ḷḷahu fik.	Thank you.
B: *bla žmil.*	You're welcome.

DIALOG FIFTEEN

A:	*s-salamu ɛalikom.*	Hello.
B:	*wa ɛalikom s-salam.*	Hello.
A:	*imken-lek tqul-li mnayn nemši l-l-busṭa?*	Can you tell me how I get to the Post Office?
B:	*b-koll faṛaḥ. šefti had ẓ-ẓenqa?* [1]	Certainly. Do you see this street?
A:	*ṭ-ṭalɛa?*	Talaa Street?
B:	*iyeh. xellik ġadi mɛaha ḥetta tuwṣel le-s-sinima d-bu-žlud.*	Yes. Stay on it till you come to the Boujlud Theater.
A:	*u-men băɛd?*	And then?
B:	*lwi ɛăl š-šmal u-xellik ġadi ḥetta telqa waḥed le-bni be-ḍ-ḍṛuž. hadik hiya l-busṭa.*	Turn left and keep going till you come to a building with steps. That's the Post Office.
A:	*ɛṛeft daba. baṛak ḷḷahu fik.*	I see now, thank you.
B:	*bla žmil.*	You're welcome.
A:	*be-s-slama*	Good-bye.
B:	*be-s-slama.*	Good-bye.

Notes

1. A street in Fez. The places mentioned in this lesson are in that city.

DIALOG SIXTEEN

A:	*ṣbaḥ l-xir.*	Good morning.
B:	*ṣbaḥ l-xir. š-ḥăbb l-xaṭeṛ?* [1]	Good morning. Can I help you?
A:	*fayn ža mekteb s-si ɛumaṛ b-le-fḍel mennek?*	Where is Mr. Omar's office, please?
B:	*ṭlăɛ l-fuq u-lwi ɛla yeddek de-š-šmal. l-mekteb l-luwwel ɛăl l-imin.*	Go upstairs and turn to the left. The first office on the right.
A:	*u-mekteb s-si ḥmed?*	And Mr. Ahmed's office?
B:	*hbeṭ l-teḥt u-ḍuṛ ɛla yeddek de-š-šmal. temma l-mekteb dyalu.*	Go downstairs and turn to the left. His office is there.
A:	*baṛak ḷḷahu fik.*	Thank you.

Notes

1. An approximate literal translation of *š-ḥăbb l-xaṭeṛ?* is 'What does the (your) feeling wish?' It is a standard polite inquiry in situations where someone may be expected to ask for something. Various contextual translations such as 'can I help you?' or 'what would you like?' are possible in English.

DIALOG SEVENTEEN

A: *s-salamu ɛalikom.*	Hello.
B: *wa ɛalikom s-salam.*	Hello.
A: *waḥed s-suʔal ḷḷah ixellik.*	A question please.
B: *tfeḍḍel.*	At your service.
A: *fayn ža mekteb s-safir?*	Where is the ambassador's office?
B: *xṛož men had l-ɛimaṛa u-sir l-hadik.*	Go out of this building and go into that one.
A: *u-men băɛd?*	And then?
B: *ṭlăɛ l-fuq u-lwi ɛla yeddek d-l-imin. temma mekteb s-safir.*	Go upstairs and turn to the right. The ambassador's office is there.
A: *baṛak ḷḷahu fik.*	Thank you very much.
B: *bla žmil*	You're welcome.
A: *be-s-slama.*	Good-bye.
B: *ḷḷah isellmek.*	Good-bye.

DIALOG EIGHTEEN

A: *mse-l-xir.*	Good evening.
B: *mse-l-xir. bġiti ši-ḥaža?* [1]	Good evening. Could I help you with anything?
A: *iyeh, fayn žat l-žamiɛa?*	Yes. Where is the University?
B: *sir men hna u-ḍuṛ ɛla yeddek de-š-šmal, f-mefṛeq ṭ-ṭoṛqan l-luwwel.*	Go out of here and turn to the left at the first intersection.
A: *u-men băɛd?*	And then?
B: *ḍuṛ ɛăl s-saḥa u-temma tṣib l-žamiɛa.*	Go around the square and there you'll find the University.
A: *baṛak ḷḷahu fik, be-s-slama.*	Thank you very much. Good-bye.
B: *ḷḷah isellmek.*	Good-bye.

Notes

1. Note the contextual translation of *bġiti ši-ɛaža?;* the literal translation 'Do you want something?' would be inappropriate English usage in this context, with overtones of impoliteness. The Moroccan *bġiti ši-ɛaža?* implies neither impoliteness nor abruptness in this context.

DIALOG NINETEEN

A:	*fayn ža mekteb l-ʔustad l-beṛnuṣi?*	Where is Professor El-Bernusi's office?
B:	*sir l-dak l-binaya. temma l-mekteb dyalu.*	Go into that building. His office is there.
A:	*l-fuq?*	Upstairs?
B:	*la, l-teɛt.*	No, downstairs.
A:	*u-mekteb l-ʔustad ɛămdan fayn ža?*	And where is Professor Hamdan's office?
B:	*xṛož men had l-binaya, ḍuṛ ɛla yeddek d-l-imin u-dxol l-hadik.*	Go out of this building, turn to your right and go in that one.
A:	*temma l-mekteb dyalu?*	Is his office in there?
B:	*iyeh.*	Yes.
A:	*baṛak ḷḷahu fik.*	Thank you.
B:	*bla žmil. be-s-slama.*	You're welcome. Good-bye.
A:	*ḷḷah isellmek.*	Good-bye.

DIALOG TWENTY

A:	*s-salamu ɛalikom.*	Hello.
B:	*wa ɛalikom s-salam.*	Hello.
A:	*še-xbaṛ ṣ-ṣɛiɛa?*	How's your health?
B:	*la-bas, l-ɛămdu l-llah. u-nta še-xbaṛ ṣ-ṣɛiɛa?*	Fine, thank God, and how's your health?
A:	*mnayn nta?*	Where are you from?
B:	*ana men ʔamirika.*	I'm from America.
A:	*šɛal hadi u-nta hna?*	How long have you been here?
B:	*žemɛa.*	A week.
A:	*ka-ttkellem l-ɛăṛbiya mezyan bezzaf.*	You speak Arabic very well.
B:	*(iwa) šwiya u-xḷaṣ.*[1]	Just a little.

Notes

1. Moroccan politeness patterns are similar to American politeness patterns in this situation. Both call for a modest disavowal of one's own skill, regardless of how well one in actual fact does speak.

DIALOG TWENTY-ONE

A: *ka-ttkellem l-ɛăṛbiya mezyan.*	You speak Arabic well.
B: (*iwa*) *šwiya u-xḷaṣ.*	Just a little.
A: *fayn tɛăllemtiha?*	Where did you learn it?
B: *tɛăllemtha f-ʔamirika.*	I learned it in America.
A: *waš hadi modda u-nta hna?*	Have you been here long?
B: *hadi yaḷḷah žemɛa w-ana hna.*	I've only been here a week.
A: *mn-ayna mdina f-ʔamirika nta?*	From what city in America are you?
B: *ana men New York.*	I'm from New York.
A: *mṛeɛba bik.*	Welcome to you (sg.).
B: *ḷḷah ibarek fik.*[1]	Thank you.

Notes

1. This is the routine reply called for in response to *mṛeɛba* 'welcome'. In so far as a literal translation is possible for this phrase it is 'God bless you'. Other replies are possible (e.g. *baṛak ḷḷah fik*) but less common.

DIALOG TWENTY-TWO

A: *hadi žemɛa w-ana fe-l-meġrib.*	I've been in Morocco a week.
B: *f-aš žiti?*	How did you come?
A: *žit fe-l-babuṛ.*	I came by ship.
B: *kif kan ṣ-ṣfeṛ?*	How was the trip?
A: *ṣ-ṣafaṛ dyali kan f-ġaya.*	My trip was very good.
B: *mnayn rkebti?*	Where did you sail from?
A: *rkebt men New York.*	I sailed from New York.
B: *waš nta men New York?*	Are you from New York?
A: *la, ana men San Francisco.*	No, I'm from San Francisco.

B:	*ka-ttkellem l-ʕăṛbiya mezyan bezzaf. tʕăllemtiha f-ˀamirika?*	You speak Arabic very well. Did you learn it in America?
A:	*iyeh.*	Yes.
B:	*iwa mṛeḥba bik.*	Welcome to you.
A:	*baṛak ḷḷahu fik.*	Thank you.

DIALOG TWENTY-THREE

A:	*mṛeḥba.*	Welcome.
B:	*ḷḷah ibarek fik.*	Thank you.
A:	*mnayn nta?*	Where are you from?
B:	*ana men ˀamirika.*	I'm from America.
A:	*kif žiti l-l-meġṛib.*	How did you come to Morocco?
B:	*žit fe-ṭ-ṭiyaṛa.*	I came by airplane.
A:	*kif kan ṣ-ṣfeṛ?*	How was the trip?
B:	*ṣ-ṣfeṛ kan f-ġaya.*	The trip was very good.
A:	*šḥal hadi u-nta hna?*	How long have you been here?
B:	*yaḷḷah žemʕa.*	Only a week.

DIALOG TWENTY-FOUR

A:	*žiti l-l-meġṛib fe-l-babuṛ aw fe-ṭ-ṭiyaṛa?*	Did you (sg.) come to Morocco by boat or by plane?
B:	*žit fe-l-babuṛ.*	I came by boat.
A:	*kan ṣ-ṣfeṛ mezyan?*	Was the trip good?
B:	*iyeh, l-ḥămdu l-llah.*	Yes, thank you.
A:	*waš hadi modda u-nta hna?*	Have you been here for a long time?
B:	*la, yaḷḷah žemʕa.*	No, only a week.
A:	*mnayn nta?*	Where are you from?
B:	*ana men ˀamirika.*	I'm from America.
A:	*mn-ayna mdina f-ˀamirika?*	From what city in America?
B:	*men New York.*	From New York.
A:	*mṛeḥba bik.*	Welcome to you.
B:	*ḷḷah ibarek fik.*	Thank you.

DIALOG TWENTY-FIVE

A: *mṛeḥba.*	Welcome.
B: *ḷḷah ibarek fik.*	Thank you.
A: *mnayn ntaʔ*	Where are you from?
B: *ana men ʔamirika.*	I'm from America.
A: *šḥal hadi u-nta fe-ṛ-ṛbaṭʔ*	How long have you been in Rabat?
B: *šheṛ.*	A month.
A: *ka-texdem hnaʔ*	Do you work here?
B: *ka-nexdem fe-s-sifaṛa l-ʔamirikiya.*	I work at the American Embassy.
A: *ɛaʔiltek mɛakʔ*	Is your family with you?
B: *iyeh.*	Yes.
A: *mṛeḥba.*	Welcome.
B: *ḷḷah ibarek fik.*	Thank you.

DIALOG TWENTY-SIX

A: *ṣbaḥ l-xir.*	Good morning.
B: *ṣbaḥ l-xir.*	Good morning.
A: *smiytekʔ*	What's your name?
B: *smiyti Richard Harrison.*	My name is Richard Harrison.
A: *mnayn ntaʔ*	Where are you from?
B: *ana men ʔamirika.*	I'm from America.
A: *ka-texdem fe-ṛ-ṛbaṭʔ*	Do you work in Rabat?
B: *iyeh, ka-nexdem fe-s-sifaṛa l-ʔamirikiya.*	Yes, I work at the American Embassy.
A: *šḥal hadi u-nta hnaʔ*	How long have you been here?
B: *hadi šheṛ w-ana hna.*	I've been here a month.
A: *f-aš žitiʔ*	How did you come?
B: *žit fe-l-babuṛ.*	I came by ship.

DIALOG TWENTY-SEVEN

A: *ˀahlen.*	Hello.
B: *ˀahlen wa sahlen.*	Hello to you.
A: *mnayn ntaˀ*	Where are you from?
B: *ana men ˀamirika.*	I'm from America.
A: *fayn tƐăllemti l-Ɛăṛbiyaˀ*	Where did you learn Arabic?
B: *tƐăllemtha fe-l-meġṛib.*	I learned it in Morocco.
A: *ka-texdem hnaˀ*	Do you work here?
B: *iyeh.*	Yes.
A: *Ɛaˀiltek mƐakˀ*	Is your family with you?
B: *iyeh.*	Yes.
A: *kif žitiw l-l-meġṛibˀ*	How did you come to Morocco?
B: *žina feṭ-ṭiyaṛa.*	We came by plane.

DIALOG TWENTY-EIGHT

A: *smeḥ-li. waš nta mġeṛbiˀ*	Excuse me, are you Moroccan?
B: *iyeh. aš ḥăbb l-xaṭeṛˀ*	Yes, what can I do for you?
A: *imken-lek tqul-li fayn žat l-žamiƐa l-meġṛibiyaˀ*	Can you tell me where the Moroccan University is?
B: *ṛa-hiya dik. mn-ayna blad ntaˀ*	There it is. What country are you from?
A: *ana men ˀamirika.*	I'm from America.
B: *hadi modda u-nta hnaˀ*	Have you been here a long time?
A: *la. hadi yaḷḷah šheṛ w-ana hna. ka-nexdem fe-s-sifaṛa l-ˀamirikiya.*	No. I've been here only a month. I work at the American Embassy.
B: *w-ana ka-nexdem fe-l-metḥef.*	And I work at the Museum.
A: *fayn ža l-metḥefˀ*	Where is the Museum?
B: *mmuṛ l-ˀutil le-kbir.*	Behind the Grand Hotel.
A: *baṛak ḷḷahu fik.*	Thank you.
B: *bla žmil.*	You're welcome.

DIALOG TWENTY-NINE

A: *šḥal hadi u-nta hna?*	How long have you been here?
B: *hadi žmăɛtayn w-ana hna.*	I've been here two weeks.
A: *ɛaʔiltek ḥetta-hiya hna?*	Is your family here, too?
B: *iyeh.*	Yes.
A: *kif žitiw?*	How did you come?
B: *žina fe-l-baxiṛa.*	We came by boat.
A: *ẓeṛtiw l-meġṛib men qbel?*	Have you visited Morocco before?
B: *iyeh, zeṛna l-meġṛib hadi ɛamayn.*	Yes, we visited Morocco two years ago.
A: *ka-ttkellem l-ɛăṛbiya mezyan bezzaf.*	You speak Arabic very well.
B: *ši-šwiya u-xḷaṣ.*	Just a little.

DIALOG THIRTY

A: *smiyt dak s-siyyed?*	What is that gentleman's name?
B: *smiytu Richard Harrison.*	His name is Richard Harrison.
A: *fayn ka-ixdem?*	Where does he work?
B: *ka-ixdem mɛaya fe-s-sifaṛa l-ʔamirikiya.*	He works with me at the American Embassy.
A: *waš hadi modda u-huwa hna?*	Has he been here a long time?
B: *hadi šehṛayn u-huwa hna.*	He's been here two months.
A: *ɛaʔiltu mɛah?*	Is his family with him?
B: *iyeh.*	Yes.
A: *ẓaṛ l-meġṛib men qbel?*	Has he visited Morocco before?
B: *la.*	No.
A: *ka-itkellem l-ɛăṛbiya mezyan bezzaf.*	He speaks Arabic very well.
B: *tɛăllemha f-ʔamirika.*	He learned it in America.

DIALOG THIRTY-ONE

A: *s-si Benett ʔustad fe-l-žamiʕa l-meġṛibiya.*	Mr. Benett is a professor at the Moroccan University.
B: *fuq-aš ža l-l-meġṛib?*	When did he come to Morocco?
A: *ža hadi šehṛayn.*	He came two months ago.
B: *kif-aš ža? fe-ṭ-ṭiyaṛa aw fe-l-baxiṛa?*	How did he come? By plane or by boat?
A: *huwa ža fe-ṭ-ṭiyaṛa, be-l-ḥăqq ʕaʔiltu žat fe-l-baxiṛa.*	He came by plane, but his family came by boat.
B: *ẓaṛu l-meġṛib men qbel?*	Have they visited Morocco before?
A: *iyeh. ẓaṛu l-meġṛib hadi ʕam.*	Yes. They visited Morocco a year ago.
B: *mn-ayna mdina f-ʔamirika huma?*	What city are they from in America?
A: *men San Francisco. ḥetta-nta men San Francisco aw-la?*	From San Francisco. You are from San Francisco too, aren't you?
B: *la, ana men New York.*	No, I'm from New York.

DIALOG THIRTY-TWO

A: *s-salamu ʕalikom.*	Hello.
B: *wa ʕalikom s-salam.*	Hello.
A: *aš semmak ḷḷah?*	What is your name?
B: *smiyti ʕli l-ḥămdawi. u-nta? (smiytek)?*	My name is Ali El-Hamdawy. And you?
A: *Richard Harrison. fayn ka-texdem?*	Richard Harrison. Where do you work?
B: *ka-nexdem fe-l-metḥef. mnayn nta?*	I work at the Museum. Where are you from?
A: *ana men ʔamirika.*	I'm from America.
B: *kont f-ʔamirika hadi ʕamayn.*	I was in America two years ago.
A: *šḥal bqiti temma?*	How long did you stay there?
B: *bqit šehṛayn.*	I stayed two months.
A: *ka-ttkellem l-ingliziya?*	Do you speak English?
B: *la, ma-ka-ntkellem-š l-ingliziya.*	No, I don't speak English.

DIALOG THIRTY-THREE

A: *s-salamu ɛalikom.*	Hello.
B: *wa ɛalikom s-salam.*	Hello.
A: *nta mġeṛbi, yak?*	You are Moroccan, aren't you?
B: *iyeh, u-nta mnayn?*	Yes, and where are you from?
A: *ana men ʔamirika. hadi ɛam w-ana hna.*	I'm from America. I've been here for a year.
B: *hadi ɛam ẓeṛt ʔamirika mɛa l-ɛaʔila dyali.*	I visited America with my family a year ago.
A: *mšitiw l-San Francisco? ana men temma.*	Did you visit San Francisco? I'm from there.
B: *la, ma-mšina-lha-š. ẓeṛna New York.*	No, we didn't go there. We visited New York.
A: *ka-ttkellem l-ingliziya?*	Do you speak English?
B: *iyeh, tɛăllemtha fe-l-medṛaṣa.*	Yes, I learned it at school.

DIALOG THIRTY-FOUR

A: *s-salamu ɛalikom.*	Hello.
B: *wa ɛalikom s-salam.*	Hello.
A: *nta mzuwwež?*	Are you married?
B: *iyeh.*	Yes.
A: *men fuq-aš?*	Since when?
B: *hadi ɛăšṛ snin.*	It's been ten years.
A: *ɛăndek ši-wlad?*	Do you have any children?
B: *ɛăndi žuž d-l-ulad u-tlata d-le-bnat. u-nta mzuwwež?*	I have two boys and three girls. And you, are you married?
A: *la-ma-mzuwwež-š.*	No, I'm not married.

DIALOG THIRTY-FIVE

A: *šɛal hadi u-nta mzuwwež?*	How long have you been married?
B: *hadi xems snin.*	For five years.
A: *šɛal d-l-ulad ɛăndek?*	How many children do you have?
B: *ɛăndi weld u-bent.*	I have a boy and a girl.
A: *šɛal fe-ɛmeṛhom?*	How old are they?
B: *l-weld f-ɛămṛu ṛebɛ snin, u-l-bent fe-ɛmeṛha ɛamayn.*	The boy is four years old, and the girl is two years old.
A: *smiythom?*	What are their names?
B: *l-weld smiytu ɛăbdu, u-l-bent smiytha ʔamina.*	The boy's name is Abdu, and the girl's name is Amina.
A: *ɛăbdu ka-imši l-l-meḍṛaṣa?*	Does Abdu go to school?
B: *la, ma-zal.*	No, not yet.

DIALOG THIRTY-SIX

A: *s-salamu ɛalikom.*	Hello.
B: *wa ɛalikom s-salam.*	Hello.
A: *še-xbaṛek?*	How are you?
B: *la-bas, l-ɛămdu l-llah.*	Very fine.
A: *še-xbaṛ mṛatek u-d-drari?*	How are your wife and children?
B: *la-bas, ḷḷah ibarek fik, u-mṛatek u-d-drari še-xbaṛhom?*	Fine thank you. And how are your wife and children?
A: *la-bas ɛlihom.*	They are fine.
B: *weldek ma-zal ka-imši l-l-meḍṛaṣa?*	Does your son still go to school?
A: *meɛlum.*	Of course.
B: *u-bentek?*	And your daughter?
A: *ɛad bdat had l-ɛam.*	She has just begun this year.
B: *mezyan.*	Fine.

DIALOG THIRTY-SEVEN

A: *šɛal hadi u-nta mzuwwež.*	How long have you been married?
B: *hadi temn snin.*	For eight years.
A: *šɛal ɛăndek de-ḍ-drari?*	How many children do you have?
B: *weld, u-žuž de-le-bnat.*	One boy and two girls.
A: *škun le-kbir fihom?*	Which is the oldest?
B: *l-weld.*	The boy.
A: *šɛal f-ɛămṛu?*	How old is he?
B: *f-ɛămṛu sett snin.*	He is six years old.
A: *u-le-bnat?*	And the girls?
B: *weɛda fe-ɛmeṛha ṛebɛ snin u-l-oxṛa ɛamayn.*	One is four years old and the other one is two.

DIALOG THIRTY-EIGHT

A: *ˀahlen.*	Hello.
B: *ˀahlen.*	Hello.
A: *še-xbaṛ mwalin ḍ-ḍaṛ?*	How is your family?
B: *la-bas, ḷḷah ibarek fik. mṛati mšat tšuf ɛaˀiltha f-ˀamirika.*	Fine, thank you. My wife has gone to see her family in America.
A: *fuq-aš ġad-teṛžăɛ?*	When is she returning?
B: *fe-š-šheṛ l-maži.*	This coming month.
A: *d-drari ka-ităɛbuk?*	Do the children bother you?
B: *la, ˀabadan, mheddnin bezzaf ɛad.*	No, not at all. They are very quiet.
A: *l-weld ka-imši l-l-meḍṛaṣa, yak?*	The boy goes to school, doesn't he?
B: *iyeh ka-imši, u-dki ḷḷah ibarek.*[1]	Yes, and he's smart.
A: *u-le-bnat ka-imšiw l-lmeḍṛaṣa had l-ɛam?*	And are the girls going to school this year?
B: *iyeh, ɛad bdaw.*	Yes, they have just begun.

Notes

1. Cf. note 3, Dialog One. It is an important cultural pattern that compliments or statements of praise should be accompanied by a deferential reference to God. Without the reference to God, such statements appear crude, and in older, more traditional social circles, they are taken as bad omens which will bring misfortune. References to God of this sort are usually not directly translatable into English.

DIALOG THIRTY-NINE

A:	*ʔahlen.*	Hello.
B:	*ʔahlen wa sahlen.*	Hello to you.
A:	*še-xbaṛ xak εaziz?*	How's your brother Aziz?
B:	*la-bas, ṛah f-ʔamirika daba.*	Fine, he's in America now.
A:	*u-xtek εăyša?*	And your sister Aisha?
B:	*la-bas, ṛaha mzuwwža daba.*	Fine, she's married now.
A:	*waš sakna fe-ṛ-ṛbaṭ?*	Is she living in Rabat?
B:	*la, sakna fe-ḍ-ḍaṛ l-ḅiḍa mεa ṛaželha.*	No, she is living in Casablanca with her husband.
A:	*ṛaželha ka-ixdem fe-ḍ-ḍaṛ l-ḅiḍa?*	Does her husband work in Casablanca?
B:	*iyeh, huwa ʔustad temma.*	Yes, he's a teacher there.
A:	*šεal hadi u-huma mzuwwžin?*	How long have they been married?
B:	*sett šhuṛ.*	Six months.

DIALOG FORTY

A:	*fayn ġadi?*	Where are you going?
B:	*ġadi le-ḍ-ḍaṛ l-ḅiḍa nšuf xti u-ṛaželha.*	I'm going to Casablanca to see my sister and her husband.
A:	*ḅḅak u-ṃṃok ġadyin εetta-huma?*	Are your parents going too?
B:	*yaḷḷah ḅḅa (huwa lli ġadi).*	Just my father.
A:	*u-ṃṃok?*	And your mother?
B:	*ṃṃi ġad-tebqa hna.*	My mother is staying here.
A:	*iyeh, fekkeṛtini, ṃṃi u-ṃṃok ġadyin l-ṭanža ġedda.*	Yes that's right, your mother and my mother are going to Tangier tomorrow.
B:	*fayn ġad-igelsu f-ṭanža?*	Where are they going to stay in Tangier?
A:	*ġad-igelsu εănd εămmi.*	They're going to stay with my (paternal) uncle.
B:	*εămmek ma-saken-š fe-ṛ-ṛbaṭ?*	Doesn't your (paternal) uncle live in Rabat?
A:	*la, hadak xali.*[1]	No, that's my maternal uncle.

Notes

1. The English word 'uncle' refers indifferently to 'father's brother' or 'mother's brother' and even, in a looser sense, to 'father's sister's husband' and 'mother's sister's husband'. Arabic has separate terms for all four relations. The term *ʕămm* 'paternal uncle' refers only to 'father's brother' and *xal* refers only to 'mother's brother'.

DIALOG FORTY-ONE

A: *ʕăndek ši-xut?*	Do you have any brothers and sisters?
B: *ʕăndi xet u-xa.*	I have a brother and a sister.
A: *mzuwwžin?*	Are they married?
B: *iyeh, b-žuž mzuwwžin.*	Yes, both are married.
A: *ʕăndhom ši-drari?*	Do they have any children?
B: *iyeh. xti ʕăndha žuž d-le-bnat, u-xay ʕăndu tlata de-l-ulad.*	Yes, my sister has two girls, and my brother has three boys.
A: *fayn saknin?*	Where do they live?
B: *xuya saken fe-sla u-xti sakna f-meknas.*	My brother lives in Salé and my sister lives in Meknes.
A: *š-men xedma ka-idir xuk?*	What work does your brother do?
B: *ʕăndu ḥanut.*	He has a store.
A: *š-ka-idir ṛažel xtek?*	What does your sister's husband do?
B: *ka-ixdem mʕa ʕămmu fe-l-ʔidaʕa.*	He works with his uncle at the radio station.

DIALOG FORTY-TWO

A: *fayn huwa xa farid daba?*	Where is Farid's brother now?
B: *mša l-ʔamirika huwa u-mṛatu.*	He's gone to America with his wife.
A: *ʕlaš?*	Why?
B: *ka-išufu ḥbabha.*	They're visiting her relatives.
A: *škun fe-ḥbabha?*	Which relatives?
B: *xetha u-xuha.*	Her sister and her brother.
A: *fayn ḅḅaha u-ṃṃha?*	Where are her father and mother?
B: *miyytin.*	They're dead.
A: *ġad-ibqaw ši-mọdda temma?*	Are they going to say there a long time?
B: *ṛebʕ šhuṛ.*	Four months.

DIALOG FORTY-THREE

A: *fayn ḅḅa l-malika?*	Where is Malika's father?
B: *mša išuf xuh f-tiṭwan.*	He's gone to visit his brother in Tetuan.
A: *škun f-xutu? tlata ɛăndu, yak?*	Which one of his brothers? Doesn't he have three?
B: *xuh le-kbir. ž-žuž l-oxṛin saknin f-le-qniṭra.*	The oldest brother. The other two live in Kenitra.
A: *waš ġad-ibqa temma ši-modda ṭwila?*	Is he going to stay there long?
B: *yaḷḷah žemɛa u-ġad-iwelli.*	Only a week, and then he's coming back.
A: *u-liyah ġad-iwelli deġya?*	And why is he coming back so soon?
B: *lazmu iwelli l-l-xedma.*	He has to be back at work.
A: *qul-li băɛda, š-men xedma ka-idir?*	By the way, what work does he do?
B: *ka-ixdem fe-l-ʔidaɛa.*	He works at the radio station.

DIALOG FORTY-FOUR

A: *fayn ġadi?*	Where are you (sg.) going?
B: *ġadi nšuf xuya.*	I'm going to visit my brother.
A: *fayn ka-iskon?*	Where does he live?
B: *ka-iskon fe-ḍ-ḍaṛ l-ḅiḍa mɛa ḅḅa.*	He lives in Casablanca with my father.
A: *ka-ixedmu?*	Do they work?
B: *iyeh, ka-ixedmu mežmuɛin fe-l-ɛanut de-ḅḅa.*	Yes, they work together in my father's store.
A: *xtek ma-sakna-š ɛetta-hiya fe-ḍ-ḍaṛ l-ḅiḍa?*	Doesn't your sister live in Casablanca too?
B: *la, xti sakna f-meṛṛakeš.*	No, my sister lives in Marrakesh.
A: *mzuwwža?*	Is she married?
B: *iyeh, hadi telt snin u-hiya mzuwwža.*	Yes, she's been married for three years.
A: *ɛăndha ši-drari?*	Does she have any children?
B: *la, ma-zal.*	No, not yet.

DIALOG FORTY-FIVE

A: *fayn ġadi?*	Where are you going?
B: *ġadi nšuf l-walida dyali; šwiya ɛăyyana.*	I'm going to visit my mother; she's a little sick.
A: *ma-ikun bas in ša? ḷḷah.*	(Polite expression used upon hearing of someone's illness; the expression is used both with and without the final phrase, *in ša? ḷḷah.*)
B: *leh la-iwerrik bas.*	(Reply to *ma-ikun bas*)
A: *ṃṃi hadi žemɛa u-hiya ɛăyyana.*	My mother has been sick for a week.
B: *yemma l-malika ḥetta-hiya ɛăyyana. koll-ši ɛăyyan.*	Malika's mother is sick, too. Everybody's sick.
A: *nṭelbu ḷḷah išafi l-walida dyalek deġya.*	Let's hope that your mother gets well soon.
B: *ya ṛebbi amin.*	I hope so.

DIALOG FORTY-SIX

A: *ẓeṛti l-meġṛib men qbel?*	Have you visited Morocco before?
B: *la, be-l-ḥăqq žeddi kan ẓaṛ l-meġṛib šḥal hadi.*	No, but my grandfather visited Morocco a long time ago.
A: *fuq-aš?*	When?
B: *hadi xemsin ɛam. u-hna kan tɛaṛef mɛa lalla.*	Fifty years ago. And he met my grandmother here.
A: *kan ka-ixdem hna?*	Was he working here?
B: *la, kan ġir ka-iẓuṛ l-meġṛib.*	No, he was only visiting Morocco.
A: *ḅḅak sidek u-lallak dzuwwžu hnaya?*	Did your grandfather and grandmother get married here?
B: *iyeh, u-men băɛd ṛežɛu l-?amirika.*	Yes, and then they returned to America.
A: *ɛawed wellaw l-l-meġṛib?*	Have they come back to Morocco again?
B: *la, be-l-ḥăqq ġad-ižiw išufuna š-šheṛ l-maži.*	No, but they're coming to visit us next month.
A: *mezyan.*	Fine.

DIALOG FORTY-SEVEN

A:	*iwa š-men xbaṛ?*	What's new?
B:	*koll-ši fi ʔaman ḷḷah. ɛad ṛžăɛt men ɛănd weldi.*	Everything's fine. I've just got back from my son's.
A:	*še-xbaṛu?*	How is he?
B:	*huwa la-bas, be-l-ḥăqq mṛatu ɛăyyana.*	He's fine, but his wife is sick.
A:	*ma-ikun bas.*	(polite expression of sympathy on hearing of someone's illness)
B:	*lah la-iwerrik bas.*	(polite response to *ma-ikun bas*)
A:	*u-wlidatu še-xbaṛhom?*	And how are his children?
B:	*la-bas, l-ḥămdu llah,*	Fine, thank you.
A:	*qul-li băɛda, yak ɛăndu žuž d-le-bnat u-weld?*	By the way, doesn't he have two girls and a boy?
B:	*la, ɛăndu žuž d-l-ulad u-bent.*	No, he has two boys and a girl.
A:	*ḷḷah ixellihom-lu.*	May God protect them!
B:	*ḷḷah ibarek fik.*	Thank you.

DIALOG FORTY-EIGHT

A:	*ṣbaḥ l-xir.*	Good morning.
B:	*ṣbaḥ l-xir.*	Good morning.
A:	*š-ḥăbb l-xaṭeṛ?*	What can I do for you?
B:	*bğina nekriw ši-dwira.*	We want to rent an apartment.
A:	*fayn, u-šḥal d-le-byut?*	Where, and how many rooms?
B:	*ɛăndna tlata de-d-drari, ʔiden xeṣṣna ṛebɛa d-le-byut de-n-nɛas.*	We have three children, so we need four bedrooms.
A:	*ma-tfeḍḍlu-š ḍaṛ?*	Wouldn't you prefer a house?
B:	*nšufu ḍaṛ u-dwira.*	Let's see a house and an apartment.
A:	*šḥal tebğì txeḷḷeṣ?*	How much would you like to pay?
B:	*nxeḷḷeṣ ši-ḥaža mwalma.*	I'll pay something reasonable.
A:	*xuya ɛăndu waḥed ḍ-ḍaṛ mezyana l-le-kra f-agdal.*	My brother has a nice house for rent in Agdal.
B:	*fuq-aš imken-lna nemšiw nšufuha?*	When can we go see it?
A:	*daba.*	Now.

DIALOG FORTY-NINE

A: *tesmeḥ-li nqeddmek l-xay?*	May I introduce you to my brother?
B: *metšeṛṛfin.*	I'm glad to meet you.
C: *ʔahlen wa sahlen.*	Welcome.
A: *bġaw išufu ḍ-ḍaṛ dyalek.*	They want to see your house.
C: *tfeḍḍlu.*	Please go in (pl.).
B: *šḥal d-le-byut de-n-nεas fiha?* [1]	How many bedrooms does it have?
C: *fiha ṛebεa d-le-byut de-n-nεas.* [2]	It has four bedrooms.
B: *tamaman lli ka-ixeṣṣna.*	Just what we need.
A: *u-fiha εăṛṣa kbira mezyana.* [3]	And it has a beautiful large garden.
B: *werrina l-εăṛṣa.*	Show us the garden.
C: *tfeḍḍlu men had ž-žih.*	This way, please.

Notes

1. Literally, 'how many bedrooms in it'?
2. Literally, 'in it (are) four bedrooms'.
3. Literally, 'and in it (there is) a beautiful large garden'.

DIALOG FIFTY

A: *ka-nqelleb εla waḥed d-dwira l-le-kra.*	I'm looking for an apartment to rent.
B: *waš baġi dwira wella ḍaṛ?*	Do you want an apartment or a house?
A: *lli kan fihom. εla balek ši-ḥaža?*	Either one. Do you know of anything?
B: *ka-nḍenn imken-li nsaεdek. fayn baġi teskon?*	I think I can help you. Where do you want to live?
A: *qeddam s-sifaṛa.*	Near the Embassy.
B: *lazem tekri dwira.*	You'll have to rent an apartment.
A: *mezyan, be-le-ḥăqq xeṣṣna ṛebεa d-le-byut de-n-nεas.*	Fine, but we'll need four bedrooms.
B: *kaynin bezzaf de-d-dwirat qṛib men hna lli fihom ṛebεa d-le-byut de-n-nεas.*	There are a lot of apartments near here that have four bedrooms in them.

A: *mezyan.*	Fine.
B: *be-l-ʔatat aw blaš?*	Furnished or unfurnished?
A: *bla ʔatat.*	Unfurnished.
B: *ka-năɛṛef waɛed d-dwira l-le-kra qeddami.*	I know of an apartment for rent near me.
A: *yaḷḷah nšufu.*	Let's go see it.

DIALOG FIFTY-ONE

A: *lqa s-si Bissel maɛăll fayn iskon?*	Did Mr. Bissel find a place to live?
B: *iyeh, lqa ḍaṛ mezyana f-agdal.*	Yes, he found a nice house in Agdal.
A: *šɛal ka-ixeḷḷeṣ de-le-kra?*	How much rent does he pay?
B: *myatayn u-xemsin derhem.*[1]	Two hundred and fifty dirhams.
A: *be-l-ʔatat?*	Furnished?
B: *la, bla ʔatat.*	No, unfurnished.
A: *had š-ši bezzaf. u-kbira?*	That's a lot. Is it big?
B: *kbira u-fiha ṛebɛa d-le-byut de-n-nɛas u-ɛăṛṣa mezyana.*	Yes, it's big, and it has four bedrooms and a nice garden.
A: *fayn žat?*	Where is it located?
B: *qeddam l-meḍṛaṣa.*	Beside the school.
A: *ɛăndu d-drari fe-l-meḍṛaṣa?*	Does he have children in school?
B: *bentu ṣ-ṣġiṛa ɛad bdat temši (l-l-meḍṛaṣa).*	His little girl has just begun going. (to school).

Notes

1. The *derhem* is the basic unit of Moroccan currency.

DIALOG FIFTY-TWO

A: *ka-nqelleb ɛla ši-ḍaṛ wella dwira l-le-kra.*	I'm looking for a house or an apartment for rent.
B: *fayn baġi teskon?*	Where do you want to live?
A: *qeddam s-sifaṛa.*	Near the Embassy.
B: *šɛal baġi txeḷḷeṣ?*	How much do you want to pay?

A: *ši-ḥaža mwalma.*	Something reasonable.
B: *šḥal men bit xeṣṣek?*	How many rooms do you need?
A: *ɛăl l-ʔaqell žuž d-le-byut de-n-nɛas.*	At least two bedrooms.
B: *ka-năɛṛef waḥed l-ɛimaṛa fiha dwira l-le-kra.*	I know a building where there is an apartment for rent.
A: *f-ayna ṭebqa?*	On what floor?
B: *s-satta.*	The sixth.
A: *mezyan. be-l-ʔatat?*	Fine, is it furnished?
B: *la.*	No.
A: *waxxa, yaḷḷah nšufuha.*	O.K. Let's go see it.

DIALOG FIFTY-THREE

A: *ka-nqelleb ɛla ši-xeddam.*	I'm looking for a houseboy.
B: *bġitih ikun ka-yăɛṛef n-negliza?*	Do you want him to know English?
A: *iyeh, ḥit mṛati ma-ka-tăɛṛef-š l-ɛăṛbiya.*	Yes, because my wife doesn't know Arabic.
B: *ʔiden lazmek ġad-txeḷḷeṣ zyada.*	Then you're going to have to pay more.
A: *šḥal yăɛni?*	Well, how much?
B: *teqṛiben xemsin derhem.*	About fifty dirhams.
A: *šḥal ka-txeḷḷeṣ dyalek?*	How much do you pay yours?
B: *ka-nxeḷḷsu b-ṛebɛin derhem, be-l-ḥăqq ma-ka-yăɛṛef-š n-negliza.*	I pay him forty dirhams, but he doesn't know English.
A: *fayn imken-li nṣibu?*	Where can I find him?
B: *daba năɛṭik l-ɛonwan dyalu.*	I'll give you his address.

DIALOG FIFTY-FOUR

A: *ɛăndkom ši-ṭebbax?*	Do you have a cook?
B: *iyeh, ɛăndna ṭebbax mezyan bezzaf.*	Yes, we have a very good cook.
A: *ka-itkellem n-negliza?*	Does he speak English?

B:	*šwiya, be-l-ḥăqq ka-ifhemha mezyan.*	A little, but he understands it very well.
A:	*ka-iṭiyyeb mezyan?*	Does he cook well?
B:	*iyeh, ṭyabu ldid.*	Yes, his cooking is delicious.
A:	*kif ṣebtih?*	How did you find him?
B:	*l-xeddam d-ṣaḥbi žebṛu-li.*	A friend's servant found him for me.
A:	*iqḍeṛ ižbeṛ-li ḥett-ana ši-waḥed?*	Can he find me one too?
B:	*daba nqulha-lu u-nɛăyyeṭ-lek ġedda.*	I'll tell him and call you tomorrow.

DIALOG FIFTY-FIVE

A:	*šḥal de-d-drari ɛăndek?*	How many children do you have?
B:	*setta.*	Six.
A:	*ḷḷah isexxeṛ.*	(polite expression after mention of someone's children)
B:	*ḷḷah ibarek fik.*	Thank you.
A:	*ɛăndek ši-xeddama?*	Do you have a maid?
B:	*la, teqḍeṛ džbeṛ-li ši-weḥda mezyana?*	No, can you find a good one for me?
A:	*iyeh, ɛămmt l-xeddam dyali ɛăndha bent baġya texdem mɛa ši-ḥădd.*	Yes, my houseboy's aunt has a daughter who wants to work for someone.
B:	*ɛăndha ši-derba?*	Does she have any experience?
A:	*iyeh, ɛam luwwel xedmet mɛa mṛat s-si Bissel.*	Yes, she worked for Mrs. Bissel last year.
B:	*šḥal bġat?*	How much does she want?
A:	*xemsa u-tlatin derhem.*	Thirty-five dirhams.
B:	*ižaṛa mɛăwwṭa hadi?*	Is that a reasonable salary?
A:	*iyeh, hadak š-ši b-aš ka-nxeḷḷeṣ l-xeddama dyali.*	Yes, that's what I pay my maid.

DIALOG FIFTY-SIX

A: *yaḷḷah nemšiw l-fas.*	Let's go to Fez.
B: *yaḷḷah. fuq-aš?*	Let's go. When?
A: *daba.*	Now.
B: *f-aš? f-l-qiṭaṛ aw fe-s-siyaṛa?* (*fe-ṭ-ṭumubil aw fe-l-mašina?*)[1]	How? By train or by car?
A: *fayn lli ꞔsen?*	Which is best?
B: *ana ka-nfeḍḍel s-siyara.*	I prefer (to go by) car.
A: *ɛlaš?*	Why?
B: *baš imken-lna nweqfu f-ši qehwa f-le-xmisat u-nšeṛbu atay.*[2]	So we can stop at Khemisset and have tea at some café.
A: *imken-lna naklu ši-ꞔaža f-le-xmisat?*	Can we eat something at Khemisset?
B: *meɛlum, koll-ši kayen temma.*	Of course, there's everything there.
A: *šꞔal de-s-swayeɛ men hna l-fas?*	How many hours from here to Fez?
B: *tlata de-s-swayeɛ, w-imken tlata u-neṣṣ.*	Three hours, maybe three and a half.
A: *ma-ši ši-ꞔaža.*	That's not much (anything).
B: *la, yaḷḷah.*	No, let's go.

Notes

1. With the independence of Morocco and the wider use of Modern Standard Arabic as the language of formal schooling, an effort is being made to replace borrowed French words with Arabic words. This accounts for such pairs as *siyaṛa* and *ṭumubil,* both of which mean 'car', and *qiṭaṛ* and *mašina,* both of which mean 'train'. The forms *siyaṛa* and *qiṭaṛ* are somewhat more bookish than *ṭumubil* and *mašina.*
2. A Moroccan town about half way between Rabat and Meknes on the route to Fez.

DIALOG FIFTY-SEVEN

A: *šefti ṣemɛet ꞔessan wella ma-zal?*[1]	Have you seen the Hassan Tower yet?
B: *la, l-daba ma-zal ma-šeftha-š.*	No, up to now I still haven't seen it.
A: *tebġi temši mɛaya?*	Would you like to go with me?
B: *waxxa, fuq-aš?*	Yes, when?

A: *daba. yaḷḷah nšeddu ṭaksi.*	Now. Let's go get a taxi.
A: *šefti ṣ-ṣemƐa?*	Did you see the Tower?
B: *la, fayn hiya?*	No, where is it?
A: *ṛa-hiya dik. šuf lhih.*	There it is. Look over there.
B: *ah, daba Ɛad šeftha.*	Ah, now I see it.
A: *tebġi ṭṭlăƐ-lha?*	Do you want to climb it?
B: *meƐlum, xeṣṣni nṭlăƐ-lha; imken-lna ndexlu-lha u-nšufu qelbha?*	Of course, I have to climb it. Can we go in it and see the inside?
A: *hadi fekra mezyana.*	That's a good idea.

Notes

1. The Hassan Tower is a famous landmark in Rabat. It offers an excellent view of the city and is visited regularly by tourists, both Moroccan and foreign.

DIALOG FIFTY-EIGHT

A: *yaḷḷah nemšiw le-ḍ-ḍaṛ l-ḅiḍa l-yum.*	Let's go to Casablanca today.
B: *ana mešġul l-yum. nemšiw ġedda.*	I'm busy today. Let's go tomorrow.
A: *f-aš?*	How? (In what?)
B: *f-siyaṛti.*	In my car.
A: *f-ayna saƐa?*	At what time?
B: *mƐa t-tmenya hakdak.*	About eight o'clock.
A: *ma-ikun-š mša l-ḥal?*	Won't that be late?
B: *mƐak l-ḥăqq. fe-š-men weqt tebġi nemšiw?*	You're right. What time do you think we should leave?
A: *fe-s-setta.*	At six.
B: *ma-ši bekri bezzaf?*	Isn't that too early?
A: *la, băḥṛa nšufu bezzaf de-l-maḥăllat.*	No, that way we can see many places.
B: *ġad-nṛežƐu f-le-Ɛšiya wella ḥetta l-l-lil?*	Are we going to come back in the afternoon or (are we going to stay) until the evening?
A: *lazem nṛežƐu fe-l-lil, ḥit băƐd ġedda Ɛăndi l-xedma.*	We have to come back in the evening because I've got to work day after tomorrow.
B: *mezyan.*	Fine.

DIALOG FIFTY-NINE

A: *fayn ġad-temši ġedda?*	Where are you going tomorrow?
B: *ġad-nemši l-ṣem Ƹet ɀessan. temši mƸaya?*	I'm going to Hassan Tower. Do you want to go with me?
A: *la, kont temma l-bareɀ, u-ġad-nemši Ƹawed băƸd ġedda.*	No, I was there yesterday, and I'm going again day after tomorrow.
B: *waxxa, nemši mƸak băƸd ġedda u-ma-nemši-š ġedda. f-ayna saƸa ġadi?*	O.K. I'll go with you day after tomorrow and not tomorrow. What time are you going?
A: *fe-t-tesƸud hakdak.*	At about nine o'clock.
B: *ma-ši bekri šwiya?*	Isn't that a little early?
A: *mnayn nšufek ġedda nttafqu Ƹăl s-saƸa.*	When I see you tomorrow, we'll decide on the hour.
B: *waxxa.*	O.K.

DIALOG SIXTY

A: *fayn mšiti l-bareɀ?*	Where did you go yesterday?
B: *mšit le-tmara.*	I went to Temara.
A: *ġad-temši Ƹawed mƸaya ġedda?*	Are you going again tomorrow with me?
B: *la, ġedda ġad-nemši l-le-qniṭṛa.*[1]	No, tomorrow I'm going to Kenitra.
A: *nemšiw băƸd ġedda?*	Shall we go day after tomorrow?
B: *waxxa. f-ayna saƸa nemšiw?*	O.K. What time shall we go?
A: *fe-t-tesƸud u-neṣṣ.*	At nine-thirty.
B: *fe-ṣ-ṣbaɀ?*	In the morning?
A: *meƸlum.*	Of course.
B: *fayn ntlaqaw?*	Where shall we meet?
A: *f-šariƸ muɀămmed l-xamis, qeddam s-sinima de-n-nehḍa.*[2]	On Mohammed V Avenue, in front of the Renaissance Theater.
B: *waxxa, iwa be-s-slama.*	O.K. Good-bye.
A: *be-s-slama.*	Good-bye.

Notes

1. This town is usually known in English by its French name, Port Lyautey. Located about 30 miles north of Rabat, it was for many years an important French naval base, also used by American naval forces in the period following World War II.

2. The scene is in Rabat.

DIALOG SIXTY-ONE

A: *smeɛ-li.*	Excuse me.
B: *š-ɛăbb l-xaṭeṛ?*	Can I help you?
A: *bġit nešri d-doxxan, imken-lek tqul-li fayn?*	I want to buy some cigarets, can you tell me where?
B: *men dak l-ɛanut hadik.*	From that shop (over there).
A: *f-ayna ɛanut? hadik lli qeddam l-ʔutil?*	(In) Which shop? The one next to the hotel?
B: *la, hadik lli qeddam l-meṭɛăm.*	No, the one next to the restaurant.
A: *imken-li nešri ɛetta l-uqid temma?*	Can I buy matches there, too?
B: *iyeh.*	Yes.
A: *baṛak ḷḷahu fik.*	Thank you.
B: *bla žmil.*	You're welcome.

DIALOG SIXTY-TWO

A: *š-ɛăbb l-xaṭeṛ?*	What would you like?
B: *ɛṭini bakiya de-d-doxxan, ḷḷah ixellik.*	Give me a pack of cigarets, please.
A: *š-men ɛăyna?*	What kind?
B: *kabir. be-šɛal?* [1]	Kebir. How much?
A: *ɛešrin ryal.* [2]	Twenty rials.
B: *u-ɛṭini ɛetta l-uqid.*	And give me some matches too.
A: *tfeḍḍel.*	Here you are.
B: *šɛal?*	How much?
A: *žat waɛed u-ɛešrin ryal bin koll-ši.*	That makes twenty-two rials altogether.

Notes

1. A brand of Moroccan cigarets.
2. One rial is worth five francs. There are twenty rials in one dirham.

DIALOG SIXTY-THREE

A: *nƐam a sidi.*	Yes, sir.
B: *bġit d-doxxan.*	I want some cigarets.
A: *š-men Ɛăyna?*	What kind?
B: *Ɛăndek d-doxxan ʔamiriki?*	Do you have American cigarets?
A: *la, Ɛăndi ġir d-doxxan mġeṛbi.*	No, I have only Moroccan cigarets.
B: *Ɛṭini bakiya d-kabir.*	Give me a pack of Kebir.
A: *tfeḍḍel.*	Here you are.
B: *šḥal?*	How much?
A: *Ɛešrin ryal.*	Twenty rials.
B: *tfeḍḍel. Ɛăndek ḥetta l-uqid?*	Here you are. Do have matches too?
A: *iyeh.*	Yes.
B: *Ɛṭini žuž ṣnadeq. be-šḥal?*	Give me two boxes. How much?
A: *žuž de-r-ryal.*	Two rials.
B: *tfeḍḍel. iwa be-s-slama.*	Here. Good-bye now.
A: *be-s-slama.*	Good-bye.

DIALOG SIXTY-FOUR

A: *ṭaksi!*	Taxi!
B: *nƐam a sidi, fayn baġi temši?*	Yes sir, where do you want to go?
A: *Ɛafak weṣṣelni l-meṭƐăm n-nehḍa.*	Take me to the Nahda Restaurant, please.
B: *ma-ka-năƐṛef-š fayn ža.*	I don't know where it is.
A: *qeddam l-buṣta.*	Next to the Post Office.
B: *ʔah, Ɛṛeft daba.*	Oh, yes, I know now.
A: *wṣelna a sidi.*	We've arrived, sir.
B: *šḥal?*	How much?
A: *setta u-Ɛešrin ryal.*[1]	Twenty-six rials.
B: *ha-tlatin ryal. xud lli bqa.*	Here's thirty rials. Keep the change.

Notes

1. Prices are frequently quoted in rials, often with the word *ryal* left out. In this context the taxi driver might have said simply *setta u-ɛešrin,* with *ryal* being understood.

DIALOG SIXTY-FIVE

A: *ṭaksi!*	Taxi!
B: *nɛam a sidi. l-ayn?*	Yes, sir. Where to?
A: *bġit nemši le-sla.*	I want to go to Salé.
B: *nɛam a sidi.*	Yes, sir.
A: *šḥal ġad-yewžebni?*	How much will it cost (me)?
B: *tlata de-d-drahem.*	Three dirhams.
A: *yaḷḷah (a sidi).*	O.K. let's go.
B: *hadi sla a sidi.*	This is Salé, sir.
A: *tfeḍḍel.*	Here you are.
B: *ḷḷah ixlef.*	Thank you.

DIALOG SIXTY-SIX

A: *tăɛmel ši-mesḥa?* [1]	Would you like a shoe-shine?
B: *be-šḥal?*	(For) How much?
A: *lli bġiti.*[2]	Whatever you want.
B: *qul-li šḥal.*	Tell me how much.
A: *ṭnaš ryal.*	Twelve rials.
B: *ṭnaš ryal! bezzaf had š-ši, ḷḷah ihennik.*[3]	Twelve rials! That's too much, good-bye.
A: *ṣbeṛ. ɛăšṛa de-r-ryal, waxxa?*	Wait. Ten rials, O.K.?
B: *la, ġad-nemši l-žiha oxṛa. qalu-li t-taman huwa setta de-r-ryal.*	No, I'll go somewhere else. They told me the price was six rials.
A: *had š-ši qlil bezzaf. ɛmel ɛăšṛa de-r-ryal.*	That's not very much. Make it ten rials.
B: *la, ḷḷah ihennik.*	No, good-bye.
A: *aži, xelleṣ lli bġiti.*	Come back, pay what you want.
B: *setta de-r-ryal.*	Six rials.
A: *waxxa.*	O.K.

Notes

1. Shoe-shine boys are much more numerous in Moroccan cities than in American cities.

2. The opening phrase of a round of bargaining. The remainder of the dialog is a typical illustration of haggling over prices.

3. Note the translation of *bezzaf had š-ši* as 'that's too much'. There is no precise equivalent in Arabic for English 'too' in the sense of 'excessively'. Thus such English expressions as 'too much', 'too big', 'too little', etc. are translated simply as 'much', 'big', 'little', etc. The implications of English 'too' in such expressions is conveyed by tone of voice, general context, etc.

DIALOG SIXTY-SEVEN

A:	*šᶜal hadi (fe-s-saᶜa) b-le-fḍel mennek?* [1]	What time is it, please?
B:	*hadi l-ᶜăšṛa.* [2]	It's ten o'clock.
A:	*waš metᶜăqqeq?*	Are you sure?
B:	*la, xellini nšuf maganti. smeᶜ-li, hadi l-ᶜăšṛa u-qṣem.*	No, let me look at my watch. Excuse me, it's five past ten.
A:	*xeṣṣni nemši l-l-žamiᶜa fe-l-ᶜăšṛa u-neṣṣ.*	I have to go to the university at ten-thirty.
B:	*tsenna waᶜed d-daqiqa u-nemši mᶜak.*	Wait a minute and I'll go with you.
A:	*naxdu ṭaksi?*	Shall we take a taxi?
B:	*la, l-žamiᶜa qṛiba bezzaf.*	No, the university is very close.
A:	*yaḷḷah.*	Let's go.

Notes

1. The usual rendering of 'what time is it?' is *šᶜal hadi?* literally 'how much is this?'. Adding *fe-s-saᶜa* 'in, on the hour, clock' after *šᶜal hadi* is optional.

2. The pattern for 'it's such and such o'clock' is *hadi* followed by a number with the definite article, as in the text, *l-ᶜăšṛa* 'the ten' and *hadi l-ᶜăšṛa* 'it's ten o'clock'.

DIALOG SIXTY-EIGHT

A: *fayn ġadi l-yum?*	Where are you going today?
B: *ġadi le-sla.*	I'm going to Salé.
A: *fe-ṣ-ṣbaḥ aw f-le-ɛšiya?*	In the morning or in the afternoon?
B: *f-le-ḥḍaš.*	At eleven o'clock.
A: *šḥal hadi daba?*	What time is it now?
B: *hadi le-ḥḍaš llaṛeb.*	It's a quarter to eleven.
A: *metḥăqqeq?*	Are you sure?
B: *tamamen.*	Absolutely!
A: *ma-bqa weqt. xeṣṣni naxod ṭaksi.*	There isn't any time. I have to take a taxi.
B: *mɛak l-ḥăqq. ḷḷah ihennik.*	You're right. Good-bye.
A: *be-s-slama.*	Good-bye.

DIALOG SIXTY-NINE

A: *fuq-aš ġad-temši l-le-qniṭṛa?*	When are you going to Kenitra?
B: *had le-ɛšiya, fe-l-xemsa.*	This afternoon, at five.
A: *ma f-yeddek weqt bezzaf.*	You don't have much time.
B: *ɛlah šḥal hadi?*	What time is it anyway?
A: *ma-ɛăndek magana?*	Don't you have a watch?
B: *la.*	No.
A: *hadi ṛ-ṛebɛa.*	It's four o'clock.
B: *ˀay! xeṣṣni nkun fe-sla fe-ṛ-ṛebɛa u-ness ɛla ši-šġal.*	Gee! I have to be in Salé at four-thirty for some business.
A: *u-f-aš ġad-temši l-le-qniṭṛa?*	And how are you going to Kenitra?
B: *fe-l-mašina.*	By train.
A: *ma-ka-nḍenn-š ġad-telḥeqha.*	I don't think you'll make it.
B: *ġad-nerkeb men temma.*	I'm going to take it from there.
A: *xyaṛ! iwa be-s-slama.*	I see! Good-bye now.
B: *ḷḷah ihennik.*	Good-bye.

DIALOG SEVENTY

A: *băɛd ġedda l-ɛid.*	Day after tomorrow is a holiday.
B: *š-men ɛid?*	What holiday?
A: *l-ɛid ṣ-ṣġiṛ.*[1]	Lesser Bairam.
B: *šnu huwa l-ɛid ṣ-ṣġiṛ?*	What is Lesser Bairam?
A: *huwa l-ɛid lli ka-ikun men băɛd ṣyam ṛemḍan.*[2]	It's the feast that comes after the fasting of Ramadan.
B: *šḥal ɛăndna de-l-ɛoṭla?*	How many days do we get off?
A: *telt iyyam.*	Three days.
B: *bezzaf, aw la?*	That's a lot, isn't it?
A: *dima hakda.*	It's always like that.
B: *mezyan.*	Fine.

Notes

1. Lesser Bairam is a religious holiday which begins on the first day of the month following Ramadan. It is the second most important religious holiday of the Muslim calendar.
2. Ramadan is the ninth month of the Muslim calendar. During Ramadan total fasting is required from sunup to sundown. No solid foods, liquids, or cigarets are permitted.

DIALOG SEVENTY-ONE

A: *ġedda l-ɛid ṣ-ṣġiṛ.*	Tomorrow is Lesser Bairam.
B: *š-ġad-tăɛmel?*	What are you going to do?
A: *ġad-nxeržu ntsaraw.*	We are going out to look around.
B: *fayn?*	Where?
A: *f-ḥadiqat l-ḥayawanat.*	At the zoo.
B: *ɛlaš ḥadiqat l-ḥayawanat?*	Why the zoo?
A: *ḥit mezyana u-kbira u-ka-itsellaw fiha d-drari.*	Because it's nice and big, and the children have fun there.
B: *š-ka-tɛămlu temma?*	What do you (pl.) do there?
A: *ka-nšufu l-ḥayawanat.*	We look at the animals.
B: *n-nhaṛ kollu?*	All day long?
A: *meɛlum. ɛăndna ɛoṭla n-nhaṛ kollu.*	Of course, we have the whole day off.

DIALOG SEVENTY-TWO

A: *š-men ɛid kan l-bareḥ?*	What feast was it yesterday?
B: *l-bareḥ bda l-ɛid ṣ-ṣġiṛ.*	Lesser Bairam began yesterday.
A: *ɛid mbaṛek mesɛud!*	Happy Holiday!
B: *ɛliya u-ɛlik.*	The same to you.
A: *š-dertiw l-bareḥ?*	What did you do yesterday?
B: *xrežna ntsaraw.*	We went out to look around.
A: *fayn mšitiw?*	Where did you go?
B: *mšina l-ḥadiqat l-ḥayawanat.*	We went to the zoo.
A: *iwa tsellitiw?*	Did you have fun?
B: *tsellina bezzaf.*	We had lots of fun.
A: *meɛlum. ɛăndna ɛoṭla n-nhaṛ*	Did you stay there all day?
B: *meɛlum, kanet ɛăndna ɛoṭla.*	Of course, we had a holiday.

DIALOG SEVENTY-THREE

A: *waš l-ɛid ṣ-ṣġiṛ ž-žemɛa ž-žayya?*	Is Lesser Bairam next week?
B: *iyeh, u-xeṣṣni nebda nṣuwweb l-ḥălwa ġedda.*	Yes, and I have to begin to make cake tomorrow.
A: *š-men ḥălwa?*	What cake?
B: *hadik lli ka-nṣuwwbu l-l-ɛid ṣ-ṣġiṛ.*[1]	The one that we make for Lesser Bairam.
A: *ka-tešbeh l-l-xobz?*	Does it look like bread?
B: *teqṛiben, be-l-ḥăqq ḥluwa. nžib-lek ši-šwiya?*	Sort of, but sweet. Shall I bring you some?
A: *iyeh, nebġi nduq mennha.*	Yes, I'd like to taste it.
B: *ġad-tɛežbek.*	You'll like it.

Notes

1. Sweet cakes made from a special wheat flour are traditionally eaten on Lesser Bairam.

DIALOG SEVENTY-FOUR

A: *tfeḍḍel, ٤mel šwiya de-l-ɧälwa.*	Have some cake.
B: *baṛak ḷḷahu fik. šnu hada?*	Thank you. What is it?
A: *hadi l-ɧälwa de-l-٤id.*	It's feast cake.
B: *٤id mebṛuk.*	Happy holiday.
A: *٤lina u-٤lik.*	The same to you.
B: *had l-ɧälwa ldida. ٤ežbetni bezzaf.*	The cake is delicious. I like it very much.
A: *iwa zid. taxod šwiya m٤ak?*	Have some more, then. Will you take some with you?
B: *waxxa, ٤ṭini ġir ši-šwiya.*	Fine, give me just a little.
A: *be-l-feṛɧat. daba nkemmesha-lek.*	With pleasure. I'll wrap it for you.
B: *baṛak ḷḷahu fik.*	Thank you.
A: *bla žmil.*	You're welcome.

DIALOG SEVENTY-FIVE

A: *ġedda ٤oṭla.*	Tomorrow is a holiday.
B: *š-men ٤oṭla?*	What holiday?
A. *l-٤oṭla de-l-٤id le-kbir.*[1]	The holiday of Greater Bairam.
B: *šɧal ٤ändna de-l-٤oṭla?*	How many days holiday do we have?
A: *ṛeb٤ ayyam.*	Four days.
B: *ġadyin tṣafṛu l-ši-maɧäll?*	Are you going to take a trip anywhere?
A: *ma-ši fe-n-nhaṛ l-luwwel.*	Not the first day.
B: *٤laš?*	Why?
A: *ɧit lazem ndebɧu l-kebš.*	Because we have to slaughter the ram.
B: *iyeh?*	Really?
A: *dima ka-ndebɧu l-kebš fe-l-٤id le-kbir.*	We always slaughter a ram at Greater Bairam.

Notes

1. Greater Bairam is the day commemorating the sacrifice of Abraham. It is the most important religious holiday of the Muslim calendar.

DIALOG SEVENTY-SIX

A: *l-aš šriti kebš?*	Why did you buy a sheep?
B: *ɛit hada l-ɛid le-kbir.*	Because it's Greater Bairam.
A: *šġad-tăɛmel bih?*	What are you going to do with it?
B: *ġad-ndebɛu u-nakluh.*	I'm going to slaughter it and we'll eat it.
A: *kollu?*	All of it?
B: *la, ġad-naklu neṣṣu, u-l-baqi ġad-năɛṭiweh l-l-masakin.*	No, we'll eat half of it, and the rest we'll give to the poor.
A: *ntuma nas kṛam.*	That's very generous of you.
B: *ka-ndiru had š-ši koll ɛam.*	We do this every year.
A: *ġir fe-l-ɛid le-kbir?*	Only during Greater Bairam?
B: *iyeh, ġir fe-l-ɛid le-kbir.*	Yes, only during Greater Bairam.

DIALOG SEVENTY-SEVEN

A: *l-aš ɛmed šra kebš?*	Why did Ahmed buy a ram?
B: *baš idebɛu nhaṛ l-ɛid le-kbir.*	So he can slaughter it at Greater Bairam.
A: *u-š-ġad idir bih men băɛd?*	And what will he do with it after that?
B: *ɛaʔiltu ġad-takol n-neṣṣ fih, u-l-baqi ġad-yăɛṭih l-l-masakin.*	His family will eat half of it, and the rest he'll give to the poor.
A: *ka-idir had š-ši koll ɛam?*	Does he do this every year?
B: *iyeh, huwa krim.*	Yes, he's generous.
A: *u-koll-ši ka-idir bɛalu?*	And does everybody do like him?
B: *la, ġir băɛḍ n-nas.*	No, only a few people.

DIALOG SEVENTY-EIGHT

A: *ɛlaš ġedda kayna ɛoṭla?*	Why is tomorrow a holiday?
B: *ɛit ġedda ɛid l-mulud.*[1]	Because tomorrow is the Prophet's birthday.
A: *hada ɛid d-le-mselmin, yak?*	That's a Muslim feast, isn't it?
B: *iyeh, bɛal ɛid l-milad ɛănd l-masiɛiyin.*	Yes, like Christmas among the Christians.

A: *š-ka-idiru le-mselmin f-had n-nhaṛ?*	What do the Muslims do on that day?
B: *ka-iṣelliw fe-ž-žwameع u-ka-iqṛaw ʔamdaح nabawiya.*	They pray in the mosques and recite eulogies on the Prophet.

Notes

1. The celebration of the Prophet Mohammed's birthday is an important Muslim religious holiday.

DIALOG SEVENTY-NINE

A: *ṭaksi!*	Taxi!
B: *nعăm a sidi, l-ayn?*	Yes, sir, where to?
A: *baġi nemši l-ḍaṛ dbibeġ.*[1]	I want to go to the New City.
B: *fayn f-ḍaṛ dbibeġ?*	Where in the New City?
A: *qeddam saحăt l-ʔeṭleṣ.*	Near Atlas Square.
B: *la-bodda nduzu عla šariع muحămmed l-xamis.*	We have to go by Mohammed the Fifth Avenue.
A: *mezyan. حett-ana baġi nšuf dak š-šariع.*	Fine. I want to see the Avenue too.
B: *tfeḍḍel.*	Please get in.
A: *yaḷḷah a-sidi.*	Let's go.
B: *waš hadi l-meṛṛa l-luwwla f-aš žiti l-fas?*	Is this the first time you've come to Fez?
A: *žit lle-hna waحed l-meṛṛa, be-l-حăqq ma-glest-š bezzaf.*	I was here once, but I didn't stay very long.
B: *kayen bezzaf ma ittšaf f-had le-mdina. xeṣṣek tebqa hna ši-modda.*	There is a lot to see in this city. You must stay here for a while.
A: *ġad-nebqa hna ši-žemعa hakdak.*	I'm going to stay here about a week.
B: *hadi saحăt l-ʔeṭleṣ.*	This is Atlas Square.
A: *mezyan, wqef حda l-عăṛṣa. temma ši-waحed ka-iعayenni. šحal žatni?*	Fine, stop by the park. Someone is waiting for me there. How much is it?
B: *ṛebعin ryal.*	Forty rials (two dirhams).
A: *tfeḍḍel.*	Here you are.
B: *ḷḷah ixlef.*	Thank you.

Notes

1. The scene is in Fez.

DIALOG EIGHTY

A: *šḥal ɛăndek fe-s-saɛa?*	What time do you have?
B: *hadi ṛ-ṛebɛa qell tulut. ma-ɛăndek magana?*	It's twenty to three. Don't you have a watch?
A: *la, ka-ixeṣṣni nešri ši-weḥda.*	No, I have to buy one.
B: *ka-năɛṛef waḥed le-mwagni ɛăndu mwagen mezyanin.*	I know a watchmaker who has nice watches.
A: *ġalyin wella ṛxaṣ?*	Expensive or cheap?
B: *ka-ibiɛhom b-taman mɛăwweṭ.*	He sells them reasonably.
A: *fayn ža had le-mwagni?*	Where is this watchmaker.
B: *ḥanutu žat ḥda s-sinima de-n-nehḍa.*	His shop is near the Renaissance Theater.
A: *had le-ɛšiya nemši ɛăndu.*	I'll go there this afternoon.
B: *xellik ḥetta l-ġedda u-nemši mɛak.*	Wait until tomorrow and I'll go with you.
A: *waxxa.*	O.K.

DIALOG EIGHTY-ONE

A: *l-žuw mezyan bezzaf l-yum.*	The weather is very nice today.
B: *iyeh. l-žuw dima hakda fe-ḍ-ḍaṛ l-ḅiḍa.*	Yes, the weather is always like this in Casablanca.
A: *waš ɛămmeṛ š-šta ma-ka-ṭṭiḥ?*	Doesn't it ever rain?
B: *qlil. kif ɛamel l-žuw ɛăndkom?*	Rarely. How is the weather where you come from?
A: *fe-ṣ-ṣif ka-ikun sxun bezzaf.*	In summer it's very hot.
B: *u-š-šta ka-ṭṭiḥ bezzaf?*	And does it rain a lot?
A: *iyeh, fe-l-berd, u-ḥetta t-telž ka-iṭiḥ.*	Yes, in winter, and its snows too.
B: *iwa qul-li l-ḥal ka-ikun bared bezzaf.*	Then it must be awfully cold.
A: *iyeh.*	Yes.
B: *ka-nḍenn nfeḍḍel l-žuw dyalna.*	I think I prefer our weather.

DIALOG EIGHTY-TWO

A: *fayn ġad-dduwwez had ṣ-ṣif?*	Where are you going to spend this summer?
B: *ġad-nduwwzu fe-s-sƐiydiya.*[1]	I'm going to spend it at Saidiya.
A: *fayn žat s-sƐiydiya?*	Where is Saidiya?
B: *Ɛăl le-bƐăṛ, l-žiht wežda.*[2]	On the sea, near Ujda.
A: *l-žuw mezyan temma?*	Is the weather nice there?
B: *lṭif bezzaf, la be-n-nhaṛ wa-la be-l-lil.*	It's very pleasant, both during the day and at night.
A: *u-kif Ɛamel le-bƐăṛ?*	And how is the sea?
B: *ha'il.*	Beautiful.

Notes

1. Saidiya is a Mediterranean resort in north eastern Morocco known for its beautiful beaches.

2. Ujda, the principal city of north eastern Morocco, is near the Algerian border. It was one of the earliest Arab settlements in Morocco.

DIALOG EIGHTY-THREE

A: *fayn ġadi?*	Where are you going?
B: *ġadi le-ḍ-ḍaṛ.*	I'm going home.
A: *yak la-bas?*	Anything wrong?
B: *ši-šwiya Ɛăyyan.*	I feel a little bit tired.
A: *b-aš ka-tƐess?*	What's the matter?
B: *ṛaṣi ka-yewžăƐni.*	I have a headache.
A: *iwa xud ši-asbiri.*	Well, take an aspirin.
B: *ka-nḍenn ka-ixeṣṣni ġir nnƐăs.*	I think I just need some sleep.
A: *iwa sir le-ḍ-ḍaṛ tertaƐ šwiya. la-bas Ɛlik.*	Then go home and rest a while. I hope you get well.
B: *leh la-iwerrik bas.*	Thank you. (Reply to a wish for recovery).

DIALOG EIGHTY-FOUR

A:	*msali had le-ɛšiya?*	Are you free this afternoon?
B:	*la, meš ġul. xeṣṣni nkun fe-ḍ-ḍaṛ.*	No, I'm busy. I have to be home.
A:	*ɛlaš?*	Why?
B:	*liʔenna ġad-iži ɛăndi n-nežžaṛ iṣleḥ-li waḥed l-bab u-waḥed š-šeṛžem.*	Because the carpenter is coming to fix a door and a window for me.
A:	*ma-lhom?*	What's the matter with them?
B:	*š-šeṛžem mherres u-l-bab xeṣṣha ttbeddel.*	The window is broken and the door needs to be replaced.
A:	*kif ɛamel had n-nežžaṛ?*	How is this carpenter?
B:	*mezyan. xdem ɛăndi men qbel.*	He's good. He's worked for me before.
A:	*u-ka-iġelli ši?*	Does he charge a lot?
B:	*la, la, ka-iṛexxeṣ bezzaf.*	No, he charges very little.
A:	*ila mšit ḥetta ḥtažitu, nqulha-lek.*	If I ever happen to need him, I'll tell you.

DIALOG EIGHTY-FIVE

A:	*bġitek tṣuwweb-li ši-xdima de-ḍ-ḍaṛ.*	I have some work at home I want you to do for me.
B:	*waxxa a-sidi. nemši mɛak nšuf?*	O.K. Shall I go with you and have a look?
A:	*yaḷḷah.*	Let's go.
A:	*had l-bab mherrsa. teqdeṛ tesleḥha?*	This door is broken. Can you fix it?
B:	*ṣbeṛ nšuf. meɛlum imken-lha ttesleḥ.*	Let me see. Of course it can be repaired.
A:	*u-had š-šeṛžem ḥetta huwa mherres.*	This window is broken too.
B:	*ḥetta huwa itteṣleḥ. kayna ši-ḥaža x̌ṛa?*	This also can be repaired. Is there anything else?
A:	*ṣafi.*	That's all.
B:	*ġedda nži u-nžib le-mwaɛen.*	I'll come tomorrow and bring the tools.

A: *šȻal ġad-yewžebni bin koll-ši?* — How much will it cost me all together?

B: *Ȼăšṛa de-d-drahem.* — Ten dirhams.

A: *waxxa a-sidi. f-ayna weqt ntsennak?* — O.K. At what time shall I wait for you?

B: *nži fe-ṛ-ṛebȻa d-le-Ȼšiya.* — I'll come at four.

DIALOG EIGHTY-SIX

A: *a le-mȻăllem, bġitek trekkeb-li ši-feṛxa l-had l-bab.*[1] — I'd like you to install a lock on this door for me.

B: *Ȼăndek l-feṛxa?* — Do you have the lock?

A: *la, nešriwha. šȻal teswa?* — No, we'll buy it. How much would it cost?

B: *ši-tmenya de-d-drahem.* — About eight dirhams.

A: *u-šȻal xeṣṣek l-l-ižaṛa dyalek?* — And how much would it be for your work?

B: *xemsin ryal. bin koll-ši žat myatayn u-Ȼăšṛa de-r-ryal.* — Fifty rials (two and a half dirhams). All together it comes to two hundred and ten rials (ten and a half dirhams).

A: *fi ʔaman llah.* — O.K.

Notes

1. *mȻăllem* 'master workman' (in some trade or profession); the *a* is a word used in addressing someone. The whole phrase *a le-mȻăllem* is as if we said things in English like 'Mr. locksmith, . . .' to a worker in speaking to him.

DIALOG EIGHTY-SEVEN

A: *ṣbaȻ l-xir.* — Good morning.

B: *ṣbaȻ l-xir.* — Good morning.

A: *ḷḷah ixellik neȻȻăt-li fayn ža ṣ-ṣuq.* — Please show me where the market is.

B:	*iyeh. baği tešri ši-ƈaža?*	Of course. Do you want to buy something?
A:	*bğit nešri ši-ṭbila.*	I want to buy a small table.
B:	*šƈal de-le-flus bğiti ddfăƐ fiha?*	How much money do you want to spend on it?
A:	*ma-bğitha-š tkun ġalya bezzaf.*	I don't want it to be very expensive.
B:	*kayen waƈed ṣ-ṣuq fayn teqḍeṛ tṣibha.*	There's a market where you can find it.
A:	*teqḍeṛ teddini l-temma had le-Ɛšiya?*	Can you take me there this afternoon?
B:	*waxxa, ntlaqaw žwayeh ṛ-ṛebƐa.*	O.K., we'll meet around four o'clock.

DIALOG EIGHTY-EIGHT

A:	*l-waƈed değya ka-idfăƐ le-flus bezzaf fe-ṣ-ṣuq.*	A person can spend a lot of money fast at the market.
B:	*iyeh. u-be-l-xuṣuṣ fe-l-baẓaṛat.*	Yes, especially in curiosity shops.
A:	*ana Ɛămmṛi ma-ka-nemši l-duk l-maƈăllat.*	I never go to those places.
B:	*mƐak l-ƈăqq. ka-iṭelbu bezzaf fe-s-selƐa dyalhom.*	You're right. They ask too much for their merchandise.
A:	*haduk l-maƈăllat măƐmulin ġiṛ le-s-suwwaƈ.*	Those places are made just for tourists.

DIALOG EIGHTY-NINE

A:	*ṣbaƈ l-xir.*	Good morning.
B:	*ṣbaƈ l-xir.*	Good morning.
A:	*waš bğiti ši-ƈaža?*	Can I help you?
B:	*iyeh. bğit ši-ṭebla ṣġiṛa.*	Yes, I want a small table.
A:	*še-ḍheṛ-lek f-hadi?*	What do you think of this one?
B:	*hadi šwiya kbira. werrini ma ṣġeṛ.*	That's a little big. Show me something smaller.
A:	*še-ḍheṛ-lek f-hadi?*	What do you think of this one?
B:	*ma-ši hadi Ɛla-š ka-nduṛ.*	That's not what I'm looking for.

A: *šefti ši-ʗaža lli ʕežbettek?*	Do you see anything you like?
B: *aṛa nšuf hadik ra-fayn.*	Let me see that one over there.
A: *hak a-sidi. mziwna aw-la?*	Here you are, sir. Very nice, isn't it?
B: *ma-ši qbiʗa. be-šʗal?*	Not bad. How much is it?
A: *xems-emyat ryal.*	Five hundred rials (25 dirhams).
B: *iwa ʕmel mʕaya ši-taman mʕăwweṭ.*	Now, you'll have to make me a reasonable price.
A: *lilek ṛebʕa-mya u-xemsin ryal.*	For you, four hundred and fifty.
B: *waxxa, hak a-sidi.*	O.K., here you are.

DIALOG NINETY

A: *kaynin le-ṣwaq f-ˀamirika?*	Are there markets in America?
B: *ʕăndna bezzaf d-le-škal.*	We have many kinds.
A: *bʗal lli ʕăndna hnaya?*	Like the ones we have here?
A: *teqṛiben. le-ṣwaq le-kbaṛ mužudin xarež l-mudun le-kbaṛ u-f-beṛṛa.*	Sort of. There are large markets outside the big cities and also in the country.
A: *u-had le-ṣwaq ka-ixedmu dima aw koll waʗed nhaṛ fe-ž-žemʕa?*	Are there markets always open or is each one open one day a week?
B: *fihom lli ka-ixedmu koll-nhaṛ, u-fihom lli ka-ixedmu ġir ž-žemʕa u-s-sebt.*	There are some that are open every day, and there are some that are open only Fridays and Saturdays.
A: *u-ka-imšiw-lhom n-nas bezzaf?*	And do a lot of people go to them?
B: *ktir-ši lli ʕăndhom l-ġaṛaḍ b-ʗaža ṭriya u-ṛxiṣa, u-lli ka-inefqu be-l-ketṛa.*	Mostly people who want something fresh and inexpensive, and who also buy groceries in large quantities.
A: *u-daxel le-mdina?*	What about inside the city?
B: *daxel le-mdina ʕăndna ʗwanet bʗal de-hna, u-ʕăndna ʗwanet kbaṛ bezzaf ka-išebhu l-le-ṣwaq.*	In the city we have stores like the ones here, and we have large stores that resemble markets.
A: *u-š-ka-ibiʕu fihom?*	And what do they sell in them?
B: *ka-ibiʕu l-lʗăm u-d-džaž u-l-xuḍaṛ u-l-fawakih u-l-ʕăṭṛiya, u-ˀumuṛ l-makla kollha.*	They sell meat, chicken, vegetables, fruit, spices, and all food items.

A: *u-dyal men had le-ɛwanet?*	And whom do these shops belong to?
B: *žollhom d-šarikat ɛamlinhom f-le-blad kollha.*	Most of them belong to companies that have them all over the country.

DIALOG NINETY-ONE

A: *šɛal bġiti f-had ṭ-ṭebla?*	How much do you want for this table?
B: *mziwna, ʔaʔ ġad-năɛmel-lek taman xaṣṣ, xemsa u-settin derhem.*	Very nice, isn't it? I'll make you a special price, sixty-five dirhams.
A: *bezzaf had š-ši, ġad-năɛṭik xemsa u-ṛebɛin derhem.*	That's too much, I'll give you forty-five dirhams.
B: *weḷḷah a-sidi ma-txerrežni! u-ɛla kolli ɛal ġad-nxelliha-lek b-settin derhem.*	I swear I can't do it! Anyway, I'll let you have it for sixty dirhams.
A: *l-ɛaṣil ġad-năɛṭik xemsin derhem u-ṣafi.*	I'll tell you what, I'll give you fifty dirhams, that's all.
B: *šuf, l-kelma t-talya hiya xemsa u-xemsin derhem. ma-neqḍeṛ-š nbiɛha-lek qell men had š-ši.*	Look, my final price is fifty-five dirhams. I can't sell it to you for less.
A: *qell men had š-ši walu?*	Nothing less?
B: *walu.*	Nothing.
A: *iwa dazet, naxodha.*	All right, I'll take it then.
B: *ḷḷah irebbeɛ.*	It's all yours.

DIALOG NINETY-TWO

A: *l-bareɛ šrit waɛed ṭ-ṭebla men dak ṣ-ṣuq lli konti neɛɛătti-li.*	Yesterday I bought a table from that market you told me about.
B: *be-šɛal šritiha?*	How much did you pay for it?
A: *b-xemsa u-xemsin derhem.*	Fifty-five dirhams.
B: *u-kif ɛamla?*	How is it?
A: *mziwna u-fe-š-šehwa.*	Very nice, and it's just what I want.
B: *iwa ila kan hakda, ma-ġalya-š b-had t-taman.*	In that case, it's not expensive for such a price.

A: *ma-ka-nḍenn-š.*	I don't think so.
B: *ḥett-ana xeṣṣni ši-ṭebla f-had š-škel.*	I need a table like this too.
A: *l-ḥanut mnayn tṣuwweqt, fiha ɛadad de-ṭ-ṭbali mziwnin.*	There are a lot of nice tables at the shop where I bought mine.
B: *had le-ɛšiya nemši. qul-li f-ayna maḥăll fe-ṣ-ṣuq žat had l-ḥanut.*	I'll go there this afternoon. Tell me where this shop is located in the market.

DIALOG NINETY-THREE

A: *fuq-aš ġad-tqellăɛ ṭ-ṭiyaṛa dyalek?*	What time does your plane take off?
B: *fe-s-sebɛa d-le-ɛšiya.*	At seven p.m.
A: *u-fuq-aš xeṣṣek tkun fe-l-maṭaṛ?*	And what time do you have to be at the airport?
B: *fe-s-setta.*	At six o'clock.
A: *ʔiden xeṣṣna nxeṛžu men ɛăndek fe-l-xemsa u-neṣṣ.*	Then, we must leave your house at five-thirty.
B: *fe-l-xemsa u-ṛbăɛ nkun wažed.*	I'll be ready at a quarter past five.
A: *lli xeṣṣek kollu ɛăndek?*	Do you have everything you need?
B: *iyeh, l-weṛqa u-t-tesriḥ, koll-ši mheyyeʔ.*	Yes, ticket, passport, everything is in order.
A: *ġad-temši qaṣeḍ l-New York, aw ġad-teḥṣeṛ f-ši-maḥăll?*	Are you going straight to New York or are you going to stop somewhere?
B: *ġad-neḥṣeṛ saɛa f-bariz u-ṣafi.*	I'll stop one hour in Paris, and that's all.

DIALOG NINETY-FOUR

A: *ṣafeṛ ɛămmek?*	Has your uncle left yet?
B: *ma-zal, be-l-ḥăqq ġad-iṣefeṛ had le-ɛšiya fe-ṛ-ṛebɛa u-neṣṣ.*	Not yet, but he's leaving at four-thirty this afternoon.
A: *ġad-tweṣṣlu l-l-maṭaṛ?*	Are you going to see him off at the airport?

B: *iyeh, kollna ġad-nweṣṣluh. ɛlaš ma-dži-š mɛana?*	Yes, all of us are going to see him off. Why don't you come with us?
A: *imken-li nemši mɛakom ila dduzu mmuṛaya.*	I'll be able to go with you if you come by for me.
B: *b-koll faṛaḥ. fayn ka-teskon?*	We'd be happy to. Where do you live?
A: *f-šariɛ tmara, ṛeqm sbăɛṭaš.*	Number seventeen, Temara Avenue.
B: *f-ayna ṭebqa?*	What floor?
A: *l-xamsa.*	The fifth.
B: *nži mmuṛak fe-t-tlata u-neṣṣ.*	I'll come for you at half past three.
A: *xeṣṣna ɛăl l-ʔaqell tulut saɛa baš nweṣlu l-l-maṭaṛ.*	It'll take us at least twenty minutes to get to the airport.
A: *dazet, ntsennak.*	Fine, I'll be waiting for you.

DIALOG NINETY-FIVE

A: *fayn šaneṭṭek?*	Where is your suitcase?
B: *ṛa-hiya dik. daba nžibha.*	It's over there. I'll get it.
A: *ma-ttɛăddeb-š. daba irfedha-lek l-ḥămmal.*	Don't bother, the porter will carry it for you.
B: *šḥal hadi?*	What time is it?
A: *ṛ-ṛebɛa u-neṣṣ. fuq-aš ġad-tqellăɛ ṭ-ṭiyaṛa?*	Four-thirty. What time does the plane leave?
B: *fe-setta u-tulut.*	Six-twenty.
A: *ma-zal f-yeddna l-weqt bezzaf.*	We have lots of time.
B: *ma-tensa-š l-maṭaṛ ṛah bɛid bezzaf.*	Don't forget, the airport's a long way from here.
A: *wala ɛalik, ġad-nweṣlu qbel l-weqt.*	It doesn't matter. We'll get there ahead of time.
B: *in šaʔ ḷḷah.*	I hope so.
A: *metʔekked.*	I'm sure of it.

DIALOG NINETY-SIX

A: *kteb-li mnayn tuwṣel l-ˀamirika.*	Write me when you get to America.
B: *ġad-nekteb-lek, u-ḥetta-nta kteb-li.*	I'll write you, and you write me, too.
A: *ka-tăɛṛef teqṛa l-ɛăṛbiya?*	Can you read Arabic?
B: *šwiya.*	A little.
A: *nekteb-lek n-neṣṣ be-l-ɛăṛbiya u-n-neṣṣ be-n-negliza.*	I'll write you half in Arabic and half in English.
B: *mezyan, ḥett-ana nḥawel nekteblek be-l-ɛăṛbiya.*	Fine, I'll try to write to you in Arabic too.
A: *u-fayn tɛăllemti tektebha?*	Oh! Where did you learn to write it?
B: *fe-l-žamiɛa.*	At the university.
A: *fi ˀaman llah.*	That's wonderful.

DIALOG NINETY-SEVEN

A: *ġedda ġad-neṛžăɛ l-ˀamirika.*	I'm going back to America tomorrow.
B: *be-ṣ-ṣăḥḥ?*	Really?
A: *iwa hadi ɛamayn ma-šeft bladi.*	I haven't been home for two years.
B: *ma-nesxaw-š bik.*	We'll miss you.
A: *ḥett-ana ma-nesxa-š bikom.*	I'm going to miss you too.
B: *u-fuq-aš tɛawed dži l-l-meġṛib?*	And when are you going to come back to Morocco again?
A: *ma-ɛṛeft. ila mken-li, l-ɛam ž-žay.*	I don't know. Next year, if I can make it.
B: *iwa ġir ma-tensana-š, u-kteb-lna saɛa saɛa.*	Well, just don't forget us, and write to us once in a while.
A: *meɛlum, nekteb-lkom.*	Of course I'll write you.
B: *f-aš ġad-temši?*	How are you going to go?
A: *fe-ṭ-ṭiyaṛa.*	By plane.
B: *iwa ṭṛiq s-slama, u-sellem-lna ɛăl le-ḥbab dyalek.*	Have a nice trip, and give our regards to your folks.
A: *ḷḷah isellmek, iwa be-s-slama.*	Thank you, good-bye, now.

GLOSSARY

aġniya pl. of *ġani*
ʔalef (one) thousand
  pl. *ʔalaf*
ʔalfayn two thousand
ʔamirika America
ana I
aš, š-, še- what (see Grammatical Note C)
aš-en huwa, šnuwa, šnu what, which
  f. *aš-en hiya, šniya, šni*
  pl. *aš-en huma, šnuma*
atay tea
ʔaxir (102) used in the expression
    fe-l-ʔaxir finally, at last
axoṛ other
  f. *oẋṛa, ẋṛa*
  pl. *oẋṛin, ẋṛin*
aži, pl. *ažiw* imperative of *ža*

b-, be- (see Grammatical Note B)
bab door
  pl. *biban*
bakit pl. *-at* package
bali old, used, worn, worn-out
  f. *balya*
  pl. *balyin*
baqi still, yet
bareح see *l-bareح*
baš to, in order to, so that
baع (*ka-ibiع*) to sell
ḅḅa (my) father
bda (*ka-ibda*) to begin
bġa (*ka-ibġi*) to want (see Grammatical Note C)
biban pl. of *bab*
biḍ (collective) eggs
biḍa f. of *byeḍ*
bin, binat between
biškliṭa pl. *-t* bicycle
bit room
  pl. *byut*
bekri early
blad (f.) town, city
bla without (see Grammatical Note A)
  bla bi- (before pronoun endings only)
  bla-ma (before imperfect verb forms)
be-l-حăqq but
ḅenk bank
bent girl, daughter
  pl. *bnat*
bqa (*ka-ibqa*) to remain, to stay
bṛa pl. *-wat* letter
berrad teapot
bṣeḷ (collective) onions
buḷa pl. *-t* electric light bulb
bumbi pl. *-ya* fireman
buṣṭa post office
buyeḍ pl. of *byeḍ*
byeḍ white
  f. *biḍa*
  pl. *buyeḍ*
byut pl. of *bit*
bezzaf very, "real"; much, many, a lot
bحal like, as, as . . . as
băعd (42) after
  băعd ġedda (59) day after tomorrow
  men băعd (42)
    (see Grammatical Note B)
băععăd men to avoid, to keep away from

d-, de- (see Grammatical Note B)
dak that (see Grammatical Notes A and C)
  dak n-nhaṛ the other day
  dak š-ši that (see Grammatical Note C)
dar (*ka-idir*) to do; to put
dda (*ka-iddi*) to take
ddabez to quarrel, to have a quarrel
deġya quick(ly), in a hurry
dheb gold
dima always
dqiqa minute
  pl. *dqayeq*
derhem dirham (basic unit of Moroccan currency).
  pl. *drahem*
drari children
duk those (see Grammatical Notes A and C)
dwa (m.) medicine
dxel (*ka-idxol*) to come in, to go in, to enter

dyal used to express possession in various ways; see the references cited in the index
džuwwež to get married

ḍaṛ house
pl. *ḍyuṛ*
fe-ḍ-ḍaṛ (30) at home
le-ḍ-ḍaṛ (31) (to)home, to the house
ḍ-ḍaṛ l-biḍa Casablanca
ḍḍeṛṛ to get hurt
ḍheṛ back
ḍiyyeq narrow
pl. *ḍiyyqin*
ḍṛeb to hit
ḍṛeb t-tilifun l- to telephone (someone)
ḍeṛṛ to hurt (someone, something)
ḍeṛṣ lesson
pl. *ḍuṛuṣ*
ḍulaṛ pl. *-at* dollar
ḍuṛuṣ pl. of *ḍeṛṣ*
ḍuw light
ḍuwweṛ *ɛla* to look for, to hunt for
ḍyeq narrower
ḍyuṛ pl. of *ḍaṛ*

faq to wake up
fas Fez
fayn where
f-, fe- in, at
feḍḍa silver
fḍuli pl. *-yin* nosy, impolitely inquisitive
fi- (62) form of preposition *f-* before pronoun endings
fiyyeq to wake (someone) up
fekk to untie, release, rescue (from a difficult situation)
fluka boat
pl. *flayek*
flus (pl.) money
fqi (m) schoolteacher
pl. *feqya*
fqiha (f.) pl. *-t* schoolteacher
feqya pl. of *fqi*
fṛanṣi f. *-ya,* pl. *-yin* French
feṛgăɛ to blow up, to cause to explode
feṛḥan pl. *-in* happy
fešš to let the air out of, deflate

gales sitting
gles to sit, to sit down
gezzar pl. *-a* butcher

ġani rich
f. *ġanya*
pl. *aġniya*

ġda dinner, midday meal
ġedda tomorrow
băɛd ġedda day after tomorrow
ġedda fe-ṣ-ṣbaḥ tomorrow morning
ġir only, just
ˀoġniya song
ġenna to sing
ġṛaṛef pl. of *ġoṛṛaf*
ġṛeq to drown
ġoṛṛaf pitcher
pl. *ġṛaṛef*
ġsel to wash
ġṭa lid, top
ġeṭṭa to cover

ha here (is), here (are)
had this, these (see Grammatical Note **A**)
had š-ši this (see Grammatical Note **C**)
hada this, this one
f. *hadi*
pl. *hadu*
hadak that, that one
f. *hadik*
pl. *haduk*
hdiya gift, present
hḍeṛ to talk
hiya she
hna here
herres to break
htemm (*b-*) to be interested (in), to be concerned (about)
huma they
huwa he

ila if
imken it is possible
imken-li (*-lek, -lu,* etc.) I (you, he, etc.) can
iyeh yes
iyyam pl. of *yum*

kamiyu truck
kan (*ka-ikun*) to be
kas (drinking) glass
pl. *kisan*
kayen there is
f. *kayna*
pl. *kaynin*
kbabeṭ pl. of *kebbuṭ*
kbaṛ pl. of *kbir*
kebb (*ka-ikobb*) to pour
kebbuṭ coat
pl. *kbabeṭ*
kbir big, old
pl. *kbaṛ*

kbeṛ bigger; older
kif-aš how
kilu (no pl.) kilogram
kisan pl. of *kas*
kla (*ka-yakol*) to eat
kelb dog
pl. *klab*
koll all, every
kollu (120) (m.) all of it
kollha (120) (f.) all of it
kollhom (104) all of them
koll nhaṛ (42) every day
koll ṣbaḥ (43) every morning
koll šheṛ (45) every month
koll ʔusbuɛ (44) every week
kma (*ka-ikmi*) to smoke
kemmel to finish
konnaš notebook
pl. *knaneš*
kra (*ka-ikri*) to rent
keslan pl. *-in* lazy
keswa suit (of clothes)
keššina kitchen
ktab book
pl. *ktub*
kteb to write
kteṛ more
kteṛ men had š-ši more (than this)
ktub pl. of *ktab*
kun if
kuṛa pl. *-t* ball
kḥăl black
f. *keḥla*
pl. *kuḥel*

l-, *le-* the
l-, *le-* to
la no
la . . . wa-la neither . . . nor
labes wearing, (having) dressed (oneself)
l-bareḥ yesterday
l-bareḥ f-le-ɛšiya yesterday evening
l-bareḥ fe-ṣ-ṣbaḥ yesterday morning
wel-l-bareḥ (31) day before yesterday
lebbes to dress (someone)
lbes to put on, to wear
leff to wrap up
lila night
fe-l-lila (129) per night, a night
llaṛeb minus a quarter (in telling time)
lli who, which, that (see the Grammatical Notes)
lli daz (m.) which passed, last
l-meġṛib Morocco
ḷeṛḍ floor, ground
lun color
luwwel first
l-yum today
lḥăm meat

ma water
magana watch, clock
pl. *mwagen*
makina pl. *-t* machine
makla food
maši going, walking, on the way
ma-ši not
mat (*ka-imut*) to die
maži (active participle of *ža*) coming
mdabza quarrel
mdad ink
medd to hand
meḍṛaṣa school
pl. *mḍaṛeṣ*
fe-l-meḍṛaṣa at school, at the school
mefšuš flat, deflated
mġeṛbi f. *-ya*, pl. *-yin* Moroccan
meġṛib see *l-meġṛib*
mġeṭṭi having covered; covered
mherres broken
mkaḥel pl. of *mkoḥla*
mkemmel finished, done
mektaba library
mekteb office
mektub written
mkoḥla rifle
pl. *mkaḥel*
mkoḥla de-ṣ-ṣyaḍa hunting rifle
melyun million
pl. *mlayen*
mleḥ salt
(*o*)*m̂m̂i* (43), *m̂m̂ek*, etc. my mother, your mother, etc.
men (*menn-* before pronoun endings) from; than
men băɛd (see Grammatical Note B)
men who (see Grammatical Note B)
mendil napkin, cloth, scarf, handkerchief
mnin when, as, while
menn- (68) form of preposition *men* before pronoun endings
meqlub turned over, upside down, backward(s)
mṛa woman, wife
mṛati, etc. my wife, etc.
mṛaḍ pl. of *mṛiḍ*
mṛat- (60) form of *mṛa* before possessive endings
mraya mirror

mṛiḍ sick
pl. *mṛaḍ*
meṛṛa (one) time, once
meṛṛa fe-š-šheṛ once a month
meṛṛtayn two times, twice
tlata de-l-meṛṛat three times
mṣaff lined up, in line
meṣnuƐ made, manufactured
mša (*ka-imši*) to go
imperative *sir*, pl. *siru*
mšaṭi pl. of *meṣṭa*
mešdud closed
mešġul busy
mešṭa comb
pl. *mšaṭi*
metfahem understanding (each other), in agreement (with)
metƐăllma pl. *-t* maid
meṭfi pl. *-yin* out, extinguished
muṛa behind
mwagen pl. of *magana*
mwessex dirty
pl. *mwessxin*
mxebbi hidden
pl. *mxebbyin*
mexnuq stopped up, blocked
mya hundred
myatayn two hundred
mezyan good
mežṛa drain
pl. *mžaṛi*
mžuwwež married
meƐlul open
meƐtaṛem respected
mƐa with
mƐăllem foreman
măƐmel factory
mƐăṭṭel late
pl. *mƐăṭṭlin*

naḍ (*ka-inuḍ*) to get up
namusiya bed
nas people
naƐes sleeping, asleep
nḍaḍeṛ (pl.) (eye) glasses
nfăƐ to be of use to, to help
(*n-*) *negliza* (the) English (language)
nhaṛ day(time)
dak n-nhaṛ the other day
fe-n-nhaṛ in the day, per day, a day
koll nhaṛ every day
nhaṛ le-xmis Thursday, on Thursday(s)
nhaṛ s-sebt Saturday, on Saturday(s)
nqa cleaner (comparative of *nqi*)
nqi pl. *-yin* clean
nsa (*ka-insa*) to forget
neṣṣ half
nta (m.) you
ntaxeb to elect
nti (f.) you
ntuma (pl.) you
nežžaṛ pl. *-a* carpenter
neƐnaƐ mint
nƐăs to sleep, go to sleep, go to bed

qaḍa to finish
qaḍi judge
pl. *quḍat*
qal (65) (*ka-iqul*) to say, to tell
qamižža shirt
qbeḍ to seize, grab, hold (on to)
qbel before
qbel-ma before (conjunction; see Grammatical Note A)
men qbel already, previously, beforehand
qeddam in front of
qehwa coffee
qlam pencil
qleb to turn over, turn upside down, backwards
qnaṭeṛ pl. of *qenṭṛa*
qent corner
qenṭṛa bridge
pl. *qnaṭeṛ*
qṛa (*ka-iqṛa*) to read, to study
qeṛƐa bottle
pl. *qṛaƐi*
qṣiṛ short
pl. *qṣaṛ*
qṣem (period of) five minutes
sbăƐ qṣam (86) thirty-five minutes
qeṣmayn (period of) ten minutes
qṣeṛ shorter
qṭen cotton
quḍat pl. of *qaḍi*

ṛabeƐ fourth
ṛafed carrying
ṛaʔis president
ṛaṣ head
ṛažel man
pl. *ṛžal*
ṛažeƐ returning, on the way back
ṛbăƐ quarter
ṛebƐa four (see Grammatical Note C)
fe-ṛ-ṛebƐa (36) at four o'clock
ṛebƐ snin (91) four years
ṛebƐ-alaf four thousand

ṛebʕin forty
ṛbăʕ-mya four hundred
ṛbăʕṭaš fourteen
rfed to carry
rkeb ʕla, rkeb f- to ride, to mount, to get on board
ṛ-ṛbaṭ Rabat
rtaḥ to rest
ṛwiḍa wheel, tire
pl. *ṛwayeḍ*
ṛžal pl. of *ṛažel*
ṛežžăʕ to return (send back, take back, bring back, give back)

sarut key
pl. *swaret*
saʕa pl. *-t* hour
f-had s-saʕa right now, at this moment
saʕtayn two hours
sebt see *nhaṛ s-sebt*
sebʕa seven
fe-s-sebʕa at seven o'clock
sbăʕ qṣam thirty-five minutes
sebʕ-alaf seven thousand
sebʕin seventy
sbăʕ-mya seven hundred
sbăʕṭaš seventeen
sefli ground floor
sinima movies, theater
sir (sg.), *siru* (pl.) imperative of *mša*
siyasa politics
siyyeb to throw, to throw away
siyyed gentleman, man
sokkaṛ sugar
sella pl. *-t* basket
sellef (*l-*) to lend (to)
smăʕ to hear
snin pl. of *ʕam*
ṛebʕ snin four years
telt snin three years
seqṣa to ask
serwal (sg.) (pair of) trousers
stilu fountain pen
setta six
fe-s-setta at six o'clock
sett-alaf six thousand
settin sixty
sett-emya six hundred
stexbeṛ to inquire, to make inquiries
seṭṭaš sixteen
swaret pl. of *sarut*
sxen hotter
sxun hot

ṣabun soap
ṣaff to line up, put in line
ṣbaḥ morning
ġedda fe-ṣ-ṣbaḥ tomorrow morning
koll ṣbaḥ every morning
ṣbiṭaṛ hospital
ṣfeṛ yellow
f. *ṣefṛa*
pl. *ṣufeṛ*
ṣefḥa pl. *-t* page
ṣġiṛ small, little; young
pl. *ṣġaṛ*
ṣġeṛ smaller; younger
ṣif summer
ṣifeṭ to send
ṣiniya tray
pl. *ṣwani*
ṣlaḥ to be of use, to be fit
ṣenḍuq box
pl. *ṣnaḍeq*
ṣnăʕ to make, to manufacture
ṣeṛṛaq pl. *-a* thief
ṣuf wool
ṣufeṛ pl. of *ṣfeṛ*
ṣuwweb to fix, to repair
ṣuwweṛ to photograph, take a picture of
ṣwani pl. of *ṣiniya*
ṣyaḍa hunting
mkoḥla de-ṣ-ṣyaḍa hunting rifle

šaf (*ka-išuf*) to see
šedd to close
šheṛ month
koll šheṛ every month
š-šheṛ lli daz last month
ši some, a few
ši-šwiya a little, a little bit
ši-waḥed someone, somebody, anyone, anybody
ši-ḥaža something, anything
ši-ḥădd someone, somebody, anyone, anybody
škaṛa satchel, briefcase
šeklaṭ chocolate
škun (63) who
škun lli (76) (see Grammatical Note C)
šelya pl. *-t* chair
š-men which, what
šni, šniya see *aš-en huwa*
šnu, šnuwa see *aš-en huwa*
šnuma see *aš-en huwa*
šra (*ka-išri*) to buy
šṛažem pl. of *šeṛžem*
šṛeb to drink
šrib (act) of drinking
šeṛžem window
pl. *šṛažem*

šwiya a little (bit), somewhat, sort of
šḥal how many (see Grammatical Note C)
šεăl to light, to strike; to turn on
šεăṛ (collective) hair
noun of unity *šăεṛa*

talet third
taman price
b-taman mezyan at a good price, for a good price
tani second
tfahem to come to an understanding, to understand (each other)
tfeṛgăε to explode, to blow up, to be blown up
theḷḷa f- to take care of
therres to get broken, to break
tilifun telephone
ḍṛeb t-tilifun l- to telephone (someone)
tkellem to talk, to converse
tekmal completion, (act of) completing
tlata (17) three
fe-t-tlata (35) at three o'clock
tlatin (88) thirty
waḥed u-tlatin (88), etc.; thirty-one, etc.
tleffet to turn around
tellaža pl. *-t* refrigerator
telt-alaf three thousand
telt-emya three hundred
telṭaš thirteen
tmanin eighty
temma there
temn-alaf eight thousand
temn-emya eight hundred
tmenṭaš eighteen
tmenya eight
fe-t-tmenya at eight o'clock
tnaber pl. of *tenber*
tnayn two (used only in compound numbers)
tenber (postage) stamp
pl. *tnaber*
tqaḍa to run out, come to an end, be finished
tqašeṛ socks
teṛžem to translate
tesε-alaf nine thousand
tesεin ninety
tsăε-mya nine hundred
tsăεṭaš nineteen
tesεud (42)
fe-t-tesεud (42) at nine o'clock
tṣaff to get in line, to form a line, to line up

tṣaweṛ pl. of *teṣwiṛa*
tṣuwweb to get (be) repaired, get (be) fixed
teṣwiṛa picture
pl. *tṣaweṛ*
ttfekk to get loose, get free, get out
ttfešš to go flat, deflate
ttekra to be rented (out), be for rent, rent
ttexlăε to ge scared, to be scared, afraid
ttexneq to get stopped up
tulut (period of) twenty minutes
tuwsaε (act of) enlarging
twessex to get dirty, to become dirty
txebba to hide (oneself)
tḥămmem to take a bath
teḥt under
tεăllem to learn
tεăṭṭel to be late, to be delayed

ṭaksi taxi
ṭanža Tangier
ṭaṛ (*ka-iṭiṛ*) to fly
ṭaḥ (*ka-iṭiḥ*) to fall
ṭbali pl. of *ṭebla*
ṭbašel pl. of *ṭebṣil*
ṭobba pl. of *ṭbib*
ṭebbax pl. *-a* (man) cook
ṭebbaxa pl. *-t* (woman) cook
ṭbib doctor
pl. *ṭobba*
ṭebla table
pl. *ṭbali*
ṭebṣil dish, plate
pl. *ṭbaṣel*
ṭfa (*ka-iṭfi*) to turn out, turn off, put out
ṭiyyaṛa airplane
ṭiyyeḥ to drop, knock down
ṭleb to ask for (see Grammatical Note B)
ṭnaš twelve
ṭreš deaf
f. *ṭeṛša*
pl. *ṭuṛeš*
ṭubis (local) bus
ṭumubil (f.) pl. *-at* car, automobile
ṭuṛeš pl. of *ṭṛeš*
ṭwil long, tall
pl. *ṭwal*
ṭwel longer, taller
ṭḥin flour

u and
ˀusbuε (43) week
koll ˀusbuε (44) every week

wad river
walu nothing

waqef standing
waseɛ wide, broad
waš (see Grammatical Note C)
waxxa even though, although
waḥed a, an; one
weld boy, son
  pl. *wlad*
wella or
wel-l-bareḥ day before yesterday
wqef to (come to a) stop, to stand
wqid (collective) matches
weqqef to stop, to stand, to stand up
weqt time
  fe-l-weqt on time
  weqt-aš when, (at) what time
weṛqa ticket
  pl. *wṛaq*
werra to show
wessex to get dirty, to make dirty
wessăɛ to widen, make wide, make wider
wsăɛ wider
wṣel to arrive
weṣṣel to take, cause to arrive, get (someone) there; to tell (the news to)
wzen to weigh
weḥda (95) f. of *waḥed*
  (*fe-*) *l-weḥda* (85) (at) one o'clock

xa see *xay*
xarež (in the process of) leaving, coming out, going out
xawi empty
  f. *xawya*
  pl. *xawyin*
xay (*xak*, etc.) my brother (your brother, etc.)
xebba to hide (something)
xbaṛ item of news, news
xobz bread
xda (*ka-yaxod*) to take (for oneself)
  imperative *xud*, pl. *xudu*
xeddam pl. *-a* worker
xeddem to operate, to work, to use
xdem to work
xedma work
xḍeṛ green
  f. *xeḍṛa*
  pl. *xuḍeṛ*
xfeq to fail
xlaq to be born
xella to leave
xeḷḷeṣ to pay
xmis see *nhaṛ le-xmis*
xemmen to think
xems qṣam twenty-five minutes
xems snin five years
xemsa five
  fe-l-xemsa at five o'clock
  xemsa u-tlatin thirty-five
xems-alaf five thousand
xemsin fifty
xems-emya five hundred
xemsṭaš fifteen
xnaši pl. of *xenša*
xneq to stop up, block (up)
xenša sack, bag
  pl. *xnaši*
oẋṛa (12), *ẋṛa* f. of *axoṛ*
oẋṛin, *ẋṛin* pl. of *axoṛ*
xerrež to take out, get out, send out, expel
xrež to go out, leave
xeṣṣ have to, must, (see Grammatical Note A)
xt- sister
  xti, my sister; *xetha*, her sister, etc.
xud, pl. *xudu* imperative of *xda*
xuḍeṛ pl. of *xḍeṛ*
xux (collective) peaches
xut- brothers
  xutek (57) etc. your brothers, etc.
xwatat sisters
  xwatati (37), etc. my sisters, etc.

yedd (f.) hand (of body only, not of clock)
  pl. *yeddin* (*yeddi-* before pronoun endings)
yum day (period of 24 hours)
l-yum today

ẓaṛ (*ka-iẓuṛ*) to visit
zaž glass (the material)
zit (f.) oil
zlafa bowl
  pl. *zlayef*
ẓenqa street
ẓeṛbiya rug, carpet
  pl. *ẓṛabi*
ẓṛeq blue
  f. *ẓeṛqa*
  pl. *ẓuṛeq*

ža (33) (*ka-iži*) to come
  imperative *aži*, pl. *ažiw*
  active participle *maži*
žab (*ka-ižib*) to bring
žarida newspaper
žayeb bringing
žbeṛ to find
ždid new
  pl. *ždad*

žib pocket
 pl. *žyub*
žuž two (see Grammatical Notes **B** and **D**)
 fe-ž-žuž at two o'clock
žnaweƺ wings
žwab pl. *-at* answer
žwayek about, around (with reference to time of day)
žyub pl. of *žib*

ƺadita accident, wreck
ƺaḍeṛ present, in attendance
ƺanut (f.) shop, store
 pl. *ƺwanet*
ƺawel to try
ƺaẓeq broke, without money
ƺda beside, next to
ƺădded to iron, press
ƺḍaš eleven
 f-le-ƺḍaš at eleven o'clock
ƺla sweeter
ƺlib milk
ƺăll (*ka-iƺoll*) to open
ƺlu f. *-wa* sweet
ƺămmem to give a bath to, bathe
ƺna we
ƺăqq truth
 be-l-ƺăqq but
ƺăqq-aš see *ɛla ƺăqq-aš*
ƺrira soup
ƺsab arithmetic
ƺsen better
ƺtaṛem to respect
ƺetta until; not a single; not even (a, any)
ƺetta waƺed no one, nobody, not anybody
ƺetta ƺaža nothing
ƺetta ƺădd no one, nobody, not anybody
ƺwanet pl. of *ƺanut*
ƺwayež clothes; things
ƺăyyed to take off, to take away, to remove
ƺăžžam pl. *-a* barber

ɛad just, just now
ɛafya fire
 pl. *ɛwafi*
ɛam (88) year
 pl. *snin*
 ɛam luwwel (31) last year
ɛamayn two years
ɛamel having put
ɛameṛ full
ɛanawin pl. of *ɛonwan*
ɛaqeb to punish
ɛaš (*ka-iɛiš*) to live
ɛawen to help
ɛayen to wait, wait for
ɛla on (see Grammatical Note **D**)
 ɛăl before definite article
ɛla ƺăqq-aš because
ɛlaš why
ɛăllem to teach
ɛmel to load, to put
ɛămma paternal aunt (i.e. father's sister)
ɛămmeṛ to fill
ɛămmeṛ never, not ever (cf. the Grammatical Notes)
ɛănd (96) (see Grammatical Note **B**; consult the index)
ɛăndna in our country (see Grammatical Note **E**)
ɛonwan address
 pl. *ɛanawin*
(*l-*)*ɛăṛbiya* (the) Arabic (language)
ɛṛef to know
ɛšiya evening
ɛăšṛa ten
 fe-l-ɛăšṛa at ten o'clock
ɛăšṛ-alaf ten thousand
ɛešrin twenty
waƺed u-ɛešrin twenty-one
ɛṭa (*ka-yeɛṭi*) to give
ɛăṭṭel to delay, to hold up, to make late
ɛwafi pl. of *ɛafya*
ɛăyni my eye
ɛžeb to please

INDEX